AN IMPOSSIBLE DREAM

Published by

Librario Publishing Ltd

ISBN: 1-904440-20-7

Copies can be ordered via the Internet
www.librario.com

or from:

Brough House, Milton Brodie, Kinloss
Moray IV36 2UA
Tel /Fax No 01343 850 617

AN IMPOSSIBLE DREAM

Some of Kenya's Last Colonial Wardens Recall the Game Department in the British Empire's Closing Years

Edited by Ian Parker and Stan Bleazard

September 2001

Librario

Dedication

We dedicate this book to a Pleistocene Africa, which we so enjoyed and sought to preserve, but which is gone. It was an impossible dream.

ACKNOWLEGEMENTS

We gratefully acknowledge the help of all who have contributed to this volume, even if some of their work does not appear in it. Our thanks to Peter Jenkins, National Park Warden and Honorary Game Warden for over forty years, deserve special emphasis. The decision to produce the book more or less coincided with the diagnosis that he had an advanced and particularly malignant cancer. Yet as he fought a losing battle over the next twenty two months, regardless of his more or less continuous pain and discomfort, he reviewed and commented on the chapters as they appeared. His own three short and unsolicited chapters were written, quite literally, from his death-bed and less than two months before he died on the 17th of September 2001. It was a grand effort.

Monty Brown, John Millard, Tony Hazeldine, Rodney Elliott, Tony Archer and our editresses, Chris Parker and Julia Lawrence made valiant efforts to render the assorted contributions into a readable whole. We thank them for their help. For help with photographs we are indebted especially to Peter Davey, Dave Richards and Tony Dyer and thank all those others to whom credits are given.

Ian Parker & Stan Bleazard,
September 2001

CONTENTS

		Page
Acknowledgements		vi
Glossary		ix
Introduction		1
Chapter 1	Early History *Parker & Smith*	5
Chapter 2	Jackson & Percival *Parker*	13
Chapter 3	Three Stalwarts *Jenkins*	33
Chapter 4	Wildlife Use in World War II *Jenkins*	39
Chapter 5	My First Expedition Down Sydney Street *Jenkins*	43
Chapter 6	Game Ranger, Maralal *Elliott*	47
Chapter 7	William Harvey's Tusks *Parker*	59
Chapter 8	Game Warden, Garissa *Smith*	65
Chapter 9	A Lion and a Leopard in Town *Elliott*	75
Chapter 10	New Directions in the 1950s: a Personal View *Simon*	83
Chapter 11	The Anti-Poaching Campaign *Parker*	93
Chapter 12	Memories from the Anti-poaching Campaign *McCabe*	105
Chapter 13	Looking Back *Brown*	119
Chapter 14	Naked Hunters *Marsh*	123
Chapter 15	Game Warden, Lamu *McCabe*	125
Chapter 16	Memories from the Coast *Carn*	137
Chapter 17	Game Warden, Marsabit *Bleazard*	145
Chapter 18	Bloody Journalist *Bleazard*	161
Chapter 19	The Galana Game Management Scheme *Parker*	165
Chapter 20	Nine Years as an Honorary Game Warden *Drury*	175
Chapter 21	The Darting Trip *Parker*	181
Chapter 22	Ukambani *McCabe*	191
Chapter 23	Roan *Coverdale*	197
Chapter 24	Lions in Suburbia *Jolley*	203
Chapter 25	The Game Capture Unit *King*	207
Chapter 26	Night Blindness & Shifta *Bleazard*	225
Chapter 27	Presidential Service *Bleazard, Brown & Marsh*	233
Chapter 28	Kavuma *Parker*	241
Chapter 29	I Was Never Meant to Be a Game Warden *Graham*	247
Chapter 30	The Kapiti Lion *Levett*	259
Chapter 31	Kipini's Ghosts *Carn*	267
Chapter 32	From Ngong to Garissa *McCabe*	273
Chapter 33	The Closing Phase *McCabe*	283
Chapter 34	Call Me Al *Bleazard*	291
Chapter 35	Policy in 1967 *Brown*	299
Chapter 36	A Tribute to David Sheldrick *Brown*	303

		Page
Chapter 37	Personalities *Barrah*	309
Chapter 38	Requiem for a White Elephant *Parker*	325
Appendix I	The State of the Game by A. Blayney Percival 1906	336
Appendix II	The Warden's Roll from 1900 to 1963	341
Index		343

GLOSSARY

English, as it is spoken in Kenya, incorporates many words from Kiswahili which can baffle the newcomer. We have put their meanings in parentheses in the text, but, in addition, also include this short glossary to help the reader.

Askari = Soldier, Policeman or an armed guard.
Bwana = in address Master, Mr or Sir. Also used for husband.
Boma = in strict Kiswahili any kind of raised, walled structure for defensive purposes, but widened to include thorn zaribas thrown together to contain cattle and other livestock, a paddock and, when spelt with a capital B, a Government (usually District) centre.
Bundu = the bush.
Debe = Originally a four-five gallon kerosene container first imported into Zanzibar from the USA in the 19th century, but now used for any large tin container of similar size.
Duka = Kiswahili for a shop or market stall.
Gogs = optical glasses.
Heshima = Kiswahili for honour, dignity, position and rank.
Kaburu(s) = a Kiswahili word for South Africans deriving from Boer.
Kanga = a guinea fowl or a colourful calico wrap-around worn by women.
Kebi = originally Kiswahili for a pot or mug, but widened to mean any old tin. The plural mikebi onomatopoeically fitted McCabe too closely for it not to be used as his nickname.
Kikoi = a cotton loin cloth or sarong worn by men.
Makuti = Palm-frond – thatching (sing. = kuti, pl = makuti.)
Manyatta = Maa, for warriors' or men's residence, commonly misused for boma.
Mchangi = probably Kikamba, in the sense of a wanderer, always looking for new places; implying restless – all of which were attributes of Eric Rundgren.
Moran = a Maa term for a young man in the warrior age grade.
Shamba = Cultivated plot, farm, ranch.
Shifta = an Ethiopian term (Amharic?) for brigand, originally applied specifically to the Habash raiders from that country, but now generally applied to bandits both generally, but also specifically those from Somalia.
Shuka = A cotton body covering worn, toga-like, over one shoulder, principally by pastoral herders.
Skitsy = School-boy slang used in Kenya, Zimbabwe & South Africa for timid or frightened.
Thunder-flash = a non-lethal British Army explosive device used to simulate grenades etc. during training, but once used extensively by East African Game Departments to frighten away big game.

Wardens and Headquarters Office Staff of the Kenya Game Department in1958.
Back row: N. Sandeman, D. Brown, K. Smith, R. Hurt, R. Harvard, S, Morris-Smith
Second row down: D. Allen, J. Barrah, R. Elliott, I. Parker, J. McKeand
Third row down: D. Smith Head of Fisheries, D. Kearney, W. Coles
Fourth row: E. Temple-Boreham, E. D'Souza, M. Menezes, Secretary, Mary Henderson,
Willie Hale Chief Game Warden end of fourth row.
Sitting in front, two Office Messengers and M. D'Souza.
(missing D. McCabe)

INTRODUCTION

Ian Parker & Stan Bleazard

Herein are memoirs of some regular and Honorary Game Wardens who served in Kenya mostly between the end of the Second World War in 1946 and Kenya's Independence in 1963. In addition, Noel Simon, who greatly influenced Kenya's conservation policy in the mid-nineteen fifties, has made a valuable contribution. Written nearly four decades later, these records are bound to have biases, the strongest being nostalgia, as it is normal to hark back to when we were supple, bright of eye and, even had it been available, viagra would have been a joke. The 'good old days' refer to a state of mind rather than any fixed point in time.

A second bias will be in the editing. When Stan Bleazard first set about getting this book written, he invited contributors to write on whatever came to mind, assuming that it would have some connection with the colonial Kenya Game Department. The subject could be serious or anecdotal, humorous or historical, about personalities or some aspect of conservation, experiences or the environment then prevailing.

We knew so wide a cast of the net would produce a varied catch. There is thus a breadth of styles and subjects. Seventeen people living in Australia, Britain, Germany, Kenya, South Africa and Zimbabwe have contributed chapters, all drawing on memories eroded by the passage of forty years. In as far as possible, personal styles were not tampered with. Facts have been checked for accuracy with written records available to us and those found wrong amended. In the interests of brevity, some repetitive material has been excised. Where two contributors agreed on the same subject, only one offering has been put forward.

Editorial license favoured articles that were descriptive, illustrated policy, or contained facts of historical value. Long tales of personal hunting adventures, of the weight of lead required to subdue some animal and descriptions of wounds inflicted, damage done and bullet penetration, were pruned heavily. For all that it was part of the job, shooting animals is shooting animals is shooting animals. Overall, hunting, like sex, enthralls the participants, but it is not a spectator sport and can be boring in the telling. For that bias we make no apology. Our aim was to produce a volume that, whatever its failings, was not boring. We have sought to give the sequence of chapters a rough but not absolute chronological continuity – in as far as possible. Mindful of economics some contributions were lightly trimmed while others were heavily pruned. Some stories we knew had appeared in print elsewhere were discarded altogether. Spelling of local and vernacular names we have left as the authors wrote them (e.g. Wasania and Wasanye obviously refer to the same people).

The Game Department was never particularly intellectual. It was a prerequisite of the permanent and pensionable Colonial Kenya Civil Service, that all officers should pass both an oral and written exam in Kiswahili if they wished to advance. Failure to pass these very simple exams stopped annual salary increments and blocked promotion. Game Wardens were exceptions. They were only required to pass the oral exam: either the written test was deemed beyond them or to be literate in the language was unnecessary in their wardenly duties. If its members had a common bond, it was disliking paper work. Even as late as 1956 when David Brown (DB) and Ian Parker were recruited, filing systems were the third fixed copy in a triplicate book, letters were written in longhand, and one was out and about more than in the office. Such a system did not leave much in the way of archives for later historians to piece together. A fundamentally thin record was rendered yet flimsier when the outgoing white order and the incoming black regime, both burned large proportions of the files containing departmental records. They had their reasons, but no thought for posterity. Consequently, the history of the Colonial Kenya Game Department is perhaps the least well documented of all sections of Government.

Not only were Game Wardens inherently reticent over paperwork, but sometimes downright quirky as well. Because its objections to game being shot on a massive scale to feed troops, prisoners and labour during both First and Second World Wars were overridden, the Department behaved as though this game use had never happened. Consequently the Annual Reports, which provide at least some history, made virtually no reference to what must, by any account, have been the most intense legal game use of the twentieth century. The subject was so little talked about that most post-war Wardens, let alone lay men, knew nothing of it. The extent of this use only became apparent through personal contacts with those who undertook the work, among whom the most informative was Bryan Jenkins, father of the Kenya National Park Warden Peter Jenkins, but also included Eric Rundgren. Further snippets and confirmation were in a file of George Adamson's annual and monthly reports for 1938-1949, one of very few saved by a member of the Department with a sense of history.

One fact that stood out as material came in was the number of Wardens who were posted to a station without any housing having been arranged for them in advance by their department. Reviewing the records, Temple-Boreham, Adamson, Smith, Brown, Parker, McCabe, Kearney, Carn and Graham were all posted to stations where their only accommodation was a tent. They had to arrange anything more substantial for themselves. Carn ended up in a converted chicken house in an Agriculture Department compound. Fred and 'Jock' Bartlett produced their first two children under canvas. No other department – Administration, Police, Prisons, Education, Agriculture etc. – created postings without treating housing as an essential element.

Yet housing wasn't the only anomaly. Many Wardens routinely dipped into their own pockets to bridge gaps when their official imprests were not topped up speedily enough from headquarters (or, let's be fair, when the Wardens themselves had been tardy in submitting accounts). Such bridging was of course reimbursed eventually. In no other department was an officer told that it was a condition of his employment that he provided his own vehicle for service in the field. Until and including the recruitment of David Brown and Ian Parker, this was mandatory. If you didn't provide your own vehicle, you didn't get the job: it was as simple as that. This rule was first relaxed for Wardens specifically recruited for the anti-poaching campaign of 1956-1957. Thereafter the rule was not enforced across the board as it had been and Bleazard, for example, was provided with a Government Land Rover. Graham in 1962 may have been the last to be told to provide his own personal transport. If someone had stood up and made a rumpus over the issue, it could not have been enforced. No one made a rumpus, however.

Game Wardens were among the most lowly paid of civil servants. Ironically, they were responsible for looking after mobile treasuries in the form of elephants and rhino whose trophies, even in the fifties, were worth millions of pounds Sterling. Without doubt, the expectation that Wardens would fend for themselves and accept paltry salaries was linked to a sense of vocation. Wardens might not be well off materially, but they had status and honour within their western culture. This *heshima* (honour, dignity) was so sought after that advertised Game Department vacancies were always hotly contested.

Yet this was a cultural phenomenon. Where it was not shared, where a Game Warden's post was seen as just a job and no more, then the obvious occurred. Being poorly paid, with no material prospects, it did not attract those with drive, intellect and ambition. And when poorly paid officials found themselves in charge of vast treasure, it is small surprise that they helped themselves - as happened after Independence. This cultural slant on post-independence events is not widely appreciated. Such recognition arises only through perceiving how colonial Wardens accepted postings without housing and provided their own transport in order to get the job: as civil servants, they were certainly different.

Finally, this volume should not be construed as an authoritative history of the Kenya Game Department though, hopefully, it may have some historical content. Neither editor can draw on personal knowledge of the Fisheries Section that was once very much part of the Game Department. Indeed few are now aware that this was so. Yet, at one point, the most obvious distinction was that its vehicles were marked Game Department (Fish). The first Head of the Game Department's Fisheries Section was Dent who, inter alia, introduced tilapia from the Athi River into Lake Naivasha in 1926. He was followed by Hugh Copley, then D. F. Smith and the last of the Colonial Fisheries Officers to head the Section was Pat Watson. When the Fisheries Section of the Game Department became a full-blown Department in its own right we have not established, but believe it was roughly about the time Kenya gained its independence. Perhaps this book may serve to stimulate a more precise review of the Game Department that redresses our deficiencies in due course.

Our editing has sought to keep faith with our common philosophy – in as far as we had one – in hoping that, if nothing else, these varied records make pleasant reading.

CHAPTER 1: EARLY HISTORY

Ian Parker & Ken Smith[1]

To be Irish, with the foresight of hindsight, it would have surprised most of us to learn that Africa's fiercest alien conservers were the Dutch. After all, it was the Afrikaner biltong hunters from '64' (Eldoret) whom we were told to be on the look out for when we were Wardens. Yet within five years of settling at the Cape in 1642 the Dutch introduced stringent game laws. Among many measures, these restricted hunting to a two-month season and outlawed the sale and purchase of game meat unlawfully obtained. Shooting birds and taking eggs was forbidden; so was merely disturbing game. Dogs had to have a heavy cudgel tied round their neck to impede them hunting. Penalties for infringing these laws included forfeiture of firearms, fines, imprisonment and corporal punishment[2]. That these laws did not in the end achieve much should have been of consequence to us, as the same could be said about the laws in our days. Yet in the lands coming under European control – including North America – after 1600, the Dutch were some two centuries in advance of conservation elsewhere.

Sometimes you 'get lucky' and such an instance was being referred to a PhD thesis by Nora Kelly[3], a Canadian lady. The only weaknesses in the thesis relate to the author's lack of field knowledge. These excepted, it is an outstanding piece of historical research that we commend unreservedly to those interested in 20th century African conservation. In very much the same vein, we independently came across five volumes titled *Preservation of Wild Animals in Africa*[4] (on which Nora Kelly had drawn heavily) which present a copious record on the subject of preserving African game that came before the two Houses of Parliament between 1896 and 1913.

Somehow, in our day, we felt that conservation had advanced and that we were at the cutting edge, yet the historical record shows that this was not so. The Imperial Government took a far greater interest, relative to its involvement in

---

[1] Kenneth Archibald Smith – Ken to most, Archibald to some – had written some historical notes on the Department's history, but died before he could see them incorporated in this chapter.

[2] For a summary of these rules, see Spinage 1991. *History and Evolution of the Fauna Conservation Laws of Botswana*. Occasional Paper #3, Botswana Society, Gaborone.

[3] Kelly, Nora. 1978. *In Wildest Africa: the Preservation of Game in Kenya 1895-1933*. PhD thesis, Department of History, Simon Fraser University. Canada.

[4] Anon 1906, 1909, 1910, 1911 & 1913. *Preservation of Wild Animals in Africa.* Command Papers being compendia of all that was presented to both Houses of Parliament on the subject from 1896 until 1913. Published by His Majesty's Stationery Office London.

governance generally, before the First World War than after it. Indeed, the history of conservation mirrors the impending collapse of the Empire and it started long before the advent of African independence.

Conscious of the recent collapse of the American bison and the passenger pigeon's extinction, the Imperial rulers were determined that East Africa's game should not disappear in similar style. The Foreign Office under which Kenya's affairs fell (until 1905 when the Colonial Office took over), kept conservation at the forefront of its interests and we have letters from the Governor of the British East Africa Protectorate – as Kenya was until July 1st 1920 – apologizing to the British Prime Minister for failing to submit the annual game returns. Nora Kelly's research in the London Archives testifies to a voluminous correspondence on the preservation of game, not from lowly civil service ranks, but between the British Government's most senior members – Prime Minister, Cabinet Ministers, Permanent Secretaries and Colonial Governors.

Between 1887 and 1895, what was to become Uganda and the British East Africa Protectorate was ruled by the Imperial British East Africa Company (IBEAC) under a charter granted by Queen Victoria. From the outset it was foreseen that game could be a major source of revenue. Equally, it was perceived that ivory would also be valuable (indeed it was hoped that the commercial viability of the IBEAC would be under-written by ivory). It was also hoped that, as in India and Burma, elephants could be tamed and used as beasts of burden on a large scale. Again, though the internal combustion engine did for this plan, we have no proof that it was basically untenable. In addition to genuinely wishing to conserve, these practical reasons made game laws among the earliest to be promulgated. When the British Government took over responsibility for governing in 1895, this policy continued and was strengthened.

In 1896, within a year of the British Government assuming power, the Acting Commissioner of the East Africa Protectorate, Clifford Crauford, (as an aside, in those days there was no Governor; the top man was the Commissioner, below him a Deputy Commissioner, next Provincial Commissioners, below them Sub-Commissioners, Collectors and last Assistant Collectors) was writing to his officers about declaring all of Kenia District a game reserve: the first to be proclaimed in British East Africa. In December 1897 this was formerly authorized by the Foreign Office. At the time, Uganda's boundary between Abyssinia and German East Africa was aligned more or less with the eastern wall of the Rift Valley (see p. 23), and reached the Kedong River just below the Kikuyu escarpment. Kenia District was all the land west of Ukambani and south of the Northern Uaso Nyiro River, including all Kikuyu country and Mount Kenya. It brought cries of protest from some officers in the field. Among them was Francis Hall (after whom Fort Hall was named) who wrote:—

> *"The most terrible news we have heard is that the whole of the Kenia District, including all these parts, is to be reserved for game, the*

regulations strictly enforced and apply to all Government officials as well as others. This is very hard lines and puts an end to all our shooting unless we apply for leave and go outside the District."[5]

Hall's dolour was somewhat alleviated when officials serving in the Kenia Reserve were allowed to shoot within it.

Both the IBEAC and the British Government outlawed commercial ivory hunting. Mr Ernest J. Berkeley of the Uganda Government wrote to the Marquess of Salisbury on November 15th 1896 outlining the regulations then coming into force. Section 2 states: -

"No licence shall be issued under any circumstances to professional elephant hunters."

Section 12 limited the number of elephants that could be shot to twelve only. Lest anyone should think that the game laws applied only to the areas administered, this was not the case. Sir Arthur Hardinge writing to the Marquess of Salisbury on the 29th September 1898 on the matter of a gun law that was to stop the killing of game wrote:–

"Its object is to prevent persons who may wish to evade the [Game] *Regulations from taking out firearms and ammunition ... under the pretence that they are not intended to be used for killing game, and then using them for that purpose in remote parts of the territory, such as the Lake Rudolf region, Boran etc., where the exercise of control over their action by Government officers may be very difficult."*

It is absolutely unequivocal that the laws applied throughout the country, whether remote or otherwise. The 1899 Game Regulations for both the East Africa Protectorate and the Uganda Protectorate were almost identical and Sections four of both reduced the number of elephants that could be taken annually on licence from twelve to two only.

Sir Harry Johnston the Commissioner for Uganda wrote to the Marquess of Salisbury on the 21st November 1900:–

"I ask permission to proclaim (temporarily) as a game reserve the area comprised within the following limits: -

The Sugota Game Reserve – Starting from the mouth of the River Turkwel where that river enters Lake Rudolf, the boundary of the

[5] Hall Papers, Rhodes House Library, Oxford.

Sugota Game Reserve shall follow the coast of Lake Rudolf southwards until it reaches the south-eastern most point of the lake. From this point the boundary shall be carried south-eastwards to the western flank of Mount Nyiro, and thence shall continue southwards along the western face of the Laikipia escarpment until it reaches the source of the small stream which flows into the north-easternmost gulf of Lake Baringo. Following this stream, down stream, the boundary of the said game reserve shall continue along the north coast of Lake Baringo, and shall thence be drawn north-westward to the westernmost source of the River Oron in the Kamasia Mountains. From this point the boundary shall be carried in a north-westerly direction along the northern flanks of the Kamasia and Elgeyo plateau till it reaches the right bank of the River Weiwei or Turkwel, and thence shall follow the right bank of the Weiwei or Turkwel down stream to where the said river enters Lake Rudolf.

This relatively vast area contains at the present time herds of elephants, giraffes, and zebras, and is the attraction of an increasing number of caravans proceeding thither often with the ostensible excuse of 'sport,' but really with the intention of killing as many elephants as possible and securing their ivory ...

"... I really think the time has come to be severe on professional sportsmen whose devastations considerably affect the value of what may prove to be an important asset in the productions of this Protectorate."

In reply to Harry Johnston's letter, Francis Bertie, replying on behalf of the Marquess of Salisbury, gave permission for the formation of the Sugota Game Reserve and further wrote:–

"With regard to the alleged destruction of elephants by private parties or professional hunters, it is the duty of all officials of the Protectorate to do their utmost to enforce existing Regulations, and to report at once any infractions of them which may come to their notice, in order that proceedings may be taken in the proper Courts."

It is in the light of the foregoing that the activities of Arthur Neumann have to be reconsidered. He may have started out shooting elephants before the laws were laid, but without question he was latterly an ivory poacher who contravened the law most thoroughly. He was a professional ivory hunter of the sort that the Governments of the day in Britain, Uganda and the East Africa Protectorate were trying to be rid of. Neumann's relationship with authority seemed ambivalent.

Monty Brown, Neumann's biographer[6], concedes that Neumann's hunting was clearly in contravention of the game laws then prevailing and records that, on one occasion in 1906, Robert Foran of the British East Africa Protectorate Police was all set to arrest Neumann and seize his ivory. The plan was stopped by Sir Frederick Jackson, the Acting Commissioner (Governor) and Neumann was permitted to sell the ivory. Jackson was one of the leading proponents of stringent game law and advocated the Northern Game Reserve should be a complete elephant sanctuary. Given his outlook and, more important, the rigid ban on commercial ivory hunting supported throughout the upper political echelons in Britain, it is difficult to see how Jackson could justify this protection of Neumann, even though they were close friends. Monty suggests that Neumann had an unwritten understanding with Jackson in which for a Nelsonian blind eye on his hunting, he would provide a stream of intelligence about goings-on in the unadministered north. That a more or less constant correspondence between him and Jackson was carried on is fact. It is an attractive supposition because it preserves Neumann's reputation, but it is unsubstantiated.

Such an arrangement would have been that much more believable, if Neumann's hunting had not been publicized. Yet he both wrote and talked about it, seemingly courting publicity. There is one way he could have got his ivory, other than shooting it, and that is trade. While elephant hunting by aliens may have been regulated, ivory was widely and legitimately traded from the native people. Could this have been Neumann's cover? Unless witnesses to him actually killing elephants could be procured, it would have been difficult to have rebutted a defence of "I bought the tusks from a native." One way or another, there has to be a more prosaic explanation for what Neumann was up to. Monty believes his suicide on the 29th May 1907 was brought about by illness and unrequited love. It was also on the eve of the north being administered. Among the first things of which the officers would have gained proof was that Neumann had broken the law on a substantial scale. Did this, too, contribute to Neumann's final act?

Karamoja Bell's claimed exploits also have to be reconsidered in the same light. He simply would not have been permitted to take elephants as he said he did and then market the ivory openly. He may have traded ivory, for which permission could be obtained, and there is evidence to suggest that he indeed did trade. Yet when one re-reads Karamoja Bell's tales and what he claimed to have shot and where, in the light of the then prevailing laws it is difficult to see any truth in them at all – other than successful writing. Take the analysis further, and relate what he claimed to have taken to the aridity of Karamoja where, for primary biological reasons, elephant densities could never have been great, and his tales are even less likely. He may have traded ivory, but to have shot what he

---

[6] Brown M. 1993. *Hunter Away: The life and times of Arthur Henry Neumann 1850-1907.* Monty Brown. London.

said he had shot, Bell most certainly did not. The impression given by Bell was that when he hunted, Karamoja was virgin territory. This was untrue. A major ivory trading route ran from Mbale on the western slopes of Mount Elgon to Maji in Ethiopia and was heavily used by Arab, Baluchi and Swahili ivory caravans long before Bell appeared on the scene[7]. The elephant along it would have been greatly harassed by the time he appeared on the scene. More important, though, the game laws were far too stringent for him to have got away with what he claimed to have done.

* * * *

Perhaps the most striking illustration of the intense official interest in conservation was the Convention for the Preservation of Wild Animals, Birds and Fish in Africa signed at London in May 1900[8]. The desire to bring about uniform game laws across the whole of Africa had been strong in London since at least 1895. It found firm support from the Governor of German East Africa – Dr Herman von Wissman (Major *à la suite* of the Army, Knight of the order of the Red Eagle, of the third class, with sword and crown, etc. etc) – and Britain and Germany jointly twisted the arms of the other colonial powers, forcing them to attend the 1900 London conference.

In those Imperial days the way the Powers went about their business triggers nostalgia of a high order. The Convention was signed with grandeur and certitude 'In the Name of Almighty God' no less (infinitely more impressive than in the name of the United Nations), by representatives from Britain, Germany, Spain, the King-Sovereign of the Independent State of the Congo, France, Italy and Portugal. Britain's self-governing Cape Colony declined to sign: its position having been summed in a memo dated June 9th 1898: -

> *" ... our laws are sufficient to protect our game, and we have hardly any game left anyway. With regard to elephants, it is feared that nothing further can be done within the Colony ... and the giraffe has long since disappeared within our colonial borders."*[9]

Despite being signed in the name of Almighty God, the Convention was soon forgotten. Nevertheless little that transpired in the hundred years following the 1900 convention was not discussed or brought up at that first great meeting. One wonders what went wrong? Perhaps two world wars and the hiatuses they caused are explanation enough, but we find it disturbing that all the ground covered by

---

[7] Yardley J. 1931. *Parergon or Eddies in Equatoria.* J. M. Dent & Sons, London gives evidence.

[8] Anon. 1900. *Convention for the Preservation of Wild Animals, Birds and Fish in Africa.* Her Majesty's Stationery Office. London. Price 2d

[9] Kelly *op cit* p. 146

modern treaties like the Convention on International Trade in Endangered Species of Fauna and Flora (CITES), was covered before, and that they have come up with little new. Proclaimed without reference to a Supreme Deity, we don't suppose they will be any more effective than the 1900 convention.

The enthusiasm to proclaim game reserves was considerable. Kenia District, was the first, Johnston's Sugota in Uganda was next, and then Lord Delamere recommended a yet greater reserve that took in most of the Sugota Reserve east as far as the Lorian Swamp. Indeed such a great reserve did exist albeit briefly taking in some twenty thousand square miles contiguous to Uganda's Sugota and north of the northern Uaso Nyiro. While such grandiose game keeping illustrates the Imperial enthusiasm for conservation, it was not practical. The Kenia Reserve was not a good choice as it included prime agricultural land much of which was already heavily settled, and that which wasn't was soon taken by incoming white settlers. All this quickly brought home how inappropriate it had been to declare all Kenia District a game reserve. In 1900 it was replaced by two larger and slightly more distant game reserves: the Northern which stretched from Mounts Nyiru and Marsabit in the north, to the northern Uaso Nyiro River in the south, and the Southern which took in all of Kajiado District.

As explained in the Annual Reports of the Game Warden for 1910-1911[10], in those days the term game reserve was an area in which hunting was not allowed. It was close to the modern concept of a national park. A game *preserve*, on the other hand, was an area in which controlled hunting was permitted. At the time the presence of large numbers of natives resident in a game reserve was not seen as an anachronism. The officials reasoned that as the game and the natives had co-existed before white men arrived, there was no reason why they should not continue to do so. The events of the twentieth century in terms of human increase and changed living standards were far beyond reasonable expectations. Incoming white settlers were seen as the real conservation problem.

Initially, the game laws were supposed to be enforced by the Imperial British East Africa Administrators and, after the British Government took over in 1895, by the Government Administration and Police. The first official specifically assigned to attend to game policy was one Richard Crawshay, who left his name attached to a scrub hare - *Lepus saxatilis crawshayi*. He did so as a member of the Administration. After him, in 1901, Blayney Percival was appointed the first Game Ranger although initially he, too, functioned as part of the Administration. He became what was initially the Game Ranger's Department and *de facto*, he headed a Department of one officer. However, though Percival was to serve the Department until his retirement in the early 1920s, and although in that period he acted as the Game Department's head several times, it was a post that he steadfastly refused to accept on other than temporary terms. His interest

[10] Anon. 1913. *Annual Report of the Game Warden for the British East Africa Protectorate for 1910 and 1911*. Government Printer, Nairobi.

throughout was to be in the field and away from desks and paper. Correctly, he saw that the departmental head's place would primarily be behind a blotter: a position, which he and his successor rangers and Wardens abhorred, but of whom few were as successful in avoiding as Percival.

Sir Frederick Jackson, true founder of the Kenya Game Department

CHAPTER 2: JACKSON & PERCIVAL

Ian Parker

Going through the correspondence relating to the preservation of wild animals in Africa between the colonial territories and London[11] I came across the following records which cast more information on early conservation in Kenya and Blayney Percival than any others of similar length. They are attachments to a letter dated March 12th 1906, from the Commissioner (Governor) for the British East Africa Protectorate Sir James Hayes Sadler to the Earl of Elgin, then the British Foreign Minister. I quote both attachments in full and present a third – Blayney's comments on the game of the British East Africa Protectorate as Appendix I.

* * * *

Enclosure 1
To His Majesty's Commissioner,
Nairobi.

Sir,

In forwarding a memorandum enclosing Mr Percival's remarks on the preservation of game in this Protectorate – with apologies for the delay – I have the honour to submit the following remarks on the question of a Game Ranger's Department.

In my estimates for such I have included a Ranger at £600 a year. I have done so because there is a widespread feeling in this country that if the question is to be taken up seriously with a view to preserving the game from extinction within the next decade or two, more particularly the rhinoceros, greater kudu, roan and sable antelopes, the buffalo and eland, all of which have sadly decreased in numbers within the last 16 years, either through diseases (rinderpest) or the advance of civilisation, an adequate and properly organised Game Ranger's Department should be established without further delay.

The 'Department' consisting, as it does at present, of Mr Percival, the Ranger, and four or six native Scouts is considered, with truth, to be little more than a farce. This, I submit, is no fault of Mr Percival.

For several years our Chief Veterinary Officer was single-handed with one Indian assistant, and the 'Department' was the subject of similar ridicule.

[11] Anon 1906, 1909, 1910, 1911 & 1913. *Preservation of Wild Animals in Africa.* ibid

Even if Mr Percival had more funds at his disposal for an increased staff of native Scouts, they would be of little use without European supervision. Our past experiences with native Police and tax collectors have proved this beyond all question. Mr Percival certainly has the makings of a very good Ranger. He is young, active and keen, a fearless rider, is inured to hardships, a complete stranger to all idea of comfort, a good sportsman, and a naturalist. I am myself in favour of his remaining as Ranger, and at a salary of £400 a year. He was originally appointed as an Assistant Collector in June 1900, and a Game Ranger in May 1901, but did not take up his duties as such until the following October, and he still appears in the staff list among Assistant Collectors. Messrs Pearson, Partington, Haywood and Maclean, all of whom were junior to him, have already been promoted to Collectorships.

Regarding the three Assistant Rangers, it is more doubtful whether an Assistant Collector now in the country would care to exchange from one branch, where promotion has hitherto been fairly rapid, to one in which it would be very remote. Should, however, a suitable candidate come forward for the post of Deputy Ranger I would suggest the salary be £300 a year. It may be considered that these salaries are too high, and that the three Assistants should rank as subordinates. Against this I would urge our experiences with Europeans on the Subordinate Staff. Before the Administrative staff was increased to its present strength, both in this Protectorate and in Uganda, our experiences with Sergeant Instructors, Police Inspectors, and other Europeans on the Subordinate Staff were far from happy. So long as they were under supervision the majority were quite satisfactory, and did excellent work, but directly they were given a little authority, and were alone, even though temporarily, the best of them went astray in one way or another.

An alternative estimate to that suggested in my memorandum would therefore be as follows: -

Ranger	£400	
Deputy Ranger	£300	or £250 for 1st year
Assistant Rangers: -		
Two at £250	£500	
Horse Allowance: -		
Four at £36	£144	
Native Scouts	£200	
Expenses	£500	
Total	£2,044	

I have, etc.,

F. J. Jackson

* * * *

Memorandum.

His Majesty's Commissioner,

I am strongly of the opinion that the steady increase in the revenue derived from game licences and fines for breaches of the Game Regulations since 1903 now justifies an appeal to the Secretary of State for a larger expenditure on the protection of the game: -

1903 ....£3,650
1904 ....£5,990
1905 ....£7,000
1906 ....£9,000 estimated

At present Mr Percival, the Game Ranger, is single-handed. He receives a salary of £250 a year, and his average annual expenses have been about £100. Game is found throughout three-fifths of the whole Protectorate in great variety and more or less plenty, and in about one fifth in great quantities. The Uganda Railway runs through country in which game is found for nearly 400 miles of its total length of 581 miles; and it bounds the Southern Reserve for the whole length of its north-eastern border for a distance of 194 miles. Yet, in spite of such rapid means of locomotion it is obviously impossible for one man with only half a dozen native Scouts to assist him, to have anything but the very vaguest idea of what is being done in the matter of poaching in the Reserve, or of breaches of the Regulations in other aspects elsewhere, even within a few miles of the line; and further afield it is impossible that he can know anything.

Few, however, will deny that poaching, shooting without licences, and other breaches of the regulations, are of daily occurrence, and are likely to continue until the Game Ranger is assisted by an adequate staff. Prosecutions have, so far, been very few, and the majority have been at the instigation of Collectors and Assistant Collectors of districts, and not on information laid by the Ranger or his Scouts. Through lack of funds at his disposal Mr Percival is at present tied down at Nairobi for about eight months in the year. Such a condition of affairs is most unsatisfactory, and compares very unfavourably with the efforts that are being made to protect game elsewhere. In the Transvaal something like £5,000 a year is expended on a small reserve under the direction of Major Stevenson-Hamilton.

2. Regarding the Boer colony in German territory, and on the border of our Southern Reserve, I am informed by Mr Ainsworth, the Sub-Commissioner, Nairobi, that this colony has now broken up, and that the Boers are now trekking northward in the hope of finding land near Nairobi. There should, therefore, be no difficulty in controlling them in future, in the matter of shooting game.

3. I fully agree with Mr Percival that the position of the Southern Reserve is in every way satisfactory, and that it covers the migration of the greater part of

the game found within its limits. There are something like 27 species of game found in this Reserve out of a total of about 56 species and sub-species known in the Protectorate.

The eastern or "Jubaland," half of the present Northern Reserve was created some years ago when the Naivasha Province formed part of the Uganda Protectorate [i.e. before 1902]. The principal object of this (Jubaland) Reserve was the protection of the elephant. It was, however, soon found that traders passing Baringo Station, and proceeding northwards into Suk and Turkana countries, were entering this Reserve from the west, in the vicinity of Loroghi, and were destroying great numbers of elephants.

Also, about that time a large so-called sporting expedition under a Frenchman named Sporck, was reported to be on its way out, *en route* for Abyssinia and the Nile via Rudolf, and as nothing further was known about the expedition and its objectives, Sir Henry Johnston declared the Suk and Turkana countries a game reserve. This was known as the Sogota Reserve of the Uganda Protectorate, and it now forms the western portion of the present Northern Reserve. This Northern Reserve is at present outside the limits of our effective administration, and until recently continued to be the happy hunting ground of Somali, Baluch and other traders who killed large numbers of elephants without let or hindrance. This destruction is now checked by the more rigid enforcement of the Outlying Districts Ordinance, and no one is allowed to enter these districts without a permit.

Until such time as the Game Ranger can visit the Northern Reserve and submit a report and recommendations, I agree with Mr Percival that it would be better not to reduce the area. The principal object of this Reserve should continue to be the preservation of the elephant, and this will probably prove feasible even if the western or Sogota half is eventually thrown open. Every species of game known to exist in the Sogota half is found in equal plenty in the Jubaland half.

4. The regulation regarding the sale of horns and skins is strictly enforced. It is, however, to be regretted that in German East Africa a considerable trade in game hides has sprung up, and within the last three years over 600 have been brought down by the railway and passed through the Customs at Mombasa, in transit. Mr Marsden tells me that many others, in sealed packages, have also passed through. Most of these hides have come from Shirati, just across the Anglo-German frontier, and as the district on our side of the boundary is known to be one of the best, though least known, of the game countries, it is not improbable that the greater proportion of these hides was obtained in British territory. I happened to be at Kisumu three years ago when the first consignment of these hides passed through and suggested at the time that this trade could, and should, be at once checked by increasing to a prohibitive rate the railway freight on all game hides, other than those obtained legitimately on a license.

5. In the revised Game Regulations the minimum weight of ivory allowed to be exported, has been raised from 11 lbs. to 30 lbs., and it is to be earnestly

hoped that this suggestion will meet with the Secretary of State's approval and sanction. I have consulted many sportsmen and all the senior officials on the subject, and all are agreed that it will prove the only effective means of preserving cow elephants and immature bulls. It will also effectually stop the endless disputes that have hitherto arisen regarding cow ivory. I may add the late Sir Donald Stewart was in favour of it, and would have recommended it for favourable consideration.

Since the German authorities have made no efforts to prevent this export of zebra and other game hides, it is improbable that they will prohibit the export of cow ivory, and there will, therefore, always remain an outlet from this Protectorate by smuggling into German territory.

This illicit trade, however, can be reduced to a minimum by our making it compulsory for all owners of ivory, whether traders or sportsmen, to register the same at one of the Government up-country stations of which there is now a complete chain across the Protectorate between Kitui and Kisumu. At least eight-tenths of the ivory obtained in this Protectorate as well as all the ivory from Manimani and Dodosa in the Uganda Protectorate comes from the countries north of our chain of Stations, and it would, therefore, be no hardship on any one to call in and register it, and receive a pass for the same from the officer in charge. The details regarding the number and weight of each tusk would then be notified to the Chief of Customs at Mombasa by post or telegram if necessary. All ivory not so registered, would be detained at Mombasa or other port of exit, until a satisfactory explanation was given.

6. Game returns are of great value in arriving at the approximate number of the various species of game killed annually, and there is no reason for believing that these returns are not submitted correctly by the majority of licence holders.

7. I agree with Mr Percival that for the present all but the simplest of cases of breaches of the Game Regulations, should be submitted to a senior official, and I would be happy to consider all such cases and issue any instructions that might be considered necessary; but I consider it would be more satisfactory if the Ranger himself was of sufficient seniority to deal with all breaches of the Regulations.

8. With regard to native hunters, I believe few, if any, are in possessions of firearms, and that they rely entirely on their own primitive methods of killing game, viz., bows and poisoned arrows, spears and pits. The Dorobo, Wasania, Waboni and a few others, who have lived for generations by hunting as a means of livelihood, may be entitled to kill game in their own districts, and even if we were in a position to prevent them, it would, I submit, be unfair to do so. On the other hand the Wakamba and the Kavirondo, who are agriculturists and also rich in stock, have been, and still are, but to a lesser extent, in the habit of organising large hunting parties and killing game wholesale outside their own districts, and I hold that these people have no hereditary right to do so. In their own districts there is no game, and it is only within the last 10 years or so that

the Wakamba have dared to leave the confines of their own districts and enter the adjoining game country, owing to their dread of the Masai. The Masai no longer molest them. The same remarks apply to the Kavirondo of the lower Nyando Valley. Up to the time of the military operations against the Nandi in 1900, these Kavirondo never hunted in the Valley for fear of the Nandi on one side, and the Lumbwa on the other; but since then, and up to quite recently, they have destroyed the game wholesale. This has, I believe and hope, been stopped. It is, however, much more difficult, if not impossible, to deal with the Wakamba referred to by Mr Percival, who enter the Southern Reserve at various points at night, and there is no chance of being able to deal with them until the staff of the Ranger has been increased.

The question of placing the Ranger in a position to deal with the matter of game preservation in a proper and effective manner is one of great importance to the country. It is acknowledged by everyone who has visited East Africa, that there is no other country in the world where game is found in such plenty and variety, and at the present moment it is indisputably one of the most important assets we have.

Great numbers of sportsmen from Europe and America are now visiting the country, and others, in increasing numbers, will follow.

Over and above the large sums of money spent and circulated through the country by them, a considerable amount of which comes back to us in the form of hut tax, the revenue alone from game licences, Customs dues on rifles, ammunition and camp outfit, railway fares and other dues cannot be less than £20,000, probably more.

Our only hope of keeping up the revenue from this source, quite apart from all sentiment in the matter of saving a rich fauna from extermination, is an efficient Game Ranger's Department, and I would strongly urge that such Department be established as soon as possible, and as follows: -

Estimates for 1907-08

Ranger	£600
Deputy Ranger	£400
Assistant Rangers: 2 at £250	£500
Horse allowances: 4 at £36	£144
Natives Scouts	£200
Expenses	£500
Total	£2,344

The Ranger should have his headquarters at Nairobi. One Assistant Ranger should be in charge of the Southern Reserve and adjacent 'open' districts with headquarters at Makindu and Kiu.

One Assistant should be in charge of the Northern Reserve and adjacent 'open' districts, with headquarters at Rumuruti or Baringo.

With an Assistant in charge of each reserve the Ranger and his third Assistant would then be able to move about from place to place as the occasion required.

The Assistant Rangers should submit quarterly reports with details as to the approximate numbers of each species of game in their respective districts or beats.

With these reports before him the Ranger would then be in a position to submit recommendations to the Commissioner in regard to the closing of a district for a limited period, or to prohibiting a particular species of game from being killed in a specified district.

At the present moment no one is allowed to kill a buffalo in the Ukamba Province[12], or a greater kudu in the Baringo District, and yet no one, not even Mr Percival, is in a position to say, or even suggest with any degree of authority, how much longer these two species should be protected. They may, or they may not, have increased in sufficient numbers to warrant a few bulls being killed on payment of a special fee.

At present the issuing of licenses is in the hand of the Sub-Commissioners of Provinces, as well as the Game Ranger. Most are issued by the Sub-Commissioner at Mombasa. This is unsatisfactory, as the Sub-Commissioners being tied to their offices are not in a position to say where a special licence holder can obtain a particular beast for which he has paid the fee of £5, and this, not unnaturally, often gives rise to a good deal of grumbling.

As a case in point: a sportsman whose time was limited, recently took out a special license to shoot a bull eland, and was recommended to go to Makindu. He went there, and successfully stalked three separate herds of eland, and then found that there was no warrantable bull amongst them, and as he had no time to go further afield he left the country without one. Again, two years ago, a well-known sportsman and naturalist, Mr Abel Chapmen, paid £30 in extra fees, but only obtained two of the beasts he had paid for, as he was not aware that he had to go to particular districts to obtain the others, and was under the impression that they might be found anywhere.

If, therefore, the issuing of special licences was left to the Game Ranger only such disappointments would be fewer, and yet I do not think it would make any difference in the number issued in future. The true sportsman would always be ready to take his chance after being advised, *on good authority*, that the beast he was anxious to obtain was to be found in a particular district

F. J. Jackson,
His Majesty's Deputy Commissioner.
Nairobi, February 13, 1906.

---

[12] Editor's note: At the turn of the century and in the wake of the great rinderpest epidemics of the 1880s and 1890s, buffalo were so few as to warrant special protection. Their rebound to being so abundant that they still rank as a very common animal, must be one of the more dramatic recoveries of any wild species in the 20th century.

Much of Jackson's data came from Percival as apparent from the following report. This raises the question of who, then, was the real engine behind the Kenya Game Department's genesis? In addition to his high station, Jackson was an eminent zoologist and arguing for conservation before Percival set foot in Africa. He first arrived on the coast in 1885 prior to Britain formally acquiring its East African territories. He came to hunt and make zoological collections, activities which were close to his heart throughout his career. As an Imperial proconsul, Jackson was something of a polymath and very influential. It was natural that he should have sought his subordinate's views and incorporated them with his own. Yet even if Percival had had the vision of founding a Department, he was neither very literate, nor a strong personality and showed a preference for being in the field and avoiding both office work and administration. Seemingly, he would have been as happy to have continued under the Administration as setting up a special Department. Given the facts it is more reasonable to award Jackson the laurels for founding the Kenya Game Department.

Blayney Percival, Kenya's first Game Ranger

Suggestions for Further Preservation of Game British East Africa by A. Blayney Percival, Game Ranger.

Revenue, 1904-05.
Approximate:

Licenses	£5,990
Fines	1,050
Confiscated Ivory	100
Total	£7,140

Expenditure:

Game Ranger's salary and expenses	£354

This seems a very small proportion of the revenue to be spent on such an extremely valuable asset to the country, and one which is increasing every year, and while it brings £6,000 as revenue in licenses (it) brings at the very least five times as much money to be spent in the country in railway freights, native porters, and the hundred and one things needed for safari. The revenue has improved year by year; in 1903-4 it was £3,605, 1904-5 £5,990, and for 1905-6 I expect over £7,000, with a further increase the year after: this in licenses alone.

Owing to the amount of settlement taking place in and around the game districts it is absolutely necessary that further steps should be taken to preserve the game. I would propose that two Assistant Game Rangers be allowed, each at a salary of £200; that they should be allowed a horse allowance of £36 each, as horses are an absolute necessity, and expenses of £100. In addition to this I think that £100 extra should be allowed to the Chief Game Ranger, this to be spent on Scouts or Police as the £100 expenses will barely cover the travelling expenses alone and leaves nothing for the Scouts. At present I am unable to keep more than four natives in permanent employ as Scouts. I would propose to station the two Assistant Rangers, one in the Southern Reserve at a point from which he could watch the boundary to prevent poaching from German territory, and also keep an eye on the road across the Seringati[13] where numbers of travellers to and from German territory pass; the other at Nakuru, in the Rift valley, from whence he could look after Likipia [sic] Baringo and Rift valley. Within a very short time all shooting in the Rift valley will be on private land, and when this happens sporting parties must go further afield. I believe that south towards the German frontier will become, with Likipia on the north, the favourite shooting grounds[14].

---

[13] Editor's note: the Seringati was what is now mostly southern Tsavo West National Park from Murka southward to the Tanzania border.

[14] Editor's note: As Kajiado and Narok districts, this is what happened; however, Laikipia was to be settled like the Rift Valley.

My estimate for the protection of game would be: -

Game Ranger's salary	£400
Expenses	"100
Police or Scouts	"100
Horse allowance	" 36
Two Assistant Rangers at £200	"400
Two Assistant Rangers' horse allowance each £36	" 72
Two Assistant Rangers' expenses each £100	"200
	£1,308

As I estimate the revenue for 1906-7 at little short of £10,000, this is still a very small proportion to be spent on preservation.

In making these suggestions I have not taken the Northern Reserve into consideration at all, as it is impossible to do anything to protect game until the country comes under the Administration in a more direct way. At present the Closed Districts Ordinance prevents stray prospectors and traders from going up there as well as the Somali and other natives, who were accustomed to trade or shoot ivory.

A. B. Percival

* * * *

With his superior's support, Jackson's urging that a Game Ranger's Department with additional officers was adopted. It came into being in 1907. However its head was not Percival, but Colonel J. H. Patterson of *"Man-Eaters of Tsavo"* fame, Percival having declined the post. Patterson was not designated 'The Game Ranger' as Jackson had favoured, but 'The Game Warden' of the British East Africa Protectorate. Perhaps this came about through no more than a wish not to deprive Percival of his title. Initially, therefore, the Head of the Department was The Game Warden and his officers were Game Rangers.

This didn't last as some Departmental officers were being referred to as Assistant Game Wardens at least as early as 1914. George Adamson called himself Assistant Game Warden, Northern Reserve when he took up his first post in 1938. Nevertheless, many if not most officers referred to themselves and were referred to generally as Game Rangers. In the Wild Animals' Protection Ordinance #18 of 1951 the head of the Department became the Chief Game Warden, and officers were obviously and legally Game Wardens. Yet despite what the law stated, we still called ourselves Game Rangers until 1958, when Willie Hale put his foot down and said that from that date forward we should conform to the law. Ranger was in keeping with the outdoor image we had of ourselves, whereas Warden was less romantic and connotated clanging doors

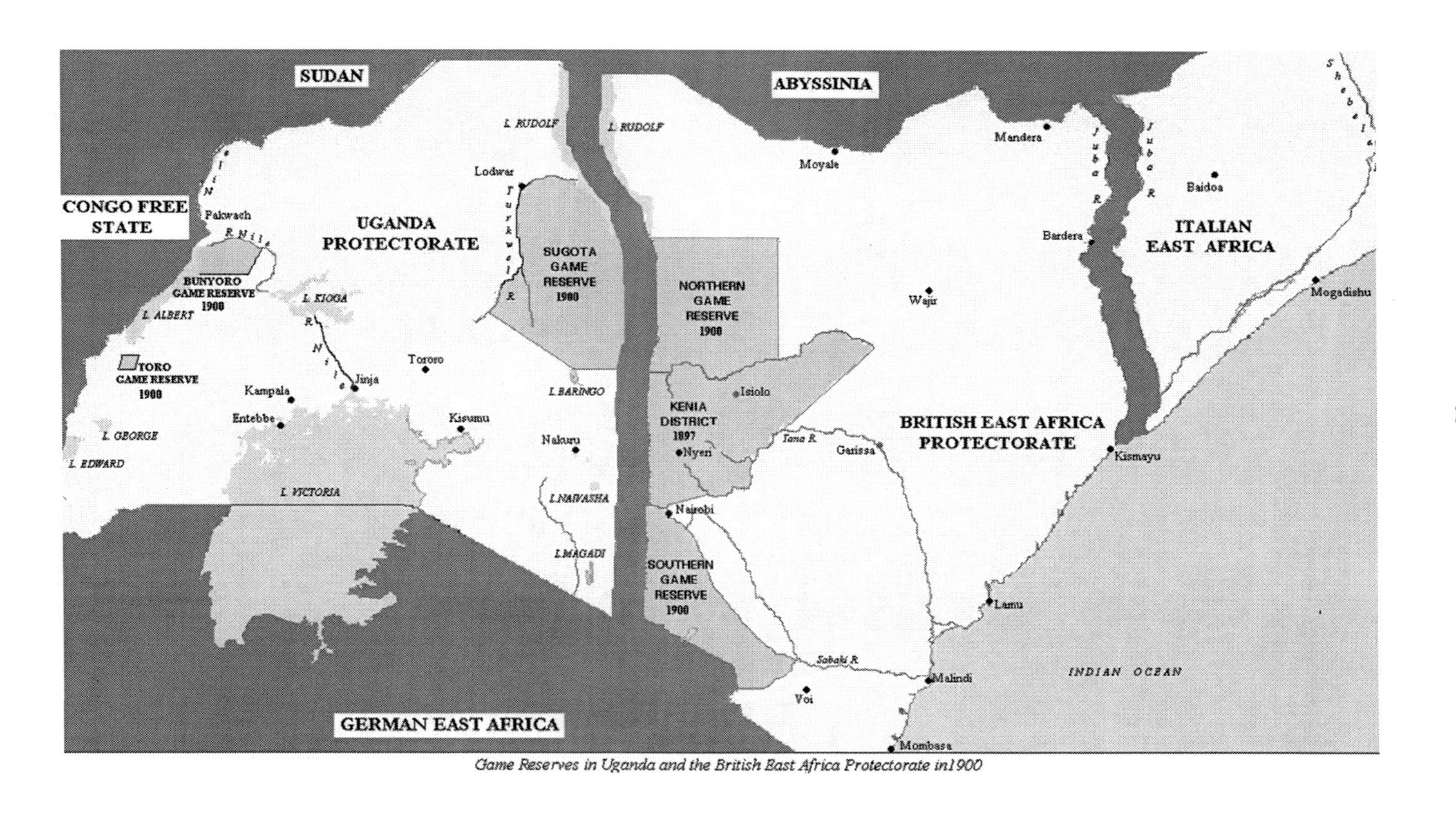

Game Reserves in Uganda and the British East Africa Protectorate in1900

and rattling keys. Most of us adopted Warden reluctantly. From the outset subordinate staff were Scouts. The area for which a Ranger was responsible was his range. When National Parks were formed matters were confused somewhat because the Trustees called their officers Wardens and their subordinate staff rangers.

From all accounts Patterson was not likeable. Prior to his employment by the Uganda Railway he had never risen above non-commissioned rank in the army. Somewhat humourless and a martinet, very much a disciplinarian in the Sergeant Major mode, he had been put in charge of the Railway slum called Nairobi in 1899. It soon split in two: that south of the Nairobi river was administered by the Railways under Patterson, and that to the north under Ainsworth of the Administration who had moved across from Machakos. Patterson's municipal claim to fame was burning Railway Nairobi to the ground to stop an outbreak of plague. It was very successful, but landed the Railway with huge claims for compensation. Patterson then volunteered for service in the final Boer War and obviously did rather well, for when he reappears he was a Colonel.

Patterson wasted no time in going off into the blue to visit the areas proposed for the Northern Game Reserve. Two friends – a married couple – accompanied him. In the course of the safari the husband accidentally shot himself. Kenya's rumour machine went into high gear and around the bars it was said that the man's death was no accident. Patterson resigned not long after his return from the safari and left Kenya. Two years or so later, he married the accident victim's widow, loosing an avalanche of "I told you so's." There was never any proof of foul play, but Kenya was without a Game Warden until 1910, when R. B. Woosnam was recruited.

In the Game Department's 1924 Annual Report it is stated:–

> *The Departmental Estimates for 1925 provided for the promotion of one of the two Assistant Game Wardens to the post of Senior Assistant Game Warden, which post had been unfilled since 1914; and further provide for the appointment of two Junior Assistant Game Wardens, in addition to the existing staff, bringing the total of officers in the Department to five.*

Woosnam's Annual Reports for 1910-1913 are excellent sources of information on a variety of subjects. Among points made were that rhino were declining. It became a self-enforcing mantra down the years. Again, despite being aware of the trend all through the century, no steps taken to stop it were successful until less than four hundred were left. Only then, and principally through the initiatives of Peter Jenkins, was it accepted that they should be concentrated in small, closely guarded sanctuaries.

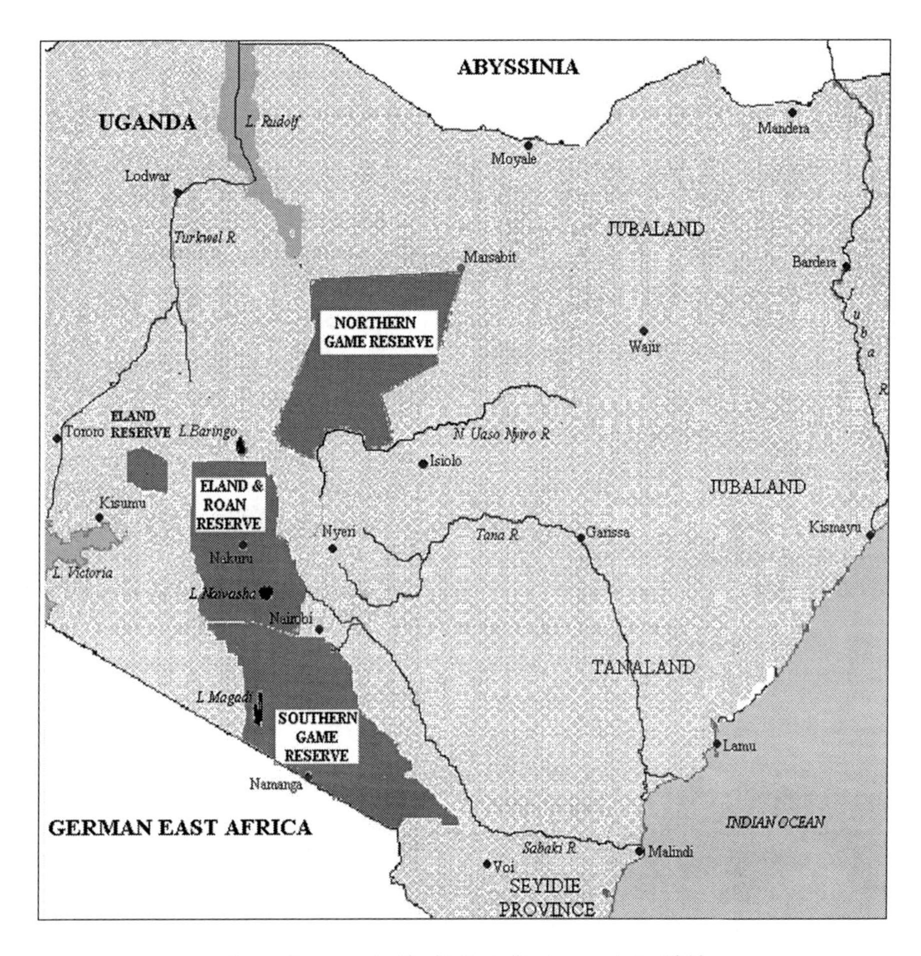

Game Reserves in the B. E. A. Protectorate in 1910

At the outset, and as indicated by Jackson's comments, Government openly accepted that the game laws were primarily to control the hunting activities of white men. They even sought to prevent the elimination of game on private agricultural land, leading Delamere to protest in the Legislative Council that:–

> *"We have seen game laws introduced here by the Colonial Office which can only remind one of the game laws of the old feudal days in Europe."*

In 1909 the game laws were redrafted but retained a section which allowed natives who had traditionally lived off game to continue to do so. The perception in vogue was that because white men found abundant game living alongside the Africans it would always be thus, providing that they were denied the use of firearms. It even prevailed where elephants were concerned. In what was broadly referred to as Tanaland, the Government introduced a policy whereby the Boni had to hand over one tusk of each elephant they killed. The rationale was rooted in a tradition that recurred across Africa that the tusk of every elephant killed belonged to the local chief. The colonial government claiming to now be the 'chief' subsumed this role for itself. The role that ivory played in the economy was enormous. Between 1887 and 1910 it and hunting revenues from sportsmen accounted for over fifty per cent of the country's income.

The size of the Department is perhaps germane to any consideration of what it was supposed to do and whether it could do it. An incomplete record of the Department is given in Appendix II but the following gives an idea of staffing through most of the colonial era: -

1906	One Officer and 4 Native Scouts
1907	Four Officers
1925	Five Officers
1927	Six Officers
1956	Fourteen Officers
1957	Fourteen Officers
1958	Seventeen Officers.

As a wry aside, the present staff in Nairobi's Kenya Wildlife Service headquarters is over 800 – even after significant retrenchment. This is greater than the whole Department in the colonial era and around double the number of rhinos in Kenya today.

In the second decade of the century, the idea that the natives would live forever in harmony with wildlife started to slip, and by the 1920s it dropped out of sight, with growing realization that things were not as they at first had seemed. What the whites were unaware of at the time was that their arrival coincided with the best years for game for perhaps a century or more. The Masai, who dominated the highland plains of south/central Kenya and northern Tanganyika had undergone catastrophe. Major internal wars that led to the collapse of the Laikipiak and virtual annihilation of the Uasin Gishu by other clans unified under Batiaan's influence reduced their numbers. This was followed in the 1880s by bovine pleuro-pneumonia and rinderpest pandemics that swept through East Africa eliminating cattle and some wild herbivores on a huge scale. Masai and pastoral numbers generally followed suit. Hardly had these events taken place when waves of smallpox brought about yet further and rather more general human reduction. Capping them was a serious famine between 1897 and 1899, followed by lesser famine in 1901, in which thousands of people starved.

This chain of disasters brought human and domestic stock numbers to what must have been a low point in terms of the previous two centuries. Competition with wildlife will have been correspondingly reduced, and game will have been bouncing back to a high point just as colonial rule took hold. Yet two decades into the twentieth century, human and livestock numbers were recovering strongly. Competition with game will consequently have been rising and influencing African farmers just as it did any other farmers. African traditional hunting was no different from any other form of hunting in its effects and the savants soon saw that game needed as much protection from Kenya's indigenous people as it did from the alien settlers. Indeed, as Africans were in a huge majority, it needed more protection from them than from the whites.

* * * *

Somewhere after 1909, the laws that specifically permitted Africans who traditionally lived off game to go on doing so, vanished from the statutes. After the First World War, the early official attitude that the game laws were primarily to control the activities of the white settlers disappeared altogether.

The First World War had brought the Game Department to a standstill. Woosnam was among its members who rallied to the colours and was killed. Once more Blayney Percival held the fort, still resisting the title of The Game Warden. In 1922 and 1923 Captain Keith Caldwell, stepped into his shoes before going off to become Game Warden for Uganda. Woosnam's substantive replacement as Game Warden - Captain Archie Ritchie – did not take up his post until 1924. In the year he took up his post, Ritchie wrote: -

> *Illegal killing by natives of valuable game animals – Elephant, Rhino and Giraffe – constitutes by far the greatest problem which at present concerns this Department; it is sad to relate that it continued on a large scale during the year...*
>
> *It is in the vast bush and Nyika countries comprising the area roughly bounded by a line running through the following places – Lamu, Lorian Swamp, Meru, Machakos, Makindu, Mombasa, an area of some 30,000 square miles, much of it unadministered and some of it unknown, that the problem of preserving the great game is one to occasion dismay, if not despair. The Wakamba, the WaGala, the WaBoni, the WaGiriama, the WaNyika and the rest, assisted by the Somali, the Arab, the Abyssinian and the Indian continue to kill, and to dispose of their ill gotten Ivory and horn ...*

The following figures show the prosecutions under the Game Ordinance during the year so far as can be ascertained

Prosecutions i.e., Persons charged	*Convicted*	*Acquitted*
378	*311*	*67*

Ritchie was so concerned by the problem of African poaching that by 1927 he had taken on a Game Ranger – MacArthur – to attend to it. MacArthur deserves greater recognition than he has so far been accorded. A champion heavy-weight boxer, a policeman – first in India and then in Kenya's Criminal Investigation Department (CID) – he went about anti-poaching in the Coast Province and Ukambani as no one else did either before or after his time. In the ten years between 1927 and 1937, he secured over four thousand poaching convictions, surely a world record? If nothing else, it made indigenous people aware of the game laws and that hunting – pretty well all hunting – was unlawful.

Again, in hindsight, official attitudes towards African hunting swung between two unreal poles. From assuming that they would never pose a threat to game and could go on using it, the pendulum swung to the other extreme of permitting no use at all. Willie Hale summed it a section on poaching in his 1953 Annual Report:–

> *"Every African is a poacher ... In Kenya one recognises no customary hunting rights, though certain sub-tribes, such as the Tharaka in Kitui, the Taita in Voi, and the Wasanye in the Coast Province, not to mention the ubiquitous forest-dwelling Dorobo, are nearly all full time hunters."*

His solution?

> *"Poaching must be stopped and, therefore, poachers must be prosecuted."*

The background to this unreasonable attitude had little to do with game and a great deal to do with security, though we Wardens were not generally aware of this. The policy of blocking African hunting occurred in only three of Africa's Anglophone countries: Kenya, Southern Rhodesia and South Africa. Unsurprisingly, these were the three where whites settlers had alienated land on any scale. While it was never stated Africans may not hunt in so many words, policies for keeping guns out of the hands of the natives had this effect. In Kenya the cost of licences was beyond average African means. If they could not afford licences, then there was no point in letting them have guns. *Vice versa*, the game laws outlawed traditional weapons (abandoning Jackson's and Percival's original belief that if they used traditional weapons they were no threat to the game) and insisted lawful hunting be done with firearms. If a man didn't have a firearm, he couldn't have a game licence. While the policy of keeping guns out of native hands was only openly acknowledged in the corridors of power and not publicized, it ensured that Catch 22 prevailed.

Kenya's anomalous position on African hunting stands out starkly when one looks at British colonial game keeping policies in the territories not opened to white settlement. Ownership of firearms by natives was not prevented, game licence costs were within local means or special licences affordable to the natives were issued. African hunters, for example, took most elephants shot on licence in Uganda. In Tanganyika a five-shilling licence permitted the holder to take far more animals than he could personally consume in a year. The outcome of Kenya's policy was that the African population was completely alienated by the game laws: an historic fact that had a potent influence in the ban on hunting started in 1977 and which still continues. While the overt rationale for this decision was that it was necessary because hunting was out of control, the country's general acceptance came from a perception that hunting was a white man's sport that thirteen years of independence had done little to dispel.

Because the Game Department never had the manpower to enforce the game laws, after MacArthur, the issue of African hunting was largely ignored. Here and there individual Wardens picked at it, but others openly admitted turning a blind eye and, only acting when ivory, rhino horn and leopard skins were blatantly taken. Lyn Temple-Boreham of Narok illustrated this classically and was quite frank about not stopping 'Dorobo' from hunting for food. MacArthur's decade of anti-poaching and the anti-poaching campaign of 1956/1957 were exceptions to a far more general attitude of *laissez-faire.*

Legend has it that Kenya's national parks are attributable to one man and one man alone: Mervyn Cowie. Like so many legends, and as Mervyn himself was the first to point out, it is at variance with fact. The idea of sanctuaries where wildlife was safe from hunting by man has been common to many cultures for millennia. The oldest conservation area in Africa is probably Menegasha in Ethiopia. While termed a park only in 1958, it has had protected status for perhaps four hundred years. The term 'national park' was introduced to Yellowstone in the United States in 1872 and while the term may have been new, that was all. The idea of sanctuaries was widespread far earlier. The list of prominent politicians, administrators and personalities advocating their establishment on a grand scale in colonial Africa is not only long but goes back to the very beginning of the colonial period. There was a grand vision of Africa as the world's great Garden of Eden in which Nature survived as it never had in Europe and North America.

In the colonial age the Afrikaners established the Sabie Game Reserve in 1898 before the Transvaal became part of British South Africa. Only later was it renamed the Kruger National Park. Article II (5) of the 1900 London Convention demanded all states establish "... reserves within which it shall be unlawful to hunt, capture, or kill any bird or other wild animal ..." The idea of parks in Africa was actually being pushed harder before Mervyn Cowie was born than after. Among those standing out was Lord Salisbury while Britain's Prime Minister. Locally, other constant advocates were white administrators like Frederick Jackson and naturalists such as V. G. L. Van Someren. Yet no one pushed harder and more effectively than Archie Ritchie, the Game Warden from 1924 until 1948. His efforts are clearest in the records of the Kenya Land Commission Report[15]. Briefly in 1933 he was made a temporary Member of Legislative Council so that he could present his ideas to this law-making body. Far more than Mervyn Cowie, Archie Ritchie laid the foundations for a formal national park system. Cowie's role, for which he is due great credit, was to thoroughly stir a slow-moving Government bureaucracy and translate Ritchie's ideas into action.

Mervyn Cowie, first Director of the Royal National Parks of Kenya (courtesy Peter Davey).

Of all the conservation policies with lasting potential that Kenya adopted, the creation of national parks was by far the most profound. Yet the principle – that big game populations could only survive if areas were set aside specifically for them – had been recognized from the very start. Initially it was thought that the Game Department could manage them and that Africans could co-exist with the

[15] Anon 1933. *The Kenya Land Commission Report* (also known as the Carter Commission after its Chairman Judge Carter). Government Printer, Nairobi.

big game inside them (bear in mind that the U.K's national parks still include much actively farmed land). Experience proved that this was not so: the sanctuaries had to be free of human residence. This meant proclaiming areas wherein people could not settle or from which they had to be removed, pitting those responsible for human welfare against those trying to conserve wildlife. This, above all other reasons, is probably why an idea so generally acknowledged took so long to come to pass. It also took time that the management of parks, once formed, called for a degree of specialization that the Game Department did not have to sink in. It was Cowie who set up such an agency – the Royal National Parks of Kenya – when the Royal National Parks of Kenya Ordinance came into law commencing on the 26th June 1945.

From very early on, the game laws made provision for creating Honorary Game Wardens. Those appointed had the legal powers of professional Game Wardens. At one time there were over two hundred gazetted honorary Wardens who not only greatly outnumbered officers of the regular Game Department, but whose presence, at least on paper, greatly increased the Department's capacities. The idea of honorary Wardens was sound, but the potential they represented was never developed. Largely acting alone and with little Departmental direction or supervision, a few honorary Wardens actively enforced policy, but for the most part they enjoyed the status and the social kudos that went with it, but did little.

In addition to the honorary Wardens, the game laws were supposed to be enforced by the Police, officers of the Administration and foresters as part of their routine duties. Enthusiasm for doing this varied very widely between individuals. Again, in theory at least, the game laws were enforced by a far larger reservoir of manpower than existed solely in the Game Department itself. Any assessment of the overall effect of Government's conservation policies should take this into account and, though no analysis of that effect has ever been objectively made, it would not be surprising if the combined influence of government officials and honorary Wardens equalled or even exceeded that of the regular Game Department establishment.

These first two chapters present a thumbnail sketch of the Game Department's background. As indicated earlier, most of us who served in it at the end of the colonial era were disinterested in anything but the life itself. Even had we wanted to know the Department's history, there was no one knowledgeable about it to whom we could have turned. For the carefree quality of our lives at the time this was probably a bonus. Looking back it was probably a weakness.

Archie Ritchie, Kenya's Chief Game Warden from 1924 to 1948.
(courtesy Tony Dyer)

CHAPTER 3: THREE STALWARTS

Peter Jenkins

Captain Archie Ritchie was educated at Harrow and Magdalen College, Cambridge, where he graduated with an Honours Degree in Zoology. He then joined the Grenadier Guards as a Second Lieutenant. Peace time soldiering and ceremonial duties bored him and he transferred himself to the French Foreign Legion as a Corporal and saw much active service with this famous French Army. When the First World War broke out, Archie rejoined his Regiment in France where he earned a Military Cross for bravery as well as a French decoration.

Archie came to Kenya in 1920 and worked for the East African Land & Development Company before joining the Game Department as The Game Warden in 1924. In very much the same way that his counterpart in Uganda, Captain Charles Pitman, was seconded to Northern Rhodesia in the mid-1930s to set up a Game Department there, Archie Ritchie was sent to Malaya for a couple of years in the mid-1930s to create an up and running wildlife conservation service there. Among other things, it underscored the influence that conservation in East Africa was having widely elsewhere. Having completed his stint in Malaya, Archie returned to Kenya and continued as head of the Game Department until he retired in 1948 to live in Malindi.

Archie was a fine figure of a man: very tall and upright, well over six foot and was a strong character with immense charm. His efforts as Game Warden did much to attract sportsmen to Kenya from all over the world. He felt it incumbent upon himself to be personally helpful to them and welcomed all who visited his office for advice. It was his habit (for which he was well known) to offer visitors to his office a pink gin or two! Small wonder that he became something of a legend to visiting sportsmen. He insisted on good sportsmanship and frowned on any unnecessary killing, recommending a good picture in preference to a good trophy. He enforced the laws firmly but fairly and rank did not deter him from what he saw as his duty: hence he prosecuted Prince Yusuf Kamal for a breach of the law as well as Jack Lucy.

Archie was a fine photographer himself and made a number of excellent wildlife films including some of animals never previously photographed. Throughout his life he continued as a keen naturalist and was held to be an authority on hartebeest.

Perhaps the sort of man he was is best illustrated by an incident off the Malindi beach in September 1959. He and the then Governor – Sir Evelyn Baring (later Lord Howick) – were walking along the shore when they became aware that two Asian girls who, having gone for a swim, were being pulled out to sea in a strong undertow and were drowning. Without hesitation, both elderly men (Archie was seventy two at the time and Sir Evelyn had a weak heart) plunged through the breaking waves and rescued the girls. In the hard swim back to shore, both nearly drowned themselves. It was a fine feat typical of two real gentlemen.

I used to visit Archie and his wife Queenie at their seafront house at Casuarina Point whenever in Malindi and got to know both well. Archie was probably the most outstanding and successful character in Kenya's conservation record between 1887 and 2001: that is the entire colonial period and the post-independence years up to the present. Apart from his work with the Game Department, he was never given the credit that he so richly deserved for being the prime mover behind the creation of National Parks in Kenya. Mervyn Cowie may have been the man who ran the parks and built up the fine organisation that it became. Yet it was Archie Ritchie using all the force of his character, his enormous charm, and his determination coupled to his prestige of office who convinced both government and the public that national parks were a necessity for Kenya. What has not been generally appreciated is that it was his secondment to the Government of Malaya shortly after he had made his case both to the Kenya Land Commission and to the Legislative Council, that slowed the process he had been driving forward so fiercely. Had he not gone to Malaya, Kenya's National Parks would have existed before the Second World War.

Archie died on the night of the 15th/16th November, 1962, at his home. I had had drinks with him in his room that evening and although he had been bed-ridden for the previous six weeks or so, he had been in very good form and we had discussed the 'old days'. He was buried at sea, just outside the territorial limit off Malindi Bay and the funeral was attended only by Vivian Taylor the Magistrate, the District Officer Malindi, Dr Rossinger, Wilson Fred the Seychellois mechanic who had looked after Archie's old Volkswagen and lighting engine, his two old servants, Bill Woodley and myself.

* * * *

G. C. MacArthur, or Mac, as he was known to everyone started his career in the Indian Army then served in the Indian Police. During this time he had, as did so many of the Raj's officers, become fluent in Hindustani. In due course he came to Kenya and joined the Kenya Police where he served with the Criminal Investigation Department (CID) and for many years was Kenya's heavyweight boxing champion. As a policeman he had a reputation for being unorthodox but successful and was credited with keeping crime in Nairobi rewardingly low.

Because promotion was slow in the Police, Mac transferred to the Game Department where Archie Ritchie was looking for someone to enforce the game laws, particularly where illicit ivory and rhino horn trading was concerned. Mac became the first Game Warden to apply himself fully to this traffic and was greatly feared, especially by the Arab and Somali dealers, whom he would approach disguised as an Indian trader, putting his Indian experience to good use.

G. C. MacArthur, Africa's most successful anti-poaching Game Warden (courtesy Tony Dyer).

Mac was to later become the most successful anti-poaching Warden Kenya (and may be Africa) has ever had. The record of convictions achieved by him and his men between the late 1920s and World War II ran into thousands. His particular stamping ground was coastal Kenya and Ukambani. When the Tsavo National Park was first gazetted, Mac probably knew that area, especially the northern section, better than any other European. He had walked over a great deal of it, spending months at a time with a few Scouts on long foot safaris, chasing elephant poachers. He was the first white man to walk from the Athi River across what became Tsavo East, then across what became the Galana Scheme to the Tana. With hand labour he cut a track from Mutha south-east to Ndiandaza on the Tiva River, then further south-east to the Lali Hills on the north bank of the Sabaki, thence along the river's northern banks to Baricho, Marafa, and east to the main coast road just opposite Mambrui, a distance of over two hundred miles. In 1948, Bill Woodley was the first person to drive the length of MacArthur's track after Mac himself, and some years later, we, in parks, reopened it.

During Word War II Mac became Archie Ritchie's deputy and retired from the Civil Service when it ended. He built Mac's Inn at Mtito Andei in his old stamping grounds, sold it to Safariland Limited of which he had become a Director, and, among other things, took the newly demobbed professional hunter, David Sheldrick, under his wing as a protégé.

Mac had a fad for loose garments with loud checks, and was very sensitive about his middle name – Cuthbert. Unlike most Game Wardens he had not the slightest interest in any form of shooting. Nonetheless he was a great field naturalist. In 1949, he showed me Ngulia Springs, and later the very first of the National Parks' self-service lodges was built there. He gave me my first bird book, Volume I of Praed & Grant's Birds of North-Eastern Africa. G. C. MacArthur died in 1950 and, despite all his great achievements in making the game laws known and enforcing him, he was soon forgotten.

* * * *

John Alexander Hunter was born in Dumfries, Scotland and came to the British East Africa Protectorate before World War I. Initially employed by the Uganda Railway as a train guard and in the Nairobi Goods Depot, delivering Goods' Arrival Notices to the merchants of the town, his heart, from the very outset, was set on hunting, and from the beginning he was known as JA.

John Alexander Hunter – JA.
(courtesy Tony Dyer).

He met and married Hilda Banbury, daughter of Nairobi's first European saddler who plied his skill in the service of Chas. A. Heyer, the German gunsmith who had premises in Government Road. Banbury was to die in a revolver accident and Chas Heyer lost his business as a result of the First World War. As a point to record before it is lost forever and although it will not change the course of history, Hilda's two younger sisters were twins and one was a very accomplished *siffleur* and in great demand for concerts. Who, today, has ever listened to a *siffleur* give a concert?

JA left the Railway and with Cecil Higgs set up a transport company with a large fleet of mule wagons. The Railway contracted them to deliver goods from Nairobi Station to outlying districts and the business was highly successful. In due course Hunter & Higgs Limited was bought by a Mr Biemer (of the furniture makers Hutchings & Biemer Ltd) for two sons-in-law – Jack Catzler and Eddie Ruben – who were in the transport business. Success stayed with them and their amalgamated transport interests grew into Express Transport Limited, still prominent in Kenya's commerce today.

After selling his transport company JA then devoted his full attention to his first interest – hunting, particularly elephant. It was not long before he was in trouble with the Game Department and seen as a poacher who had to be neutralised. Confronting him head-on as was typical of him, Archie Ritchie gave JA a serious warning. As a result of this JA swapped elephant poaching for the quieter business of professional hunter. He joined a fellow hunter, Rowland Shaw and their firm was called Shaw & Hunter Limited. Among their employees as Accountant and Stores Assistant was a youngster – Donald Ker, who subsequently went into the field on several safaris with JA as his second hunter. In the fullness of time, Donald Ker joined up with Syd Downey and Jack Block to form the well-known company of Ker & Downey Safaris Limited.

JA left Shaw & Hunter, with Donald Ker as the Company's senior hunter. In due course the Company gave up hunting altogether and set up a gun shop in Nairobi's Hardinge Street. It later changed its name to Kenya Bunduki Limited and is still in existence.

JA conducted several highly successful safaris as an independent and also worked for Safariland. Yet, for all his success as a professional, hunting, rather than looking after clients, remained JA's interest. When, in 1942, Archie Ritchie offered him employment as a control officer (presumably in the philosophy of having a potentially bad poacher on one's side rather than in opposition), JA joined the Game Department and stayed in it until he retired in the late 1950s. He served principally in Ukambani and in neighbouring Kajiado. JA's name is remembered today for having shot one thousand black rhino in and around Makueni, to make way for agricultural settlement. At the time, when these animals were so common, it was not considered an issue of particular note.

Like Mac some seventy miles down the road to Mombasa, JA spent his retirement running a roadside hotel – Hunter's Lodge – on the Mombasa/Nairobi road at Kiboko, in the area in which he had served the Department for over quarter of a century. He died there in 1963.

Peter Jenkins, National Park Warden & Honorary Game Warden for over forty years, aged eighteen, shortly after being signed on as a Junior Assistant National Park Warden. (courtesy Sheila Wren).

CHAPTER 4: WILDLIFE USE IN WORLD WAR II

Peter Jenkins[16]

The Second World War wildebeest and zebra control started in the Simba-Emali area. It had three roots. The first was to provide meat for labour and prisoners of war. The second was pressure from the Administration to provide free meat for famine-stricken and starving Kamba. The third to reduce competition between Masai stock and game for limited grazing. The Game Department sent a temporarily employed Control Officer to shoot them – I think his name was Harris. Animals were simply left in the field where shot and the Kamba were free to collect such meat as they were able. It was a complete debacle and was quickly stopped by Archie Ritchie, the Game Warden. Next he asked my father, Bryan (Pop) Jenkins to take over. He agreed providing that all meat and hides were utilised. Pop received no salary but could sell the meat and hides, was given a special petrol allocation (the wartime ration was four gallons a month) and the Game Department supplied firearms and ammunition. Henry Higginson, a Gilgil farmer, put in £500 and became Pop's sleeping partner, and a Ford V8 three ton truck was hired from the Allison brothers of Subukia.

The weapons supplied were all military: either British .303 Mark III service rifles, or captured Italian Army 8mm and .256 rifles. Pop preferred the 8mm once sighting problems had been overcome. These Italian weapons were routinely sighted to shoot three feet high at one hundred yards range. This was solved by providing them all with new foresights that we made from warthog ivory. The military hard-point 'solid' ammunition was converted to soft-point by splitting the nose – the split and dip method. This job was allocated to Pop's partner's son – Phil Higginson – and myself, and we prepared fifty rounds each per day. We were also permitted to do some of the actual shooting. The Italian .256 carbines were only used for close-range coup-de-grâce work: they kicked like a mule, had a flash like a twenty-five pounder, roared like a cannon and left us twelve and thirteen year-olds black and blue!

All meat was salted and air-dried, where possible in shade and disposed of through the War Supplies Board for one shilling a pound. Zebra fat was rendered down and sold. Hair from zebra manes and tails was used for brushes and the heavy zebra hides themselves were exported to the USA to be used as leather in machine belting. All this produce was railed from Emali station which, in those days, consisted of the station building and Jafferali's duka only (Jafferali later moved to Sultan Hamud).

[16] Editor's note: This is a particularly important record from probably the only surviving individual able to speak with first hand experience of what was the most extensive legal game use in Kenya's history. It was clearly something that the Department wished to forget as the records disappeared and the policy was rarely talked about after World War II.

The first season started at Simba, but at the District Commissioner's request we moved to Selengai. Shooting was done in four week blocks separated by no-shooting periods of six to eight weeks. On average twenty to twenty five animals a day were taken, all between 0900 and 1200 hours; all shooting was from a vehicle; Pop would not allow chasing and tended to concentrate on small groups to keep disturbance minimal. One recollection stands out strongly. In those days the density of rhino in the Mashuru-Selengai-Emali area was very high and to see ten to fifteen different animals a day was normal. They were so abundant that they were a significant factor during our work. On one occasion I was treed by one for four hours which prevented us retrieving six downed wildebeest in the vicinity. Despite firing shots to frighten the rhino away, it went to sleep under the tree in which I was marooned.

After the first year Henry Higginson opted for Pop to buy him out. The Allison's truck was returned to them and my father acquired an ex-South African Army Ford V8 truck from Hughes Limited, through the good offices of the War Supplies Board. These were arguably the best trucks then available. With a new engine, a wooden body exchanged for the original metal structure and good tyres, it gave us good service.

In 1944 the Administration pressed for our operation to be transferred to the Loita Plains[17] in Narok District, where Pop's work continued intermittently until after VJ day in 1945. Work was carried out in the Subatai area and was only possible when the migration moved onto the Loita (therein lies a point - the migration then was different to that today). A second Ford truck and an Italian Prisoner of War taken on as a driver/mechanic/skinner allowed offtake to be raised to forty a day. The bagged meat was collected by an Asian transporter Kushi Mohamed (of Narok & Uaso Nyiro) every ten to twelve days and driven to railhead at Kijabe. The hides still went for machine belting in America.

When not at school I joined Pop at Loita and from 1945 onwards was entrusted to shoot on my own from the second truck driven by the Italian. My best day was twenty eight mixed wildebeest and zebra in about two hours.

My father stopped his cropping work at the end of 1946. All the statistics of offtake, meat and hides disposed of etc., were sent as monthly reports to the Game Department by my father, but he never kept any for himself. From memory I think that our total offtake from both Selengai and the Loita was some 6,000 head of zebra and wildebeest in just over four years. Yet while Bryan Jenkins stopped cropping, the programme continued under Major Lyn Temple-Boreham (TB), the Narok Warden. He soon tired of this work and it was handed over briefly to a temporarily employed control officer. This gentleman distinguished himself by mistaking some Masai donkeys for zebra and writing-off the Game

[17] Editor's note: The Administration's demand that game be reduced to lower pressure on Masai stock in both Kajiado and Narok Districts gives the lie to the oft-stated idea that Masai interests did not conflict with those of the game.

Department truck assigned him. At a time when such vehicles were worth their weight in, if not gold, then ivory, this was a terminal error where his employment was concerned. He later went on to be a professional hunter, but to the end of his days never got rid of the nick-name of 'Punda' (i.e. donkey) acquired during his short stay in the Game Department. How TB disposed of the meat from the cropping he carried out I do not know, but by 1947 the War Supplies Board must have closed down. Also lost to history is how TB persuaded the Administration that game reduction in the interests of Masai cattle was no longer necessary. Had the game been so reduced that it was no longer competing with stock?

Throughout my father's time culling game, there was no Game Department presence in either Kajiado or Narok[18]. He kept Ritchie and the local District Commissioners closely informed of what he saw and heard. He made frequent visits to the Talek and Mara areas in which very few Masai were ever seen. We never saw cattle or elephant in the Mara, Siana Hills or Sand River areas. Pop acted as a *de facto* Game Warden and was called on to provide services. At one time hyaena were a problem around Ngore Ngore. In attempts to get rid of them over fifty lions were poisoned. In the wake of this debacle Pop was asked to take over the control work and agreed, providing that no poison was used and all animals that had to be killed were shot.

I never had much information on the wartime game shooting elsewhere. What I knew came second hand. Nevertheless the greatest amount took place around Nanyuki, in the Rift Valley, Kinangop Plateau and in Laikipia, and much of it was very contentious. Unlike in Masailand where we worked, the game in Laikipia was seriously reduced and never recovered. This was intentional as game was seen to be in competition with European farming. Species particularly affected were zebra, oryx, and giraffe. Much of the meat was delivered to the Prisoners of War Camps fresh. Many people were involved, among them Game Wardens – Adamson and Rundgren for example, Honorary Game Wardens, as well as many others well known in the game field such as Alick and Boyce Roberts, Roy Mayers, Carr-Hartley and the Randall brothers.

---

[19] Editor's note: TB was away with the K.A.R., first in Abyssinia, then in Burma, where he reached the rank of Major and won an MC.

Sydney Waller and his gun bearer (courtesy Tony Dyer).

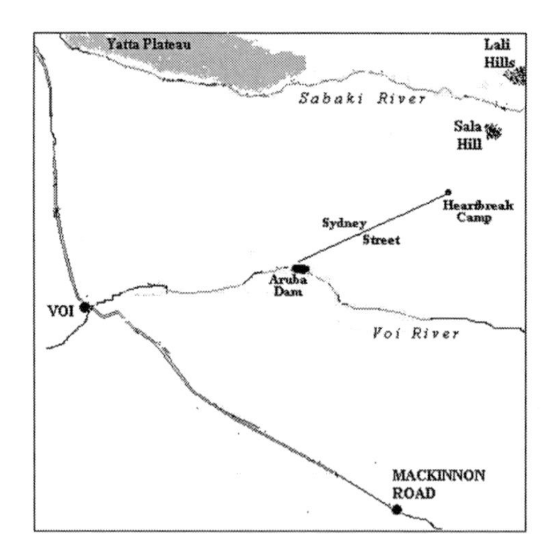

The Location of Sydney Street

CHAPTER 5: MY FIRST EXPEDITION DOWN SYDNEY STREET

Peter Jenkins

Few today can envisage the enormous problem that locusts caused in the first half of the 20th century, or realise the damage they can inflict. They were the farmers' bane and the ruin of many. The only way of controlling them in those days was to find where a swarm had bred and when the hoppers, as the immatures were known, emerged and before they could fly, place bran poisoned with arsenite of soda across their line of march. Locust Control Officers were stationed in remote dry areas where the locusts laid their eggs, and with their staff scoured the bush searching for hoppers. They were perhaps responsible for providing more access tracks into remote territory than any other group of men in Colonial Kenya's history.

Sydney Waller gave up professional hunting just before World War II, joined the locust Control Department, and was stationed at Voi. When he retired some time before 1948, he stayed on at Voi, living in an old corrugated iron shack on Voi Sisal Estate about four miles out of town opposite the civil airstrip on the Nairobi road. He fell on hard times and became a virtual hermit and I remember him in his twilight years when I first went to Tsavo. He was a big, quiet, unassuming man – who loved to chat with us youngsters whenever we called. He died a lonely man in his old corrugated iron shack about 1951. Few, if any, of the modern hunter/guides will ever have heard of Sydney Waller.

One of the locust control access tracks Syd made with hand labour, ran from Voi along the north bank of the Voi River to where Aruba dam now is. From Aruba it headed northeast towards the Galana in a straight line before ending abruptly in dense bush, having got nowhere! This last straight section some twenty miles long was known as 'Sydney Street'.

The first time I drove along Sydney Street was a few weeks after I was posted as a Junior Assistant Warden, to the newly gazetted Tsavo National Park in 1948. At the outset, there was only one Tsavo National Park that was split into two – East and West – a little later. We set off early one morning from Voi to do our first recce into what, later, became known as Tsavo East. I was driving a horrible Dodge lorry: it was like an oven as the engine was inside the cab. Seated in stately splendour in the back on camp chairs were the Warden Ron Stephens, the District Commissioner and Lionel Hartley. Perched along the truck's sides were ten local worthies to provide manual labour when needed.

Of course neither the Warden nor I had ever been there before and Steve was exploring his new park. As it turned out neither the DC nor Lionel Hartley had been there either, though both had lived in Voi for several years. Lionel, brother to the famous game trapper Carr-Hartley, was building what is now the Park Inn (then the Voi Hotel) for Safaris Africa Limited (a subsidiary company of Safariland Limited) and it was not long after this trip that he was persuaded by a so-called Major Astles to locate a dead elephant. They crashed into Mazinga Hill just outside Voi soon after take-off and Lionel was killed instantly. Astles had never been a Major, but was a Sergeant Major from the Army Ordinance base at Mackinnon Road. He moved to Uganda and, years later as Bob Astles was closely associated with Field Marshal Idi Amin Dada, sharing in his infamy.

The track had not been used for years, was seriously overgrown, very rough and the bush so thick one could see for only a few yards on either side. We ground along in low gear with repeated stops to either remove trees knocked across the track by elephants, or to allow the boiling engine of this abortion of a truck to cool down. No one had any idea where the track went to or ended. After some four hours of tedious going it terminated in a wall of bush and we turned around to grind our way back to Voi. Apart for four or five dikdik, a few ground squirrels and hundreds of hornbills, we had seen nothing but thick bush. I, for one, was beginning to wonder about the Great Tsavo National Park!

It was now coming up to mid-day and the heat was intense. In the cab you got burned on anything metal. The excited morning chatter from the crew in the back had long stopped, senses dulled by the roaring, graunching noise from the engine and gear box, compounded by the relentless ear-drilling sounds from millions of cicadas.

My three seniors were rapidly losing interest in this grand recce of the new park. Glowing red from sunburn like over-ripe tomatoes, sweating like hogs, becoming progressively more bad-tempered, they alternately dozed fitfully or shouted advice to me above the noise and creaking emitted by this heap of a vehicle about what gear to engage, or instructed me not to hit so many holes. We ground along, never above ten miles an hour and were only half an hour from Voi when, rounding a sharp corner with an impenetrable wall of bush on either side, were confronted by an enormous bull rhino in the middle of the track.

His response was instantaneous: he wheeled round and charged. As the engine of this contraption was beside me in the cab, there was nothing of substance in front of me and I did not fancy that horn coming inside with me! In lightning reflex, I swung hard right, ploughing into thick *Sanseviera*, losing what little forward momentum we had. The rhino grazed the left side, gave a tremendous snort that abruptly wakened the three seniors slumped in their camp chairs.

He then hit us abeam with great force, just behind the cab on the left side. There was a resounding crash followed by the sound of splintering timber from the body and the truck canted violently to the right. The three were thrown out of their chairs into a tangled heap on the floor, where they were then trampled by the locals who in a panicky stampede tried to distance themselves from the rhino's side, heedless of who might be underfoot. The right door of the cab flew open with the impact. The African driver sitting on the left in quick reaction grabbed the waist band of my shorts and prevented me being thrown right out. In mid-air, half in and half out of the cab, I lost control, the dense sanseviera brought the truck to a complete halt and the engine stalled.

The rhino now had a stationary object to work on, and he made good use of the opportunity. Three or four attacks followed in rapid succession on the rear of the vehicle – one of which removed the back toolbox with a rending of metal. Pandemonium! The rhino puffed and snorted while the vehicle shook and rocked, timber shattered, with pieces flying everywhere like missiles. Everyone was yelling and, above the commotion I could hear Steve shouting from beneath the shambles, "Get going, get going!"

Get going my foot! I was still half out of the cab as the driver frantically tried to retain his hold on my shorts. The vehicle lurched violently under each impact, threatening my precarious position as I desperately tried to claw and scrabble back inside onto a seat that had become dislodged – just to add to my problems. Steve was still bellowing movement orders the while!

After what seemed an age, but which was in fact probably less than a minute, I managed to get back inside. Unusually for that heap, the engine fired the first time, and we shot forward bulldozer fashion, through the bush. The rhino now started on the back end. Another violent crash removed the tailgate, this time causing panic at the rear and a charge from all in the back to get as far forward as possible, once more flattening Steve and Co. More roaring from Steve somewhere on the truck floor, "Go faster! Go faster!" and accompanied by the locals shouting the Kiswahili equivalent: "*Fanya mbio! Fanya mbio!*" Yet we were barely moving, ploughing through dense bush, trying to work back to the road. Several more jarring hooks came in rapid succession – then he hit us hard underneath, lifting up the rear end and jerking us backwards as he extracted his horn which had jammed in the underslung spare wheel carrier.

Steve suffered a mega sense of humour failure when he eventually surveyed the shattered timber, holes in the floor and bent metal to the Park's new and only lorry. The DC's dignity was dented and he had a badly grazed face where one of the locals had planted a size twelve tyre sandal in his haste to remove himself from the rhino. Lionel Hartley thought it all hilariously funny and could not stop laughing, which added to Steve's ill-humour. One local had a bad cut on the jaw from a flying shovel and was very subdued, while the others jabbered at the tops of their voices and I collected a rocket for not getting going quicker.

So ended the Parks' first journey down Sydney Street. In 1949, after Tsavo East had come into being under David Sheldrick with Bill Woodley as his Junior Assistant Warden, Syd's track was extended. The point at which the extension commenced is still apparent today as a change in direction towards Sala Hill on the river. This is where Bill's base camp was. It was the first big road project carried out by the park staff in Tsavo East and at the time a major undertaking. Keeping a labour gang of over one hundred men supplied with water and rations which had to be carted in a single, ramshackle World War II truck, was a logistical nightmare. It took several months of tedious work, cutting through the featureless, waterless bush that teemed with rhino, which frequently scattered the workers far and wide, before the track eventually reached Sala. Not least among the events which took place was that the workers went on strike. Small wonder Bill's camp in the bend at the end of Sydney Street was called Heartbreak Camp.

Today Sydney Street is a wide road and part of the main access through Tsavo to the north coast resorts at Malindi and Watamu, down which tourist minibuses hurtle trailing clouds of red dust. Few belting along it, usually breaking the park speed limits, will ever wonder about the beginning of this route and even fewer will care! One thing is for sure; none of today's visitors will ever see a rhino! That, then, is the story of Sydney Street.

'The Major' – Rodney Elliott, Game Warden Maralal (photo R. Elliott).

CHAPTER 6: GAME RANGER, MARALAL

Rodney Elliott

(This chapter is taken with permission from Rodney Elliott's unpublished autobiography)

Maralal was the headquarters of Samburu District which lies to the east of the Rift Valley between what were the 'White Highlands' and Lake Rudolf (now Lake Turkana). The township lies on the southern slopes of Maralal Mountain some seventy miles north of Rumuruti. In effect, the southwestern quarter of the district is an extension of the highlands further south. The southeastern quarter and northern half are dry lowlands typical of the rest of northern Kenya, but broken by three soaring mountain ranges - Nyiru, the Ndotos and the Mathews. All three and Maralal have cool, forested, heights. The District belongs primarily to the Samburu, a northern section of the Masai, but there were also other pastoralists - the Turkana, Rendille and Boran - whose herds graze parts of it.

From the earliest colonial days Samburu District was marked as an excellent game area. Indeed long before the First World War, almost all of it was designated as the Northern Game Reserve in which no sport hunting was allowed. The region used to be plagued by the 'Habash', who were gangs of Abyssinian buccaneers led by Amhara or Oromo 'Galla' who raided far and wide out of their highland fortresses in Ethiopia for slaves and ivory. For Kenya, a benefit from the Italian conquest of Ethiopia in 1936, was that Habash raiding virtually stopped.

When the case for national parks was put to the Kenya Land Commission in 1933, its protagonists wanted, above all else, to have the Northern Game Reserve proclaimed as the country's premier park. In those distant days they felt that the local people's interests could be successfully married with those of a national park. Later, when Kenya's parks were proclaimed after the Second World War, the Administration disagreed and was not prepared to subordinate human interests to conservation and the national park authorities had to look to Tsavo for their major dry country real estate.

Under the National Parks Ordinance 'National Reserves' could be proclaimed; these were a sort of halfway house between park and non-park status. In them human interests had precedence over wild animal conservation, but conservation affairs were taken away from the Game Department and put in the National Park authority's hands. As a sop for denying the Northern Game Reserve full park status, the Government did gazette a substantial part of northeastern Samburu and contiguous southwestern Marsabit District including Marsabit Mountain as the Marsabit National Reserve.

Thus in 1955, the eastern part of Samburu was technically in the National Reserve and game affairs under a Park Warden, Jerry Dalton who had based himself near Isiolo. Jerry, a thoroughly decent character, had been crippled by poliomyelitis and was unable to be active in the field. Both for this reason and the ambiguous status of national reserves, he was given neither the funds nor staff to do much. When I arrived at Maralal he was keen that I should take over control of game affairs within that part of the Marsabit National Reserve that lay within Samburu District, which I did. Subsequently, in the early 1960s, much of the Marsabit National Reserve was degazetted, returning to Game Department control while Jerry Dalton retired.

I originally had difficulty persuading Willie Hale to let me base myself at Maralal. Initially he had posted me to run Samburu from Rumuruti just outside at the district's southern edge. This was still in the land ranched by Europeans and too similar to Nanyuki with all its game control problems for my liking. And apart from anything else, the Game Department camp there was infested with rats. One night I woke with one impertinent rodent nibbling my moustache! I retaliated by putting down abundant rat poison. It led to something of a Pyrrhic victory because the rats then died in the house's hollow walls and the resulting stench was so awful that I had to move out.

The white ranchers around Rumuruti had a reputation for being among the most eccentric in Kenya and more prone to 'go bush' than anywhere else in the country. There was an element of truth in this. When handing over the area to me, my predecessor Roger Hurt, suggested I visit one of these eccentrics (rancher called Mills) as he was giving a party which would be memorable. It was. Only two people attended: Mills and his manager newly arrived from England. Luckily, I had declined, because the manager laced Mills' whiskey with strychnine, which gave him a particularly horrible death. The manager had forged a false will in which Mills left him the ranch. The murder was readily detected and the manager ended his days going through a trapdoor at the end of the hangman's rope.

While Willie Hale eventually agreed with my arguments for a base at Maralal, it meant that I had no house and all my staff lived under canvas. Fortunately for me the foresters posted to Maralal - successively Bill Beer and John Wreford-Smith - were bachelors who kindly allowed me to bunk down in their quarters. It was six years before Government provided the funds for a Game Warden's quarters and even longer to house my staff.

No other civil servants in Kenya were expected to be as self-reliant as we Game Wardens. When I joined, the basic equipment provided for each field station was a tent, two chairs, a table, a camp bed and a canvas bath. Transport provided was a three-ton truck. Smaller vehicles such as Land Rovers had to be provided by the Wardens themselves, although mileage travelled in the course of duty was paid for out of the station transport vote at predetermined government rates. A double-barrelled rifle usually of .470 calibre was provided as a personal rifle for each Warden in addition to several .404s and a dozen or so old military .303s that were issued per station. The older-established stations had Game

Department houses - for which government charged rent. Office equipment was confined to a triplicate book of the old foolscap size, some file covers and a safe.

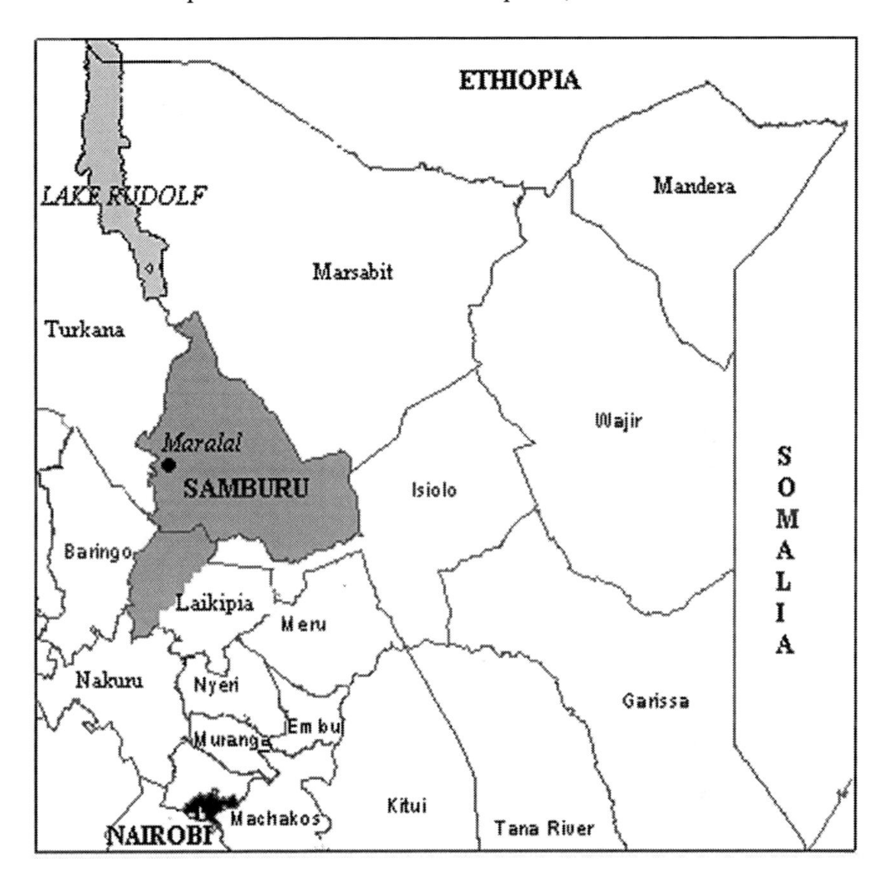

Maralal Game Range: Samburu District & Western Laikipia

Clerks were unheard of. Our correspondence was written, longhand, in our triplicate books. The original went to the addressee, the duplicate could be sent as a copy to other parties such as our headquarters, and the triplicate kept in the book for reference.

Each station had a dozen or so Game Scouts - ranked as Scout, Corporal or Sergeant. They were issued with khaki military 'askari' type uniforms, though when I joined, the Department had no badges.

Most stations had a cash imprest account that covered cash outlays made in the course of official duty – such as paying rewards for information or minor purchases. From time to time most Wardens had to temporarily finance work out of their own pockets. Even though this was eventually reimbursed, there was no doubt that government took advantage of the fact that Wardens were in the Department more from vocation than for gainful employment!

Scanning through my correspondence gives an accurate picture of my work in 1955. On the 7th May I wrote to Willie Hale about game matters on the 95,000-acre Laikipia Ranch managed by a Mr Southey. Southey had a reasonable attitude towards game: he liked its presence, but he tried to keep buffalo numbers down, as he feared they were a source of cattle diseases, and to provide meat for his labour. On average he shot one a week. I recommended that Southey be allowed to sell forty buffalo hides a year.

On the 14th May I wrote about Inspector G. E. Touche of the Kenya Police Reserve who had pleaded guilty to shooting game from a motor vehicle and for which he had been fined shs 300, given a month in which to pay or, in default, serve one month in jail. His licence was automatically revoked and he was barred from taking out another for three years. At the time that he committed the crime two other white Police inspectors had accompanied him. There were always bad hats who took advantage of their official status to break the game laws, but the Mau Mau Emergency had led to a general relaxation of the rules. The Department tended to look the other way when men on patrol augmented their rations by taking a buck for the pot now and then. However, the Emergency was winding down and it was time to tighten up, so I took a serious view of Policemen breaking our rules.

Several days later I reported charging a Samburu – Lebesoi Lelisimon – for spearing a buffalo for which he had been fined shs 200. I was at the same time investigating farm guards who had allegedly killed a giraffe, a rhino and a female eland. Because cattle rustling by young Samburu out to prove themselves was endemic, most white ranchers armed their cattle guards. From time to time these guards turned their weapons to poaching - as in this instance.

On the 23rd of May I wrote that a Mr Burton had been fined shs 150 or three months in jail in lieu for shooting a female eland without a licence. I had also arrested a Police constable for poaching.

On the 6th June I caught one G. Fox of the Desert Locust Control Organisation for shooting an eland unlawfully. He said that it had been an accident: he had been shooting at a Grant's gazelle but hit the eland by mistake. That he should take me as sufficiently foolish to believe this was so irritating that I charged Fox with a second offence: shooting at an oryx while within 200 yards of his vehicle. Fox caved in, admitted the offences and asked if the matter could be resolved out of court by 'summary punishment'.

On the 10th August I wrote to Gilbert Sauvage, an animal trapper, asking if he could stock two dams near Maralal with hippo. I thought having a few hippos in them would add a nice touch. I suggested that, if Willie Hale agreed, Gilbert could catch hippos where they were unwanted and take some of the hippos caught while releasing the others into my dams on a one for one basis in lieu of a fee.

On the 2nd September three Turkana hunters were convicted and given eighteen month sentences for setting snares, possessing arrow poison and causing unnecessary suffering. I threw the book at this lot because they had previously been convicted of killing a giraffe. The DC trying the case agreed with me.

On the 9th of September an angry letter to Willie Hale concerned a newly fledged professional hunter – R. W. Ryans[19] – who on his first safari for Ker & Downey Limited wounded and lost a rhino. Instead of following it up himself and making every endeavour to kill it, staying on its tracks until nightfall if necessary, he had left two trackers to do so while he went back to camp with his client. The incident happened at 10.30 in the morning and when I arrived in Ryans' camp at 14.30 I caught him with his feet up and a beer in hand. By the time that I was through Ryans certainly felt that his professional licence would be revoked and his hunting career over.

On the 12th September a letter to headquarters notified Willy that a well-known and very likeable professional hunter, had been fined shs 2,000 for taking a greater kudu illegally. He had had no licence for a kudu when he had come upon one in an area where they were not allowed to be shot in any case. Stupidly he had shot it. Hiding the horns up a tree and getting rid of the hide down an aardvark hole, he had then taken out a licence and come to me for advice on where he should look for kudu. Unfortunately for him I already knew what he had done. His conviction automatically meant that the man lost his licence to take out safaris. I had asked Willie Hale to notify his counterpart, Gerry Swynnerton, in the Tanganyika Game Department of the conviction to prevent the man from hunting in that country too. The two Departments co-operated closely in such matters so that a conviction and loss of licence in one country usually meant that its consequences applied in the other (and Uganda too). In the same letter I reported an un-named Samburu had been fined shs 500 for killing a cheetah. I took unlawfully killing any of the spotted cats seriously – though not when they had been killing stock. Cheetah can be nuisance where small stock are concerned.

On the 21st September professional hunter John Cook reported wounding and losing a rhino. After Cookie described the event I was satisfied that he had taken all reasonable steps to rectify the mistake and that no blame attached to the hunters. Indeed I was sufficiently satisfied to endorse his request to headquarters that his client be allowed special licences for an ostrich and a Grevy's zebra. Later I was not so happy as Cookie had neglected to tell me that the rhino they wounded and lost had been a female with a large attendant calf and I regretted accepting Cook's story.

When not on safari, John Cook used to send his gun-bearer scouting round the game lands for big elephant - a perfectly legal step to ensure that when a client

---

[19] Editor's note: this was Bill Ryan who went on to become a well-liked and respected Ker & Downey hunter. Rodney had mis-spelt the name, adding an s.

arrived they did not have to spend time looking where there was nothing to look for. It had been on one such venture near Suguta Marmar that the elephant being spied upon saw, chased and killed Cookie's gun-bearer. I visited the scene and followed up the animal. I deliberately gave it my wind to see how it reacted. If a habitual rogue and it came looking for me, I would shoot it. This turned out to be the case, for the elephant charged us immediately it was aware of our presence, even though we were some way off, so I killed it.

But to return to my 1955 duplicate book: later on the same day I had looked back through my triplicates and it seemed that the hunters were not being nearly careful enough and I wrote to my boss pointing out that professional hunting safaris had wounded four big game animals in the preceding four months and asked him to register his strong displeasure to their Association.

On the 1st October I wrote to W. Thoms Esq., allowing him to keep a cheetah as a pet if he could tame it, and also that he could keep a stock-killing leopard's skin. I told him that I would personally arrange for the necessary permits to be issued. Thoms was a good landowner who took care of the wild animals on his property and was the sort of person whom I felt should not only be encouraged, but also allowed to make some money out of game. If he was permitted to sell the leopard skin it would bring him some recompense for the stock it had killed.

At the end of that month four American missionaries, M. Donohew, J. M. Retherford, F. Reeve and a Mr Yutzy, were taken to court for unlawfully killing a Kenya hartebeest. I was not the only Warden who had found that missionaries – particularly American missionaries – among the worst offenders for breaking the game laws. Seemingly they felt a dog collar gave them licence to break the rules!

My first Annual Report was written on 4th January 1956. It was all of two pages long with an additional page of statistics covering the first seven months in my new post. My staff comprised a Driver and 12 Game Scouts, all of whom lived under canvas. Four elephants had been shot on control, three buffalo and a larger number of zebra. We monitored 12 safari parties that had hunted in my area and shot six elephants, eight rhinos, fifteen buffaloes and seven leopards. Seven white men had been taken to court, 13 Africans but no Asians. I had endeavoured to count the game on the Leroghi Plateau and El Barta plains. I think that this was probably the first such game count ever done in Samburu. I undertook it because government was trying to introduce rotational grazing schemes to the local herdsmen as a strategy in managing their grasslands. Those responsible complained bitterly when carefully conserved grass was then consumed by 'my' game. I wanted some idea of just how many game animals were involved and whether the claims were justified. The count showed that they were, but while the game numbers were not as serious as made out, the issue did need resolving. This was one of the elements that formed my policy of trying to get as much income from game back to the Samburu to offset the costs of its presence.

The next seven years were more detailed repeats of that first year. By and large the professional hunting fraternity played by the rules and some of them were Honorary Game Wardens. Yet there were some exceptions. Three cases I recall clearly. The first concerned one of the better-known elders of the business: Bunny Allen. His client wanted a picture of an elephant charging. Finding one, he had set up the client with her camera, and then thrown stones at the elephant. The charge he got was rather more serious than he had wanted, and he had had to open fire. He had failed to stop or drop the charging animal and his gun-bearer then saved both the hunter's and the client's lives by dropping it stone dead. Unrepentant, Bunny took the tusks without reporting the matter to George Adamson in whose area the event took place. Later he claimed them on a licence subsequently taken out in his own name. At a time when Africans who killed elephants unlawfully were going down for several years, he should have got the same sort of sentence. Unfortunately, I was not present when the Criminal Investigation Department (CID) of the Police prosecuted him for me, and he got away with a mere slap on the wrist and the loss of his professional hunters licence for a year. I think it was grossly unfair that he was not punished more severely.

I had had my eye on another hunter whom I did not trust. Hoping to catch him out sooner or later I visited his camp to find him gone. I could see where hides had been salted, then pegged out to dry. Licking the palm of my hand then placing it on the ground where each hide had been, a sample of hairs stuck to my damp palm (this trick was a tip from Jim Corbett, famed for his destruction of man-eating leopards and tigers in India, and whom I got to know when he lived in Nyeri). By examining them carefully, I could tell what animals had been shot. One was a greater kudu, which were not allowed to be shot in this particular area. Looking carefully about the campsite, I recovered a kudu's fresh lower jawbone. With me at the time was my good friend Reino Hoffmann, who was Professor of Anatomy at Nairobi University. The hairs and the jaw were taken to his University laboratory and confirmed as coming from a greater kudu.

Next I checked whether the hunter and his client had had a kudu licence on the day that we collected the evidence: they had not, but a few days later, they had bought one. Knowing this I went to Zimmermann's, the local taxidermist, and asked if the hunter had brought in any trophies recently. He had and there, sure enough, was a kudu skull minus lower jaw. This exactly matched the lower jaw we had recovered at his camp and both obviously came from the same animal: a point Reino could easily prove in court as an expert witness. Then I checked whether the hunter had submitted his game register. He had and claimed a kudu shot nearly three hundred miles away from where we found our evidence, some days after we collected it. There had been no ban on shooting kudu where he said he shot it for a very good reason: greater kudu did not occur there. This case never came to court as the professional hunter got wind of it and fled the country.

The third case concerned another well-known professional hunter: Peter Leth. Assisted by Peter Saw, then newly recruited to the Game Department, I had stopped Leth's vehicle to find him, his girl friend and a prominent Nairobi trophy dealer with a load of three hundred leopard skins. With a jail sentence of up to five years and a fine of £1,000 for the first illegal leopard skin and a further year or a further £250 for each subsequent illegal skin, it seemed that if their consignment was illegal, each could be sentenced to 304 years in the 'slammer' or a fine of £75,750, or a mix of these two possibilities. It was a spectacular seizure. Yet the case never went to court![20]

The skins had been brought into Kenya from Ethiopia and Somalia on the dealer's behalf. We could not prove that they had been acquired unlawfully in either country of origin. In all probability, given those two countries' lax conservation, they were legal. Kenya law, however, required the skins to be declared to Customs at the point of entry. This had not been done at Moyale where they entered Kenya, which was my ground for seizing the consignment.

Intelligence information had warned me that the consignment of leopard skins would be entering Kenya, so we had had time to prepare a reception. We sought Police advice on what procedures needed to be followed to import the skins legally as well as where to set the ambush. The Police said that they had to be declared to the Moyale Customs, yet did not tell me that the Moyale Customs staff had recently been withdrawn and the station degazetted. When the leopard skins arrived, there was *no* Customs presence at Moyale. In such circumstances the correct procedure was for the importers to declare their cargo to the nearest alternative Customs post - which was Nairobi.

Of course the dealer, who knew his law, protested that they were on their way to do this when we had interfered. That was his defence and we could not disprove it. The Department's legal advisors said that there was no case to answer. We *should* have known the Customs situation: after all, this leopard skin project had been known in advance. I knew when it had arrived at Moyale. I knew when it arrived at Marsabit further into the country and the ambush was laid knowing that it had left Marsabit and was on its way south. We *should* have continued the surveillance and pounced only if not declared to Customs and Game Department in Nairobi. The Police should have told us of the Moyale Customs Post closure.

Yet the Game Department had not been the only interested party in this particular case. The Police had asked me to accept one of their men on the roadblock and, unbeknown to me at the time, his objective had not been leopard skins. What *he* sought lay in the trophy dealer's brief case: a bundle of letters to addresses in Nairobi from men detained in the north by the Government for

---

[20] Editor's note: In fairness to the professional hunting fraternity it should be noted that the majority of its members were law abiding and many were Honorary Game Wardens. It was in the nature of wardens' jobs to seek out those who were not, hence an unintentional bias in their recollections.

political reasons. The trophy dealer had picked them up while coming through Marsabit and was a clandestine courier: Police Special Branch – the country's intelligence service – was obviously more interested in this cargo than in spotted cat skins. It has crossed my mind since that the Police (who had been so helpful about informing of the importers' progress from the border onward) deliberately misinformed me about the Customs situation in Moyale because they wanted an interception made *before* the dealer/courier got into the highlands where the letters could have been dropped off anywhere in Kikuyu country.

If the Game Department initiated the vehicle's interception looking for illicit trophies and the letters were 'found' as an incidental by-product of this wildlife matter, it would nicely conceal prior Police awareness of the clandestine mail route. It was just before Kenya's independence when intelligence on detained politicians' thoughts and access to their mail was of primary interest to the government. In such circumstances using the Game Department as a cat's paw would have made sense. Whether or not the Game Department secured a conviction was of no concern to Special Branch. It wanted the letters and got them. That was what mattered. I never heard what happened to the Asian for involving himself in a highly contentious political activity.

An area of particular interest for me was the white farmers' and ranchers' attitudes towards game. I felt strongly, perhaps influenced by my own leanings towards ranching or farming, that the more they made from game, the more they would like having it on their properties and the more they would stop trespassers taking it. There were so many ways owners could legally get rid of wild animals (e.g. fencing, removing cover, denying water supplies etc. etc.) that we could not stop them if that was what they really wanted. Where game on private land was concerned, the landowners' will to have it, counted above all else.

By 1960 all 'my' landowners who wanted them had quotas of animals that they could lawfully take and sell. These quotas did not include elephants, rhinos or leopards, but focused on zebra, buffalo and the antelope – particularly impala and Thomson's gazelle. In as far as I was able, I left the allocation of quotas and issuance of sale permits to my Honorary Game Warden – David Partridge. After all, he lived on the land, knew the area and its game and, as important, knew the people to whom the quotas were being given. The system worked and saved me having to spend time on the settled ranches.

A second area of particular interest involved the local Samburu. Where they were concerned, I took my cue from Lyn Temple-Boreham (TB), the Game Warden of Narok whose district I had looked after twice before I moved to Maralal. Our laws were unrealistic where the tribesmen were concerned. They lived among the game and to some, like the 'Dorobo', hunting was their way of life. If any people had a moral 'right' to hunt, they most certainly did. Because of this I turned a blind eye towards animals taken for meat and traditional use, with traditional weapons and techniques. All I required was that such hunting should not be blatant. In return for this unwritten concession, however, I expected them to report to me all that they learned about other people hunting in my area. Consequently, like TB, I had many informants scattered through the district. Their enthusiasm was honed with monetary rewards for good information and I liked to think that, at least where white people were concerned, it was not easy to do much in my area without me hearing about it.

If locals hunted blatantly I had no option but to prosecute them, and my blind eye never covered killing the three species whose trophies were most valuable: elephant, rhino or leopard. Yet even here I tried not to cut across tradition. While it was technically illegal for the Samburu to possess ivory in any form, I took no action against the many who openly wore ivory ornaments. As long as they didn't kill elephants overtly I was not concerned. When they were troubled by stock raiding predators or a truculent elephant or buffalo, I encouraged them to take the necessary measures themselves, thus saving the Department the bother. So long as they informed me of their actions and surrendered the trophies as soon afterwards as practically possible, I was content.

Had I been a young Samburu moran (warrior) I would have welcomed the excitement of killing a stock-killing lion with my spear. An incident in Narok when I was standing in for TB illustrates the attitude we shared. I had been in my office one morning at Narok when two Masai morani asked to see me. A lion had killed one of their cattle nearby and they had it surrounded not far off. Would I

The traditional way of taking lion: from Roosevelt[21]

[21] Roosevelt T. 1910 *African Game Trails*. Scribner's Sons, New York. p. 352

come and kill it? Taking a heavy rifle and a tracker I set off with them and we did not go far before coming across an impressive ring of morani surrounding a large patch of 'leleshwa' (*Tarconanthus camphoratus*). The men were spaced ten to fifteen paces apart and if the lion was indeed in there, it could not get out unseen. As they had things well planned, I asked their leader what he wanted of me.

"Just go in and chase it out to us," he had replied.

I agreed, but pointed out that it was not a mouse and if I saw it and could take a good shot at it, I would do so. And if it came for me, likewise, I would shoot it, which caused some laughter. I also asked him to make sure his men did not hurl their spears and 'simis' (short swords) at my Scout and me. The waiting Masai would know that we had entered the circle when they heard the call of a certain bird that the Scout imitated well. With that the leader went round the cordon and gave his instructions. Having done this, the call was given and we went in.

The Scout and I never saw the lion as it bolted ahead of us, into the waiting cordon and was speared. Before expiring, however, it seriously chewed up one Masai and injured another not quite so badly. The morani were well pleased, as would I have been had I been one of them. The satisfaction from such an affray must be immense. Those in the right place had faced a charging lion with a spear - a far stouter effort than taking it on with a rifle. To top it off, a Game Warden had been available to take casualties to hospital where they both recovered with scars worth talking about for the rest of their lives. I did have the lion cut open to examine the stomach contents and confirmed that it had, indeed, eaten a cow.

As with the white farmers, I felt African support for conserving could only benefit if game was profitable to the people. Consequently I was ever on the look out for means to obtain money from wildlife into the local District Council's coffers. Kenya was divided into over eighty hunting blocks or 'controlled areas'. Hunters and their clients would book blocks then pay a 'controlled area fee' to the relevant District Council for animals shot (after Independence, African District Councils became County Councils). These fees were additional to what was paid to the central government for licences. This went to the local government councils in whose areas the animals were taken. It was not a lot of money and I wanted them to receive much more. Thus in some of the blocks in my area I banned vehicles. Instead, hunters and clients had to use horses or camels which, in turn, they had to hire from the local Council. Initially the hunters grumbled (they made good money by charging their clients mileage: the more their vehicles motored the more money they earned), although in the end, the horse and camel hunts were popular and the Council did make a lot of money.

William Harvey and his great tusks.

CHAPTER 7: WILLIAM HARVEY'S TUSKS

Ian Parker

They could have been called Galogalo Kafonde's tusks, or Winston Guest's or MacArthur's for that matter. All three were involved with them one way or another. So, too, were Bror von Blixen and the aviatrix Beryl Markham. It doesn't really matter as all these principal actors are now dust. The tusks themselves were sold to the American Museum of Natural History and at 189 and 178 pounds (85.7 & 80.7 kg) are the biggest known to have come out of Kenya.

The largest confirmable[22] African elephant tusks are in the British Museum of Natural History in London and weigh respectively 226½ and 214 pounds. According to John Millard, who swears convincingly that it is the truth, they came from a small volcanic crater called Legumishira, on the northwestern slopes of Kilimanjaro, late in the 1800s. John should know because nearly a century later Legumishira was on his land. The largest taken by a sportsman weighed 198 and 174 pounds, from an elephant shot by Powell Cotton on the shores of Lake Albert in Uganda near the turn of the century. Next in size comes a Tanzanian pair that was taken in 1971 weighing 192 and 189 pounds. Not far behind them was a pair from the Malawi border which weighed 185 and 183 pounds, from an elephant killed by H. Manners in 1953.

In the twentieth century several million elephants died at the hand or through the influence of man, yet less than half a dozen are known to have yielded tusks that individually weighed over 180 pounds[23]. Out of two hundred or so elephants shot annually on licence in Kenya between 1925 and 1970, on average maybe five had tusks which weighed over 100 pounds apiece. In every five years maybe four had tusks heavier than 120 pounds. In every twenty there might be two that were heavier than 150 pounds. That is the backcloth to William Harvey's tusks.

It started with Winston Guest: an American sportsman with an eight handicap at polo. As a multimillionaire he had the wherewithal to indulge his passion to bag a world record elephant. In 1936 the famous Swedish professional hunter Bror von Blixen had taken him and his sister, to hunt elephants on the eastern end of the Yatta plateau which, in 1948, became part of the Tsavo National Park. Blix had contracted Beryl Markham, the decorative and very competent flyer[24],

---

[22] The biggest tusk 19th century ivory trader and slaver Jumbe Kimemeta acquired weighed 264lb (120 kg), and he obtained three heavier than 220 lb each. Reported by Höhnel von L. 1894. *Discovery of Lakes Rudolf and Stefanie. Vol II.* Longmans, Green & Co. London. p. 142.

[23] The Wata elephant hunters like Abakuna Gumundi and Galogalo Kafonde and Kamba such as Elui and probably some others took ivory of this order, but having sectioned the tusks in the bush and discarded their butt-ends, we have no measure of just how big they were.

[24] Beryl Markham .1942. *West with the Night.* Houghton Miflin.

to spot for them and guide them towards any suitable trophies she might locate. Even at this early stage, not everyone thought using an aircraft sporting and, as a point of interest, Winston's brother Raymond had refused to accompany the safari for this reason. The partnership between Beryl and several hunters that included Blix and JA (J.A.Hunter) resulted in a patchwork of airstrips in Tsavo East National Park and out into the drylands of what later still became the Galana Game Management Scheme. Many of them were resuscitated two decades later in the anti-poaching campaign of 1956-1957.

Directed by Beryl, Winston, his sister and Blix, with their trackers and gun-bearers had come upon two monsters. Winston had dropped the bigger animal and the party was off after the second bull. Catching up with it, Winston's sister killed it. With tusks weighing over one hundred and thirty pounds apiece, it was a magnificent trophy. All were agreed, however, that it was small compared to that which had fallen to Winston's bullet. Alas, when they returned to the site of the first shot, that elephant had gone. Only stunned, it had recovered and fled. They followed the elephant for two days. Eventually it crossed the Sabaki River and they lost its spoor amongst the tracks of other elephants close to Sala Hill on what is now the Tsavo Park's eastern boundary. Unbeknown to them, they must have been within a mile of where it lay dead.

A bullet that merely stuns an elephant is seldom fatal. Someone of Blix's experience would have known this and that the chances of finding Winston's elephant were small. In the circumstances, two factors may have accounted for their persistence. The first and most obvious was the sheer size of the escaped elephant's tusks. They followed it in the hope that they might come up with it again despite knowing it had not been mortally hit. The second is that either Winston or Blix had in fact placed a second bullet in it, giving them hope of finding the elephant dead. That it obviously died within a day or two of escaping, suggests the latter possibility. The safari ended and a disappointed Winston returned to the United States.

In 1936 Galogalo Kafonde, was in his late teens or early twenties and was already considered an ace hunter among his own people. Later he figured prominently among those wanted during the 1950s anti-poaching programme. Very late in 1936, or possibly as 1937 broke, he came across two huge elephant tusks near Sala Hill. The elephant that had borne them had been several months' dead. Somewhat more than a foot of both tusks still rested within the skull, retaining the greenish staining characteristic of decomposed connective tissue. The rest of the two feet that had once been in the skull were bleached by the elements, acquiring the longitudinal hairline cracks known as 'shakes' that in the living and newly dead elephant, only occur on ivory outside the animal's head. In the living animal, shakes never occur on that part of a tusk that is within the skull where it is protected from external influences.

The weight of each tusk was so great that Galogalo ingeniously lashed each to a bundle of dry logs and floated them downstream to his home at Kisiki-cha-

Mzungu on the Sabaki. This was the stuff of legend and was soon talked of throughout his Wata (Waliangulu) community.

William (Bill) Harvey and his wife arrived in Mombasa from Britain in the mid-1920s. Hard working, enthusiastic, big-hearted and determined to succeed in the land of his adoption, he epitomised many colonials. Like them, he had small regard for red tape or inconvenient bylaws. Shortly after arriving in Mombasa he had written to his brother John, and told him of the El Dorado into which he had fallen. His enthusiasm was contagious and his brother sold his business, packed his furniture including a grand piano, and set sail with wife and son for Mombasa and great fortune. Bill met them and took them to their new abode. On perceiving the makuti-roofed, mud-walled shack his sister-in-law had burst into tears – such was the difference between what was before her and what she had been led to expect. Her husband, an altogether steadier man than Bill, then joined the railways, which he served for forty years.

Bill Harvey ran a successful butchery and did well. His wife - equally big-hearted and ambitious – delivered a huge meat pie to the bachelors in the Mitchell-Cotts mess, where the journalist Edward Rodwell had digs. While earning their gratitude it also ensured that they placed their custom with the Harveys' butchery. Rodwell recalled that while Bill was generally popular, he was often in trouble with the law for ignoring tiresome rules. He did not feel that official meat inspectors were any more competent than he when it came to deciding what was or was not fit for public consumption. Nor did he agree that delivering meat in the boot of his car detracted from its quality or put customers at undue risk as the hygiene specialists claimed.

Like many in those days, Bill knew one could make good money by taking out an elephant licence, shooting a decent bull and selling the ivory. In early 1937 he had gone to shoot his elephant on the Voi River not far from Voi township. No doubt he employed a local Wata tracker as was the custom, and no doubt through this tracker he learned of a huge pair of tusks recently found near Sala Hill on the Sabaki. He offered to buy them, concluded a deal with Galogalo, and the tusks were his. Shooting a hartebeest, he daubed its blood on the butt ends of the tusks to make them look freshly killed, and re-appeared in Mombasa, claiming to have shot the elephant that had borne them.

Bill Harvey was not shy and having initially had them in his house (where his nephew John remembers them), had Edward Rodwell (the Editor) put their photograph in *The Mombasa Times*, and then displayed them in his butchery where Rodwell saw them. Word of tusks that size went about town fast, attracting traders, hunters and ivory *aficionados*. He was offered thirty shillings a pound for them (more than 50% over the going rate) which he did not accept. Unfortunately, among those whose attention was drawn to the monster tusks, was MacArthur, the anti-poaching Game Warden. He saw immediately that they had not come from a newly shot elephant. After an unhappy interview, MacArthur seized the ivory and Harvey lost his tusks.

The local community was dismayed. Bill Harvey had admitted to finding the tusks and not shooting the elephant that had borne them. While this wasn't quite 'kosher' by the game laws, the animal was already dead and taking its ivory surely saved a living animal? Mombasa sided with Bill Harvey and thought MacArthur a spoilsport. Bill never let on, of course, that he had bought the tusks from Galogalo. Had that come out, it is virtually certain that MacArthur would have prosecuted him. As it was, the matter blew over and after Bill Harvey died in 1943, few recalled the magnificent tusks he so briefly owned.

Yet the tale does not end there. Word of an elephant skeleton yielding giant tusks circulating among the hunting fraternity soon reached Winston Guest in America. He quickly sent a man by ship to Kenya to claim them. Voi was only forty seven miles from Sala where the tracks of elephant were lost. Surely the tusks had to be his? In his mind there could never have been two such pairs.

The Game Department was not convinced. There was no evidence to connect Harvey's tusks to an elephant whose tracks were lost forty seven miles or so from where they were purportedly found. Had it been known that they were in fact found within a mile or so from where Blix and Guest had lost the tracks of their quarry, and that they came from a carcass whose age corresponded roughly with the time that had elapsed since they had thrown in the towel, then Guest's man would almost certainly have taken Harvey's tusks back to the United States with him. Ironically, by the end of 1937 they had arrived in New York, the Game Department having sold them to the American Museum of Natural History[25].

Around campfires some still recall the huge pair of tusks and romantic formula makes them ever bigger. A fresh tusk starts drying out immediately it is removed from the newly dead elephant and will eventually lose about five percent of its original weight. The heavier of Harvey's tusks weighed 189 pounds a year or so after the elephant bearing it died. It could therefore have weighed 198 pounds when fresh and equalled the biggest tusk taken by Powell Cotton. It would have been a sportsman's world record, for those from Legumishira were taken by a commercial ivory hunter, or even, perhaps, from a dead elephant. Be that as it may, the figure registers. Years later recalled around another campfire, the teller forgets whether it was a fresh or dry weight. Taking it as dry, a listener would have opined that fresh it weighed 208 pounds. With the same inexorable logic, a decade on at another campfire, it becomes 218 pounds. Tusks and fishes that get away had much in common.

Over the years, I heard the story from several sources. There was Bill Woodley who first told me of having heard of a huge pair of tusks that were floated down the Sabaki. Later, there was Galogalo himself. There was John Harvey – Bill Harvey's nephew – who saw them in the Harveys' makuti thatched house. Edward Rodwell knew Bill Harvey and as Editor of *The Mombasa Times* placed the photograph of them in that paper, saw them in Harvey's Butchery and

---

[25] Anon. 1937. *Annual Report of the Kenya Game Department*. Government Printer, Nairobi.

knew all about their confiscation. Peter Jenkins heard it directly from MacArthur and Tony Archer who hunted with Winston Guest's brother Raymond, knew the family's version from him. Having spoken with them all and perused the official records, this is perhaps as close as anyone can now get to the truth. That, then, is the tale of William Harvey's (Galogalo Kafonde's, Winston Guest's or MacArthur's as you will) tusks: the biggest known to have come out of Kenya.

Galogalo Kafonde, who found the great tusks.

Kenneth Archibald Smith, Game Warden Garissa

CHAPTER 8: GAME WARDEN, GARISSA

Ken Smith[26]

After leaving service with the King's African Rifles, I moved from Junior Manager of a 20,000 acre ranch at Ulu, to a plantation at Kilifi. In 1949 I became an Honorary Game Warden adjacent to the Sokoke-Arubuko Forest under the wardenships of Jack Bonham, Don Bousfield and Gordon Harvey. After a period as a Temporary District Officer in the Ol Kalau areas and Kipipiri during the Mau Mau Emergency, I applied for one of two vacancies in the Game Department. Both Barrah and myself were successful, being selected, we learned later, from dozens of applicants. I recall only one snag to this success; it was Col. Sandeman telling me I had to provide my own transport. The early Land Rovers were in vogue at a frightful £750 each. Nevertheless, with a cable to U.K and help from stalwart friends, I raised the funds and started on a way of life I felt worthwhile in achieving wildlife conservation goals that were important to me.

On joining the Department in 1955 I was sent to Fred Bartlett at Nanyuki primarily to obtain experience in buffalo lore and control on which Fred was recognised as an outstanding authority. Early in 1956 I was sent north to Isiolo in the Northern Frontier District (known as N.F.D.) to join Senior Game Ranger George Adamson who was responsible for Isiolo, Marsabit, Moyale, Mandera, Wajir, Garissa and the Upper Tana River Districts (seven districts): a vast nomadic, biblical area with its magnificent ranges of mountains, hills and luggahs crossing hot plains. I recall saying to George Adamson how I wished I had been born in his generation and had had his experiences in the north of Kenya. He replied "I wished the same, to have been born into the period of Livingstone - Selous - Pretorius - Gordon - and others of that ilk."

With only four or five Scouts per district one recalls the Governor's comment to the Colonial Secretary in 1906 about the department being a farce. However, George was by necessity, greatly assisted by his colleagues and friends in the Administration, Police and the Veterinary and Livestock Services, who helped the Game Scouts in their duties. Much later, as the 1950s drew to a close, George's huge range was broken up: Marsabit and Moyale came under Stan Bleazard based at Marsabit; Garissa, Wajir, Mandera and upper Tana River came under me based at Garissa, while lower Tana River and Lamu came first under Tony Carn at Lamu. Later still both came under Dave McCabe at Malindi. Yet in

[26] Towards the end of March 2001, Kenneth Archibald Smith fell and broke his leg at Lamu, was flown to Mombasa Hospital where, within twenty-four hours he died of a heart attack. He left an incomplete set of notes on the history of the Kenya Game Department and his personal service in it from which the Editors have derived the following account.

1955 these changes were still a way off. Kenya's ten game ranges as they were at the end of 1956 are in the figure below.

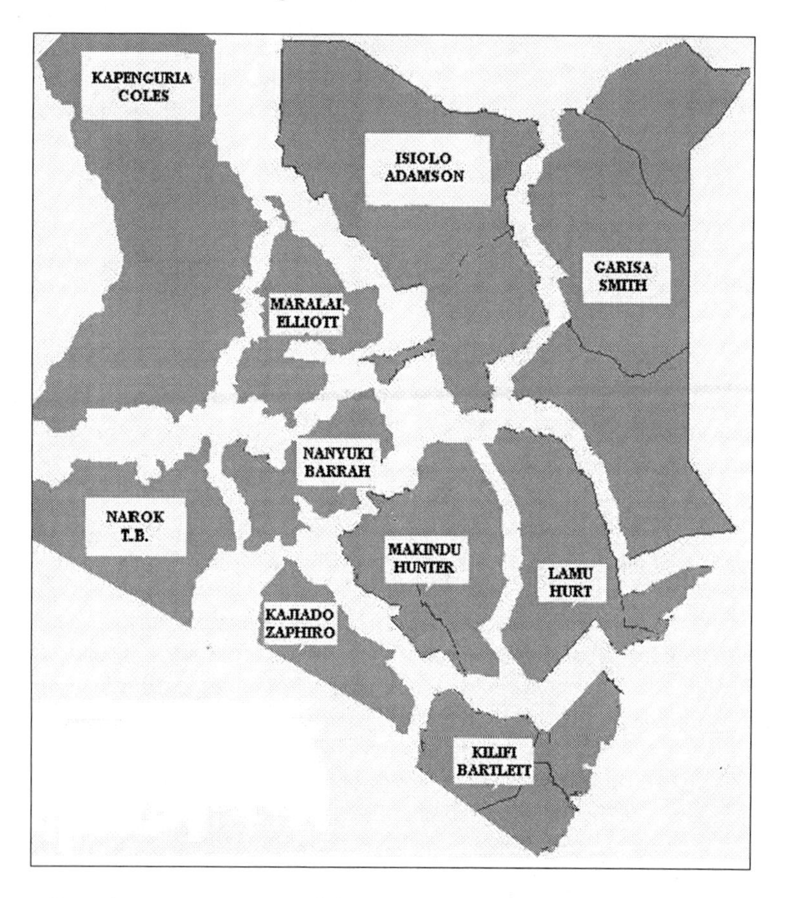

Kenya's ten game ranges and their Wardens as they were at the end of 1956.

I was with George for several months with a view to eventually taking over part of the N.F.D. Lion were numerous and caused considerable loss of livestock and not infrequently took up man-eating. My first field experience with George was dealing with a man-eater that had killed two women and one man at Iskot Kinna near Garbatulla. George established a shady camp in the area and told the Chiefs to put the word out for all the young men and herders to report in haste any fresh tracks, while we stood by. A male lion in the man-eating group left a distinctive track because he had a disabled paw which he slightly dragged.

A report came in and led by a fine Scout tracker we were shown the lion's track. The follow up led to the Melka Lorni range of rocky kopjes and bush. Tracking was difficult. Suddenly we were charged by a furious lioness, who was shot. Found to be heavily in milk, she was back-tracked to a cave where three tiny cubs were found. Sorrowfully we returned to camp where George's wife Joy took charge of them. Thus I was in on the very beginning of the Elsa saga. Despite several tries, we never did find the lion, who was perhaps Elsa's father.

At other times George used another method for despatching stock killers that was far removed from the old slit-trench manner at ground eye-level used by Selous. Taking his old bush lorry to the area where livestock had repeatedly been attacked and having studied the area and knowing the winds, a zebra was shot and dragged around and tethered to a stake in the open. The lorry with its driver and a Scout in front, and George and myself in camp chairs in the open back, sighted the car lights on the zebra. Branches were placed around the lorry to break up the silhouette, with everyone in position by dusk and ready for sight or sound. Pre-arranged signals on the cab were one tap, stand by - two taps lights on. There were false alarms when hyaenas and jackals interfered, but the system worked and we laid low a couple of stock killers. Sips of whiskey were allowed to fend off the evening chill as we waited.

So the apprenticeship carried on with patrols of over a week or more to investigate elephant killings by Borana youths, a favourite pastime to prove their manhood in spearing forays and impressing the local maidens, by presenting them with elephant tail-hair bracelets. After a memorable entry into the Game Department I left to report to Nairobi headquarters.

Jack Bonham, Game Warden Malindi (courtesy Trish Luke)

Gordon Harvey, Game Warden Kilifi (photo Peter Davey)

I was told to visit Embu, Mwingi in Ukambani and Garissa to assess and select a new station. After visiting these districts I had no hesitation in settling for Garissa. Isiolo was one gateway to the NFD and Garissa the other on the largest river in Kenya, the Tana. Garissa was also the headquarters of a vast district of the same name with a full complement of Government officials. The town was rambling but immaculate and a focal point for the riverine Korokoro and Malakote, and for the Somali clans of the Aulihan, Abdwak and Abdulla. Somalis, Arabs and Asians ran all the various trades, supplies, cattle, transport etc. It was a sign of the times and the independence under which we operated, that the Department's newest Warden was sent out to decide where the Department's newest station should be.

My house and headquarters was a large barn-like mud and wattle white-washed structure with a riverine rush roof thatch. My staff was one Sergeant, one Corporal and four Scouts at the new headquarters, two Scouts at Mbalambala ninety miles upstream, three in Wajir District and three in Mandera District: a total of twelve men to cover over 19,530 square miles (50,000 km^2). My transport was my own Land Rover and trailer, four camels and a large riverine canoe. Prior to my arrival the Scouts had very occasionally seen George Adamson, and in as far as they received any supervision at all, it had come from the officers of other Government Departments as a favour to George. For the most part, however, they had been on their own.

The Scouts had one uniform each, a pill-box hat, a 1914-18 rifle and looked like remnants of that war, but were fine and disciplined nevertheless. My initial goal was to get our ministerial stores to issue me with a truck, more uniforms and funds for housing. We never could get enough of basic items like uniforms, so I got myself appointed to local Boards of Survey (which authorised the disposal of worn out uniforms and equipment from Administration and Police staff). From these I selected and extracted the better items. Friendly colleagues in both Administration and Police put in items which still had a useful life. Kit such as Kepi Hats (I had a supply of elephant-head hat badges) Merduff shirts, webbing, bandoliers, puttees, water bottles etc. Sandals and bandoliers with defects were sent to a saddler. The result was a morale booster to both my Scouts and myself.

I was not the only Warden who bought items of basic equipment like badges out of my own pocket. It made two points: (i) how the Game Department was treated very much as a Cinderella when it came to providing equipment and (ii) the *esprit de corps* and sense of self sufficiency with which Wardens overcame this lack of logistical support. One consequence of this independence was that Game Scouts of no two ranges were turned out in quite the same way.

There was much anti-poaching work to be done, but an inadequate staff with which to do it and so it tended to be left till last. Control work took greater priority, understandably in the eyes of the people and the Administration, because damage by wild animals attacked that basic of life: food production.

Along the river, hippos, buffalo and elephant damaged shambas of maize and rice. Throwing thunder-flashes at these marauders helped a little, but they were costly and difficult to obtain. Regrettably, we relied on that old stand-by of shooting marauders. While the damage done to crops was occasionally spectacular, by far the worst damage was done by baboons, which were numerous and widespread along the river. Their overall damage to crops was greater than all the big animals put together. They also took chickens and on occasions caught and tore up lambs and kids.

Baboons were so detested by farmers and Government alike that Garissa County Council funded three teams of three Council Scouts each, who were armed with twelve bore Greener shotguns and .22 rifles with one of each team carefully taught to use poison (usually arsenite of soda). Each team's sole task was to destroy as many baboons as possible.

Baboons: they may reflect much that is human, but they were by far the worst agricultural pest the Game Department had to deal with (photo Peter Davey).

Crocodiles constantly took people and livestock along the Tana and were a threat that was as much part of riverine life as motor accidents in a city suburbs. We shot offending individuals as and when we could, but the only long-term solution would have been their extermination. That would have been against Departmental policy and, in any case, beyond our very limited capacities.

Away from the river, stock-killing lion attacks were frequent and widespread with herders often mauled defending their stock. Lion varied their methods of attack. One was of following a herd after watering. While returning to their night bomas, the lions stalked stragglers. I remember on one occasion we stalked the stalkers and were successful; but only once. Night attacks on bomas were also common. The pastoral Somalis and Boran usually hunted down these stock killers themselves and did not need Departmental help.

Hyaena were a nuisance everywhere, taking both livestock and people. They were particularly bad around Wajir where they commonly entered the flimsy nomadic dwellings to maul and injure people. Our solution to hyaenas was poisoning – mainly with strychnine.

With the division of Kenya into controlled area hunting blocks in 1957/58, those Garissa blocks that included riverine stretches became very popular hunting areas. Four of the 'big five' trophy animals (elephant, buffalo, rhino, lion and leopard) were common: leopards were the exception as the species had been snared heavily in the past. A goodly number of elephants produced heavy ivory. Oryx, Burchells and Grevy Zebra, were plentiful. Francolin, guinea fowl, and sand-grouse provided superb shooting.

I insisted that two species of game were fully protected in Garissa: black rhino and the hirola (or Hunter's antelope). While rhino were not uncommon, from what local people said I gained an impression that there were fewer than in the past. The hirola is a handsome animal found only in south-east Garissa and across the border in a limited area of Somalia, and I thought in view of this relatively small range, they should not be a sportsman's trophy.

Once the controlled area blocks were established, as was the case widely across the country, hunters had to pay a cess additional to their licence fee for every animal shot. The Game Department then handed this over to the local District Council in whose jurisdiction the respective controlled area was. The controlled area fees paid to Garissa District Council are what funded the "Game and Vermin" teams that were committed to getting rid of baboons. In effect, hunters were paying for two sets of licences: one to the Central Government and one to the Local Government Authorities. This arose from rising realisation that the local people who lived with the game had to benefit from it, if they were to develop any sympathy for conservation.

The foregoing is all to do with the basic systems and in no way conveys the pleasure I experienced from being a Game Warden. The variety of jobs, the open air life, the companionship of other station officers all made for a carefree and immensely enjoyable existence. Often safaris were undertaken with other district officials and as they went about their routine business, I would attend to game affairs. One such memorable safari was a joint Administration/Game Department column with lorry, camels with water, provisions and tentage, to trace the 1923 border between Kenya-Italian Somaliland (now Kenya-Somalia Border) from Kolbio east to the coast at Ras Chiamboni near Kiunga, passing through the largely unexplored, dense Boni Forest.

Ken Smith closed rhino hunting in the Garissa range in 1955 at a time when they were still thought common animals elsewhere in Kenya. He was among the first Wardens to take such a step. (photo 'Gertie' of Amboseli by Peter Davey)

The border trace had been cut when Britain ceded 'Jubaland' to Italian Somaliland, but traversed such remote country that no officials had passed along it, other than perhaps during the Second World War, for a very long time. We expected to experience difficulty in locating it, but to the contrary, it had obviously been used for decades as a narrow camel track and one wondered how much ivory and rhino horn had gone along it over the years?

The dry, lowland stations in the NFD were not renowned for feminine company: indeed they were essentially bachelor postings. One had to provide one's own off-duty entertainment. Each station had its own club with distinctly idiosyncratic rules and titles. Thus there was the 'Garissa Curling Club' with a swimming pool and bar and a replica curling stone. Its office bearers were a

President, Secretary, Treasurer and Sweeper. I was President for 3 months and Sweeper the next three months.

Wajir had its famous 'Wajir Yacht Club' which, among other things, collected hats from all visitors including the Duke of Windsor, Valerie Hobson and General Cunningham. Invariably the question of where club members sailed arose and an arm would encompass the wide expanses of arid camel country surrounding Wajir, "there … we sail on ships of the desert," would be the standard reply.

Mandera had its 'Whaling Club' on the Ethiopian-Somalia Border and Isiolo had its 'Bath Club'. All had their rituals and both dinner and guests' nights. At the Curling Club, formal dress was bow tie and kikoi (sarong). The club had a pet orphaned male black and white ostrich 'Buni' who delighted in a bunch of lucerne dipped in a pint of beer every Saturday at 1300 hrs. He loved parades and uniforms and would walk up and down the lines of men at attention, pecking at brass buttons. Once the Provincial Commissioner came from Isiolo to rehearse a ceremonial parade in preparation for a visit by the Governor. As the PC inspected the Guard of Honour, Buni joined him, strutting up and down the lines sedately, as dignified as a Governor himself, to the great amusement and joy of the large crowd who also loved parades. Later, Buni was successfully returned to the bush as with adulthood he became aggressive.

* * * *

In 1960 I went on leave and on resuming duties was posted to take over TB's Narok range while he went on leave. As well as looking after what is now the great game area of the Masai Mara National Reserve, this involved dealing with people in the agricultural highlands and game matters affecting Masai, Kipsigis, Kikuyu and Jaluo people in addition to white settlers. It covered wheat farms, tea estates, lucerne crops and large herds of Masai cattle, and trying to arbitrate between white farmers around Lake Naivasha, where one group liked hippos grazing their lawns and the other hated them grazing their crops.

I experienced elephants in the Chepalungu Forest, which TB had warned were the fiercest in Kenya. I confirmed this almost to my terminal cost. The elephants in the large thick forest were frequently hunted, speared and harassed by the Kipsigis farmers whose shambas they visited. Such a herd was carefully followed up, but not carefully enough. They scented us and without warning charged as a group in vegetation so dense that one could hardly see a yard. The two Scouts and I were on the edge of a vertically-sided gully and, while neither we nor the elephants could see one another properly, all three of us were physically buffeted over the lip down into the coarse bush below. The elephants could not follow us over the edge and without question the presence of the gully saved our lives. We were all three torn and scratched by the vegetation through which we fell, but otherwise unharmed. Betty, the wife of the local District

Officer, David Round-Turner, patched us up and fortified us with David's medicinal whisky.

I joined John Burton, Inspector of Police Bomet on a Kipsigis hideout on the Upper Mara River, where we recovered a good haul of ivory, rhino horn and leopard skin. This is worth recording because, even in the colonial era, and in the range of the man who was, arguably, the best Warden in Kenya, poaching for these valuable commodities was not rare.

I enjoyed this brief period running Narok and getting first hand experience of the great wildebeeste migration which has been described so many times. Yet I was happy to be returning to the NFD where, in 1961, I took over Isiolo from George Adamson who was retiring.

The year was in the mould of my Garissa experiences and included reporting an outbreak of anthrax in elephant at Kinna, destroying a rogue elephant at Garbatulla, arresting eighteen Boran youths from a manyatta at Sericho for killing elephant, poisoning hyaena at Merti, and checking on rhino on Mt. Lolokwi (Sabacho) who were as nimble as mountain goats.

In 1962 I started taking steps to get the land south of the Uaso Nyiro made a local County Council Game Reserve. This was opposite the Samburu County Council Game Reserve that Rodney Elliott, Game Warden at Maralal, had already established. If I were successful, it would make both banks of the river protected. It involved locating a source of funding, approaching both Administrators and local County Councillors and playing politics at a level I had never experienced before. These plans did not come to fruition until March 1965.

As Independence approached in 1963, Somalis stepped up their agitation for the NFD to be ceded to Somalia and started outright guerrilla warfare before it was actually granted on December 12th. Their activity put our Game Department outposts at risk and I had to draw these in and concentrate my Scouts around headquarters in Isiolo. From now on, it was impossible to set out on a carefree safari. Instead every move had to be undertaken with the security situation in mind and aware that ambushes were common throughout the District.

The situation cramped our style considerably, though it did not make us particularly anxious. We, in the Game Department, were usually armed and felt that we could take on any Somali 'shifta' gangs who offered a fight on better than even terms. In mid-1964 they made a night attack on the Warden's house, offices and armoury. We exchanged fire and sent up flares. There were no casualties on our side and I doubt on the other side either. The shifta retired after about an hour of wasting ammunition.

After Independence in 1963, the Game Department was rapidly Africanised and greatly expanded. When I had joined in 1955 there were Game Wardens, senior Game Wardens and the Chief Game Warden. It was a simple, three-tiered system, in which Neil Sandeman, as Game Warden Headquarters, acted as the Chief Game Warden's deputy. There were also a few officers who were signed on as game control officers, which was a lower rank than Game Warden and usually temporary only.

As part of the Africanisation process, the officer establishment of the Department was expanded. Starting at the lower end was game assistant, Assistant Game Warden, Game Warden (several grades), senior Game Warden, divisional Game Warden, deputy chief Game Warden and Chief Game Warden. Having all report to and be directed from headquarters would have been ridiculous. A more conventional administrative structure was devised that basically followed the civil service pattern in which district officials were subordinate to and worked under the supervision of provincial officials, and only provincial officials communicated directly with the central headquarters.

While there were still too few Wardens to have one in every district, the country was organised into 'Divisions' that roughly paralleled the Adminsitrative provincial levels. In May 1965, I was posted as one of the Divisional Game Wardens to command the Southern Division which took in the ranges of Kiboko, Kajiado, Ngong, Narok and Homa Bay: in a word, all of southern Kenya outside Coast Province. Subsequently I became Divisional Warden for the Coast.

This final stage of my service with the Game Department was very different to my early years as a Game Warden. It was far more being a conventional civil service pen-pusher, who was desk-bound or attending endless meetings. The work was principally supervisory, rather than 'hands on' and I think that like those colleagues who served on after Independence, we did so, not because we liked the work (I certainly didn't), but because we wanted to ensure the new African Wardens had the best possible start in taking over their responsibilities.

Now, in my twilight years, I look back and my most pleasurable memories are recollections of colonial Garissa, of the imperturbable Tana, the grandeur of a stark biblical land and a band of officials, with Somalis and riverine tribes and clans, Arab and Asian traders all forming a finely meshed community in which there were sometimes fiery relations but in which we were always respectful of each others' rights. It seems so different to today, and so long ago.

CHAPTER 9: A LION AND A LEOPARD IN TOWN

Rodney Elliott

(this chapter is taken with permission from Rodney Elliott's unpublished autobiography)

It must have been in the late 1950s when, having just driven down from Maralal, I walked into Game Department headquarters to be met by Neil Sandeman, the Deputy Chief Game Warden. "Just the man," he said. "Go immediately to Milimani Road and get things under control. There is a lion loose in town and what with all the people gathering to see the fun, someone is going to get hurt."

I pointed out that I had neither a firearm nor any of my Scouts with me. Neil had said I should not worry as he would be down shortly with an appropriate weapon. It was imperative that someone responsible went to the scene immediately to prevent an accident happening. So I went to Milimani Road.

For some time the Police had been receiving a trickle of reports about people seeing a lion in the vicinity of Nairobi's Anglican Cathedral of the Highlands. For the most part they were not taken very seriously and on more than one occasion the reporter had been admonished to go home to bed and sleep off the effects of whatever party he had been attending.

Milimani Road ran roughly east-west through a heavily wooded residential area. At its eastern end it joined what was then Delamere Avenue (now Kenyatta Avenue) which is one of the city's main thoroughfares. With an overall upward slope from east to west, it was in a shallow valley so had rising ground on both sides for its entire length. The road ended in a T-junction at its westerly end.

Driving west up the gradient of Milimani Road, I saw no crowd. However, at the T-Junction I parked and on disembarking became aware of many subdued voices on higher ground on the other side of the road forming the cross of the T (today called Ralph Bunche Road). To reach them I walked over the T and onto a path that seemed to lead in the general direction of the voices.

Hardly had I set out when there was a report from a heavy rifle, a bullet kicked up dirt not far from me and ricocheted away into the distance with a savage whine. The idiot who had fired the shot clearly had no gun discipline and was a danger to everyone. From the sound of the shot I was fairly sure that it had hit nothing before striking the ground in front of me.

Cupping my hands to my mouth and in my best barrack-square voice, I expressed my opinion of the shooter, ordered him not to fire again and announced to all and sundry that I was a Game Warden and in charge of rounding up the lion. With that I went towards the sound of voices to an excited crowd higher up the slope. There, Police seemed to have the crowd under control. I restated that I was in charge and wanted no independent initiatives.

The lovely garden through which Rodney Elliott followed the last lion to be shot in central Nairobi. It was killed near the base of the tall building in the background: now appropriately named 'Simba Flats'.

Leaving the group I commenced casting towards where they said that the lion had last been seen, which was of course in the direction from which I had just come. I soon found the tracks of a relatively small lion travelling at speed back towards the T-junction. Unarmed and aware of how effectively the big cats can conceal themselves in the scantiest cover, I proceeded cautiously, scanning all the abundant cover through my binoculars. I hadn't gone far when a young woman with a child on either hand approached me from the general direction in which the tracks led. Excitedly she asked "have you seen it?"

Advising her that I had not, I asked her to go back to her car, go home and listen to events on the radio. This was not the place to be with two young children. I forbore to tell her that I was actually standing on the lion's tracks.

The lady departed and I proceeded on the trail to find that the lion had recrossed Ralph Bunche Road just to the south of the Milimani Road junction, heading back towards town. I felt that, frightened by all the activity and the shot fired at it, the animal would want, above all else, to lie up in thick cover. Leaving the tracks I reconnoitred ahead to see the lie of the land and what cover it provided. Moving parallel to Milimani Road it was obvious that the most likely stretch was not more than three hundred yards long and in the low ground close to the road itself, for it was there that trees and shrubs were most dense. Midway up the slope there were rather too many houses and flats.

Having established the most likely area I withdrew and found that Neil Sandeman had arrived and was among a posse of armed men, among whom was Steven Ellis, Warden of the nearby Nairobi National Park from which the lion had undoubtedly come. Feeling that it was 'his' lion I suggested that he should take command. He knew of the animal: it was a young lioness that was something of a wanderer who had left the park and taken to scavenging Nairobi dustbins for a living. He felt that it was only a matter of time before there was an accident in which she killed a person and that she should be shot as expeditiously as possible. Steve asked if I would complete what I had started.

I explained where I expected the lioness to be and positioned the posse of gunmen at the downhill, easterly end of this area. I would then go to the other up-hill end and work slowly towards the posse line. The posse went to its appointed position, I took a 12-bore shotgun loaded with SSG and went to my starting point.

On my recce I had noted a tree overlooked the stretch in which I thought the lioness would be hiding and my first move was to climb it. From this vantage point I saw a fairly deep drainage ditch ran parallel to and some thirty to forty paces from Milimani Road, which was now packed with vehicles head to tail. I could see into quite a lot of the ditch and spotted the lioness lying as flat as she could make herself, facing the stop line. Nearby was a clump of cactus, which would give cover so that I could get close to where she was. The wind was blowing favourably so she would get no warning of my approach.

Descending the tree I went quietly and quickly to the cactus clump a mere twelve paces or so from the lioness. Easing myself sideways, her hindquarters came into view below me. The downward angle was excellent as any shot, which might miss the animal, would enter the far bank of the ditch and not the assembled vehicles on the road beyond. Easing further sideways her flank was in view and with all my attention on it I saw her hindquarters suddenly tense up. Looking up to find what had caused this, I saw an Alsatian dog approaching her from in front. Obviously she was on the brink of either charging or fleeing, both of which could upset matters dramatically. To pre-empt either I threw caution to the winds, took another step sideways so that more of the lioness came into view and placed my shot just behind her shoulder. The lioness vanished down the ditch and there was a barrage of shots from the posse as she came into its view skidding along on her chin and clearly done for.

Later I asked Neil Sandeman if the shots from those in the stop line had been necessary and he felt that they had not. No one wanted to take a chance and all who fired did so just to make sure.

I did not stay long enough to see what happened once I knew the lioness was dead, but apparently the crowd from the cars that had jammed Milimani Road solid, swarmed into the property to see the victim and trampled a once lovely garden into complete ruination. In such cases the Game Department commonly let the person who had dispatched a nuisance animal to have its skin. On this occasion Neil gave the skin to the owner of the property where the lion was killed as small compensation for the damage done to it. Once tanned the pelt hung in the hall of his block of flats for many years. For all I know, it may still be there!

* * * *

There was a sequel to the Nairobi lion. An animal trapper had lost a leopard, which somehow escaped from its cage. A lady up by Westlands, scarcely two miles from Game Department headquarters, had just reported that a leopard had killed eighteen of her geese, or so she thought. Neil assumed this might be the escaped animal and asked me to take immediate action.

If it was the escaped leopard, it was habituated to humans and not frightened of them. In an urban environment it might start taking more than geese and could even be a danger to people. Leopards do not often become man-eaters, but when they do, they are formidable. The likelihood of leopards killing humans seems the outcome of people's abundance compared to that of other potential prey: the two factors being inversely related to one another. Thus man-eating leopards have been more common in India with its high human density, than has so far been the case in Africa. The hunter/author Jim Corbett, detailed the extraordinary success of the man-eating leopard of Rudraprayag, which, in a span of years, took over one hundred people. In western Kenya, where people are dense and wild animals few, man-eating by leopards crops up every few years and it is also reported with some frequency from Malawi.

Leopards are more catholic in their diet than virtually any other large predator. The most commonly found remains in their droppings are of small rodents. Seemingly they are congenital rat eaters. So, too, are they inveterate scavengers - which is what makes them so easy to bait and trap. They love carrion. Yet they are also capable of taking animals far larger than themselves. The most amazing case of which I had evidence concerned a large male leopard killing a full grown bull eland - an animal that probably weighed over 1,000 kg, while the leopard itself is unlikely to have weighed much more than 100 kg. Had I not visited the site and seen the evidence with my own eyes, including the leopard himself with the abrasions he received, I would not have believed the tale.

Neil Sandeman was right to want this city cat back in a cage - or dead. The lady who had lodged the complaint lived near the Westlands roundabout between what is now the Uhuru Highway and the Nairobi River. Arriving at the house I found her distraught. Obviously very fond of her geese, having had them for many years as sentries, she was incensed that all eighteen should have been killed at one go. Not one bird had been left alive.

The leopard departed with a goose - quickly enough established from its tracks - was easy to follow as white goose feathers sign-posted the way, having been knocked out wherever the goose was dragged past or through a bush etc.

The trail led towards town and into thicker vegetation on what was then part of Chiromo Estate. I sensed that the animal would lie up here, so I sent to the Game Department for a leopard trap, which soon arrived. Wiring a goose to the trigger as bait, we set it near to the thicket. That night the leopard tried to recover its purloined prey and was caught.

Leopard, perhaps the most adaptable of Africa's big cats (photo Peter Davey).

Next day, hearing this, the original owner arrived to reclaim his animal. Neil expressed his happiness to oblige once the man had settled with the owners for eighteen geese. Wild animals cannot be owned and therefore no one can be held responsible for their actions. However, the owners of tame animals are responsible for them and thereby liable for damages. Faced with this legal nicety, the trapper thoughtfully took another look at the leopard in the trap and decided that it did not, after all, really look like the one that had escaped.

We had laughed at that. Yet while I think that, on this occasion, the leopard was the one which had escaped, there is a sting in the tail of this story. Some years later a similar event happened. Another caged leopard escaped from its confines. The public demanded that it be caught as it was an unacceptable risk having a wild leopard free in a city. Several traps were set at suitable sites about Nairobi. In due course three leopards were caught, none of which was the escapee!

The city still has a very inconspicuous population of peri-urban leopards that live off rats, stray dogs, cats and rubbish. Was it not for the fact that occasionally they take well-loved pets and draw attention to their presence, they would remain virtually unknown[27].

I cannot conclude without recording for posterity one final leopard episode. It concerned a young scientist who was studying the species. He needed to place radio collars on as many as possible so that he could follow their movements at all times of day or night and thereby determine the home ranges and the extent of their territories. His study was being made in the Tsavo Parks and thither he took the most up-to-date leopard trap. Technically it was altogether an excellent piece of work from which neither leopard nor lion, nor any other mammal too large to go through the holes in the weld-mesh could escape.

Taking it to a nether region of Tsavo far off the tourist routes, the scientist set his trap. At the last moment he felt a minor detail needed attention, so he entered it to make the adjustment. It called for more than two hands, so he bid his assistant join him. And it was while they were applying all four hands to the matter at issue that they accidentally tripped the drop door. With a crash it came down behind them. They found out then just how escape-proof the trap was. I was not exaggerating when I said that no mammal could escape it - man included!

The accident happened early in the morning. For hours the two men in the trap wriggled and probed and schemed and devised to no avail. There was no way out and eventually they resigned themselves to their imprisonment, hoping that the very unlikely would happen: someone would fortuitously pass their way or a search would be mounted for them. It obviously passed through their minds that months later their bleached bones might be found in the trap. It was an unpleasant prospect and as the sun rose to its zenith so did their thirst. Unlike the sun's heat, however, their thirst did not diminish as the day wore on.

Back in camp the scientist's newly employed cook was the only person less happy than the erstwhile leopard trappers. He was a native of western Kenya where people are exceedingly numerous and wild animals have all gone. Not quite knowing what a park was when he signed on, the emptiness and wild beasts amongst which he now found himself horrified him. All through the day his fear rose. First his Bwana failed to return for breakfast, then lunch, tea and now dark had fallen and he was all and most awfully alone. It was then that he started shouting for help. He must have made quite a noise because it carried through the night air and far away though the leopard trap was, it was faintly picked up by the two now settled as best they could for the night.

---

27 Editor's note: In August 2001, as I was editing this book, a leopard visited my property on Malima Road, in Nairobi's Langata suburb and killed four ducks. Several nights previously it visited Martin Forster's property also on Malima Road and killed his geese. Two weeks subsequently it took Dr Dieter Röttcher's German pointer. In mid-September it took one of his Jack Russels. I.P.

They answered him and a mournful dialogue of shout and counter-shout directed the cook towards them. More frightened of being alone at night in camp than risking encounters with big bad animals, he made his way through the dark to his employer and released the two prisoners. Thus what could have become a very nasty accident was resolved. The moral of the story, I suppose, is trappers should ensure they have a way out of their own traps! All's well that ends well, and the somewhat wiser scientist has withstood endless ribbing down the years since his unusual experience. And that, thankfully, is as it should be.

Leopard portrait (photo Dave Richards).

Noel Simon.

CHAPTER 10 : NEW DIRECTIONS IN THE 1950s

Noel Simon

On my first visit to Kenya, in 1942, wild animals were almost everywhere in abundance. Huge herds of zebra and other plains game could be seen from the train as it crossed the Athi Plains. On the Kinangop and the floor of the Rift Valley, in the Northern Frontier District (NFD), indeed almost throughout Kenya, it was the same. But when I returned after the war the great herds were sadly diminished, having been slaughtered, among other things, to feed the tens of thousands of Italian prisoners of war held in Kenya. While this was taking place, the Athi Plains suffered the ill-fated wheat growing scheme. Intended to contribute to wartime food production, several thousand acres of the Athi Plains were ploughed and sown to wheat. The green shoots attracted immense numbers of wild animals, which were shot in the interests of crop protection. But as fast as one group of animals was eliminated, others came in to take its place. It had been a high price to pay for a wheat-growing scheme which failed dismally to produce any wheat at all.

After the Second World War I returned to farm in Kenya. From the outset I was interested in wild life (in those days we still spelt it as two words), and felt intuitively that it must be the country's greatest asset. Yet at all points there seemed to be conflict between the game and development: a conflict that the game was clearly losing. The side effects of some of the measures taken to deal with problem animals were sometimes almost as bad as the problem itself. Take locusts, for example, which posed a constant threat to Kenya's agriculture. One of the ways of dealing with this menace was to spread poisoned bait across the locust hoppers' line of advance. This was highly effective, but it also caused enormous losses among birds, either through consuming the bait or by devouring the poisoned locusts themselves. Ground-dwelling birds, such as francolin and guineafowl, were particularly vulnerable. Early reporters at the beginning of the century described game birds in extraordinary abundance. Alluding to a place near Lake Nakuru, at the confluence of the two Nderit rivers, Chapman[28] wrote: -

> *...mere words could hardly do justice to the profusion... Francolin and guineafowl were more plentiful than grouse on a Scottish moor, while quail were so numerous that half a dozen would spring up at every step.*

---

[28] Chapman A. 1908. *On Safari.* Edward Arnold. London.

While locust poisoning was not responsible for the game bird decline around Nakuru, it did seem a primary cause across much of the NFD and one from which some species may have never really recovered. Throughout my first decade in Kenya, I was growingly aware of the difficulties of preserving the country's game. My first venture into active conservation was founding the Kenya Wild Life Society at the end of 1955. I can do no better than quote myself in two paragraphs from the Society's First Annual Report for 1956.

> *The idea of the Kenya Wild Life Society can claim to have been conceived in No 12 Banda at Ol Tukai. Since arriving in Kenya shortly after the end of the War, I had always wanted to visit the game areas, but owing to the heavy preoccupation of establishing a farm with all the work such an enterprise entailed, it was not until September, 1955, that my wife and I could find the time to take a holiday and head off for Amboseli. It has often been said that imagination is better than realization. The picture in my mind of a unique faunal sanctuary wherein the interests of wild creatures predominated was rudely shattered.*
>
> *The case of Amboseli is only one example to me of many similar difficulties facing the Game Department and the National Parks Trustees and I became more than ever convinced that a properly organized body of well-informed opinion could be of the greatest value and support to both organisations.*

My thinking led to an article in the *Kenya Weekly News* in November 1955 in which I set out the idea and asked for public support. It was underscored by a forceful leading article by Anthony Cullen. The idea caught on and in December 1955 a formation committee of Mervyn Cowie, Syd Downey, Dennis Mathews, Donald Ker, Jack Block and I established the Kenya Wild Life Society.

Pledged to help both Parks and Game Department improve their standing, the Society's arrival on the scene, introduced a new element – coordinated public opinion. The Society's two publications, *Wildlife* and, later, the scientific *East African Wildlife Journal*, led to greater awareness and understanding of the issues involved among both the general public and the scientific fraternity. The Society could both support and criticise as circumstances demanded, and bring pressure to bear on government in ways that neither the National Parks nor the Game Department could undertake for themselves. By forming and focusing public opinion the Society became influential.

An example of what could be achieved through collaboration and exercising the Society's influence occurred when the Serengeti Committee of Inquiry was held in 1956. The Trustees of the Tanganyika National Parks (virtually all of them government nominees) had to face the fact that although the Serengeti was a park in name it nevertheless failed to meet the criteria necessary for national park status. National parks are by definition areas from which all human interests are excluded. But when the Serengeti was established as a national park in 1940, the Masai who were then living in the park were allowed to remain. By 1951 they claimed rights of occupancy. Government responded with an undertaking to restrict access to those Masai who had acquired rights prior to 1951, and to induce them to leave by augmenting water supplies outside the park's boundaries, an undertaking that was never honoured. The difficulty was exacerbated when, in the early 1950s, a cycle of dry years caused large numbers of additional Masai to enter the park and the Tanganyika Government was unable to restrict numbers to those possessing rights before 1951.

The conflict of interest between the Masai and park authorities could not be allowed to continue. The Trustees therefore concluded that the park should be divided in a way that would leave them with an area, which although smaller, had the virtue of being free from human interests. At first the Masai agreed to the Trustees' proposals but, later, changed their minds. Government felt it would not be prudent to press the Masai to accept, and put forward counter proposals, based on such concessions as the Masai were prepared to make, which naturally enough were very few. Thus the only boundaries acceptable to the Masai fell short of the Trustees' minimum requirements, and the Government reduced them still further.

Right up to the last moment the Trustees had supported the Government's proposals as the only feasible solution, on the grounds that any other course would only make the Masai more obdurate. But in an extraordinary, last minute volte-face, they completely reversed their position and joined with the Society, thereby uniting those opposed to the Government's plan and greatly strengthening our position. Faced with an increasingly cohesive opposition, the Tanganyika Government agreed that a Committee of Inquiry, chaired by Sir Barclay Nihill, should investigate the matter and recommend what should be done to resolve the matter.

Representing the Wildlife Society, Dr L.S.B. Leakey, Clive Salter QC and I sat through the entire Inquiry. When my turn came to speak, I suggested that should the Committee of Inquiry decide to excise the Ngorongoro Crater from the park, consideration should be given to compensating the parks by extending the park boundary northwards to link up with the Kenya Mara area. This 'Northern Extension' covered 2,000 square miles that, then, encompassed the greater part of the area used by the Serengeti plains game in the course of their spectacular migrations[29 & 30].

---

[29] Editor's note: The annual migration of the mid-1950s did not enter what is now the Mara National Reserve. While animals crossed the international boundary between Kenya and Tanganyika, at times in numbers, there were essentially three annual movements (i) between the Mara and Kenya's Loita Plains, (ii) between Ngorongoro Crater and the southern short grass Serengeti Plains and (iii) between the Lake Victoria corridor east to the short grass

The excision of the Ngorongoro Crater, the park's prime attraction, duly came about and was unquestionably a major loss. Fortunately, the concept of the Northern Extension uniting the Mara area with the Serengeti plains, was accepted by the Committee of Inquiry, and, both ecologically and politically, represented a distinct gain for the Park and its fauna.

The Kenya Wild Life Society was not only influential from the outset, giving me considerable satisfaction, but it brought me into the local conservation arena.

* * * *

In 1956 I joined the Royal National Parks of Kenya as Executive Officer and was upgraded to Deputy Director when Jack Hilton left. I resigned from the National Parks in February 1958. During this brief period, my position was enhanced by wearing two hats – those of Deputy Director of the National Parks and Chairman of the Kenya Wild Life Society. It was also perhaps the most dynamic two years in Kenya's conservation history for it encompassed three major philosophical breaks with the past: the anti-poaching campaign, the Waliangulu Scheme and the formation of the Game Policy Committee. For the first time conservation policy and its *raison d'être* was subjected to more rigorous intellectual enquiry than had happened previously. It was coupled to a drive to get things done and not merely talked about.

The anti-poaching campaign and the Waliangulu Scheme are dealt with in greater depth elsewhere in this volume, so suffice it that here I record only my personal connections to both programmes. In 1955 we had no clear idea of how many elephants there were in Kenya. The former Game Warden Archie Ritchie had at some point in the past, given as his opinion that the national total might be around 12,000 and the figure had stuck. Had anyone looked at ivory production as documented in the Customs records, it would have been patently obvious that the population had to have been a great deal larger.

In 1953, the American Fulbright Scholar, Hal Buechner, had paid Tsavo a brief visit from Uganda. In an aerial count between the Voi River and the Nairobi-Mombasa railway, he had counted 3,000 elephants. At the time it was known that there were other elephants elsewhere and that 3,000 could not be the total. With Buechner's count as the base, it was felt that there were probably at least 4,000 in Tsavo East and West combined.

In 1955, David Sheldrick estimated that native poachers were killing around 1,000 elephants annually in and around the two parks. This figure, believed to represent twenty five percent of Tsavo's overall elephant population, set alarm-

---

Serengeti Plains. For a variety of reasons (i) and (iii) melded into the great north-south migration of the late 20th century.

[30] See also Pearsall W. 1957. *Report on an Ecological Survey of the Serengeti National Park, Tanganyika.* Oryx 4, 71-136.

bells ringing. The general belief was that unless poaching could be contained it was only a matter of time before Tsavo's elephants ceased to exist. But the national parks had neither the manpower nor the financial resources to do much to improve the position. David Sheldrick, Warden of Tsavo (East), was combating the poachers with one Field Force of thirty men. At least two more Field Forces were necessary if progress was to be made. At this juncture my two hats once again served me well.

Attempts to induce government to take appropriate measures to rid the park of the poaching menace had gone on for months without achieving any satisfactory result. Indeed, a strong body of opinion insisted that the true position in the Tsavo National Park had been exaggerated and that there was therefore no need to make money available for anti-poaching purposes. In September 1956, Mervyn Cowie, despairing at the lack of progress, handed responsibility for persuading the Government to mount an anti-poaching campaign to me. I went to see the Governor, Sir Evelyn Baring, the Commissioner of Police, Sir Richard Catling, and several ministers to put the case to them. They responded magnificently and, within three months, Government had agreed to allocate money for a full-scale campaign against the poachers.

The Governor, the Attorney General, Chief Justice, the Chief Conservator of Forests, and several others issued important directives on the subject. Government agreed to place the Ivory Room at Mombasa under Game Department control. Fresh legislation was drafted, and other measures taken, too numerous to detail here. David Sheldrick was given overall responsibility for running the field campaign, while Superintendent Rassie Potgieter of the CID was in command of an urban campaign against the illicit trophy buyers.

The primary aim of the field campaign was first to clear the two Tsavo National Parks (East and West) of poachers then, once that had been achieved, to cross the park boundary into the lands around the parks. Results exceeded all expectation. It had at first been estimated that it would take two years to clear the park of poachers. In the event this aim was largely achieved in nine months. Tsavo East was virtually free of poaching for the next fourteen years or so. In Tsavo West the results were less complete, but poaching was considerably reduced. Where the Tsavo Parks were concerned, the campaign was a remarkable, landmark achievement.

The Waliangulu Game Management Scheme was a logical follow-on to the anti-poaching campaign. It would benefit the Waliangulu people by guiding their hunting propensities into legal channels and safeguard their culture. Less widely appreciated was that from the very outset the scheme would also have been a device to avoid a proliferation of elephants and consequent devastation of habitat in the Tsavo East National Park by 'cropping' them in the game management zone[31]. Unfortunately, the Kenya Government's negative attitude meant losing the opportunity for testing the scheme's potential. Much of the blame for this missed opportunity can be laid at the door of the Treasury for refusing to support the scheme, but the Game Department was also at fault for being barely luke warm about it.

On becoming a member of the National Parks staff I was immediately struck by the lack of any clear-cut statement of conservation policy, both within the service itself and nationally. Neither the National Parks nor the Game Department did much to rectify this. In 1956, however, Government created a national consultative body: the Game Policy Committee with the specific purpose of drawing up a long-term policy for conserving the country's fauna. The idea was first class, but the manner in which it was put to use was not. The committee took three years to issue a report, and when, in 1959, it at length appeared – as Sessional Paper No 1 of 1959/60 entitled *A Game Policy for Kenya* – it proved of little value. While the Government paid lip service to the importance of wildlife as a valuable cultural and economic resource, it appeared to have neither the will nor the means to support its own policy. In point of fact, most of the proposals required comparatively modest financing. As the Sessional Paper admitted, it did not bode well for the wildlife of Kenya if the relatively small sum required to safeguard what the government itself recognized as an important natural asset could not be found.

* * * *

On joining the Parks, I was also struck by the wide differences in the functions and attitudes of the two organizations responsible for Kenya's wildlife - the Game Department and the National Parks. Of course there were bound to be differences between the two: it would have made no sense for each to have been a carbon copy of the other for they had different functions. Yet the differences that separated them seemed greater than what they had in common, so much so that the two organizations often appeared to be pulling in opposite directions.

Whereas the National Parks were in the business of protecting wildlife, and of non-interference with nature, the Game Department was perceived to be largely preoccupied with enforcing the Game Regulations, in issuing hunting licenses, and in 'control' work (i.e. shooting animals that killed livestock or damaged crops). Some members of the general public, however mistakenly, looked upon the Game Department as an instrument of game destruction rather than conservation. Cooperation and coordination between the two organizations were

[31] Editor's note: The logic here was straightforward, but the facts on which the case rested were flawed. Later findings showed that there was rather limited movement between Park and Scheme and that reductions, if they were needed, would have to take place in the park itself. It is of note here

minimal. Some of this seeming unwillingness to make contact stemmed from the Game Department's status as a government department, while the National Parks Service was a quasi-independent organization with its own Board of Trustees.

That this state of affairs, accepted as immutable, was to a great extent a reflection on the characters of the two heads of their respective organizations. Willie Hale, a former District Commissioner, was at that time Chief Game Warden, and ran a fairly easy-going department in which the hierarchy of command was sometimes difficult to discern. Mervyn Cowie was Director of the National Parks and ran a rather more conventional organisation in which everyone's position, relative to each other, was clear-cut. Stemming from a deep-rooted fear that the Government might take over the National Parks and merge them with the Game Department, Cowie had a barely-concealed antipathy towards the Game Department. The relationship improved when Ian Grimwood became Chief Game Warden, as he was more open to new ideas than his predecessor, more positive in his approach to problems, and recognized the importance of collaborating with the National Parks. Nevertheless, there were good grounds for Cowie's fears: after independence amalgamation actually took place. With hindsight the case for and against having two separate conservation entities has never really been clearly determined and issues have been decided more by the eloquence and personalities of the various proponents.

Personally, I was convinced that, economically and culturally, Kenya's wildlife was the country's greatest asset, and that successive generations were under a moral obligation to do everything necessary to safeguard it. Yet I did not believe that safeguarding it necessarily meant preserving any *status quo*. I was among those who believed the way forward lay in conserving rather than preserving wildlife. The difference between them is fundamental. Preservation implies protecting every living thing regardless of the ecological consequences, while conservation entails wise use, which includes controlling numbers as a legitimate form of management. It also recognizes that the so-called 'balance of nature' no longer exists, and has to be replaced with prudent management, which recognizes that it is perfectly reasonable to harvest the fruit as long as the tree itself remains intact, and able to yield another crop the following year.

With such an outlook I found it extraordinary for the Game Department to have ignored the possibilities of obtaining sustained yields of protein from wildlife. It should have been in the forefront of researching the most suitable methods of its use. Failure to assess this potential is a criticism that can fairly be laid at the Game Department's door. Yet the National Parks were equally chary of research. The first Fulbright Scholar to come to East Africa was Dr George Petrides, who undertook a study of the Nairobi National Park, published in 1955 as *Kenya's Wild Life Resource and the National Parks*. Mervyn Cowie had been looking for scientific support for some of his own theories, and when this failed to materialize he determined never to have a scientist on the staff. Cowie's attitude played no small part in all subsequent Fulbright Scholars by-passing Kenya and going instead either to Uganda or Tanzania.

Lake Nakuru National Park with its massed flamingoes around the shoreline, was originally created as a bird sanctuary (photo Rolf Davey)

One of the biggest gaps in Kenya's park system was the lack of one specifically for birds. Since Kenya possessed a magnificent avifauna, this seemed a glaring omission. A location of prime potential was Lake Nakuru, which the eminent American ornithologist, Roger Tory Peterson, described as the finest bird spectacle he had seen in a lifetime of bird watching. Not only were indigenous species abundant, but also Kenya was winter home for many palaearctic migrants. Among them were the Eurasian ducks – chiefly pintail, garganey teal, and shoveler - from western Asia where, since the end of the Second World War, vast reclamation projects, especially in the Ukraine, drained much of their wetland breeding grounds. This, and the fact that Russian-bred ducks and geese also had to run the gauntlet of thousands of hunters along the length of their flyways had caused a progressive decline in migratory ducks entering Kenya. I thought a system of sanctuaries to provide refuge for migratory birds, along the length of the principal flyways was an international obligation. I was not alone in this outlook and no one was more in favour of setting up bird sanctuaries and parks than John G. Williams of the Coryndon Museum.

It was with this in mind that, on behalf of the Kenya Wild Life Society, I convened a public meeting in Nakuru on 17th November 1957. The hall was packed, not a seat to be had. I invited Dr Louis Leakey to open the meeting, followed by John Williams, the Coryndon Museum's ornithologist. The meeting was asked to approve a resolution that the greater part of Lake Nakuru should become a bird sanctuary. A lively discussion ensued and the motion was carried by a huge majority, and a small committee appointed to work out the details.

The very person one would have expected to be most enthusiastic about the new park was the Director of National Parks. But strangely enough Mervyn Cowie was at first opposed to it. His antagonism arose from a concern that the parks' resources were already at full stretch and that unless the annual Government subvention for running them was increased he was unwilling to accept this additional commitment, however desirable it might be[32]. This difficulty was eventually resolved, and Lake Nakuru became Kenya's first national park primarily for birds[33].

Looking back, there were many other developments that made the years 1955-1959 more productive than any before or since. African involvement and participation was at the forefront of the local conservation mind. In addition to the genesis of the Waliangulu Scheme, controlled areas fees from sport hunting started to flow into African District Council coffers. An important milestone was the Meru District Council's decision, taken in the late 1950's, to set aside more than seven hundred square miles of their land as a District Game Reserve – the first in Kenya to be established by and for the local people. It was later upgraded to national park status. Following on this came talk of the Masai setting up their own game reserves, which culminated in, first the creation of the Trans-Mara Game Reserve and, eventually, the Masai Mara Reserve. In various articles in Wildlife magazine and in my book, *Between the Sunlight and the Thunder: the Wild Life of Kenya,* published in 1962, I advocated making the greater part of Masailand a Masai Park, to be run by the Masai themselves for their own benefit. This would have had the effect of linking up with Tsavo and other adjoining national parks to form an immense block of land, some 40,000 square miles (102,400 km^2) in extent, reaching across the international boundary into

---

[32] Editor's note: As apparent in Bleazard's records elsewhere in this book, this was in fact Mervyn Cowie's stock response to any suggestions of acquiring more land. While it irritated those making the cases for new parks, it had a certain logic. I am unaware of any case in which the Cowie reaction actually prevented an area becoming a park in the long run.

[33] Editor's note: Lake Nakuru National Park now has a complement of game animals and few people today are aware that it was established primarily for birds.

Tanzania where wildlife and domestic livestock would live together in traditional Masai fashion. It would also have helped preserve Masai culture.

Today, fifty years on, it is fascinating to read of somewhat similar ideas emanating from the South African Peace Parks Foundation, designed to link already existing parks and game reserves into extensive blocks of land in which wildlife would be safeguarded, reaching across territorial boundaries. They are ideas that first saw the light of day in that flurry of conservation thinking that characterized the mid-late 1950s. Naturally, the question arises, why this five-year period should have been so productive?

The answer is perhaps not so much that these years were a pinnacle of achievement but rather that years both before and after were troughs. In the early 1950s, Kenya's affairs were dominated by the Mau Mau rebellion. In the 1960s MacMillan's gale of change once again pushed conservation into the background. Yet whatever the reason, those few years were very stimulating.

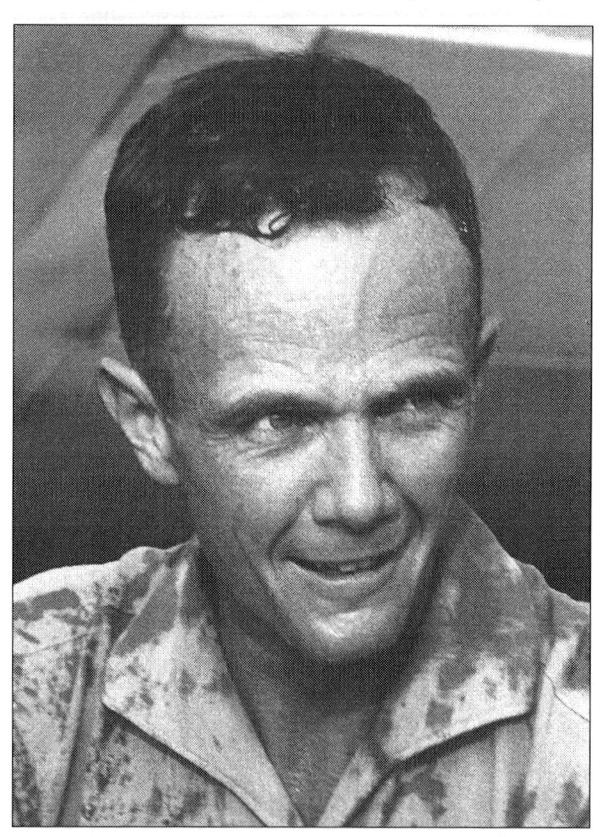

Ian Parker

CHAPTER 11: THE ANTI-POACHING CAMPAIGN

Ian Parker

There were actually three great anti-poaching campaigns in Kenya during the twentieth century. First there was MacArthur's which was rather a one-man show. He and a mere handful of stalwart Scouts captured and jailed over four thousand 'poachers' between 1927 and 1937[34]. Mark you, the work was relatively easy because the natives were unaware that poaching was in any way wrong. After MacArthur they at least realised that they shouldn't talk to white people about any hunting that they might do.

Then there was what has widely known as the Sheldrick/Woodley campaign in 1956 and 1957. Next running from mid 1963 until the early seventies was the Somali shifta battle. Whereas MacArthur, Sheldrick and Woodley genuinely dealt with people who were foremost meat and trophy hunters, this was not so with the shifta. True, they poached, but they had a far wider political agenda of which poaching was only part.

Where strong personalities are involved, their names come to be associated with certain events. Thus we talk or write about MacArthur's anti-poaching work, whereas he was not alone. His head Scout, Diwan bin Ahmed (who died in 1931) may have initially been due at least as much credit[35] as Mac, and his other Game Scouts were also due much credit (or blame – depending on your point of view) for what was achieved. We tend to refer to the Sheldrick and Woodley campaign in the mid-fifties and to Elliott's anti-shifta activities, even though they, themselves, would have pointed out that others, both in the ranks, and among Wardens, deserved recognition.

The anti-poaching campaign I write of here is that with which I was personally involved in the nineteen fifties. Its taproot went back through the MacArthur era (1927-1937) to the arrival of colonial rule. From these earliest days the Administration was aware that specialised ivory hunting tribes peopled the coastal hinterlands from the Juba River in what is now Somalia, to the Umba River on the Kenya/Tanganyika border. In the north they were the Bon (a.k.a. Boni or Waboni), north of the Tana delta the Dahalo (Africa's most northerly click-speaking group) and from the Tana south to the border the Wata (a.k.a. Waliangulu, Wasanye). Tucked away behind the Shimba Hills was yet another group – the Digiri – who, today, are on the verge of losing their identity through absorption into the Digo and Duruma people.

The degree to which their cultures were connected with elephants and ivory is unlikely to have been ecologically as much as commercially founded, given their

[34] Anon 1927-1937. *Annual Reports of the Kenya Game Department.* Government Printer, Nairobi.

[35] Anon 1930. *Annual Report of the Game Department.* Government Printer, Nairobi.

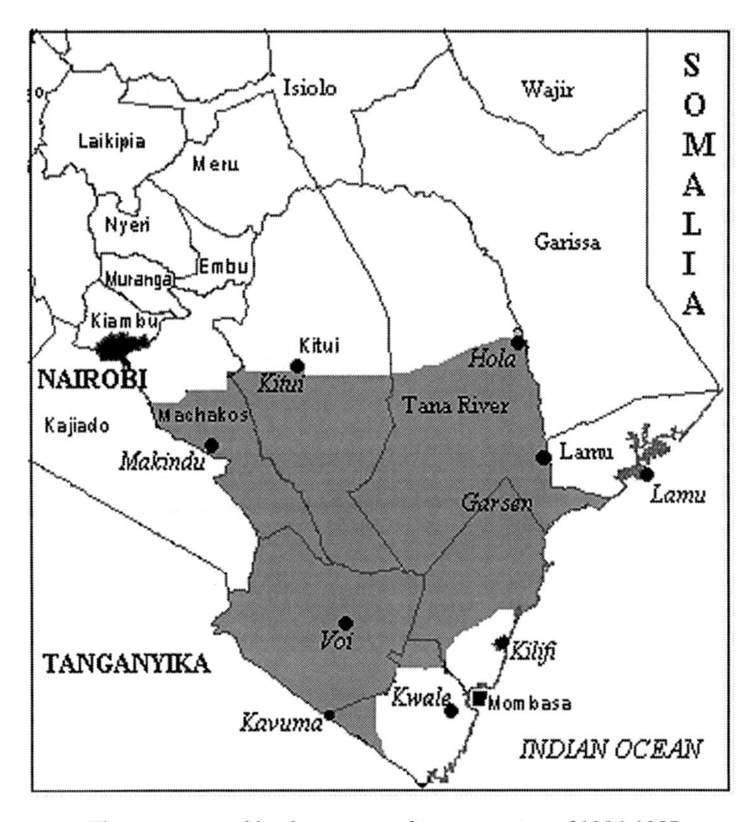

The area covered by the anti-poaching campaign of 1956-1957

proximity to the coast and its sea connections with distant civilisations that wanted ivory. The early colonial administrators were so well aware of this that they did not try to stop it as much as use it. Thus the Boni were allowed to hunt elephants on the condition that they surrendered one tusk of each elephant killed to the Government[36]. While this arrangement did not last, it was nonetheless revealing of prevailing official attitudes. Yet, for all that the government was aware of their existence and what they did, there seemed to be a recurrent amnesia on the subject. MacArther pulled this coastal elephant hunting back into the official consciousness during the 1930s, but as soon as he relaxed his anti-poaching work, the issue was forgotten.

Thus when in 1948 Billy Woodley a brash young Warden with a truck and a diary (he and Peter Jenkins were ordered to keep a diary by the first Tsavo Warden – Ron Stephens), reported large scale elephant hunting along the Sabaki, in Tsavo National Park, he was disbelieved. Hunting, as he described it, was on a

[36] Anon. 1913. *East Africa Protectorate: Annual Report of the Game Warden 1910-11 &1911-12.* Government Printer, Nairobi.

scale beyond imagination and he was, to his consternation, severely criticised. No one wanted to believe what he said: even MacArthur who two decades earlier had roped in poachers not in their hundreds, but thousands. It is possible (Bill himself used the word likely) that the antagonism he met with had a different origin: he had come too close to an ivory racket being run by a Ranger in the Game Department[37]. Indeed Woodley nearly lost his job.

What saved him was the division of Tsavo into two parks – Tsavo East and Tsavo West – and his posting to the former under David Sheldrick. David quickly checked his subordinate's statements and confirmed that the hunting by Waliangulu, Kamba and Giriama was every bit as extensive and open as Woodley had reported. Both of them were so ignorant of earlier records that they believed the Administration was unaware that such a people as the Waliangulu existed. Part of this confusion may have arisen from the different names by which they were known: Wata by themselves and the Orma, Wasanye (the smiths) by the coastal Swahili, and Waliangulu by the Mijikenda people. The depth of official ignorance is also apparent in failure to appreciate that many place names across the coastal hinterland and along the coast itself north from Kilifi, are all derived from the Oromo spoken by the Wata (e.g. Arabuko, Teso, Roka, Mida, Dida, Gede, Malindi, Jilore, Galana among hundreds, are all Wata place names).

Once reported by Sheldrick and Woodley, the issue of elephant hunting in the coastal hinterlands became fixed in official minds. Initially law-enforcement was planned along the lines that prevailed in South Africa's Kruger National Park. A series of Ranger posts were distributed across the park and staffed by small groups of rangers who would patrol the areas around them and, by their presence, deter poaching. The system was logical. The rangers would become familiar with their local areas and, through this familiarity, be an effective Police force.

It took several years to appreciate that the system did not work. If rangers could keep an eye on poachers, the opposite was also true. The fixed Ranger post could be watched, the movements of its men observed and which direction the patrols took noted so that hunting could be carried out elsewhere. More important, small numbers of rangers could both be intimidated by larger gangs of poachers and bribed to turn blind eyes towards them. Further, with men distributed in small numbers and widely separated, they were difficult to lead and supervise. Officers were too distant from their men.

In the years when this was becoming apparent Sheldrick and his assistant Woodley, together with other Wardens like John Lawrence, were absorbed with developing a park infrastructure. Woodley, for example, spent time in Nairobi

---

[37] Editor's note: Coincidentally and independently, I obtained similar evidence on the same Ranger a decade later. Yet, by then he had been dead for some years and collecting conclusive evidence would have been an academic exercise for which there simply was no time. I.P.

being trained to drive road graders by the firm who supplied them (Gailey & Roberts Ltd) and then applying his training by grading roads in the Nairobi National Park. In consequence, while they knew illegal hunting was going on in and around Tsavo East, it was not given overriding priority in Sheldrick's schedules for attention.

In 1952 Woodley was conscripted for six months military training in the then Southern Rhodesia. No sooner had he returned from this than the Mau Mau rebellion broke upon Kenya and he was called up for full-time military service with the Kenya Regiment, which kept him away from Tsavo for most of the next three years. The Mau Mau-induced state of emergency not only deprived Tsavo East of Woodley, but also placed a damper on development generally. Only as the rebellion was becoming contained and its end in sight did Sheldrick have the latitude to turn his attention fully onto bringing poaching under control.

Thus, while Sheldrick may have decided as early as 1952 that the Kruger model of fixed outposts manned by small Ranger units was inappropriate and that an alternative system of law enforcement was called for, he was not in a position to implement his alternative until late 1954. From his army experience and the very military set of his mind, he reasoned that better results would be achieved if his entire law-enforcement staff were concentrated. Based at headquarters, they could be deployed anywhere in the park without warning and in strength enough to tackle big poaching gangs. His men would be under close supervision, removed from being under poacher observation and less able to make arrangements with them. Acting as a platoon-sized Field Force, under his direction, David correctly felt law enforcement would improve rapidly.

Bill Woodley, returning from military service in mid-1955, brought with him experience that had earned him an MC, and a considerable knowledge of intelligence gathering. Assuming command of the Tsavo East Field Force, he and Sheldrick made anti-poaching their top priority. From then on development was rapid. The real extent of elephant and rhino hunting became apparent for the first time. So, too, was it obvious that its suppression would benefit greatly if poachers could be pursued beyond the borders of the parks, back to where they lived. In more recent jargon, their thinking embodied the principle of 'hot pursuit'. And it was Woodley's perception, more than Sheldrick's, no doubt reflecting his recent military experiences, that poachers – like guerrillas – would always be more vulnerable in their homes, off duty so to speak, than when in the field and on guard.

As these attitudes set and they started putting together a network of informers among the communities both east and west of Tsavo, Sheldrick also commenced publicising poaching, the number of people involved and estimates of elephants and rhinos killed annually. In a pattern that has since become the hallmark of conservationism, a crisis was created with predictions of extinction. David's

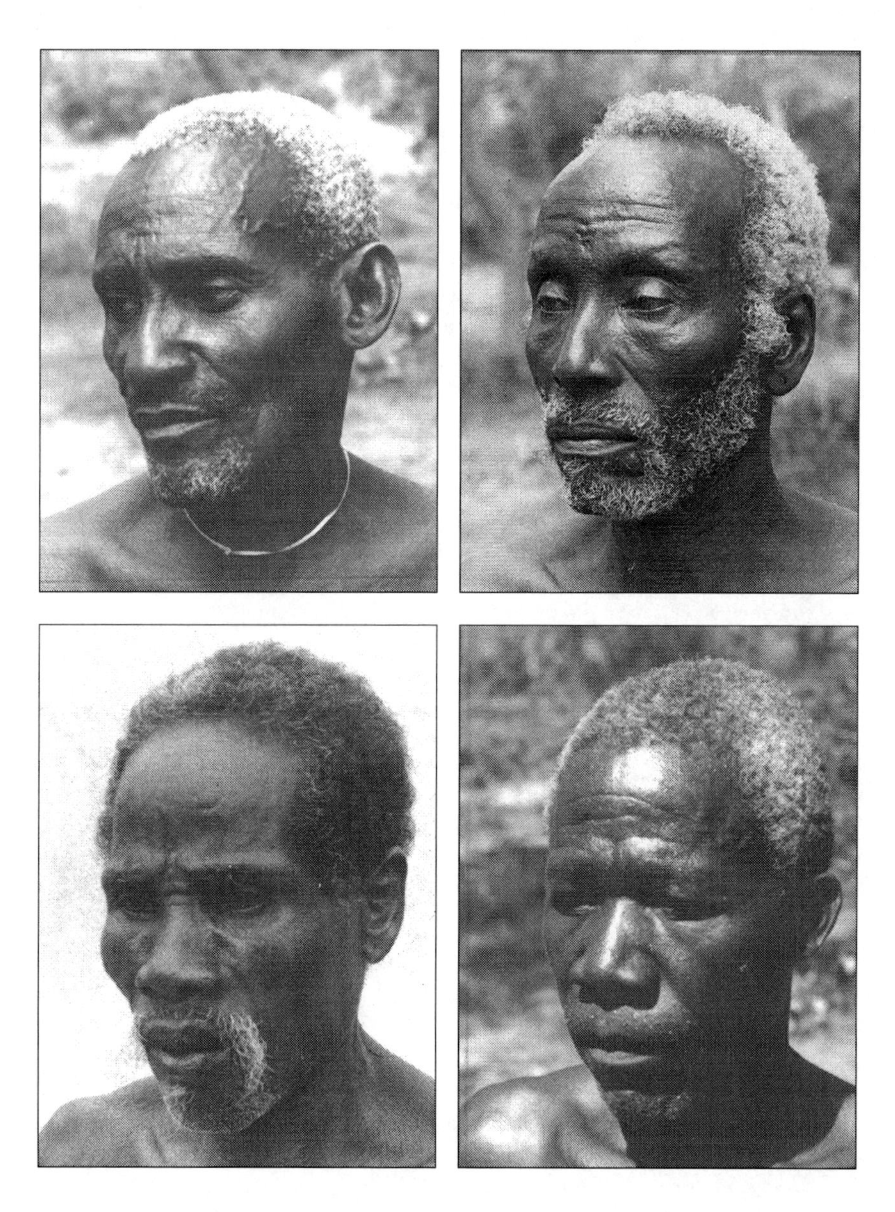

Left to right, top Abajila Guyo and Dido Galogalo; bottom Guyo Ashako and Jefa Meri: four men picked up during the anti-poaching campaign for offences against the game laws. Ironically, the Wardens responsible greatly admired them for their hunting skills (photo Bill Woodley).

unabashed champion was Noel Simon, ex-Royal Navy Fleet Air Arm, whose flair for public speaking and writing whipped up public concern about poaching in Tsavo. Less closely connected with David Sheldrick, but also a publicist with influence, was the journalist Anthony Cullen, then writing for the Kenya Weekly News. The publicity came to the attention of one man who could take action: Sir Evelyn Baring, Kenya's Governor.

Sir Evelyn Baring, son of Lord Cromer, the British ruler of Egypt as the 19th century ended, was Britain's Proconsul in Kenya. In the Imperial mould, Sir Evelyn demanded action, not just from the National Parks, but also from his government as a whole. It was he, better than Sheldrick and Woodley, who saw that nothing short of a full-blooded campaign involving the Administration nationwide was called for. It was he who ordered such a campaign be set in motion, initially in Coast Province and Ukambani and later elsewhere when these two areas had been cleaned up. Baring's Directive circulated to all Administrative Officers is worth quoting in full:–

> *I am disturbed by the grave threat to Kenya's wild life caused by the activities of poachers. These activities have recently become so extensive as to present a serious danger to the preservation of the game populations of the Colony. Though it is primarily the responsibility of the Game Department to protect the Colony's game, it is the duty of all officers to help in preventing poaching: this duty is of special importance because the staff of the Game Department is small and cannot, with the many functions it has to perform over wide areas, give undivided attention to poachers.*
>
> *2. The Wild Animals Protection Ordinance (No. 18 of 1951) makes provision for the preservation and control of wildlife. Under section 8 of the Ordinance it is an offence to hunt, kill, or capture any game animals, except in accordance with the conditions of a licence granted under the Ordinance. It is intended to introduce more stringent provisions.*
>
> *3. Under section 12 of the Royal National Parks Ordinance (Cap. 215) it is an offence to enter a National Park without a valid permit, to possess a weapon, explosive, trap or poison, or to kill, injure, capture or disturb any animal in a National Park.*
>
> *4. I wish all officers, and particularly those of the Administration and of the Police, to make themselves familiar with the relevant provisions of these Ordinances and to take all possible measures to put down poaching. I am sure I can rely on*

all officers to apply themselves to this task. Kenya's game population, although unhappily diminished during the past two decades, is still a great natural asset and it is of the first importance that it should be protected.

2nd January, 1957. *(signed) E. Baring, Governor*

The reaction of the Kenya Wild Life Society, as expressed in Noel Simon's first Annual Report[38], is also worth recording verbatim: -

We in Kenya are indeed fortunate in having in the person of Sir Evelyn Baring a Governor who is so vitally interested in the question of fauna preservation, and we have much for which to thank him. His Excellency's directive can I feel be described as a milestone in our endeavours, for it marks a fundamental decision in the attitude of the Administration, and recognition of the need to conserve the Colony's diminishing wild life.

As is so often the case, Evelyn Baring's Directive did not mark the beginning of his endeavours, but the formal tidying up of what he had actually started months earlier. By the time that his Directive came out he had ordered all policemen to apprehend and prosecute poachers, demanded that magistrates award deterrent sentences for poaching, that the Police appoint a senior officer supported by an appropriate subordinate staff to concentrate on illegal ivory and rhino horn dealers, and that the Kenya Police Air Wing place a pilot and aircraft at the disposal of the anti-poaching forces operating out of Tsavo. While, to their credit, Bill Woodley and David Sheldrick unquestionably set the events in train that led to the anti-poaching campaign of 1956 and 1957, Sir Evelyn Baring elevated their ideas into something greater and made the whole programme into an altogether more significant project. A man of many parts and achievements, he was never given the credit that was his due for the anti-poaching campaign. Indeed, with history's hindsight, it would be appropriate to refer to it as the Baring anti-poaching campaign of 1956-57.

* * * *

Written as I have presented events above implies a greater sense of order and foresight than actually was the case. There was never a point at which Sir Evelyn or anyone else laid a neat plan on a table and said this is what I want and this is how we shall do it. Aside from the Governor's command that all departments of

[38] Simon N, *1957 First Annual Report 1956*. Kenya Wild Life Society. Nairobi. P. 15

government concerned should act, events tended to come together in a somewhat piecemeal fashion. My own personal involvement bore this out.

Two posts in the Game Department were advertised and the successful applicants came from the Administration: one from the pukka side in the form of David Brown (known to all as DB), and the other from the non-pukka Mau Mau Emergency side in the form a D.O.K.G. (District Officer Kikuyu Guard) – me. We both had to buy new Land Rovers: mine registered KFL 929 and his KFL 930. DB was sent to learn about control work at Nanyuki; my training was to read the previous decade's various station monthly and annual reports. Having done this I was equipped with a tent, bed, wash basin, camp chair and table and a .475 with a broken right firing pin (this was not apparent at the time). My orders were to go to the Makindu range, base myself in Makueni, try and find some of JA's (i.e. JA Hunter's) Game Scouts (JA was then the Warden Makindu Range and, at the time, on leave in the U.K.) and catch poachers. There was no house or accommodation, I should live in my tent.

Obediently I set about my duties and in my first morning's work at the end of September 1956 arrested sixteen men for illegally possessing game trophies – mostly in the form of skins. That afternoon they were all sentenced to six months in jail with a two hundred shilling fine in addition. From my lowly position I felt that I had done rather well. Others were not quite so appreciative. Unbeknown to me, Bill Woodley accompanied by Dave McCabe (he was yet to join the Game Department officially) together with the National Park Field Force from Tsavo East had planned a series of raids based on weeks of intelligence gathering and my morning's work had well and truly upset their applecart. Every man and his brother were aware of anti-poaching activity. Unfairly, I thought, I was criticised for what I had done. However, as no one had told me that the Tsavo team would be operating in 'my' area or outside the parks for that matter, I wasn't sure how I could have divined that they would be.

My 'territorial rights' had been infringed and I drove down to Tsavo to see David Sheldrick to put matters straight. This I did and asked (demanded ?) that in future I be warned of impending action in 'my' area. Insufferably cocky, I did not create a favourable impression. In fact it was McCabe and Woodley who had jumped the gun. The plan[39] whereby they were authorised to operate outside the Tsavo Park had yet to be formalised. When that took place, it was agreed that not only would the National Parks' Field Force operate outside the parks as necessary, but that two more such units would be formed and staffed by members of the Game Department. All three units would come under David Sheldrick's command.

[39] Police Minutes of a Meeting held at Colony Police Headquarters at 10 a.m. on Wednesday, 10th October, 1956, to Discuss Methods of Combating Game Poaching

In due course the three units came into being and were variously staffed by DB, Dave McCabe, Major Hugh (*Callotis*) Massey, Denis Kearney, Peter Jenkins and myself. My time was short. After several incidents attributable to 'youthful lack of judgement' (among them arresting a station master and briefly bringing the railway to a halt) I was transferred to do buffalo control at Nanyuki.

The anti-poaching *modus operandi* was simple. Informers would be sent into an area, collect information on who had been poaching and what. When a reasonable body of evidence had been assembled, a Field Force would move into the area at the dead of night and arrest all listed. Interrogations would start immediately. Befuddled and confused, a prisoner would be faced with evidence of his activities. If possible it would be presented in such a way that he felt one of his close acquaintances had provided the information. This made him more likely to divulge something about the supposed informant. Few, if any, could match Bill Woodley in this interrogation work. The keys to success were speed, questioning people before they had time to concoct alibis or speak with their fellows and great patience. It started as soon as the captives were apprehended and went on until all evidence possible had been gathered. As information came in it was acted upon. Posses were sent out to bring in new names. The work was continuous for several days before running out of steam, whereon the force returned to its base to prepare court cases and start the next operation.

Much of this anti-poaching work was unpleasant. Waking up households in the middle of the night, terrifying women and children, then getting men to split on their companions, smacked of Gestapo technique. What made it all the more unpleasant was that most of us admired these African hunters who, with bow and arrow, took game that we wouldn't approach without a heavy firearm. It was yet more unpleasant because, with the Wata especially, they were so proud of the culture and prowess that it was not in them to deny hunting. Ignorant of our legal system, without legal aid to help them, they usually pleaded guilty, seeing it as the honourable thing to do. We did this unpleasant work because we believed that it had to be done if poaching was to be stopped. Wrongly, we thought poaching would bring about elephant and rhino extinctions – at least locally. And in truth, we were also young and serious thinking was what superiors were for.

In parallel with the Field Forces under Sheldrick, a Senior Superintendent of Police from the Criminal Investigation Department (CID) whom we knew as Rossie Potgieter (but whose name was more likely Rassie – the Afrikaans abbreviation of Erasmus) worked with a team of investigators based in Mombasa and went after the buyers. Combined, the two programmes convicted 429 African hunters, 47 full time or part time African middlemen who bought tusks, rhino horns and leopard skins from these hunters, and 23 Asian or Arab traders who exported the commodities illegally from Kenya[40].

---

[40] Ian Parker unpublished text: *What I Tell You Three Times is True*.

These results only suppressed poaching in Tsavo East National Park. In this limited area it was effective and poaching ceased to be a problem there until mid-1971, a period of fourteen years. Elsewhere it made local hunters far more wary than they had been, but that is all. They continued to hunt and even in Tsavo West poaching levels did not diminish greatly[41].

Once the poachers who had plagued Tsavo East had been taken care of, David Sheldrick's (and the National Parks organisation as whole) interest in managing anti-poaching further afield waned. Towards the end of 1957 he relinquished command of the operation, the Police Air Wing aircraft was withdrawn and the Game Department assumed responsibility for managing the two Field Forces. Without an overall commander and, more important perhaps, without anyone organising intelligence gathering and running an informer network with the same competence as Sheldrick and Woodley, the whole operation wound down.

Rassie Potgieter was retired early for reasons never published, but about which Kenya's rumourmongers speculated pointlessly. The anti-poaching campaign quite literally faded away and, as had been the case before it started, it was down to individual Wardens to 'anti-poach' if that was their predilection.

The primary lesson that came out of Baring's anti-poaching campaign was clear and relevant to poaching generally across Africa. The way to control it is through plain, plodding, routine detective work, not out in the wildernesses, but back where the hunters have their families and homes. They always return to them and when at home are not on guard. Further, this is where others learn of their doings or such phenomena as sudden wealth can be observed. Bill Woodley and David Sheldrick proved that this is where they are easiest to catch and where evidence of their activities is most easily obtained. In most cultures, but particularly those which rely on hunting ability, poaching is not like paedophilia and kept ultra secret. To the contrary it is talked about and hunters are lauded.

Strangely, although David Sheldrick appreciated this, when Tsavo was next invaded, he never raised the point. In 1971 a bad drought struck Tsavo, eastern Kenya and northeast through Somalia. Elephants died in thousands. Their ivory was there to be collected for all of it was far beyond the Park's small Field Force's ability to recover. Under the drought's spur, the Kamba along Tsavo's western border risked being caught and word that Tsavo was an El Dorado of free ivory overcame their reluctance to invade the park. Driven by the drought, they entered in such numbers that only a small proportion risked being arrested. Once the advantage of numbers was appreciated, they stayed on and poached when the drought-produced tusks ran out, and the work of '56 and '57 became an inconsequential memory.

---

[41] Peter Jenkins *in litt.*

There were compounding factors. The Collectors sanctioned to gather ivory around the country (see Chapter 39) provided a ready market for all tusks recovered. Once tusks or rhino horns were over the park boundary, they were safe. It was improbable in the circumstances, that government would have allowed a parks' team loose outside its own domain. Whatever the reasons, David restrained himself to advocating a boosted anti-poaching team to operate inside the parks. It was as though the very significant success of the nineteen fifties had never happened and the principle underlying it had been forgotten.

The Mkamba, Ndibo Molu, one of the most successful middlemen between the Wata and Kamba hunters and the Asian ivory buyers in Mombasa

David McCabe: 'Kebi'

CHAPTER 12: MEMORIES FROM THE ANTI-POACHING CAMPAIGN

Dave McCabe

In early 1956 the Mau Mau Emergency was winding down rapidly and my army 'demob' took place during the same period, leaving me at a loose end as my previous employment in agriculture had, during the intervening years of the emergency, fallen away. I was due some weeks of leave from the Security Forces and spent them with Bill Woodley, Peter Jenkins and/or David Sheldrick, safariing, giving them a hand. All three were senior staff of the Tsavo National Park (East) whom I had known for many years. These Park Wardens told me the Game Department was recruiting Wardens to run the new Field Forces being formed and urged me to apply for one of the posts.

The selection board surprisingly accepted me in preference to one or two perhaps better-qualified candidates. Assigned to the anti-poaching campaign commanded by Sheldrick, I returned to the Parks H.Q. at Voi. While waiting for the Game Department Field Forces to be set up, I worked with Bill Woodley and Peter Jenkins for the next few months in the National Park Field Force already formed. We ranged as far afield as the lower River Tana, the South Coast, Kitui and Makindu Districts. Many of these safaris were reconnaissances although, as the Parks Field Force was with us, we also raided poacher settlements.

* * * *

The people we had to deal with in these game lands were mainly Wata, Boni and Wakamba. The Wata lived from the Tana river south to near the Tanganyika border. The Boni lived from the Tana north to the Somali border and the Kamba lived to the west of the Tsavo Parks. All three groups hunted rhino and elephants almost exclusively with bows and poisoned arrows. Wata and Boni were similar, although their languages differed. Both used larger and more powerful bows than the Wakamba further inland.

Wata and Boni arrows were about a metre in length and fletched with four flights in contradistinction to those of the Wakamba, which are smaller and fletched with only three flights. Considerable trouble was taken making these arrows and those of the Wakamba, in particular, were beautifully crafted and decorated. Arrows in all cases followed the same pattern. The tang of the arrowhead was fixed tightly to a short (six inch) poison shaft, around which the poison was smeared. The poison shaft, in turn fitted less tightly into the main arrow shaft. The principle was that once head and poison shaft were buried in the target, the wooden shaft of the arrow parted company with them and fell to the ground to be collected later for re-use, leaving the poison in the animal to do its

Boru Duri with Wata bow and arrows (photo Alan Root)

work. Many poachers filed their own marks into the tang of the arrowhead as personal identity marks.

On occasions these marked arrowheads were recovered from rotted carcases and from them it was possible to identify the poacher since the "signature" would be familiar to fellow poachers. The Wata/Boni bows required so powerful a pull that it was not possible to draw them without long practice. I cannot recall any white Warden being able to draw in one of these great bows to its full extent. The owners could, but not by pulling straight. Bow and arrow were pointed skyward and the draw started as the arrow was brought down into the aim using all the muscles of the arms, shoulders and back on one huge heave, the arrow being released as it came into line with the target. Occasionally one would see burn scars on the archers' shoulders. These burns were deliberately inflicted, it seems as a sort of counter irritant to the pain of muscles tearing when drawing these huge bows. When not in use, the arrowheads and poison were wrapped in a strip of softened dik-dik skin. This protection prevented deterioration of the poison and was a precaution against personal accidental injury. The covering was removed before the arrow was used.

The poison was made from *Acokanthera* trees. All members of this genus contain very poisonous cardiac glycocides, the most toxic of them coming from the Horn of Africa's *A. schimperi* and inland Kenya's *A. fresiorum*. The former yielded a glycocide called ouabain (named by a Frenchman after the Somali name for the tree – *wabayo*), while the latter a very similar form called Acovenocide A. There is no known antidote to this group of poisons (to which digitalis is related). Bits of the tree – bark, leaves roots and wood – are boiled, new material constantly being added to the liquor and the well boiled bits removed. Eventually the highly concentrated liquor is boiled down to a black, tarry consistency. Each poison maker had his own special touches adding items such as spiders and pieces of snakes to the concoction.

The efficacy of the poison, apart from relating to the skill of the manufacturer, depended on the speed with which the poison dissipated into the bloodstream. If this is rapid a victim may only run a few hundred yards before collapsing. Conversely, an animal ineptly struck may not die for some days. Before my time the ace poacher Galogalo Kafonde killed three elephant with three arrows loosed in quick succession near the Sabaki River. All died within sight of each other.

Members of the coastal Giriama tribe made the most lethal poison. In their heyday the Wata poachers at Kisiki-cha-Mzungu, a village on the Sabaki not far from the Tsavo Park boundary, retained a well known Giriama poison maker on a semi-permanent basis (Kisiki-cha-Mzungu is self explanatory and refers to a survey beacon erected by Lugard in 1890 when exploring the Sabaki for the Imperial British East Africa Company before Kenya, or the British East Africa Protectorate, as it was first known, officially became a Crown Colony). Not only were the residents of Kisiki renowned for hunting skill, but also for their capacity for alcohol. This they obtained by tapping doum palms for their sap. When fresh this is a not unpleasant tipple but after a few days fermentation it becomes stupefying toddy. To tap a doum palm, one has to climb to the fronds at the top of slender branches that are prone to snap under the weight of a man. The Wata reduced the risks by connecting several branches together with a scaffolding of poplar stems. The extent of the doum palm toddy business was very apparent from these scaffoldings that at one time were in every mature palm between Lugard's Falls and Kisiki-cha-Mzungu – a distance of nearly fifty miles. It was a measure of Galogalo Kafonde's status in Wata society that, in his heyday, he engaged the services of a personal palm tapper.

* * * *

Eric Rundgren, then a professional hunter, reported that the very atmosphere of the lower Tana stank from poaching, there were carcasses everywhere and complained that the tracks of "every worthwhile bull elephant were overprinted by those of a human," manifestly a poacher. So little anti-poaching work had been done since MacArthur's day twenty five years earlier, that the people no longer believed hunting to be illegal. He reported one small village north of Karawa at the Tana delta where, quite openly, the inhabitants had shown him recently taken tusks and made no attempt to conceal their bows and poisoned arrows. Billy Woodley decided to move camp to Karawa with part of the Parks' Field Force. Several Somali rangers dressed in civvies were sent off the next morning to have a smell around. They returned the following day having visited two Wata villages some distance northwards. After chatting to the inhabitants for a bit they casually mentioned ivory. These poachers must have been aware that poaching was illegal but one must doubt that they had ever expected to encounter the opposition in person, especially in the form of two or three scruffy Somalis. Whatever, they produced some tusks and the rangers noticed several bows etc in the huts.

After de-briefing our men we decided to raid both villages that night. To this end a patrol of rangers together with Bill and me set off hoping to arrive on target at about 2.00 a.m. However, our estimate was badly out and we didn't reach the poachers village until around 4.30 a.m.

One man detailed to watch the surrounds of the village almost stumbled onto a lady who had come out on an early de-watering exercise. She let out enough of a shout to awaken the other inhabitants before heading for the horizon. It didn't matter. The village was small consisting of only half a dozen or so huts and no one else got away. Some six pairs of tusks (I think) plus a number of bows and quivers of poisoned arrows were seized. The males of the village were handcuffed and told to identify their own ivory and weapons. At this stage, and for some time into the future, most of these poachers showed no reluctance to admit possession of trophies and weapons. This was a contrast to experience with their colleagues to the south where denials and evasions made successful prosecution difficult or impossible in the absence of corroborative evidence.

The second village was empty, its residents having been warned of our presence by the lady who ran away from us, so we returned to Karawa. There the prisoners were further questioned and court charge sheets prepared. The interrogations, at which Bill was a past master, delved into many aspects of poaching and some comprehensive information on other poacher villages, names, activities etc were forthcoming: all quite amicably. The information was recorded and added to a very comprehensive card index system at the Voi headquarters. From before the start of the anti poaching campaign comprehensive notes had been kept concerning poachers and their activities. All arrested poachers were photographed and all information from informers and interrogations of poachers sent on to Voi where Daphne Woodley, Bill's wife (later to become Daphne Sheldrick), collated the information and maintained a card index system. As this developed it became increasingly useful in confounding uncooperative poachers during interrogation. Not infrequently they were so impressed by what was known that they gave up and admitted not only to the misdeeds of which they were accused but sometimes even volunteered information compromising other poachers whom they assumed, or had been told had sneaked on them.

Bill then left for Malindi, the nearest centre with a Magistrate's court, while I continued raiding. From the information gleaned during these interrogations we knew of a Wata village on the banks of the Tana River, which I visited a night or two later. The raid was a total failure. Before we could get into position the alarm was given. No doubt news of our previous efforts had gone ahead of us. In no time the whole village was in an uproar with women screaming and armed poachers boiling out of huts. I could hear the snicking of rifle bolts as the Parks rangers began to get excited. Fearing that things were getting out of hand and realising that no good could come out of continuing the raid, I managed to prevent any shooting and ordered a withdrawal.

Apropos of this, it may be worth recording that a couple of years later a similar situation arose when a Police C.I.D. contingent from Mombasa searching for an illegal ivory buyer, raided a village called Egakumbi. On that occasion the situation did deteriorate into an exchange of rifle fire versus poisoned arrow. One poacher I know was killed and I think one or more were wounded. At the time this raised quite a stir. As a precaution to avoid such situations arising in the first place, Parks staff was trained differently from the conventional civil Police.

Continued interrogations gradually filled our store of information. One or two names repeatedly cropped up and we realised that these were of men of considerable standing in the poaching fraternity. One, Abakuna Gumundi appeared to be the doyen of the lower Tana poachers so efforts were concentrated on finding this gentleman.

Although news of Abakuna's whereabouts was not too difficult to obtain, follow ups invariably failed, as we were always one jump behind. Then, when we were back in Malindi with the Field Force for a break and to restock our fuels, rations etc., a message came from the Police to say that they had a man waiting at the Police Station who said that he wished to speak to "Bwana Bilu" (as Woodley was known by poachers from Ukambani to the coast). Without knowing whom we would find we drove to the Police Station. A slim, slight, very fit man of about thirty introduced himself as Abakuna Gumundi and said that he understood that we had been looking for him. A huge surprise indeed: he said that he had given himself up because he was tired of continually being obliged to shift around in order to keep one jump ahead of the Serikali (Government) as were his womenfolk in keeping up with him[42].

I have sometimes wondered whether Abakuna, a very intelligent man, was not at the time beginning to realise that the freedom to wander at will over many thousand square miles helping himself to whatever game he wanted, and which

[42] Editor's note: The real reason was that one of his wives was having a complicated pregnancy and needed medical attention which Abakuna had to arrange. Source A. L. Archer, who was a great friend of Abakuna.

Abakuna Gumundi, one of the greatest Wata elephant hunters. He was eventually murdered by Somali shifta (photo A. Archer).

he and the others like him, had enjoyed, was coming to an end. We spoke to Abakuna; or rather Bill did mostly, for many hours. Absolutely fascinating; he made no effort to conceal any of his activities and was happy enough to discuss matters concerning many of his colleagues.

Abakuna was far more value to us at liberty than he would have been in jail. He mentioned a cache of, I think, fourteen tusks buried in the bush well inland and provided a man who had been with him when the elephant were killed, who knew the site. Bill had to return to Voi and took Abakuna with him. I took a few of the Parks Field Force, the guide and some locally recruited porters to recover the ivory. We understood it was some hours walk from Adu, a small settlement at the end of a bush road where we spent the night. We set off on foot at first light the following morning. As we could expect little or no water in the bush this late in the year each man was carrying extra water and the porters also had been temporarily issued with borrowed water bottles. In addition and as a precaution, rations for a night out were taken along. We also had a portable radio transmitter/receiver in contact with Voi headquarters, which by now had become standard bush equipment on anti-poaching work.

The "some hours" turned out to be the understatement of the year. We spent two nights out, the second without food and with very little water. Although we had come across a small pool of smelly water on the way out and replenished stocks, we somehow missed this on the return journey and had some discomfort with thirst as a consequence. One of the porters became distressed and was unable to carry his load of the recovered ivory so I was obliged to lug this along myself as I was the only unloaded member of the patrol. Fortunately none of the tusks was very heavy, probably about 30lbs at the most.

Shortly after recovering the ivory we heard an aircraft in the distance. This was Punch Bearcroft and Bill Woodley whom we then guided overhead by radio. They expressed surprise at how far from Adu we were, and after ascertaining that we were not in any difficulties dropped a parcel which they claimed would be useful on foot safaris in a hot climate. This arrived on a coloured streamer. After much unwrapping I discovered a condom in a matchbox. It was a leg weary, hungry and thirsty patrol that got back to the transport and its welcome clean water at Adu the following day. The leg weariness was even more pronounced the next morning. Punch Bearcroft later estimated that we must have walked some 120 miles in all on this little expedition. He was amazed that anyone could navigate to a specific point over this distance in such featureless flat bush country. So was I.

* * * *

Up until this point I had been working with Bill Woodley and the National Parks Field Force. When the finance for two Game Department teams came through, one lot of recruits were to be principally Somalis from Garissa, the other from the pastoral Samburu and Turkana. Ian Parker collected those from Garissa while I, having drawn equipment including a lorry from Nairobi, set off for Samburu and Turkana on a recruiting trip. This took a couple of weeks, and the thirty odd recruits, mainly raw Samburu and Turkana but including one or two recommended retired ex-K.A.R.soldiers, were soon based in a tented camp near the Voi Parks airfield.

Full kit was issued to each man but only after removing the body dressing of rancid sheep fat and generally sanitising some of these wild gentlemen. It was also necessary to remove the elaborate (and frequently fragrant) coiffures of many before they could wear any uniform headgear. After some discussion all had their skulls shaved. This latter, strangely enough, resulted in several instances of men passing out after some hours' exposure to the sun. The whole mob was then subjected to intensive military foot and arms drill training, with field schooling modified for their specialised anti-poaching roles.

Initially there were language problems. However, Africans seem adept at picking up foreign tongues and the present instance proved few exceptions. Towards the end of this training period David Brown, destined to be my 2 i/c, arrived on the scene at Voi. "DB" as he became known had transferred from the Provincial Administration. I had had no experience at all of Government administrative or accounting procedures so DB's arrival was a godsend. Other arrivals were Major Hugh Massey (nicknamed '*Callotis*' after the fringe-eared oryx *Oryx beisa callotis* because hairs grew out of his ears) and Denis Kearney. The former, an ex Hussar, had in fact already worked for a very short while with Bill Woodley and me along the coast. He was considerably older than anyone else in the organisation. Denis, known to all of us, was ex-Kenya Regiment with an excellent record in intelligence work during the Mau Mau rebellion.

The two Field Forces were known respectively as Hola Force in the care of DB and myself and Makindu Force with Denis and Hugh Massey. Both had their own transport. Hola Force was to operate Kilifi northwards to the Somaliland border and inland to include Tana River District. Makindu Force was to control poaching over pretty well the whole of Ukambani (i.e. Machakos and Kitui Districts). National Parks would continue to look after things within their own boundaries. Overall David Sheldrick from Tsavo East's headquarters at Voi would retain command and co-ordination. DB and I with Hola Force then spent some months keeping up pressure on the Wata poachers of Tana River District and to a lesser extent on the Boni of Lamu District.

We forsook Hola and initially moved camp out some twenty miles into the bush to the junction of two old locust survey tracks at Mutiboka, rather a lonely place but away from the populated areas of the river. Later we moved to Minjilla, a small hill on the roadside near the junction of the Malindi - Lamu road and the Garissa turn off and a couple of miles from Garsen with its ferry to cross the Tana en route to Lamu. Bill and I had used this site before and found it convenient for work on the lower Tana. One disadvantage was the mosquitoes.

These pests were prolific all along the lower Tana, but the Garsen area was of particular note. Another vicious insect was a dully multicoloured tabanid fly shaped rather like a bee but considerably larger and with a quite fearsome proboscis. They appeared to be territorial as, after killing those in the immediate vicinity, they were not replaced and one became free of their attentions. Later, in 1957 DB went off on overseas leave. He never returned to the Field Force so from then on I was on my own.

* * * *

September 1957 saw a joint Parks/Game Department safari to the inland area between the Galana and Tana Rivers. Except during the rains and for a while afterwards there is little or no surface water in this wild and uninhabited bush. Between the coast and Ukambani, this huge flat, hinterland is completely featureless, except for two adjacent small hills, Dakadima and Dakadikacha. For some time reports from poachers, mainly Waliangulu, had suggested that the area contained much dead ivory (i.e. from elephant that had died either naturally or at the hand of poachers but not found). We planned that I would make my way in from the Tana near Hola with one lorry whilst Bill Woodley and Denis Kearney with a lorry and Land Rover would work their way in from the Sabaki River in the South. Each Unit would provide about twenty rangers/Scouts who would walk as the lorries would have to be fully loaded with forty gallon drums of water plus rations, equipment and petrol. For celebrations on meeting up at the Dakadima hill rendezvous, each of us would take along a case of beer. In addition to the drums Bill had been able to borrow a Public Works Department water cart, which could be towed by the Land Rover.

From the late 1920s until the end of the 1930s, Bror von Blixen had frequented this area looking for trophy elephants for his clients. Following in the footsteps of Denys Finch-Hatton he had taken up reconnaissance from the air, mainly using Beryl Markham as pilot. First using Finch-Hatton's airstrips he had put in another set even further out in the blue – at Ndiandaza, Sala and, furthest out of all, at Dakadima. With JA's help, he had even spanned the Sabaki at Sala hill, making a temporary pontoon bridge out of forty-four gallon drums attached to steel cables. From this crossing point he had cut a trail to Dakadima, seventy miles away. It was this trail that Bill and Denis would follow with their team.

To my knowledge, it had only been used twice since the war broke out in 1939. First Bill Woodley and Peter Jenkins in about 1955 had hunted along it (Bill was on a private elephant hunt during which he shot a large tusker). Bill and I had travelled along it while elephant hunting earlier in 1957.

For the ivory search, the men split into pairs. Before setting out to scour the countryside for tusks, each man was issued with tracer ammunition. They were given strict instructions to stay together. These were precautions against becoming lost - a very real risk indeed. Even the poachers to whom this country was 'home ground' took special measures against getting lost in it. When hunting they would tie a long stick, with a bunch of grass at the tip so that it stuck out of the tallest nearby tree to project well above the canopy. These beacons enabled them to find their camps.

Each pair of Scouts or rangers was instructed to stick together, and should they become lost to stop altogether until dark when they should fire off the tracers skywards at intervals. A watch would be kept at camp after nightfall, which would respond by sending up flares from a Very pistol as a guide back to camp. Inevitably on a few occasions men did get lost but the signal arrangements worked until one evening when one man of a pair returned alone. He and his colleague had separated. The other man was in a distressed state when eventually found a day later, having long since finished his water.

Euphorbia robecchii: the broken branch tips betrayed where vultures had perched, suggesting the likelihood of a carcass nearby

As had been predicted by the poachers, a considerable quantity of ivory was found, using the Waliangulu knowledge that a useful guide to the possible whereabouts of carcases was provided by tall 'hadama' (Euphorbia robecchii) trees. Because they stuck out beyond Commiphora canopy, vultures selectively used them. The tips of the top branches were fragile and broke under a vulture's weight. Where many had used a tree, as would be the case when a carcass was nearby, its top had a flattened appearance. While not foolproof, these signs made it worth searching in the vicinity.

I cannot recall how long we spent on this safari; neither can I remember the number or weight of tusks recovered. I do however have a photo of Bill and Denis with some of the ivory laid out after returning to Voi. There are four pairs of 'large' tusks of which the largest weighed 133 lbs (60 kg) each. Another photo is of three rows of tusks. Unfortunately, these rows go out of the frame. The tusks of some fifty elephant, and the horns of about thirty rhino can be seen.

Some of the ivory and rhino horn collected on the Dakadima exercise (photo McCabe).

I wish that I could recall the ratio of these to the carcases from which the trophies were recovered[43]. The vast majority of tusks collected were in good condition showing little or no sign of the deterioration associated with weathering, insects etc. from long exposure to the elements[44]. So these animals must have died from one cause or another within the last year or two.

* * * *

The Wata and Kamba poachers themselves seldom, if ever, sold their trophies direct to the illegal exporters. That trade was confined to Arab and Asian businessmen mainly in Mombasa. Contact between poachers and dealers was usually via a middleman who inspected trophies in the bush and arranged purchase and onward transport to Mombasa.

In those days, most tusks were not exported whole from Kenya. The first steps in processing were undertaken in Mombasa with tusks being sectioned into pieces suitable for specific uses, and having the outer 'bark' (a trade term) removed. The least valuable parts were the butts, that is the hollow end pieces, to that point beyond which the first three fingers of the hand held side by side would not go, and the tips. Again, these were cut off at that point where the tusks were as thick as the first three fingers held side by side. To avoid buying these least desired parts of the tusks, the dealers only bought tusks, without the tips and butts which were left in the bush. This meant all ivory bought illegally was prime. Thus many poachers' hideouts were scattered about with discarded butts and tips.

Although in the past there had been some prosecutions involving these dealers, most cases collapsed due to legal technicalities during arrest or subsequent preparation of the case. Unlike the poachers who were rarely defended by a lawyer, a competent barrister always defended the traders. For example, one night in 1954, one of the older Wardens, Gordon Harvey, mounted a classic 'sting' operation. While a dealer was nearby in the bush haggling with the middleman over a sack full of rhino horns, Gordon had crept into the rear seat of his car. The sack of horn was then thrown into the boot of the car and the owner climbed into the driver's seat. He found himself unable to drive away as

[43] Editor's Note: The total ivory collected was 446 whole tusks weighing 3,734 kg, with a further 772 kg of butt ends and tips. The ratio of skeletons with ivory to those without was 1:5 (i.e. one in six). The total weight of ivory recovered by the three anti-poaching Field Forces between November 1956 and December 1957 was 11,690 kg whose value exceeded the cost of the anti-poaching programme between these dates. See Holman D. 1978 *Elephants at Sundown – the Story of Bill Woodley*, W. H. Allen. London.

[44] Editor's Note: Later work indicated that natural elephant mortality running at 3%-5% annually would always have been a large source of ivory. The records from Tsavo East itself for the years 1957-1971 when there was virtually no poaching made this point cogently. The deterioration on tusks left in the open was also highly variable and good ivory has been recovered after 40 years in the bush, while serious weathering has occurred on some tusks after only eighteen months.

Gordon had removed the ignition key and also had him by the neck from behind. The defence pleaded successfully that as the driver did not have the car keys he was not in possession of the car and therefore could not be in possession of the rhino horns in the boot.

Late in 1956 an Indian businessman was arrested in Mombasa in possession of a number of tusks. I cannot remember the precise details of the investigation but the case revolved around a pair of cow tusks, minus their butt-ends and tips. The businessman argued that they were legal tusks bought at the Mombasa auctions, but could not produced the butts or tips because they had been thrown away. Bill Woodley knew, however, from whom he had bought the tusks: it was none other than Galogalo Kafonde. Galogalo agreed to show him the butts and tips that he had removed in the bush and they recovered both butts and both tips from where the dealer had never been. When the defence challenged the prosecution to match them to the tusk centres in question, Bill Woodley was able to do so to the court's satisfaction. The lawyer (Mr O'Brien Kelly, an Irishman with a pathological dislike of Wardens and game law, and a long record of successfully defending clients against game charges) was then unable to prevent a conviction.

This happened just after the Governor had directed the courts to take poaching cases seriously and new stiff penalties for poaching and illicit dealing had been promulgated. These were applicable and the Indian was sentenced to a hefty fine plus a prison sentence. His attempts to swap the prison part of it for a further fine were rejected whereon he ranted and raved and burst into tears. Not long afterwards another dealer was successfully convicted and when he appealed his sentence, the Appeal Judges not only rejected the appeal but also significantly increased his prison sentence. Very salutary though these convictions were, they undoubtedly drove illegal trophy dealing deeper underground. Nonetheless, they cheered us up no end as it seemed very lop-sided justice for us to be throwing the poachers in jail, while the richer men who stimulated them to break the laws got away free or, at worst, lightly.

David W. J. Brown: 'DB'

CHAPTER 13: LOOKING BACK

David Brown

I joined the Kenya Game Department in 1956. For two years before that I was District Assistant in the Provincial Administration. After one glorious year in the Samburu District of Northern Kenya as assistant to Terry Gavaghan, I had been moved to urban Nairobi as the Officer in Charge of the Nairobi Tribal Police Force. I yearned for a return to the open spaces of Africa, to the bush and its magnificent wildlife. Idly perusing the Official Gazette, I came across a notice of vacancy for Game Wardens (2). Off I wandered to the District Commissioner's Office, there informing Ginty Tannerhill of my intention to apply.

Ginty reached for a Staff List, examined it and then said: - "Its not much of a job: only £850 a year. You have to be the Chief to get onto Super Scale. Much better prospects in the Administration. You might be Governor one day."

The rugby season had finished and being bored, I applied despite the good advice to the contrary. After a month or so I was duly summoned to interview. Willie Hale, the then Chief Game Warden was a Selection Board Member, his trousers just being anchored to his waist by his colourful Charterhouse tie. Years later I often saw the same tie disappearing out of a Game Department office window whenever Joy Adamson approached to beard Willie in his den.

John Webster, the Permanent Secretary for Forestry and Wildlife, was also an interviewer. I forget who the third member was. Willie himself was a former District Commissioner and I think he was getting a bit brassed-off with some of his Wardens who either could not, or would not put pen to paper to provide him with some indication of what was happening in their areas of responsibility. Probably for that reason and after having discovered that both my father and grandfather were gamekeepers in England, he recommended my appointment.

I was to spend three months being taught by Fred Bartlett to hunt buffalo, elephant and other animals that were interfering with agricultural production on the slopes of Mount Kenya, and another three months with George Adamson as a student of bushcraft and anti-poaching techniques. As it happened I only had a month with Fred before he was transferred to Kilifi on the coast. He only lasted a year there before accepting one of the many lucrative offers for him to become a white hunter. With a wife and fast growing family to support, it was a wise move at the time, but the Department lost an exceptionally gifted hunter. Jack Barrah took over from Fred and gave me more first class tuition. In particular I remember being very surprised at how unfit physically I was, not withstanding just having completed a strenuous rugby season.

My appointment with George Adamson collapsed because I was redirected to take part in the anti-poaching campaign already described in previous chapters. Ian Parker and I were the first two Game Wardens sent to serve under David

Sheldrick. I was initially and ostensibly Second-in-Command to Field Force Commander Billy Woodley, but in fact was the avid pupil and grateful follower of the already renowned Bwana Bilu. The only disagreement I can recall was Billy's practice of smoking a Clipper cigarette whenever a breathing stop was called, during our many prolonged walking safaris through stinking hot semi-desert country. Billy steadfastly maintained his thirst was thereby quenched. Certainly he drank very little but I am sure such abuse must have contributed to his subsequent ill health.

After serving with Bill and the National Park's Field Force, I then joined Dave McCabe running one of the two Game Department Field Forces based on the Tana. In fourteen months most of the Waliangulu tribe responsible for the elephant poaching in and around the Tsavo Parks had been rounded up. I served with '*Kebi*' until due for home leave at the end of 1957.

Upon my return in 1958, the Game Warden Headquarters, Colonel Neil Sandeman, went on leave and I took his place. This meant occupying an office next door to Willie Hale as his Number Two with particular responsibility for the large weapons' armoury and the allocation of hunting areas to the professional hunters, still then referred to as 'White'. Willie helped himself to a handful of my cigarettes every morning from August onwards and then proudly presented me with a box of fifty for Christmas. When my five-month stint was up and I was eagerly awaiting news of where my new Station would be, Willie suddenly decided to retire. This disaster meant Neil Sandeman became the Acting Chief Game Warden and I was stuck as his deputy for nearly a year, until Ken Smith was cajoled into doing time in Nairobi and I bagged Garissa in Northern Kenya on the banks of the Tana River.

After three adventurous years moving up and down the Tana in various ways and into the sparsely populated hinterland, it was back to the Ngong Hills where one's main duty was to keep straying animals in the Parks and Reserves and to enjoy the buffalo and colobus monkeys on the Hills. I became reasonably adept at trapping leopard, which were at first released in the Nairobi Park. But since I kept catching the same ones, they had to be sent further afield. One such was reported to be at the Baring Biscuit Factory, in down town industrial Nairobi. I took the report with a pinch of salt expecting the beast to be a serval cat, or some other innocuous puss. The last sighting was said to be in a tiny store next to the gents' urinal. When pulling away old boxes and debris I was astonished to see an unmistakable leopard's rosette but four feet away, in the corner behind some bicycles. A hasty silent retreat was made. A cage was summoned and placed in the doorway to entrap one of the biggest leopards ever caught, which in fact had been released into the Nairobi Park only a few days before[45]. Clearly there was no room for any more there.

---

[45] Editor's note: DB's early finding that leopards caught, transported and released quickly returned to their points of origin was appreciated by a number of other wardens, but it must have taken a

By this time Ian Grimwood had become the Chief Game Warden with Neil as his deputy and disaster struck again. Neil retired and I was recalled to Head Office in Nairobi once more. My Administration background was proving something of a disadvantage to some one who really wanted to be in the field. Initially, I hoped that my position as deputy would be temporary and that someone more inclined to sitting behind a desk would be found. Unfortunately, this ws not to be. Before such a person could be found, Ian fell out with the African Permanent Secretary of the Ministry for Tourism and Wildlife under which the Game Department now came, and retired. Being on the spot I was put in the Hot Seat and was Chief Game Warden from 1964 until 1968 with assistance from two splendid deputies in Jack Barrah and Stan Bleazard.

These were difficult times. After two years of Independence there was understandable pressure to replace European personnel with locals. Population growth and land hunger was threatening animal habitat just about everywhere. An anti-hunting lobby was gathering strength. Joy Adamson wanted to protect every animal everywhere. United Nations and other `experts' wanted to show us how to manage our wildlife and parks. I saw my role as a buffer and to keep my field officers as free from interference and red tape as possible.

In 1968 I, too, was retired to facilitate localisation of the Civil Service. One of my last duties was to chair a meeting of the Trustees of the Kenya National Parks. The meeting was addressed by Dr. Richard Laws, a scientist funded by the Ford Foundation to conduct a comprehensive study of the Tsavo Park with particular reference to the elephant population. After consideration of Laws' evidence, the Trustees concluded that to maintain the Park in its then state, it was essential that elephant numbers be controlled. Indeed, there were already far too many for the vegetation to sustain. Since many of the Trustees had to retire after that meeting, those present felt unable to make a decision which would be binding upon the new, incoming body. The meeting's conclusion was therefore termed a recommendation to the new Board, to advise the Minister of its views and formally recommend the appropriate action.

In the event nothing was done and history records thousands of elephants perishing during the next significant dry period (1971). After the meeting I kept asking myself whether such a terrible event might have been avoided if Billy Woodley had not unravelled the Waliangulu elephant hunting practice. No doubt someone else, probably David Sheldrick, would have done so. As it happened, both elephant and rhinoceros were later to be brought even closer to extinction by slaughter for monetary gain with the use of sophisticated modern weaponry.

During those latter years it was impossible not to offend many persons concerned with wild animal welfare in one way or another, but those in my own

---

further ten years or so and confirmation through radio-tracking before it was generally accepted that trapping-transporting-releasing was, by itself, not an appropriate solution to troublesome leopards.

Department I am sure understood and appreciated what I was trying to achieve. As a parting gift they presented me with a magnificent oil painting, by the now renowned Canadian artist and biologist Robert Bateman, depicting Ahmed the famous Marsabit elephant. It remains a treasured memento.

The truest test of a Warden's hunting competence was success after buffalo in the Nanyuki range (photo Peter Davey).

CHAPTER 14: NAKED HUNTERS

Tony Marsh

Tony Bond was a Livestock Officer and his long time friend Peter Stonier was an Assistant Agricultural Officer. Both men worked in the Kitui District of Kenya during the early 1950s. Both owned heavy rifles and they decided to use a weekend hunting rhino on the lower reaches of the Athi River which had dried up to the extent that only intermittent pools were left for the various game animals to drink. The time-honoured method of rhino hunting was to follow the course of the river and look for tracks of any likely looking beast and follow it up.

During the dry season of the year the temperatures in the river bottoms were very high indeed and the two hunters decided after a while to remove all their clothing, retaining only hats and gun belts. There was no fear of displaying their nudity as there were no resident Wakamba in the area and it was far from where casual travellers might stumble on two men clad in hats - one about 5ft 4ins tall and the other over 6ft 2in - walking along a sand river, each with a heavy rifle over his shoulder.

On rounding a corner in the riverbed the hunters came upon two people lying sun-bathing on a rock just at the edge of the river both of whom were even more scantily clad than the hunters. As one of the sunbathers was a lady the intrepid hunters, being gentlemen, removed their hats, bade the two on the rock a pleasant "good morning" and carried on looking for rhino spoor. The identity of the two sunbathers was never revealed, but this tale soon spread far and wide amongst the hunting fraternity.

I recently called in on Tony Bond just outside Kimberley, where he and Stonier bought adjoining farms and grew garlic and onions very successfully for many years. Over lunch in a local restaurant I checked out the incident of the naked sunbathers and Tony confirmed that it was indeed true.

Tony (Nyani) Bond, who hunted rhino dressed only in a hat, shoes, gunbelt and watch, (photo John Fletcher).

CHAPTER 15: GAME WARDEN, LAMU

Dave McCabe

The anti-poaching campaign ran down quickly after David Sheldrick relinquished overall command, though that had never been the official intention. When the Field Forces were originally set up, it had been planned that they would become permanent aspects of the Department. Many of the subordinate staff becoming redundant while those who did not were shared out among the established Game Department stations. I, myself, was posted to take over as Game Warden Lamu and Tana River Districts from Denis Kearney who had resigned from the Game Department and joined the National Parks.

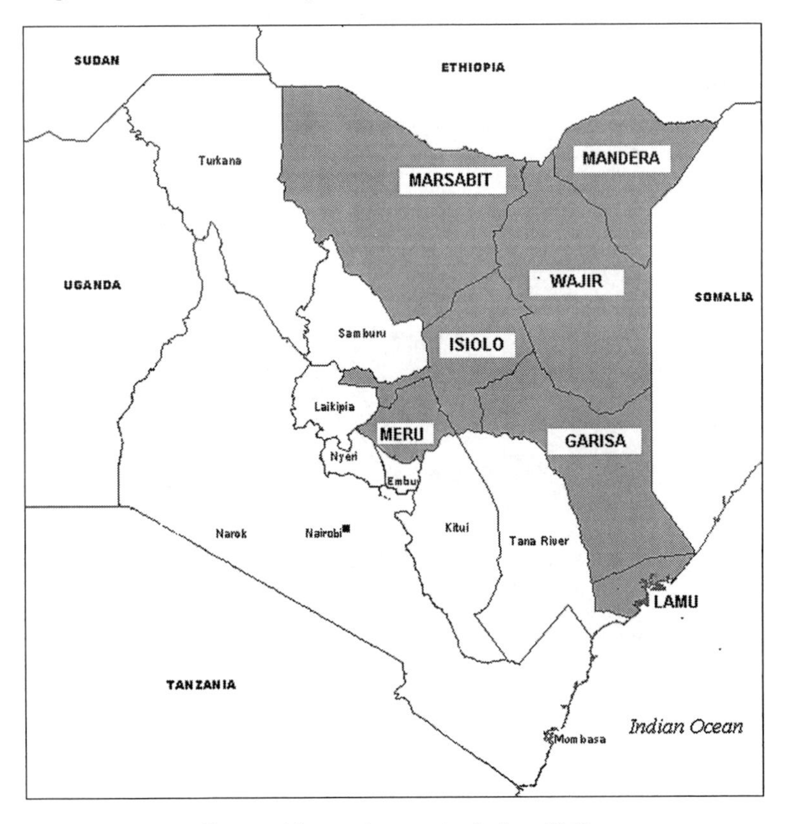

George Adamson's range in the late 1940s

Lamu District had, for a long time, been Kenya's most active elephant control area. Despite this it had never had a Warden with specific responsibility for the District until in the mid-1940s, when it was placed under George Adamson and under whom it remained until the very late 1940s. He was essentially a token Warden for he lived over five hundred miles away at Isiolo at the northern foot of Mount Kenya. In all the time that he was the Warden responsible, I do not think he managed to visit Lamu more than three brief times. A glance at the map that shows George's range illustrates why.

The Game Department answered the Administration's progressively more strident calls for help to stop elephants damaging crops by asking Jack Bonham, based at Malindi, to help out. When he could not do this and had to attend to his own range south of the Tana River, it sent in off-duty professional hunters or Honorary Game Wardens to kill a quota of elephants on a share of the ivory basis. Among their number were Bob Foster and Eric Rundgren.

I knew Eric well: a character who was unquestionably a great hunter. Equaling this, however, was his habit of treating clients with contempt and ridicule to the point of extreme rudeness. This they either enjoyed or couldn't take at all. The number who came back for more as well as recommending Eric to their friends showed that the reputation had probably gained much in the telling.

Tony Henley who did two years in the Kenya Game Department before moving to Uganda (courtesy Tony Dyer).

One of the elephant 'bounty hunters' was Tony Henley who started *ex-officio*, but was taken on briefly as a Game Ranger and based in Lamu District. After him, Don Bousfield served until the outbreak of the Mau Mau rebellion, and when he was called up there was a gap of several years before Roger Hurt became Game Warden Lamu. When, in 1957, Roger took over Kilifi to let Ian Parker investigate the proposed Waliangulu Scheme, a man called Maurice Grey ran the station for the months that he was away. He only lasted in the Department for a few months, and the only person in the Department who seemed to know him was Ian. Roger Hurt returned to Lamu in February 1958. He shortly thereafter went on leave and was replaced by Denis Kearney and then myself in 1959. I was followed a year or so later by Tony Carn.

Lamu was the Game Department's Cinderella in which the main activity was shooting elephants along the coastal cultivated settlements from Tana River northwards to Kiunga on the Somali border and along the banks of the Tana River. This activity came to a head annually when crops were ripening from June onwards. This period also coincided with influxes of elephant from further inland, attracted by ripening doum and borassus palm fruit. Both are prolific in many coastal areas. Seasonally, the demand for elephant control was so intense that, even with a Warden in residence, the Game Department still brought in 'bounty hunters' to help out.

Since no specific arrangements or instructions were given to these hunters, other than "that's your area, shoot up to one hundred elephant before a given date" I doubted its effectiveness in protecting crops. Yet it was Departmental stand-by strategy, used more for its political than any real value in control crises. Apart from the annual peak periods, some game control was necessary for most of the year to safeguard plantation crops such as bananas.

My two best Scouts were a Bajun, Sergeant Kibwana, and an Ogaden Somali, Cpl Dineh. Kibwana was an ex-World War II naval rating with a sound sense of discipline. He had been issued with probably one of the last double-barrelled .600 rifles used by the Kenya Game Department. This cannon had been made by Manton of London, a long defunct firm. Now and again it fired both barrels simultaneously ('fanya rivet' in Kibwana terminology) invariably knocking Kibwana off his feet. He was very competent on elephant control, having accompanied Rundgren on numerous occasions. He told me Eric had once held him, Kibwana, by the ear to prevent him doing a bunk when things became rather too hot for him and elephants were all about them.

The coastal settlements between Lamu and the border could only satisfactorily be reached by sea. One smelly and uncomfortable trip to Faza by dhow was enough for me; I am not a mariner. Thereafter I used to scrounge a lift with the DC's launch on its periodic trips along the coast. This meant that I had to conform to someone else's schedule that either allowed insufficient or too much time before having to return to Lamu. This was unsatisfactory. Consequently I had to leave virtually all supervision of Game Department affairs north of Lamu to Sergeant Kibwana with whom I checked at intervals by making road trips to Kiunga on the Somali border and Mkokoni a few miles to the south. They were the only points on the coast accessible by road.

Cpl Dineh was quite the most outstanding member of the subordinate staff that I had come across during my entire career with the Game Department. He was a quiet man, totally without bull, an excellent shot and lacking any of the arrogance so often associated with his race. I brought him to Lamu as i/c of the few Scouts and stores etc. Lamu being an island, it was practical to keep all the Station's supplies, equipment and transport on the mainland and essential to have a sound man looking after the depot.

I heard there were very interesting coral formations in the sea off Kiunga so I took a mask, flippers and harpoon gun and borrowed an outrigger canoe along with its owner to have a look. The information was not exaggerated. It was really marvellous with gin-clear water down to a depth of thirty feet. Fish were everywhere and masses of crayfish. On one occasion I had a Scout from Kilifi District with me in the boat. I knew he could swim, albeit weakly, and as he wanted to have a look underwater, had lent him my mask. He was straightaway in difficulties requiring assistance back to the boat. After draining himself he admitted blind panic at the thought of "falling to the bottom of the sea!"

Once, while camped at Kipini a Scout and I looked over a banana plantation damaged by elephants. A number of banana plants had indeed been flattened. The owners asked that we ensconce ourselves in the plantation that night and wait for the elephants to arrive. I was not keen as, a short while previously I had had an alarming minute or two after being foolish enough to enter a crop of standing maize in the dark to get at some marauding elephant. At the first shot, fired from close range, the whole mob had stampeded, a number of them right over the place where the Game Scout and I were standing and we were lucky not to have been run down. So, on this occasion I declined the suggestion and promised to return the following morning to follow up any elephant, had there been further damage. I was appalled the following morning to find the entire plantation of about two acres written off. I felt bad about this, which, I think, was the most extensive crop destruction that I was ever to see. I could imagine the owner's feelings, feelings unmitigated by the death any of the elephants responsible.

Baboons were everywhere a serious pest. Adequate control over them was never achieved. Poisons of various kinds worked until they learned to avoid poisoned baits, which they quickly did. Denis Kearney had initiated a rather successful system using dogs to chase the baboons into trees. Once treed, a man on the ground could use a shotgun with good effect until the baboons abandoned the tree or trees, and when on the ground the dogs and a second man with a spear could kill more. This system eventually failed when replacements for injured dogs became hard to come by.

The Boni Forest that stretched the length of the coast hinterland from the Somali border to near Witu, was zoologically and botanically the most attractive feature of the Lamu range. Despite its name it was only clumps or patches of timber interspersed with tall, *Hyparrhenia* type grassland. Difficult country when the grass was grown and obscured one's vision, it was park-like after the annual burn-off when the grass was bright green and short. The forest held a good scattering of elephant, buffalo and smaller game. Late one evening I saw a small herd, about six or eight individuals, of an antelope species which I think were sable. Having never heard or read of this species hereabouts either previously or subsequently, perhaps I was mistaken[46].

For some reason, probably connected to the nature of the soil there is a dearth of surface water in much of the Boni Forest. One of the few large pans it did contain dried out almost completely late in 1959. As it was the last remaining water for some distance around, it was becoming a graveyard for elephant and buffalo. When I first visited it there were already some carcases of both species lying about and the periphery of the pan had become a nasty sticky mess with the centre no more than liquid mud. Two weeks later there were more dead elephant and buffalo around it and the air noisome with the stench of rotten flesh.

Particularly noticeable was the total loss of reaction from animals as we walked past within a few yards of them. The pan itself was a terrible sight, there being dead and dying animals both in and all around it. On this occasion I noticed that on one side of the pan there was a steep bank on which I sat and watched for much of the rest of the day. Time after time elephant or buffalo passed below us, almost within touching reach of a rifle barrel, seemingly oblivious to our presence. On the other sides of the pan there were several elephants struggling vainly to extricate themselves from the mud. One bull elephant passed beneath us and waded into the liquid mud up to its belly before trying to drink. No good. To my surprise it waded out even further before trying again. Then appeared to give up as it collapsed onto its side and slowly sank below the surface, its trunk being the last part to disappear. I filmed this and also took a few still pictures.

Our side of the pool seemed to have a firmer bottom and here we noticed a thin film of water overlay the thickening mud. Elephant calves had somehow learned to drink this by skimming the surface with the tip of their trunk instead of immersing it below the surface.

Locals said the pool had never before dried up. Despite having been urged to have a copy of the cine film made, I never did and eventually (inevitably?) lost the entire spool of, I think, six hundred feet.

Where the Boni Forest merges with the dry NFD vegetation, there were some large tuskers, as there were also in the south around Witu, but a rather striking impression I gained in my time in the Lamu Range was both the small stature and a disproportionate number of immature elephants in the Boni Forest. This was particularly noticeable north of Lamu. There is evidence that Somalis had hunted the area very heavily indeed during the Second World War. When British Forces captured Italian Somaliland, the Kenya Police initially played a

[46]Editor's note: Jackson 1930 *Early Days in East Africa*. Edward Arnold & Co., London reported seeing several herds of sable in the Lamu hinterland c. 1885 and he was a very accurate and reliable observer. I therefore believe that Kebi did see sable. It is not widely known that sable occurred between the Sabaki and Tana Rivers in the extreme east of what became the Galana Game Management Scheme in country that was not dissimilar to some of the Boni Forest. Even in the 1980s their presence, too, was all but unknown to white men.

prominent role in its administration. The Police reported from the ivory on hand that in 1942 at least 3,000 elephants had been killed in the area of southern Somalia, Garissa and Lamu Districts. This might account, at least partially, for the apparent abundance of young animals. Yet there may have been nothing new about this as early in the twentieth century, Karamoja Bell mentions hunting for ivory as being largely a waste of time in the Boni Forest. Rundgren, Foster, Henley, Bousfield and Bonham all said that Lamu elephants were small. The suspicion lingers on that the Boni elephant may be genetically a small race. Maybe, one day, someone will look into the possibility, if there are any left now.

* * * *

I saw interesting ruins both near Kipini and on the coast just inside Somalia near Kiunga. The Kipini ruins are fairly well known but the Somalia ones are not. The countryside was deserted when I came across them, but obviously at one time the area must have been well settled. There were the remains of fair sized stone enclosures suitable for cattle but too big for sheep or goats. Also, still in good repair, were Arab-type tombs. These were open roughly square structures with walls some twelve feet in height with small minarets at the corners. On, I think, two of these towers were saucer-like indentations where some object resembling a dinner plate had been removed. Their removal had been by chisel or screwdriver, the marks of which appeared to be fresh[47].

None of the local people knew anything about the history of these relics. I mentioned them to the Mombasa archaeologist in charge of Fort Jesus and Gedi, Dr Kirkman. He had heard of but had never seen the ruins. He mentioned that the ceramics had been removed before the First World War by Capt. C.H. Stigand and thought they were sent to a British museum. I subsequently visited the place again and took some photos. On this occasion a small Somali woman and boy were there, with a camel. Remarkably, these ruins are built of stone, not of coral as one would expect. I never saw any stone anywhere near the place. Local Bajun thought the stone came from Kilwa in Tanganyika several hundred miles to the south, a strange theory.

In 1959, the beaches along the Kiunga coast were quite magnificent, invariably deserted except for the occasional person searching for ambergris. Looking north along the coast one can sometimes see the most extraordinary mirage of a thicket of enormous inverted palm trees sticking well above the

[47] Editor's note: Kebi missed out here. The indentations were likely to have held Chinese ceramic plates of considerable antiquity and value. In the early 1990s, Tony Archer & I spent time on Pemba Island in the wake of a Japanese gentleman who had been going round all the ancient houses swapping old Chinese wall plates for nice, new, colourful mass-produced plates. Each Chinese plate was thought to be worth more than $3,000. I.P.

horizon. This phenomenon, which is known locally as *Fatah Morgana*, has never been explained to me.

While on the subject of ruins, I was once guided to two graves in a patch of thick bush in the vicinity of Golbanti on the South bank of the Tana. I could just read the name Houghton and the date 1886 on the weathered headstones. The Houghtons were a missionary husband and wife murdered by the Masai and are mentioned in one of Rider Haggard's novels. At the time in the wake of the great rinderpest outbreak, the Masai were raiding as far afield as the Kenya coast where they were referred to as Wakwafi.

Lion of the north: cattle killers and occasional man-eaters (photo Peter Davey)

Like so much of the white man's early history in Kenya, the Houghtons' murder is now all but forgotten and I take this opportunity to reawaken the event. Sir Frederick Jackson was on Manda Island when the Houghtons' cook and a small boy called Makau arrived after fleeing from Golbanti and Jackson obtained a first hand account of what had happened. This is how Jackson recorded the event[48]:–

> *The cook's account was as follows: Some six weeks previously a large band of Masai had raided the Gallas* [Orma], *annexed a very considerable number of cattle, and had come down the river until quite close to Golbanti, when Houghton, instead of following the example of Mr Wakefield and other missionaries, who, though willing to afford refuge in their stations, and ready to beat off an attack, never actively interfered with the raiders so long as they kept their distance, very unwisely issued a certain number of guns to his people, and allowed them to go to the Gallas' assistance.*
>
> *That appeared to have so incensed the Masai that a certain number of them determined on coming back purposely to attack Golbanti.*
>
> *When they arrived, early one morning, Houghton was on the roof of a church he was building, and when the alarm was given by an old woman who came running into the stockade, Mrs Houghton ran out of her house, and tried to close the heavy gate, but a moran managed to get there first, push both her and the gate back, and promptly speared her. Houghton, in the meantime, scrambled down from the church, and ran to her assistance, but seeing that he had come too late, tried to get back to the roof, but was speared as he was climbing a ladder. In all, eleven natives were killed inside the stockade, the cook and Makau only saving themselves by jumping into the river and swimming across. A local native, unarmed, and taken by surprise like everyone else, had sought safety by hiding, but on the moran's near approach and fearing detection, he got up and ran. But the moran ran faster, and just when within range of his spear, the pursued man suddenly turned round and grappled with him, held him tight and shouted until a friend, also unarmed, came running up, wrenched the spear from the moran and killed him; and that spear, presented to me by the cook, is now in my possession.*
>
> *The above narrative, coupled with the fact that the Masai had come direct to Golbanti, and effected a complete surprise, and made little or no attempt to raid cattle on their return journey,*

[48] Jackson. F. J. 1930. *op cit.* p. 106

tends to support During's [a missionary] *opinion that it was a deliberate act of reprisal.*

* * * *

Doum palms whose sap and fruit inebriate both elephants and men.

When the fruit of the many doum and borassus palms north of the Garsen - Witu road was ripe, the elephant went round shaking these huge plants to get the nuts down. The ground beneath them became so littered with fermenting fruit that it could be smelt at a considerable distance. The elephants were not averse to the fruit in this state and after a surfeit became partially intoxicated and unpredictable in their behaviour. I found this worth bearing in mind when on control work in these localities, as have others.

Lions were a particular nuisance on the route along which cattle from the NFD and Somalia were driven to the coast. No doubt the livestock was the principal attraction, but man-eating was not rare. The lions of Ijara, almost on the edge of the Boni Forest at the eastern end of Garissa District, had a bad reputation in this respect. On one occasion they were also partially responsible for the failure of an effort to arrest an ivory buyer at Ankish, some miles north of Lamu - Ijara road.

I had sent two men (one of them a poacher who had recently sold a pair of tusks to the buyer) with some marked ivory for sale to an Arab (known as 'Buggerlugs' because of the large tufts of hair protruding from his ears). However, they spent the entire night up a tree taking refuge from three lions. The lions were still there when Ken Smith (then Game Warden Garissa) and I arrived next morning to follow up the bogus poachers to Ankish. Once the lions had moved off we went ahead with the now delayed plan but failed again when we found that the Arab buyer was not at home. We did, however, discover a number of looped ropes submerged in a nearby creek. These, the poacher said, were used by Buggerlugs to conceal ivory under the water.

On the long walk back to the Land Rover Ken became afflicted with "cheek-chafe". This painful condition is caused by chafing of the skin between the cheeks of the bum while sweating (an affliction to which the overweight are particularly prone). In extreme cases the sufferer is obliged to walk holding the buttocks apart. It can be avoided by wearing boxer type shorts with the lining removed and without underpants, i.e. to allow the air to circulate (a solution not recommended in mixed company!).

On another occasion, while driving to Nairobi from Lamu to hand in a worn out Land Rover for scrap, I arrived at Ijara realizing that the petrol I was carrying was insufficient to reach Garissa one hundred and ten miles away. Not wishing to return to Lamu, I bought a debe (four gallon tin) of paraffin at the tiny Somali duka at Ijara, which did not stock petrol. By blending this with the petrol I hoped to have sufficient to reach Garissa. What a hope! After a few more miles, with the engine becoming hotter and hotter and more and more smelly, the Land Rover finally gave up altogether. Traffic being a rarity, the only option was to seek assistance from an earthmoving unit, engaged on bulldozing water holes for the stock route at Madahaduni a few miles the other side of Ijara from whence I had just come. A mile or two beyond Ijara I noticed the tracks of three lions superimposed over my recent tyre-marks and going in the same direction as myself. Not so good. After a short distance the tracks left the road. A little later I looked back to see two lions walking about 200 – 300 yards behind me. Were these two of the original three? Where was the third? Or were they another two lions? I wished I had not left my rifle in the Land Rover with the kitchen toto.

What were these lions up to? They would hardly be wandering about in this heat had they fed recently and I thought of "missing" Somalis. They never came any closer and, on the umpteenth occasion on which I looked back, had disappeared. Perhaps the white skin and strange smell worried them!

The lions hereabouts, in common with those of the semi-desert NFD variety, seldom grew any mane, their usual adornment being confined to a scruffy kind of fringe or less. The number of lions congregating along the Somali Stock Route in those days was quite extraordinary. While walking through the night to seek assistance from the Livestock officer i/c the Ijara Stock-holding Ground (who was Peter Saw, later to become a Game Warden himself) to rescue my family from a bogged down lorry some miles down the road, there were lions roaring and grunting, near and far, from all points of the compass.

I sat up one night for a habitual goat eating lion near Pandanguo (literally meaning 'lift your clothing' i.e. a wet-land). After a few hours I could no longer take the mosquitoes so returned to camp and went to bed. As bait we had a live goat which was now tethered to a small tree within a few yards of my tent. Some time later I was obliged to step outside to answer a call of nature. I could make out the indistinct shape of the goat nearby but was rather puzzled by another vague object to one side of the tent. At the time what followed seemed to be in slow motion; the second object shot across my front a few yards away, snatched up the goat and disappeared, all without a sound. The rope, more a piece of heavy string, had snapped. This lion was later shot after being caught in a gin trap while trying to enter a goat boma. It was an old beast well past its prime.

In January 1960 I was transferred to Simba in Ukambani. Lamu, still the Cinderella, was left without a Warden for five months until July when Tony Carn arrived. It had been an interesting year and the Lamu and Tana River Range had some unusual flora and fauna. Yet it was a difficult station for a married man with a young family as I was. Fresh supplies were scarce. While Dr Fatal Patel did us well, the rather basic medical facilities were a strain, and the delays and frustrations of ferrying from the island to the mainland added to the problems. As a station, Lamu was in all respects better suited to a bachelor.

Tony Carn

CHAPTER 16: MEMORIES FROM THE COAST

Tony Carn[49]

These notes are culled from my monthly and annual reports of my early years in the Game Department. First I was posted to Lamu, where I served from July 1960 until December 1963. I returned to the coast in January 1967 when I was posted to Malindi, staying there until April of that year. In May I went to Kwale on the South Coast, serving there until December 1967.

I officially transferred from the Forest Department into the Game Department on the 1st July 1960, was posted to Lamu, where I took up my duties on July 11th. My responsibilities also covered Tana River District which, with Lamu, accounted for more elephant shot on control than all other districts combined.

Coming from the relatively disciplined and well-organised Forest Department, I was a shade surprised at the far more lax ambience of the Game Department. This had its positive aspects as we Wardens were very much our own bosses; but it also had drawbacks. In my first monthly report some of them were very apparent. My complement of Game Scouts for the two Districts was twenty five. Their travel and safari allowance claims had been outstanding for six months. No leave roster existed and for the past two years most of them had had no leave. Housing was in very poor shape. I managed to cadge some of the 'mabati' A-frame huts from the DC Tana River who was closing down the notorious Hola Mau Mau Detention Camp. The Game Department had no house for me and I was accommodated, courtesy of the District Agricultural Officer, in one of his temporary quarters at Hindi. Among my first administrative moves was to put in for money to improve these quarters, which leaked and required re-thatching.

Lamu, with its ancient connections to Arab and Islamic administration, was divided into three Mudirates: Kiunga, Faza and Witu. Each was under a Mudir, rather than a Chief, as was the custom in a coastal strip that was still nominally Zanzibar territory, but leased and administered by Kenya's British Colonial Government. The Tana River flowed for the most part through arid vulturine guineafowl country. As the single linear source of water, all permanent settlement was strung along it, separated by stretches of riverine forest of varying thickness. With wild animals coming in from the dry country to water on the river, they were forever damaging cultivation along both river banks.

Most of my first month was spent travelling around the two districts to familiarise myself with my staff and the nature of the work they undertook. However it did not take long to settle in. Looking back through my reports, it is

[49] Editor's note:– Tony's sight has so deteriorated that he can no longer write easily. However, he still has copies of his reports from Game Department days and made them available for me to produce this chapter on his behalf. I. P.

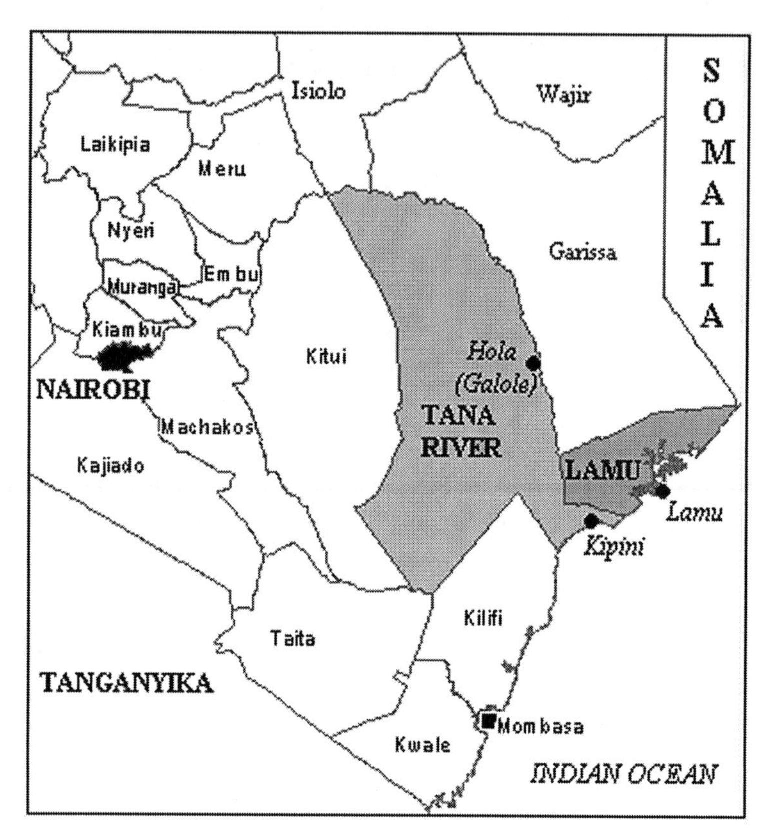

Lamu Range; the upper part of Tana River was looked after by the Warden at Garissa and most of the south-western horn was in the Tsavo Park.

clear that each month brought crises, which, at the time, dominated one's existence. Yet rereading these fading documents, they have a certain sameness about them. Although Lamu and Tana River have never been thought of as among Kenya's 'great' game districts, this is perhaps because they are not open country like the Masai plains, and consequently their game is not readily visible. Yet the control statistics tell clearly enough of both game abundance and its more or less continuous interaction with people. Where elephant were concerned, Tana River District was probably the Mecca for hunters who wanted really big tusks.

As expected, elephants raiding crops were my main headache and in the 903 days I was Game Warden Lamu, my Scouts and I shot 476 elephants and lost two wounded. While there was some seasonal variation in the rate at which we shot elephants, it works out over all at a slightly greater rate than one elephant every two days. In my 1962 annual report after having documented eighty bull elephant and thirty cows taken on control I wrote:–

"These figures give some idea of the elephant control carried out by myself and the Scouts, and I do not think that we can tackle the elephant problem any better with the staff and guns available. Each year we are endeavouring to reduce the elephant population, but in actual fact I think we only collect the surplus, and that the breeding herds are largely untouched by our present measures. This fact is borne out by the very large percentage of bulls shot as against the number of cows..."

In those days there seemed to be some confusion over whether the purpose of control was merely to punish crop raiders or to actually reduce elephant numbers. It is now history that we could, in fact, have drastically lowered their numbers by knocking out whole herds, as was demonstrated both in subsequent elephant culling programs and the wave of poaching that was to characterize the 1970s. It was inconceivable at the time that in less than two decades, elephants would be diminished to a mere fraction of what they had been in the 1960s.

In addition to elephants, we took thirty six buffalo, thirty five lions and thirty one hippos over the same period. Put another way, excluding elephants, we shot one of the other big five every nine days. A peculiarity of Tana River district was the number of waterbuck that we killed on control: seventy five in my stint as the area's Game Warden. In addition to these 'regulars' we also took two leopard and two rhinos that were causing trouble. Forty years on, no one could possibly think of shooting a black rhino on control. In those days, however, they were so abundant that it was a decision any Warden could make without reference to a superior. Today the mere suggestion would bring an international outcry. For the record the control data from my reports are in the following table.

TABLE 1

Animals shot on control in Lamu & Tana River Districts July 1960-December 1961

Year	Elephant	Buffalo	Hippo	Rhino	Water buck	Lion	Leopard
1960	75	4	15	–	13	9	1
1961	129	10	9	1	34	19	–
1962	126	8	3	–	28	2	1
1963	146	14	4	1	–	5	–
Total	476	36	31	2	75	35	2

In addition to what we in the Department saw as control work, there was 'vermin' control. This covered those smaller animals like baboons, vervets and bush pigs that, at least in our minds if not the law, did not quite qualify as game species. Indeed, in my 1962 annual report I wrote: "No one is directly responsible for vermin control, beyond the shamba owner ... it is not generally realised that the Game Department has no onus to deal with vermin." With hindsight this was more a statement of our Departmental attitude than reflecting anything embodied in law. Technically, if an animal was classified on any of the Wild Animal Protection Ordinance schedules, it was unavoidably Game Department business. Yet if we had turned our attention to controlling baboons effectively, we would have had little time for anything else.

How officals travelled in Tana River District in 1934 (photo Noel Kennaway).

In my first year I did in fact put a lot of effort into tackling baboons (as described by McCabe), which, according to the Agriculture Department, did more damage than all other wild animals combined. The compromise position reached by the end of my tenure was that both Tana River and Lamu African District Councils employed baboon poisoners who were paid, at least partly, from controlled hunting area fees received from visiting sport hunters. In addition to the baboon poisoners, we had arranged for the Councils to pay farmers some compensation for damage inflicted by game. Lamu set aside one thousand shillings (£50) a year for this purpose and Tana River District one thousand five hundred (£75). Even taking the relative strength of the currency in those days, one can but marvel at how totally inadequate such compensation was. All it did was to establish our sympathy for farmers who lost their crops!

Preventing poaching was a routine Departmental responsibility, but with our commitment to game control work, it was not given the attention that it might have been. Having to spend our time chasing shamba raiders on the one hand and trying to catch people for hunting on the other was not without irony. Although the Department's anti-poaching units who operated independently of us Range Wardens may have arrested some poachers in Tana River District, I was only aware of 30 convictions for offences against the Game Ordinance between July 1960 and December 1963. When one appreciates that there were Boni and Sanye living in both districts and that their culture at the time was still based on hunting, it is clear that we only scratched the surface of our law enforcement responsibilities. Most of the convictions were for possessing arrow poison, though we also had half a dozen or so for unlawful possession of leopard skins – in the hands of Somalis.

As recounted by Dave McCabe in his anti-poaching chapter, Bill Woodley, Denis Kearney and he and their teams had combed the dry country between the Sabaki and Dakadima hill and collected a substantial amount of ivory[50]. It was part of Wasanye lore that there was always ivory to be taken out of these dry lands. I made two safaris into the hinterland of Tana River District in 1961 and 1962. On the first occasion I collected 568 kg (1,249 lbs) of ivory and on the second 900 kg (1,980 lbs). An overseas survey team cutting traces through this same dry bush handed in 115 kg (254 lbs). In the Galana Game Management Scheme between April 1960 and June 1963 the tusks of 233 elephants were picked up[51]. At the time we all thought that this ivory must, in some way, have come from animals that were wounded by, but escaped from poachers. In those days we really had no idea of how many elephants there were. Later, when aerial counting had come into its own, it was estimated that Kenya must have had between 150,000 and 200,000 elephants in the 1960s, of which a significant proportion were in Tana River and Lamu. With hindsight, the amount of ivory that could be gathered in the bush was as much the product of natural mortality and abundant elephants, as it was of any other reasons – among them poaching.

One way or another, ivory dominated game matters and in 1963 I calculated that the elephants we had shot on control had produced 1,955 kg (4,300 lbs) of ivory minimally worth £3,200 (maximally, it may have been worth £4,300). All of this, which exceeded what my game range cost Government, went into central funds with nothing returned to manage the resource that produced it.

Two factors distinguished my term as Game Warden Lamu from that of my predecessors. It spanned Kenya's last three pre-independence years and was thus an intensely political period. First, the emerging African politicians began featuring prominently in District life. Given the clash between the local people

---

[50] See p.116 for Dave McCabe's figures.

[51] I. Parker 1964. *The Galana Game Management Scheme*. Final Report

Waterbuck, of which seventy five were shot on control while I was at Lamu (photo Peter Davey).

and game, it was hardly surprising that these new local leaders took an interest in the matter and that this was heavily biased towards their constituents' interests and against the Game Department. Their interference did not make for peace!

Second, the Somali problem reared its head. On the threshold of independence, the Somalis wanted Britain to cede northeastern Kenya to Somalia. In 1963, the violence they promised if denied their request broke out. Among other consequences, this threw all Somalis in Government service, among them our Somali Game Scouts, under a cloud of suspicion. It also meant that all my outposts close to Somalia and vulnerable to attack, had to be closed and our men concentrated. Presaging events to come, it did not bode well.

* * * *

I left Lamu at the end of December 1963 and did not return to the coast as a Warden until 1967, when I did a four month stint as Game Warden Malindi followed by an eight month session at Kwale. By then, four years after independence, the Game Department was a very different organisation to that I had originally joined. It had become far more a conventional civil service Department and had developed a clerical section which, earlier, had been non-existent in the range stations. It was far bigger, with several ranks of Wardens in ranges where originally only one had been responsible for several districts.

Game control still figured as a prominent, probably the most prominent, feature of Game Wardening at the coast, though it was not quite such an aspect of our work in Kilifi and Kwale as it had been in Lamu and Tana River. In my year at the coast the Department shot forty nine elephants, eight buffalo, three hippo, two waterbuck, one lion and one bushbuck on control. At the time I did not appreciate that this was the twilight of the great game control era as, within the next decade, the elephant populations which had given rise to it, collapsed.

After Kwale I transferred inland and served out my remaining years at Isiolo. There our main preoccupation was anti-poaching against Somali shifta gangs. In the intervening years between 1963 and the 1970s, the troubles associated with Somalia's claims over northeastern Kenya had escalated into a guerrilla war, and then faded back into disorganised banditry, which continues until the present.

Stan Bleazard at Marsabit

CHAPTER 17: GAME WARDEN, MARSABIT

Stan Bleazard

There was always intense competition for Game Department and National Park vacancies and it took me five years to secure one. Academic qualifications were not demanded and there were no formal job specifications for Game and National Park Wardens. The qualities looked for were several: a keen interest in nature, a liking for wilderness and ability to live alone, initiative, a proven independence, and leadership abilities (usually manifest in military experience), were among them. Particularly important were honesty and strong character references from established Game Wardens, Honorary Game Wardens or from respected members of the Establishment.

My personal ambitions were realised in 1960, which for me, was a hallmark year. In February, Uganda's Attorney-General Dreschfield and Senior Park Warden Frank Poppleton interviewed me in London for the position of Warden in that country's National Parks system. Having travelled widely in Uganda, I knew the country well, and had made big game hunting safaris to Karamoja and to the Chambura fly area and two climbing expeditions in the Ruwenzori Mountains. For me it was certainly a plum opportunity. Only simultaneous news of a vacancy in the Kenya Game Department held me back and after a few days I withdrew my candidacy as a Uganda Park Warden, preferring another try for the Kenya position instead. In June I attended a successful interview before a Board of the Public Service Commission in Nairobi. Naturally when I received the news I was elated.

I approached the small Game Department offices next to the Coryndon Museum, on the hill overlooking the Nairobi River with a sense of joy. I was to meet Col Neil Sandeman the Acting Chief Game Warden, who would tell me where I was being posted and brief me on my work. As I climbed the stairs to the veranda of the old wood and iron building, my eye had been caught, as it would countless times in the years ahead, by a very fine buffalo head mounted on the wall outside. Through an open door I saw a man with a short cultivated moustache sitting behind a substantial office table. Forming a bower behind him stood a matched pair of enormous tusks. As I approached his doorway, he fixed me with a beady stare. One eye seemed slightly displaced and perhaps should have worn a monocle. I announced who I was and was surprised by his small stature when he rose to shake my hand, which he gripped firmly then sat down again rather awkwardly. Years later I learned he had suffered acutely from piles, which accounted for his sometimes-brusque demeanour.

With minimal pleasantry Neil had brought discussion quickly to the point. I was to take over Marsabit and Moyale Districts from Senior Game Warden George Adamson, who had previously run them with other Districts of the Northern Frontier Province from Isiolo. All matters concerned with the Wild

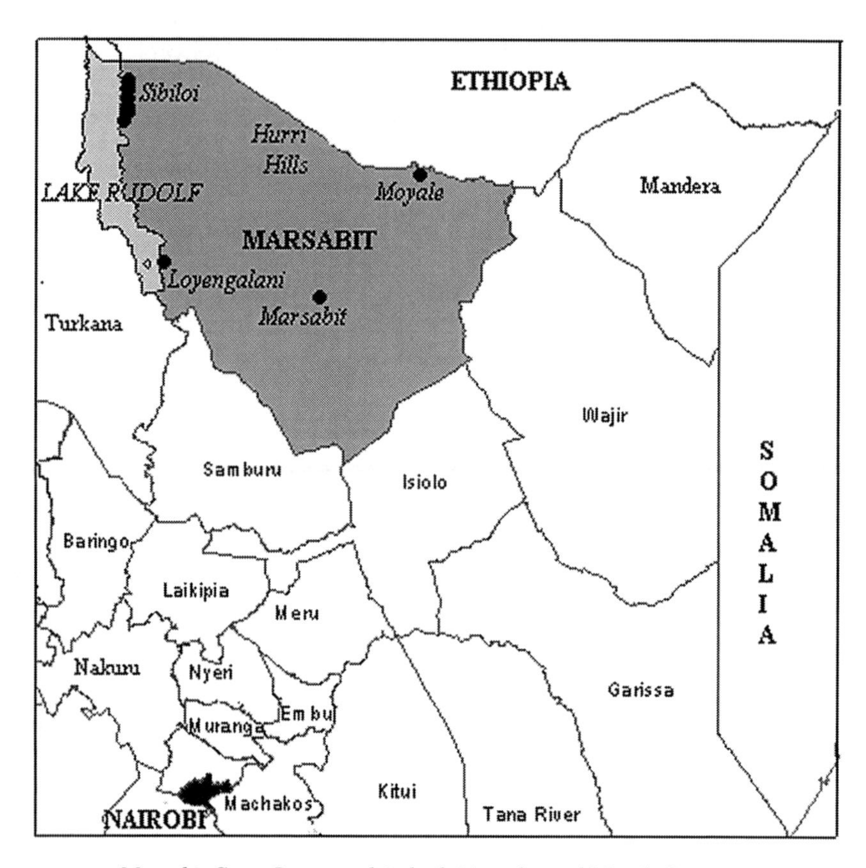

Marsabit Game Range took in both Marsabit and Moyale Districts.

Animals Protection Ordinance in the two Districts would be my responsibility. There was considerable poaching in both, particularly of giraffe, he emphasised, which would need my urgent attention. I was to establish a base at Marsabit and my duties in particular, would be to implement the recommendations of the 1956 Game Policy Committee with respect to the Marsabit National Reserve, and to pursue a course, which would lead to Marsabit Forest Reserve ultimately becoming a National Park[52]. I should also try to ensure that as much habitat as possible outside the forest be included in the eventual national park. I was also to examine the prospects for a National Park along the alluvial shore plains of Lake

[52] Editor's note: In this chapter of Bleazard's recollections, the point Jenkins makes of Ritchie's role in the genesis of national parks is remade. Most of Kenya's national parks and reserves were first suggested by wardens of the Game Department. Although it meant control of such sanctuaries passed to the 'opposition' National Parks, or to County Councils, these wardens clearly saw park status as the ultimate conservation goal.

Rudolf from Alia Bay northward. These proposals he assured me, would take much negotiation with local authorities. In Moyale District, I was to try and inhibit the trade in colobus monkey skins entering Kenya legally from Ethiopia, because sheer numbers indicated totally inadequate protection for these beautiful and inoffensive creatures across the border. Complaints about stock raiding lions had become too numerous and would need to be dealt with.

The Government, Neil informed me, had recently permitted licensed hunting in both districts, particularly for professional safaris, which had for many years previously been denied access to most of the NFD. In consultation with George Adamson, and as a priority, we must describe, map and set conditions for the areas where hunting could occur. He had handed me a sketch map as a guide, which I studied while he answered the telephone. While he was thus engaged I glanced around the room. By the entrance door, a glass fronted cabinet displayed memorabilia, which include amusing telegrams and miscellaneous notes. A one US dollar currency bill, doubtless the subject of some past bet or gesture, was pinned to the papers. Someone had vividly sketched a cartoon of an angry rhino chasing a party balloon. On separate walls hung two large very fine leopard skins, one melanistic. My eye caught a world record bushbuck head on a shield high on the far wall. There were two grand, well-upholstered leather couches, surely not meant for exhausted hunters reporting sanguine events, I mused.

The Colonel then made two surprising and for me disappointing pronouncements. Hitherto every Warden had used his own private vehicle for work and was entitled to claim a set mileage allowance from the Government for its use. I was to be the first Warden issued with a Government Land Rover, and he recommended I disposed of my own, a cherished diesel model. A similar situation arose over my prized Jeffery .450 No.2 double-barrelled rifle. He would not be able to supply me cartridges of this calibre as I had expected. Instead, I would be issued a .470 double for which there was ample ammunition. However, I left the office basically well pleased, but wondering how George Adamson, whom I had never met, would feel about my posting[53].

Interestingly, in 1927 my father Jim Bleazard aged just twenty had twice walked with baggage camels from Meru to Marsabit and back, While camped for six months on the mountain, he had met the Eastman Kodak Expedition of Martin and Osa Johnson and of course, Blayney Percival, the first Game Ranger, was with them. Jim had regaled me as a boy with stories of the place, so I was naturally delighted that Neil Sandeman had posted me there. A buffalo head

[53] Editor's note: At the time Stan Bleazard would not have been aware that the Adamsons' preoccupation with Elsa and her cubs had eclipsed George's effectiveness as a Game Warden and consequently his superiors wanted him to retire. George had spoken of doing so, but was taking his time about it as, being a Warden gave him many privileges that were useful where his lions were concerned. Stan's posting reduced his once huge range to a single district and was, *inter alia*, a gentle nudge to make up his mind.

The Warden's wooden bungalow had been condemned before his arrival (photo Stan Bleazard).

obtained at Marsabit by Jim adorns the Kenya Regiment Association premises near the Nairobi Club in Nairobi. In the course of the next several days, moving around the various agencies of Government arranging administrative details, I met Dave McCabe, Game Warden Simba, whom with his brothers, I had known since our youth. He had been in town to get the Government Chemist's analysis of poison on some arrows for evidence in a prosecution he was bringing against a poacher. I told him about my posting to Marsabit and enquired how I should handle any situation which might arise when I met George Adamson. The only thing I had to fear he had said was Joy, George's belligerent wife, whom I should avoid altogether if possible. George was apparently considering retirement, which event he said would be heartily welcomed by all at headquarters because of the havoc Joy invariably wrought when the Adamsons came to town. She so criticised all and sundry and expected all to do her bidding that the junior clerks referred to her as Mrs Game Warden.

I sold my .450 rifle for £100, the same as I paid for it in Uganda two years previously. Today it would be worth many times that sum. Having completed the transaction and drawn stores and equipment for my new station, I left on the 340-mile journey to Marsabit and the Northern Frontier Province.

After crossing the unpredictable Milgis luggah, Marsabit first appeared as a low range on the northern horizon. As I proceeded across the flat and often barren Kaisut desert, for many miles this range seemed hardly to grow. Eventually, however, it filled more and more of the horizon until the road started a gradual ascent. At one point the soil colour changed abruptly, from red earth and sandstone to grey with lava boulders. The density of vegetation increased markedly, particularly to the east of the road which obviously acted as a break to fires from the lowlands coming up the slopes. West of the road such fires had kept trees down and allowed an almost uninterrupted western view across pale parched grasslands to Mount Nyiro and Mount Kulal eighty miles away, both of which seemed to rise with us. In the evening, large flocks of guinea fowl fed along the roadside and an odd duiker ducked for cover as we approached. Finally the forest loomed, a remnant of centuries of attack by fire, it stood dark and aloof over Marsabit volcano's broad summit and so concentrated my gaze that I almost missed three bull elephants browsing at the road verge. They were all large-bodied beasts carrying good ivory. Suddenly the road formed an ox bow into the mountain where an old military concrete pillbox, a reminder of World War II, overlooked the deep Ulanula Well, whose permanent water has always provided for thirsty livestock in times of drought. Our way then swung easterly onto a fertile plateau skirting the forest. Shortly we came to a fork, one branch leading to a line of dukas, the other to the District Offices where I announced my arrival to Peter Browning, the Acting District Commissioner.

A tall, imposing man, Peter welcomed me with such exuberance that I was a trifle nonplussed. In due course I appreciated that in Marsabit's isolation, he craved the stimulation of an intellectual and had hoped I would be a kindred spirit. No doubt I disappointed him as I have never been overtly cerebral. Iain Ross, his District Officer, who I had met when he was a youth in Uganda, had taken me to my quarters and on the way we renewed acquaintance. My new home was a red roofed cottage with black plank walls, quaintly set at the forest edge, with the vestiges of a flower garden within which was a central rose bush. It was a two-room abode built by District Commissioner H. B. Sharpe in about 1928 and although it had been uninhabited for a long time, the place still smelt of smoke. The location looked ideal but inside there was disappointment, for I could see through the walls in several places where termites had done their worst. Closer examination revealed even more serious damage. Long ago, the building had been condemned and was scheduled for destruction. Yet, where others might complain, Game Wardens were not so fussy and easier to please. Now that I had arrived it was given a reprieve. There was ample space nearby to build staff quarters and an equipment store.

Not unhappily, I unloaded my limited possessions and set up camp within, to spend the first night of what I hoped would be many in Sharpe's cottage, and the most interesting time of my life.

* * * *

In the next few days I became acquainted with my surroundings. The Marsabit forest has a tree community similar to Nairobi City Park's and the Karura Forest's, with brown olives, *Crotons* and *Premna* common. Though not immediately obvious, big game was there in plenty and I was astonished one morning to see the snow peak of Mount Kenya, about one hundred and seventy miles south. I found Lake Paradise exactly as described by Osa Johnson forty years earlier, and surprisingly, even the foundations of the Johnsons' buildings were still evident. Small herds of greater kudu inhabited the drier western fringes of the forest, particularly the slopes of Marsabit's many small calderas.

The arrangement and demarcation of hunting blocks had taken longer than headquarters anticipated. I tried to get help from George Adamson, but each attempt to meet him failed. Finally I decided to camp in the vicinity of his house compound near Isiolo and wait, rather than search for him somewhere on the Kinna River where he was reportedly on safari. It was a pleasant spot. Before dawn each morning, melodious scrub robins began calling from within the *Euphorbia* hedge that surrounded the Adamsons' house. The first day was spent on administrative matters at Provincial headquarters in Isiolo. In the evening I tried out the Department's .470 Rigby double rifle, shooting at a target in the luggah near the house. The weapon handled and grouped well. Over the weekend I climbed and explored the nearby Karisia Hills, which held a healthy wildlife population. I came upon klipspringer on every suitable rock slope and there were frequent rhino kick sites. On the first day I saw a small herd of elephants in a valley known as the gap, and two solitary bulls feeding and moving in the same direction as the herd.

On the second day I was surprised to find the same number there. In the afternoon on the way downhill I disturbed an old buffalo. Rising from his siesta in deep shade he came out to confront me at about thirty paces, nose high into wind, which was coming from behind me. He was visibly annoyed and pawed the ground preparing to charge. I slid the safety catch of the double forward, raised the rifle to my shoulder and waited, confident I would survive his attack and that he would not. His hooves propelled clods to his rear and a cloud of red dust arose almost obscuring him. Suddenly he stopped, glared at me for a second, then turned tail. Halting after a few steps, he turned around to see if I followed. I held my position and he wheeled away and was gone.

The nights in camp were noisy. An impala ram grunted working hard to keep his harem in order, while zebra whinnied through the night. Scavenging hyaena wailed to each other as they sought some morsel. A leopard called majestically once from the hills and every night lions roared in the distance. I slept, as usual, with the tent flap open to let in cooling air and let me watch the brilliant star lit vault above from my pillow. About the third night, very late, I was pleased to hear vehicles arriving. Knowing my task would at last be completed in the morning, I turned over and dozed to the sound of gear and baggage being offloaded. The sound of activity ceased and I fell asleep. Next thing I knew was the smell of acrid hot breath in my face through the mosquito net. Dimly, I made out the shape of what I thought was a hyaena which began to rock the camp bed by pushing its forehead on the canvas underside. Unsure what was happening, I was momentarily paralysed with fear. Wishing to protect my precious rump I hastily reach for my .38 Special, which lay next to me in the broad pocket of the tent wall. Just as my hand closed on the revolver's handle, someone coughed in the darkness nearby.

"You got Elsa there Julian?" George Adamson called. Still frozen with fear I was unable to immediately respond.

Eventually I got out a frantic bellow "Yes, for Christ sake get her out of here." It mattered little who he thought I was.

Julian McKeand, an ex-fisheries officer, was now a Game Warden working under George 's direction, who, when I met him later, told me that he had had a similar experience, adding that Elsa was more inclined to shove any occupant off the bed and stretch herself out on it and in the process ruin any mosquito net, than to hurt its occupant. As George had a reputation for mischievous pranks, I will never know if the incident was intended or not. The following morning started out well enough. I joined George with Elsa for a pre-sunrise walk along the track that leads to the gap. The lioness knew the way well and often left us to investigate scents and opportunities out of sight, only to rejoin us almost unseen, at least by me. George was aware of her behaviour every minute, stopping occasionally to wait for signs of her when he was mentally out of touch. We had talked of many things as we proceeded. His knowledge of wildlife was, of course, profound and I could not help admiring this modest unassuming man. We came upon a freshly spread rhino midden beside the track which George examined briefly. The same spot had been used for as long as he could remember. In the distance, a giraffe watched us and the lioness, never browsing for as long as we were in sight. Just before reaching his house on our return George dropped a bombshell. He intended asking for a transfer to Marsabit.

Naturally I was stunned and unhappy with the news. After breakfast, in a somewhat strained atmosphere, we completed our business. It was before noon and I considered an immediate departure. George however invited me to lunch, which I initially declined with as much good grace as I could muster. In his unassuming way, and obviously trying to smooth my ruffled feathers, he made it plain how very disappointed Joy would be, inferring the wrath of God will fall on him if I did not accept. Not wishing to offend, I acquiesced but secretly dreaded meeting the dragon. I need not have worried. I met a healthy, vibrant woman who must have been a peach in her youth. I enjoyed an excellent curry lunch served on a central carousel, during which Joy dominated a conversation which ranged over every conceivable topic. Most of the time George remained silent, though his eyes twinkled throughout the meal. He was an excellent raconteur when she allowed him time.

Afterwards I was treated to a piano recital. As she played the keys she was visibly tense, sometimes angry, sometimes joyful. I did not recognise the piece and hid my ignorance. George came to my aid, murmuring Chopin when she was not looking. Joy suddenly broke off and stood, interlocking her fingers in a stretching exercise. Almost in tears, she lamented never having time to practise her music, then insisted on showing me some of her watercolours, mostly wild flowers, which of course were excellent and though I did not recognise many of them, I had praised the true colours and fine lines I saw. It was after three before I got away. Elsa was lying, paws up, under an acacia tree in the garden where she had been since mid morning.

* * * *

The five-hour journey back to Marsabit allowed plenty of time for reflection. The Adamsons were a highly intelligent and talented couple but with very different personalities. Joy had an endless capacity to create tension that George counter-balanced to some extent with one to create ease. The hospitality they gave me was in no way unusual though I felt sure some effort had been made at short notice to diminish my reaction to George's wish to take over Marsabit. I could not believe headquarters would transfer me elsewhere so soon to accommodate his wishes, but doubts lingered. By the time I reached the acacia woodlands of the meandering Merille valley where my father had camped thirty years earlier, I fretted that I might now never do the same. Determined to see as much of the range as possible in case I was transferred, I spent the following day completing descriptions of hunting block boundaries and posting them off to headquarters. Then I set out on a ten-day safari to the Merille valley and the foothills of the Mathews and Ndoto ranges, Ol Doinyo Mara and Mount Kulal.

The lowlands through which I had travelled were gripped by intense drought. Yet towering above them, the lonely, lofty NFD mountain peaks imparted a surreal sense of stubbornness and permanence: that they would remain and overcome whatever transpired. It was reflected in the bull elephants, rhino, giraffe and oryx that dwell in their shadows, surviving on what little sustenance there was on the desolate hot plains, and clinging to shrinking water holes until completely dry before being forced to higher elevations. No sooner had I completed this first trip, than I set off on another longer safari across the Chalbi Desert to Alia bay and Lake Rudolf, then north to Ileret.

Recent rain had turned the Tula Bor plain a shade of green that gladdened any wildlife enthusiast's eye. There were some three thousand topi, together with hundreds of both Burchell's and Grevy's zebras, oryx, Grant's gazelle and giraffe. Lesser kudu and gerenuk were common in the bush fringes. Lion, leopard and cheetah were present, and of course hordes of hippo and croc in the lake. In the morning and evening, a pair of northern ground hornbills strode across the plain. I watched a carmine bee-eater try to hitch a ride on one and failing, trying to settle instead on a Heuglin's bustard. Failing again, it clung to the neck of a gazelle that tolerated the passenger only briefly.

Topi were present in their thousands along Lake Rudolf's north-eastern shore. (photo Peter Davey)

Travelling on to Saberei, I saw numerous tall dust devils across the border in Ethiopia. Rising from a dry lakebed, they seemed stationary and gave a pinkish tinge to the cloud base. In the distance I saw the last vestige of water that was Lake Stefanie[54]. On the Dukana plains I was surprised to spot a herd of over

[54] Since Stan's visit the lake has both increased and decreased more than once. Ed

eighty Grevy's zebra in the dry Bulal watercourse. Almost home at Gof Redo I met a herd of greater kudu and a pair of Heuglin's bustard. Working seven days a week I visited many places in my range, including some in Moyale District where, as predicted, lions were a nuisance.

At one I tethered a live goat as bait, and a pride of seven lion arrived just after dark. The bait was quickly attacked and they commenced quarrelling. By spotlight I shot a scrawny old lioness, which briefly scattered the pride. After a short pause they soon returned, undaunted. To my disgust two lions started to feed on the dead lioness, so I shot one of them too. It scarcely moved, so I shot its companion as well. District Commissioner Clive Smith and the locals were happy, but such slaughter nauseated me.

Back at Marsabit my men had to live continuously under canvas unless I arranged quarters for them. I also needed a store so I turned my hand to building. Cedar poles for construction had to be fetched from Mount Kulal so I had planned my next safari there. On the point of departure, Ian Grimwood the new Chief Game Warden announced by telegram that he intended visiting me, so I delayed leaving. Major Grimwood arrived late in the afternoon and insisted on setting up his own camp away from the township. He invited me there for a sundowner during which we discussed matters, particularly progress in resolving boundaries of the Marsabit National Park. This was my first acquaintance of him and I was favourably impressed. He provided generous tots of Scotch and we talked late into the night. I was delighted to learn that George had decided to retire, which settled my tenure at Marsabit. In the morning we met with DC Peter Browning to discuss proposed National Parks at Marsabit and Lake Rudolf. He was supportive, promising to write to the Provincial Commissioner.

Over the next four years I completed a store and staff housing, repaired Sharpe's old house so that it was at least weatherproof, established five outposts with two huts each and physically demarcated the proposed Marsabit National Park boundary with a firebreak. I made at least one foot safari of about ten days every year, using camels to carry water and gear. This allowed me to enter areas impossible to reach by vehicle. By visiting far-flung manyattas, I believe our presence helped prevent poaching. I learned about and saw important natural waterholes. Of more importance, I developed a feel for the land and its fauna. On patrol it was rare not to see or hear a leopard every day, also caracal. Rhino too were common in many places. I recognised a kind of local symbiosis between nomads and the elephants who had used these ranges for centuries. This was reflected in place names for hill features and waterholes. Arba Jahan (Oromo for five elephants) and Mata Arba (Oromo for ear of elephant) are two prominent features seventy-five miles East of Marsabit that formed the boundary with Wajir district. Overall I tried to spend most of my time in the field and as little as possible dealing with the bureaucracy.

Responding to urgent appeals from the DC Moyale to deal with two man-eating lions, I left Marsabit 10th December 1961 in deteriorating weather for a safari memorable not least for discomfort. Within twenty miles I caught up with my lorry that had started some hours before me. It was bogged in unstable ground but the Land Rover eventually dragged it clear and we continued, making slow progress in wet conditions. Crossing the Dida Galgalu we were caught well and truly by thunderstorms of immense proportions. Late in the afternoon, when attempting yet another rescue of the lorry submerged to its radiator, I miscalculated approaching rain and delayed putting up canvas. Too late I gave instructions to make camp. First one tent then another was blown away and finally my own flew away, like a magic carpet, over the horizon as a violent downpour started and continued into the night. I tried to sleep in the back of a Land Rover that was too short. It was also held fast in the mire and leaning badly. I remembered Reggie Destro's trite aphorism that any bloody fool can be uncomfortable on safari. We progressed about half a mile on each of the next four days and after running repairs to a number of mechanical problems, the weather allowed us to reach Moyale finally on the 16th.

We proceeded to Funanyata, the area of the reported man-eater, where we learned that a young man had indeed been killed, though not eaten. That morning another youth had been mauled defending his cattle and taken to Moyale. While making camp an old man arrived with news that the offending lion had been seen and a hunting party was already on the way to deal with it. Not really convinced that anything positive would ensue, I took him in the Land Rover to a manyatta a few miles away, where we collected another man to guide us further. Another mile or so on we met the hunting party spread in a wide circle, within which they assured me the lion was hiding. It was open ground with scattered low bush only inches high and I had doubts. Scanning the area I saw nothing, even with binoculars. I drove forward a few yards and made another survey; still nothing and I was even more sceptical. Then I saw him crouching low and glaring at me about thirty yards away. Perhaps recognising its perilous situation, the lion growled menacingly. I had neglected to assemble my .470, which lay behind the seats in its case, so without more ado I used my No 4 .303 service rifle and shot him through an eye. It was an old lion with a deep spear wound to the gut, which probably accounted for it being caught in the open.

Next day we moved camp to Kubi Tari where more lion trouble had been reported. After some days patrolling and making enquiries, we learned that a man had been injured weeks previously while interfering with a lion that had been feeding on an oryx. I felt that was insufficient reason to shoot another lion, and with the weather holding, I dispatched the lorry back to Marsabit on Saturday 23rd December. With two Scouts, I investigated Chera flood plain. There was no grazing and the place was devoid of game and livestock. Demo Dera, a distinct landmark looked tantalisingly close. Checking our map I estimated it was only twelve miles away. A well-known waterhole lay beyond and I decide to take a look. Leaving the Land Rover mid morning, we crossed a zone of serrated alluvium where there were numerous ponds, all drying out in the fine weather.

Beyond the alluvium we came upon a series of difficult lava ridges that I had not anticipated and which we crossed in searing heat, reaching the top of Demo Dika, a smaller hill, in the early afternoon. It was hardly any cooler and the waterhole was not yet visible. However, we pressed on and crossing a saddle saw a fine greater kudu bull. Klipspringer whistled at us during the final ascent of Demo Dera, which we completed by 4 p.m. From the summit we could see the large waterhole of which I had heard. It was made by the hill on which we were forming a natural barrage across a drainage line. At the water were some cattle whose herder was singing, unaware of our presence. Marsabit was clearly visible on the horizon southwest and I scanned the surrounding country briefly before commencing our return. Total darkness caught us between lava ridges in thorn bush through which it was difficult to pick our way, so we halted and waited an hour for the moon to rise. It was still stiflingly hot while we rested.

When we resumed, my lead Scout guided us unerringly over the ridges, but it was difficult going in the lava and we stumbled frequently. With no breath of wind, each piece of tuff dislodged sounded unusually loud as it tumbled down the scree below. About midnight we descended onto the plain where it was cooler, the going easier, but the night still silent. Very soon our footsteps were in water and no matter in which direction we turned, we could see the moon's reflection. Evidently very distant rain of which we were unaware and which may have even fallen days earlier had arrived and flooded the plain in our absence. We pressed on into water waist deep, rifles over heads. Each of us taking duckings as we stumbled into submerged holes. With the changed landscape I was doubtful of ever finding our vehicle. Eventually the water became shallower and with uncanny ability the Scout took us directly to where the vehicle, first recognisable from the outline of the Land Rover's canvas hoops, still stood on dry ground. It was three a.m. and we lay down exhausted and slept on the hard earth. After an hour I awakened in panic thinking more water might soon arrive. My companions were snoring but I roused them, figuring this was no place to spend Christmas.

* * * *

While I wanted to be on safari in the field, much time was spent either on prosecutions or on negotiation for the two parks. When the Royal National Parks of Kenya were officially formed after the Second World War, it had been their ambition to locate their major national park in northern Kenya, taking in most of what in 1900 had been the Northern Game Reserve, including the Mathews and the Ndoto Range. In 1933, Archie Ritchie had pressed this case strongly

Ahmed, small in body but great in tusk was a special ward on Marsabit Mountain (photo Stan Bleazard).

to the Kenya Land Commission[55]. However, the Administration had blocked the proposal arguing (correctly) that the area's residents could not be dispossessed of their lands, and the National Parks had to content themselves with Tsavo instead. Nevertheless hopes of having northern national parks never died and the creation of the Marsabit National Reserve in which the fauna was under the Parks' jurisdiction served as a gesture of sorts. When the Marsabit National Reserve was eventually conceded to be a pipe dream and de-gazetted, and when the

[55] The Kenya Land Commission Report 1933 *ibid.*

creation of Marsabit National Park was mooted, two park rangers stayed on in Marsabit and regularly patrolled the proposed Park to maintain a presence. Billy Woodley, Warden of the Mount Kenya and Aberdare Mountain Parks, visited Marsabit about three times a year as part of this policy. Yet it fell to my lot as a Game Department official to put in the groundwork for what became Marsabit and Sibiloi (on the shores of Lake Rudolf) National Parks.

Everyone was supportive of the proposals to make Marsabit Mountain and the Lake Rudolf northeast shore national parks. All except Mervyn Cowie, that is, who although in favour said he could not possibly take on more parks without a corresponding increase in his budget from Government. Cowie was, of course, playing politics: the greater the body of support for the new parks, the greater the pressure on Government to fund them and the more demanding he could be. Yet not all of us understood his tactics. Ian Grimwood tried to persuade him that he would have a better lever to gain more funds by taking Marsabit and Sibiloi on the lakeshore as parks, as they would cost him nothing to run because they could continue to be managed on a daily basis by the Game Department.

We could only get into many parts of Marsabit and Moyale by walking and using camels (photo Grete Davey).

In July 1965 I accompanied the Board of National Park Trustees led by Chairman Dr Hyder on an air safari to Ileret and Marsabit to inspect the ground. It seemed at last that the proposals were close to fruition. But new opposition arose. Logie, Kenya's Conservator of Forests, objected to losing Marsabit Forest Reserve. In October and November 1966 I attended two further meetings about the proposed parks in the Ministry of Tourism & Wildlife. I suspected the official intention was to await Logie's imminent retirement, before proclaiming both as national parks, which is what eventually happened.

Many interesting people came to visit, including the Governor Sir Patrick Rennison, Wilfred Thesiger, Bill Holden, Charles Lindberg, Stuart Keith of New York Natural History Museum, Ionides with Billy Woodley, Reggie Destro, Dr Doug Clarke of Ontario, Syd Downey, Japan Consul Tom Hayashi, Malin and Connie Sorsbie, Edmund Blanche with John Dugmore and of course Col Mervyn Cowie, Director of the (then) Royal National Parks of Kenya.

My base on Marsabit's forested mountain, situated amidst extensive arid wastes, was always a gem to return to after dusty safaris to Lake Rudolf, El Yibo, Ngoronit, Serolevi, Korondil, Ajiftu, El Kejata, Laradabach and Arabel, the Hurri Hills – all poetically named. My range was as wild as any part of Africa and I loved every minute I was in it. All these magic places had their special interest and their big game, supplemented each year by huge numbers of Palaearctic avian migrants. After brief rains the desert bloomed with millions of wild flowers, which turned the landscape into a magnificent kaleidoscope of colour. Roads being limited I hired camels and travelled the way my father did. In some years up to a hundred lives were lost in tribal skirmishes, mostly from Ethiopian incursions. In other years diseases such as rinderpest, anthrax, measles and brucellosis were common.

On Wednesday 7th February, 1962, I made camp near Harar Bamba waterhole to deal with a stock raiding lion. Gurar Police Post was about fifteen miles away, above the escarpment near the international boundary with Ethiopia. No lions had visited the waterhole overnight, so we set off on foot to visit Chufa pan where elephants had been, then to Karadusi pan where a lioness had drunk. We followed her spoor for a couple of miles until obliterated by cattle tracks. We then visited a number of manyattas for information and to spread the word that we were in residence searching for the lion that was causing trouble. Next day we visited Chalalaka and Ajoli pans, and other nearby manyattas. Returning late afternoon a little weary from the day's patrol, I sat down to relax in my camp chair and noticed we had a stranger squatting in camp.

The man had risen, come towards me, and greeted me before holding a stick with a folded paper clamped in the split end. I hesitated a moment, savouring the tradition of a bygone age and until he flicked the stick in a gesture of insistence. As soon as I withdrew the paper he squatted in front of me, to await my reply. It was a standard Kenya Police radio message form which read: "Your attendance required for legal conference Nairobi seventeenth February Game." The message was plain enough though I could not for the life of me think why I should be needed at a legal conference. I noted the matter in my diary, then signed the paper and folded it up. The man stood and held out his stick for me to replace the paper. As soon as I had done so he saluted and set off for Gurar[56] from whence he had come. It was a vignette out of a past age and typified an NFD ambience of not being in the twentieth century.

During my four years at Marsabit, I was always aware how privileged I was to be doing something worthwhile and that, with the political tides then running, would soon be no longer possible for the likes of me. I wanted to conserve as much wildlife as possible, hoping that following generations of indigenous people would find the same value in it that I did. I cherished my acquaintance and amity with northern Kenya's tough nomadic people. I relished having gone to places seen by less than a handful of my race and even though I visited them a dozen times, they never lost their appeal. Almost every white, colonial, civil servant who served in Kenya's great NFD, was caught by its sublime aura.

[56] Editor's note: This may be the last recorded instance of an official message delivery by cleft stick.

CHAPTER 18: BLOODY JOURNALIST

Stan Bleazard

From time to time most Game Wardens had to entertain the likes of Governors and VIPs. We often had unwanted official or semi-official guests thrust upon us, and were treated as sort of 'unofficially official' tour guides and professional hunters. With Marsabit being so remote I managed to escape the attentions of all but the most genuine visitors. Yet one cannot win all the time and I did have one gentleman foisted on me who broke my run of luck. His reason for visiting northern Kenya, I seem to recall, was as a representative the Fauna Preservation Society. Like much else he said, this subsequently turned out untrue.

But to return to the beginning: it all started at the behest of Ian Grimwood. Would I hire ten baggage camels and a leader for someone to make a safari from Laisamis to Loyengalani on Lake Rudolf. Later, it was suggested I meet this person and escort him along the lakeshore from Loyengalani to Alia Bay, then back to North Horr. The arrangement had little appeal, except that I tried each year to make at least one camel safari to remote areas. I had not previously covered this relatively easy route and company might make it more interesting.

The 'Major' (Rodney Elliott) introduced me to John Hillaby on Wednesday 5th December 1962, the man with blond hair and a beard who I was 'booked' to accompany along the lake to Alia Bay. He expected everything to be laid on for him and I was there to do his bidding. Next, he quibbled at the small per diem Government charges of sh3.00 for the leader and sh1/50 per camel that I asked him to pay. When I made it clear, no money no camels, Hillaby produced the cash immediately. It put a focus on his character. Given my first impressions I would have been happy to opt out of all arrangements at this early stage.

Having arranged the camels and their handlers, Hillaby's safari started in Elliott's Maralal District. I was not due to join it until he later entered my Marsabit range. Late in the afternoon 1st January 1963 I set off from Marsabit, having sent my lorry ahead to North Horr with men and rations. Passage across the Chalbi desert proved hard going and the clutch on the Land Rover began to slip. It was after nine when I arrived. After flushing out the clutch housing next morning to no avail, I decided to leave the Land Rover at the Police Post and proceed to Loyengalani in the lorry. There was no sign of Hillaby when I arrived and I had to wait some time for Guy Poole the manager of the 'Oasis Lodge' to appear. He told me he had unfortunately fallen out with Hillaby who had moved camp to Balo Laga.

At Balo Laga I met Hillaby shirtless and black-eyed, his pale face and body showing bruises, indicating that he had indeed had quite a 'falling out'. The real reasons for the contretemps only emerged when Hillaby told it to a friend, who recounted it to me years later. In the privacy of his diary, Hillaby had referred

A view of Lake Rudolf and the lake shore from Porr Hill, past which we walked with Hillaby (photo Peter Davey).

to Guy Poole's wife as "a fat old whore". When he had been away from the Lodge, this worthy lady had been in to tidy and clean Hillaby's room and, coming across the diary had read it. Finding the reference to herself, she had taken the diary to her husband in a state of great excitement. He was so enraged that when Hillaby reappeared, and without so much as a word, Guy smote him in the eye and followed it with a most thorough battering – the evidence of which I could now see. Yet that was not all the Pooles intended:, they were going to sue Hillaby for defamation and many other things besides. The diary was their evidence and Hillaby had had to depart leaving it in their possession.

At the time I did not know the detail. All that Hillaby told me was that, while acknowledging that he had insulted Poole, he implored me to return with him to the 'Oasis' to recover his diary. I did not see it as any business of mine to do so and when I told him we should continue without it, he was absurdly threatening.

I stopped unloading the lorry while I made some tea and considered the situation. During the stand off, a boomslang had somehow got inside a Scout's haversack lying on the ground without anyone seeing it do so. It naturally caused a lively diversion when discovered. Using a fishing rod and line with a noose technique shown to me by Ionides, I caught the snake and released it at a safe distance. After a couple of hours Hillaby approached me more humbly and again implored me to try to retrieve his dairy. He now told me that part of his work was as a Fleet Street journalist (so much for representing the FPS) and, appreciating the importance of his diary to him, I agreed to see Poole alone.

Grevy's zebra, a common animal at Alia Bay when I walked with Hillaby (photo Peter Davey).

When I met Guy Poole about sundown, he was in no mood to negotiate, saying only that the diary was already in the hands of his lawyer in Nairobi and that he intended to sue Hillaby for assault. I returned to Hillaby without his diary.

We set off next morning, Hillaby with straw hat, shirt, khaki shorts and canvas shoes for an easy ten-mile walk along the beach to a camp below Porr. My men and I moved in full patrol gear prepared for any eventuality. This was, after all, a volatile area and the relatively frequent forays by marauders from Ethiopia were the reason why Government felt Hillaby needed an escort. That first day was without incident. When we went on, starting before it was fully light next morning, I noticed with some amusement that Hillaby travelled with shirt but no trousers or underpants and this was to be his mode of dress from then on. How he chose to dress was of course entirely his affair, and because he insisted on walking far ahead of the slow camels, he was sometimes out of our sight in any case. Yet, choosing to be clad on top but naked below was so eccentric that I could not help but ask why. This brought a rude response and thereafter my companion's attitude was distinctly offensive. I wondered what would happen if we met a Gelubba raiding party (they took male genitalia as trophies) and I wished a camel fly would bite him where it would hurt most.

Passage for camels was not possible along the shore at the foothills of the dark Longondoti Range (long and dirty George Adamson called them). We had to head back the way we had come and find a way inland and round the East side of the range. On this route we met plenty of game, including giraffe, oryx, topi, grant, both kinds of zebra and signs of rhino. It was here Hillaby could have met his Waterloo, for he stumbled alone and completely unarmed onto a sleeping lion. He was lucky and I saw him streaking up the side of a barren hill minus hat, while the lion made off at a canter in the opposite direction (no doubt appalled by what it had seen). Thereafter he wore trousers, but never mentioned the encounter. We reached Alia Bay on 13th and North Horr four days later. From there Hillaby continued his safari southwards alone, along the east side of Mount Kulal to points beyond in Rodney Elliott's range.

In mid February I received a letter from the Major who queried if Hillaby owed any money for camel hire. He had met Hillaby again who told him he had purchased the camels and therefore owed nothing. I replied immediately giving the facts. The Major was not about to let this slippery customer get by without paying[57]. Later in the month, when he reached Wamba where we had first met, Hillaby wrote me a letter, including an open cheque. "The sum should include," he wrote, "an extra ten bob (for you)."

This insulting tip rubbed salt into an already open wound! Later I learned that Government had subsidized his trip to write a book publicising northern Kenya. It appeared as *Journey to the Jade Sea*[58] which, I am told, sold rather well.

---

[57] In contrast to Stan Bleazard's view of Hillaby, Rodney Elliott said that he found him a decent enough fellow who later returned Rodney's hospitality in his London club.

[58] Hillaby J. 1963. *Journey to the Jade Sea*. Library of Congress card 65-11478. Simon & Schuster. New York.

CHAPTER 19: THE GALANA GAME MANAGEMENT SCHEME

Ian Parker

The Galana Game Management Scheme was spawned by the 1956/1957 anti-poaching campaign. Woodley then Sheldrick both experienced a strong ambivalence about arresting the Wata and locking them up for doing no more than pursuing their traditions. If anyone had rights to hunt, surely it was these natives? Though they had successfully stopped poaching in Tsavo East, law enforcement along the lines taken to achieve this was not a long-term solution.

Noel Simon catalysed their thoughts with information on how the native peoples of Canada were allowed to hunt traditionally. He argued that there was no reason why similar provisions should not work for the Wata. As Simon, Sheldrick and Woodley mulled over such thoughts in mid-1957, I became Game Warden Kilifi. As most of the Wata lived in Kilifi District, I became involved in their fortunes as I, too, did not think throwing them in jail was a reasonable solution to their 'poaching'. The upshot was that I joined in proposing the Wata be allowed to hunt some elephants lawfully. Little did we know that a remarkably similar proposal had been made about 1925 by the then District Commissioner, Kwale, a Mr Sharpe[59], or that it had been thrown out by the Game Department.

Noel Simon summed our thinking in a seminal paper that he submitted to Kenya's Game Policy Committee[60]. Sheldrick's addendum to this paper warned:-

> *"There is no doubt that if the Waliangulu were to think that this scheme was for the benefit of Europeans or other tribesmen it would fail ...."*

As Willie Hale, the Chief Game Warden, was a member of the Game Policy Committee, the paper came to his immediate attention and, initially, he thought it a good idea. So much so that he committed me to make a feasibility study of the proposal, while Roger Hurt stood in for me as Game Warden Kilifi. In October 1957 and with Bill Woodley as guide, I toured all the main Wata settlements to learn something about them.

Before my findings were submitted to him in January 1958, Willie Hale had already reversed his earlier support for the concept:–

---

[59] Kelly, Nora. 1978. *op. cit.*

[60] Noel Simon. 1st August 1957. *Future Conservation Trends.* A paper submitted to the Kenya Government Game Policy Committee.

"Frankly, I do not think this scheme will work. I consider that the correct solution is to attempt to convert the Waliangulu to Agriculture and get them to settle in places such as Hola." [61]

Copies of my report were distributed to the DCs in Kilifi, Kwale, Taita and Tana River as well as to the Provincial Commissioner in Mombasa. Having completed my mission, Willie H. ordered me to resume duties as Game Warden Kilifi and Roger Hurt went back to Lamu. Where the Chief Game Warden was concerned, the idea had been examined, found wanting and rejected. That, in his opinion, should have been the end of the matter. He had failed to take Simon's or Sheldrick's reactions into account and they went to work behind the scenes to reverse Willie's rejection. Even worse, he had been unaware of the Administration's wholehearted support for the proposal.

These omissions were brought to his attention down several channels. The Ministry of African Affairs insisted that the proposal be tried. Later, under Simon's prompting, the ecologist Frank Fraser-Darling drafted the following resolution that was passed at the IUCN's 10th Assembly held in Athens:–

"This Assembly of the IUCN notes with approval the pilot Game Management Scheme being planned for the Waliangulu tribe in Kenya, whereby the economic welfare and cultural patterns of the tribe will be sustained, and records its full support of this attempt to show that protein production is possible by game management from areas of low or non-existent agricultural value. The scheme provides an opportunity of obtaining valuable scientific and sociological data from this form of land use."

The Nuffield Foundation offered £10,000 to get the Scheme started. To cut a long tale short, the Game Department was told to implement what, at the time, was called the Waliangulu Scheme, while Sheldrick and Parker were appointed members of a small committee chaired by the DC Kilifi to start things moving. Such was Government interest in the concept that Sir Evelyn Baring, the Governor, took the time to attend one of our meetings in Malindi. As the architect of the previous anti-poaching campaign, he was also aware that mere law enforcement would not stop illicit hunting.

Against such robust and wide support, Game Department opposition was ineffective. The Ministry of Forest Development, Game & Fisheries took the Department's position initially, but with the Governor and African Affairs supporting the concept, it quickly caved in. The East African Professional Hunters' Association under John Lawrence's chairmanship objected to the idea.

---

[61] Letter GA 3/5/6/38 of the 30th October 1957. Chief Game Warden to Game Warden Kilifi.

However, the vehemence of its opinion was not so much apparent on paper, as in the colourful invective John used in the New Stanley Hotel's Long Bar.

The Scheme had become something of a personal cause with me and, to put it mildly, this did not make me popular at headquarters. Willie Hale retiring in the midst of it all did not help matters. In a nutshell, a highly irregular situation had developed in which the Department's youngest Warden was negotiating with other Ministries and the Governor himself over both his Departmental and Ministerial Heads. The anomaly was appreciated with some amusement in the higher echelons of Government. Once the Scheme was irrevocably a *fait accompli*, my unusual position was ended by a courteous and much appreciated personal letter from our Permanent Secretary John Webster in which he informed me of Government's approval and ended with the words: -

> *"I would like to congratulate you on all that you have done in the preparation of this project, and to wish you the best of luck in carrying it out."* [62]

Neil Sandeman was the Acting Chief Game Warden and took a different attitude, maintaining that I had been intolerably insubordinate. Organising the 'opposition' was, in his eyes, unacceptable and he never forgave me. While there was some ground for Neil's case, it was overstated and he grossly under-estimated the behind-the-scenes influence of Sheldrick, the more open championing of Noel Simon and the Administration's demand that the project go ahead. Neil (and some other colleagues) failed to understand that, at a very fundamental level, support for the scheme reflected a general belief that the Game Department's policies towards Africans had been wrong.

This was realised by some prominent Wardens like Lyn Temple-Boreham and Rodney Elliott who, as already been mentioned, turned blind eyes to poaching for meat. It is no coincidence that in the same period as the Waliangulu scheme was attracting limelight, the Department divided Kenya into over eighty controlled hunting areas from which fees would derive and be channelled into African District Councils. Rodney Elliott in Maralal was pushing for landowners to have quotas of animals that they could cull and whose trophies they could sell. The first locally managed game sanctuary - the Meru County Council Game Reserve (which was subsequently to become a National Park) – came into being through the initiative of Larry Wateridge in the Veterinary Department's Tsetse Section. That people in game areas had to benefit from wildlife was penetrating the Game Department skull, but pressure for change was all from its grass roots. Conversely, its leadership was outstanding for conservatism. This did change later under Ian Grimwood and even more under DB.

---

[67] John Webster letter to Ian Parker 22/4/1/8 of 29th April 1959 copied to the Ag. Chief Game Warden.

* * * *

The foregoing is a thumbnail outline of the Game Management Scheme's genesis. Yet between producing the initial plan in 1958 and implementing the scheme on the ground in April 1960, changes occurred in the planning. At the time, I was hardly aware of them. If I had been, I greatly under-estimated their significance. The original proposal envisaged the Wata continuing to live more or less as they did traditionally and, within set quotas, hunting as and when they wanted, albeit with rifles and not bows and poisoned arrows. The two government officials responsible for the scheme's development were to have had supervisory roles; primarily ensuring that the Wata did not over-shoot allotted quotas and helping dispose of produce such as ivory for the best possible prices. It was a simple plan that would interfere little with the way the people lived.

When the scheme started, however, the freedom we all sensed so important to the Wata was grossly curtailed. They would be scheme employees. All the shooting would be supervised and timed by the two white officers running the scheme. Elephant meat would be dried and sold, rather than consumed locally (because the locals did not have the money to buy it). In essence the two officers would act as managers treating the 3,000 square mile area as a great ranch with the Wata as their employees. It was radically different from what was originally proposed and much more complicated. Sheldrick had warned in 1957 that if the Wata did not think the programme was for them it would not work. Like the rest of us he, too, seemed to forget this premise.

Even now in hindsight and with access to the various relevant documents from those distant times, I am not sure how or why our original plan became so subverted. Government was against the Wata having general access to rifles: they had to be under the supervisory officers' control. We had to teach them how to use firearms. The IUCN resolution that supported implementing the scheme illustrated, if not an actual change in thinking, then a shift of bias in its reference to protein production and game management as an alternative to conventional agriculture and ranching. The germ of Simon and Sheldrick's original proposal was wholly social – let the natives hunt. Relating land productivity to conservation was a new line that became fashionable over the next two decades. We were swept along with the need to show production and profitability and healthy balance sheets, which complicated the project. If I was aware of how my own outlook had changed, it was at best subliminal and I accepted it on the premise that once running we would be able to straighten things out.

I cannot recall when the name Waliangulu Scheme was dropped in favour of Galana River Game Management Scheme, but I do remember that it was my decision to drop River from the title on finding that Galana means just that in Oromo. Newly married to Christine Mowat, we arrived to set up the Galana Scheme in April 1960. The track MacArthur cut in the 1930s along the north bank of the Sabaki from Baricho to Kitui, and a trail from Lali Hills to Dakadima made by Blixen just prior to the Second World War, were the only 'roads' in the 3,000 square mile wilderness. Peter Jenkins showed us where the Tsavo East boundary lay and helped us find a house site above the highest known flood levels. In the first five days camped on the Sabaki's north bank we were stung four times by scorpions. Yet, after this painful initiation, the next four years were perhaps the most enjoyable of our lives.

There were dramatic moments. With a six week-old baby the 1961 floods swept our house away and we were stranded in tents for the next three months. We had to be self-sufficient. We eventually broke out to the north-west by driving through Tsavo East north of the Sabaki, via Ithumba, Kitui and Thika. Those '61 floods were a land-mark event in East African ecology, whose effects have yet to be properly quantified. Among the numerous riddles they produced were patches of sorghum across the landscape between the Sabaki and Tiva rivers. The seed could not have been carried by water, because water did not flow widely across the land. It is too heavy to have been blown in by the wind, and must have been lying dormant in the soil since a wetter era centuries ago.

Tony Seth-Smith. Inset, his uncle Martin who was a Game Warden in 1913. The Seth-Smith family was the only one that had two generations in the colonial Game Department.

For much of our time on Galana, Tony Seth-Smith and his first wife Renny, were our companions. Our nearest town was Voi. The Sheldricks acted as a most welcome base and we were included on the Tsavo East radio network under the call sign 'George Monkey' assigned us by the irrepressible Denis Kearney. Every morning at 0700 hrs we were in daily radio contact with the outside world.

The financial foundation of the scheme was an annual quota of two hundred elephants. These would be shot, their flesh dried and sold and their ivory sent to the Ivory Room in Mombasa. The Scheme ivory was sold separately from all other lots and the revenue received was returned to the scheme as a grant from the Treasury. We also sold elephant ear and belly skins for leather: in the wisdom prevailing, later proved wrong, that rest of the hide was too thick to use.

Although subsequent research was to show that between five and ten thousand elephants lived on Galana, we never secured our annual quota of two hundred elephants. We had grossly under-estimated the difficulty of taking elephants to a predetermined schedule in the thick *Commiphora* woodland that characterised the area. With visibility averaging fewer than fifty paces, there was no option but

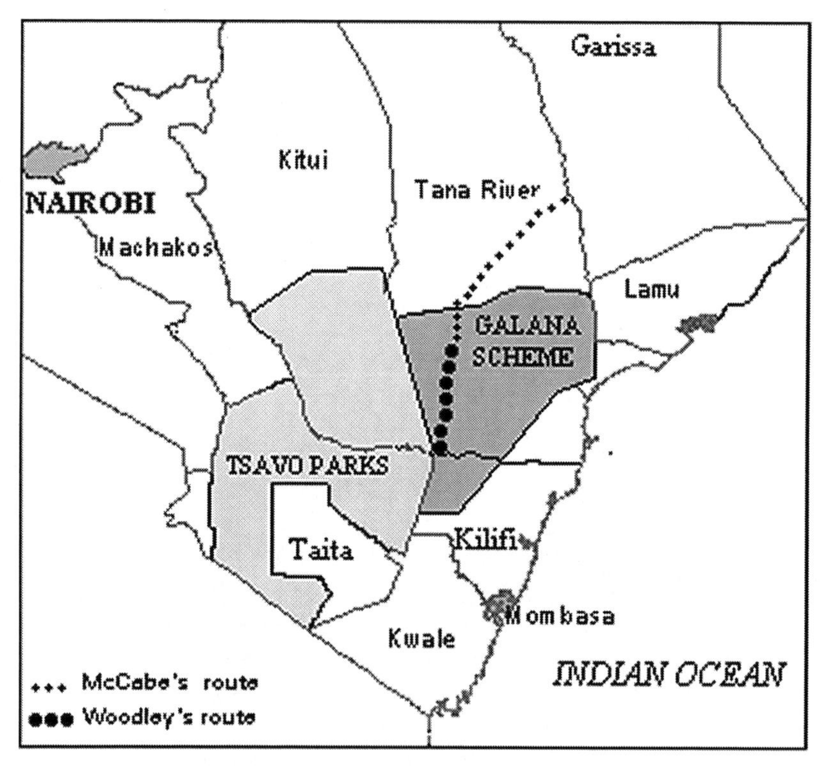

The Galana Scheme area & the Tsavo National Parks. Also shewn are the routes taken by by McCabe & Woodley on their September1957 ivory collecting safari (see p.113).

to follow tracks. However, when the elephants habitually moved down wind all day as they did during the dry weather (probably a local tradition in response to centuries of hunting by the Wata), this was not very fruitful. The facts listed are:- years 3.5; elephant killed - total 274 (males 136, females 138); ivory produced 6.3 tons (average weight per animal 23 kg, per tusk 11.5 kg); dried meat produced 37 tons of which 31.8 tons sold @ shs 1.96 per kilo, 0.9 ton to cultivators in compensation for crop damage, the balance consumed by employees or destroyed by pests; elephants sold for zoos 4; crocodiles taken for skins 52; leopards taken for skins 4.

'Produce' from the Galana Scheme: sacks of dried meat and ivory.

Development included three hundred and sixty three km of graded roads and a further two hundred and seventy seven km of motorable, hand-cut tracks. The extent of these roads would have been far greater, but for the 1961 floods which wiped out almost all the work done to that date. A monthly average of seventy two Wata men (who had one hundred and fifty eight dependants) had been employed and earned a gross income of £8,571. Total earned income from sale of produce was £21,557. Total expenditure, which included the £10,000 capital grant from the Nuffield Foundation, was £29,000. If the capital was repaid over 30 years (not unreasonable in Kenyan ranching terms) with 5% interest, the project showed a minuscule profit of £8 in its first three and a half years.

There was an additional commercial activity that should have been considered in any economic appreciation of results. Prior to the scheme few safari parties ever hunted the area. Once we had opened it up with tracks, they used it regularly. Taking the prevailing daily charges levied by professional hunters as a yardstick, the income generated from safari hunting in the Scheme during the period 1960-1963 at least equalled the scheme's income from sale of produce. Combined, the gross income generated exceeded £40,000, and in overview, wildlife use had been unquestionably profitable in these formative years. However, there was a hitch over safari hunting. Headquarters adamantly refused to allow any income from it to be credited to the scheme. Even controlled area fees normally sent to the relevant local authority were denied it.

In terms of land use development and the sheer scale of the project, it was unreasonable to have expected so novel a concept to show profit within its first four years of operation. Further, even in the relative values of the times, £10,000 was a ridiculously small capital with which to develop 7,680 square kilometres. I thought then and still do that in terms of showing that there was potential in game management as a land use, we had done pretty well.

Times were changing. Independence was upon us. Our future as British expatriates in a Kenyan civil service was uncertain. I had taken no leave other than an annual fortnight since I joined the Kenya Regiment in 1954. In these circumstances and under the threat of losing my long leave accumulated over nearly ten years, I applied for what I was due in mid-1963. This was not so much to go on holiday as to write up the scheme's results and lay new plans. The final paragraphs of the report sum my conclusions: –

> *"... It is also doubtful whether Government, with its massive commitments in other fields, is able to contribute large sums for capital development at this stage. Now the Scheme is established, and three years of Government pioneering have revealed the various possibilities in the area, it seems correct that private enterprise should be invited to take over development and exploitation. Returns from this type of land can only be obtained through heavy investment. The area's potential is sufficient to warrant this.*
>
> *It is therefore recommended that, providing the Government's responsibility to create employment for the local people can be satisfactorily transferred, serious consideration should be given to future development being carried out through private enterprise."*

Ian Grimwood, our Chief Game Warden at the time, agreed with this view and authorised me to find investors willing to take over Galana. Ray Ryan (an American oil man) of the Mount Kenya Safari Club was interested and a proposal was put to Government that would introduce cattle into the area to be run jointly with game. By early 1964, negotiations had reached an advanced stage when Ian reversed an earlier acceptance that the company Ryan was putting together would have a free hand in its game management: he now maintained that all management decisions regarding wildlife would have to have Game Department sanction. Consequently Ryan's proposal collapsed.

Ian's volte-face was brought about by factors that had nothing to do with the validity of the Ryan proposals that he had earlier accepted. State House had ordered the Chief Game Warden to sanction some ex-Mau Mau members to 'collect' ivory hidden during the Mau Mau rebellion a decade earlier and to sell it. Rightly, as history has proved, Ian saw that such freedom would bring an uncontrollable avalanche of illicit ivory onto the market. He could not disobey the order, but he fought hard to keep as great a measure of control as possible over how it was implemented. He could not on the one hand argue for maximal control over an enterprise in black hands, while on the other he permitted minimal control in another for white investors. To be consistent he sacrificed the Galana proposal.

While all this was understandable with hindsight, it was not so at the time and I resigned, terminating the scheme's second phase. The third phase ran for the next three years – 1964 to 1967 – under a succession of Wardens that included Dave McCabe, 'Coley' Coles and Mike Imbert. As predicted, the programme limped along, hampered by lack of development capital and a government that could not make up its mind how best to proceed with it. However, during this time, seeds planted by the Ryan proposal germinated and a very similar project was put to Government by a consortium headed by American Martin Anderson and which included Mike Prettejohn, Gilfrid Powys and Tony Dyer. This was accepted and Galana Game & Ranching Limited came into being with a thirty-three year lease of what had been the Galana Game Management Scheme north of the Sabaki. The small area of the scheme that lay south of the river also in due course became a ranch – Kulalu.

* * * *

The fortunes of Galana Game & Ranching Limited warrant a volume on their own. Suffice it that in the practical aspects of managing game and cattle (building up a herd of 28,000 high quality Boran cattle), the company succeeded, fulfilling all predictions. In handling Kenya's politics and the infiltration of Somali shifta who, *inter alia,* murdered Ken Clark, the Company's Game Manager, it was not so successful. The Company's lease was terminated ahead of time and the land taken by Kenya's Agricultural Development Corporation and now sinks back towards the oblivion in which we found it nearly fifty years ago.

With hindsight and taking all things into consideration, the Galana Scheme failed. It failed primarily because we lost sight of the original, very simple goal, which was to let the Wata (Waliangulu) continue their traditions as hunters. Instead, we tried to organise them and show then a 'new' way. We did not perceive the irony in young white men who had never lived off elephants trying to teach people of the world's only elephant-hunting culture how to do so. Looking back, all one can add to a plea of *mea culpa*, is that we did it with the best of intentions (which, so we are told, line the route to Hell).

Would the plan have worked had we stuck to our original simple objective? If we had allowed the continued use of long bows and poisoned arrows, the answer is probably, during the colonial times, but less likely once independence had truly asserted itself. We were ignorant of the advanced technology behind the Wata longbow and arrow poison. At the hands of a good hunter, most arrowed elephants were dead within fifteen minutes. The discomfort they experienced would have been greater than a bullet through the brain, but not that much greater than an anaesthetising dart fired by a veterinarian. That not all were good hunters is of course true, but swapping bow and arrow for rifle – which is how we argued, did not rectify being a bad hunter.

After independence it is unlikely that the integrity of the area could have been maintained as a hunting ground. It is unlikely that the Wata would have developed sufficient social cohesion to resist the Somali shifta any better than Galana Game & Ranching Limited. It is even more unlikely that they would have been able to resist Game Department corruption any better than the National Parks who had the advantages of being organised and equipped to enforce law.

Today the catch phrase through the Third World is 'community conservation' as though the idea is a great new finding. The Galana Scheme is evidence that the Kenya Game Department was moving along these lines nearly fifty years ago. Indeed, come to think of it, it is still the largest government-initiated venture in this sphere yet tried in Africa.

CHAPTER 20: NINE YEARS AS AN HONORARY WARDEN

Mike Drury

I was fourteen years old and Capt. Ritchie was visiting my parents on their farm in Limuru, when I asked him for a position in the Game Department when I left school. He had replied that, it was best that I wait until I left school and see what portents the future held. I left school and shortly thereafter received call up papers for military service, which took care of the next two and a half years.

My first experience of buffalo hunting was with my friend Jack and a British army PT instructor on the slopes of Mount Kenya. Approaching the edge of the forest we saw a lone bull grazing a few metres from the tree line. Jack and the instructor stalked the buffalo using a patch of giant heather for cover, leaving me on the vehicle, watching. The buffalo grazed his way, slowly, into the forest and disappeared. Leaving the vehicle, I joined the two hunters and we followed the tracks into the forest. There were two canopies: one high off the ground formed by the tree crowns; the other from ground level to a height of about ten feet. This lower layer was so dense that it severely restricted lateral visibility. My companions climbed a tree hoping to see down into the thicket. Propping my rifle against the trunk to have both hands free, I had tried unsuccessfully to join them. Having failed, I was standing at the base of the tree feeling superfluous.

At this point the PT instructor said, "I'll go a bit higher and see what I can," which, he did, shinning up another ten feet. As he did so, the buffalo exploded out of the bush in front of me and I was in the fork of the tree, ten feet up, my rifle still in my hands. To this day I know not how I got there but my first experience of buffalo hunting was behind me.

On the completion of my military service I drifted through several jobs, none of which I found compatible. Then, in 1956, I entered Kenya Government service, responsible to the local African District Council for water supplies on what was known as the B1Yatta irrigation system in Ukambani. In the same year I was made an Honorary Game Warden, and at last was able to spend some time doing what I had wanted to do since aged fourteen.

My first surprise came when the Department could not provide me with a suitable rifle for big game control. In this dilemma I persuaded a cousin to sell me his .350 Rigby Magnum. The first complaint I received was of a rhino destroying crops. Taking my new acquisition and twenty rounds, a Game Scout with an old No. 1 .303 rifle (ex British Army) plus my sister who wished, foolishly, to accompany me, I set off. Arriving at our destination we found the complaint was justified and crops were considerably damaged. With an assurance that the rhino was not too far away, we picked up its tracks and followed for about two miles into a very thick and thorny patch of bush that, from the extent of trampling, was obviously well used by rhino and buffalo. On this day, however, there were only two rhino in residence.

The usual warning was given by tickbirds, which compromised our position and all hell broke loose. The two rhino crashed around sounding like two steam locomotives labouring up a steep incline with wheels slipping. When I was upright, visibility was zero and apart from the violently shaking bush I could see no rhino. When I sat down I could see only lower legs and feet. I waited in vain for a head to appear so I could kill the animal with a brain shot. Fortunately, this never happened as the rhinos took off.

It was an ordinary morning with everything going as it should be when a gentleman arrived at my office. Elephants had destroyed his shamba during the night and he wished me to kill them all. Collecting two Game Scouts and equipment sufficient for a night out we set off. Arriving at the shamba we found it devastated. We followed the elephants' tracks for about two miles until they entered thick bush well interspersed with wait-a-bit thorn. As we proceeded, most of the time bent double to get through the dense undergrowth, there was a thundering silence broken only by the occasional scraping of a branch across our clothing. Suddenly, with a crack like a rifle shot, a branch was broken very close ahead of us. We froze. The crown of a tree not far from us moved, but I could see nothing of the elephant. My palms grew wet, sweat trickled off my brow, and I felt sure the elephant would hear my breathing and heart beating. Suddenly the head appeared, very, very close: side brain shot: I was confident.

Squeezing the trigger, down he went, but he was up and running before I got to him. I followed as fast as I could. As he came into a small open piece of ground a short distance ahead, I took a hip shot which brought him down but he was up again, but now virtually static. Only his head was partially visible and I went again for a side brain shot to down him. It didn't work and I tried a third time, yet he stood. I was getting the angle all wrong, so telling my Game Scouts to sit down and wait for me, I moved slowly round to the front of the elephant and he, finally, went down with a frontal brain shot. I went down from total relief, my first elephant hunt over.

The old man and his family, who had lost their crop, were pleased to have the meat, but it was small recompense for what they had lost. This was the only occasion in over nine years that I ever saw a standing crop completely wiped out.

We had been out several nights on anti-poaching ambushes without success when we received a request for assistance from a man who had 50% of his paw-paw trees annihilated by elephant. Following tracks, Sergeant Musembi with my .500 and myself with a .475 No.2, we caught up with the herd in thick *Combretum* and wait-a-bit thorn bush. A young bull carrying small ivory was half angled towards me with a second very large animal standing, with only his rear end visible out of a large thorn bush. If I took the young bull with a side brain shot, the rest including the very large animal whose backside I could see would run off in the direction that they were already travelling in. With my first shot the young bull went down, but only briefly. I finished it off with my second barrel, but simultaneously as I fired, I felt the muzzle blast of Sergeant Musembi's .500 in my back. Turning I asked, "what the bloody hell are you doing?" Musembi had just pointed. Eight paces away, a second elephant lay dead.

Intent on despatching my own elephant, I had been unaware that the larger animal that had been stern towards us had wheeled and come straight for us. The muzzle blast I felt on my back was Musembi's second shot, I had not even been aware of his first shot. The second animal was a large bull carrying ivory of one hundred and two and ninety-seven pounds. When we checked him over the reason for the charge became obvious, his one front foot was absolutely putrid from one of the most evil forms of trapping I ever came across, namely, a piece of four by two inch wood from which eight inch long metal spikes protruded. Buried in soft or sandy soil in an trail, the spikes lamed any elephant unfortunate enough to stand on them, reducing its mobility and making it easier to kill with a bow and poisoned arrow. I had made the classic mistake of taking something for granted: that the big bull with the spiked foot would run with the others. It would have cost me my life but for Sergeant Musembi whose reliability and courage was typical of my Scouts.

On another occasion Sergeant Musembi reported two leopard casualties being treated in the local dispensary. There I found two brothers so badly ripped and bitten that I took them to hospital in Thika.

It transpired that during the night a leopard had taken a sheep from their boma and early in the morning they had followed its tracks. This was easy as the leopard left a clear trail where he had dragged the sheep. Not far from their abode they came across the sheep carcass lying next to a small gully, which emerged from a patch of thick bush. In single file they went to collect the remains and as the leading man bent to pick up the sheep the leopard attacked. The man went down with the leopard on top tearing at him. The second man attacked the leopard and diverted it from his brother, but got himself badly mauled. The two men assured me that in the fracas they had cut the leopard's throat, producing the knife allegedly used, as proof, a small single bladed Joseph Rogers knife of the type we used to have when I was a boy. Improbable though it sounded, as one of them was an ex-Game Scout, I did not totally disbelieve their throat-cutting story.

I sent two Scouts to where the incident had occurred with instructions to find out what they could, but not to enter the area where the fray took place until I arrived. Returning from the hospital, I collected Sergeant Musembi and armed with one single barrelled Stevens 12 gauge shotgun and one .375 rifle we set off, hopefully, to find one dead leopard with its throat cut.

Musembi and I arrived at the scene of action to find the two Game Scouts had picked up a blanket left by one of those attacked but had seen no leopard. There was the gully in which the sheep's carcass had been found, and signs of a scuffle.

Where the leopard had left the fray there was some blood on the grass, but not in such quantities as to suggest a cut throat. With all the coming and going that had taken place we felt the leopard would no longer be near and that there was not much we could do, and set off home.

SUNDAY NATION

Game warden
off a
by le

By SUNDAY N

THIRTY-THREE-YEA
an honorary game
Plateau, was recoverin
beth Hospital, Nairobi,
savaged by a wounded
kos, last week.

Wincing from the pain of a badly twisted ankle, his arm swathed in bandages, and with 24 stitches in his face, Mr Drury told me that the leopard had mauled two Africans who were following it up after it had taken a sheep.

"One of them very courageously tried to cut its throat as it attacked the other, but he was also seriously injured."

On Thursday Mr Drury went out after the leopard, accompanied by a game scout carrying a shotgun. "Before I left, my wife Elizabeth, told me to be careful," he recalled. "She didn't want to take me into hospital in the same state as the two Africans."

He caught up with the leopard in broad-bladed grass which cut visibility to a minimum. "First thing I knew was hearing it roar," he said "and I had the 375 magnum almost up to my shoulder when he was on me."

After shooting hurriedly Mr Drury's rifle was swept out of his hands, and the leopard raked at his throat. "I knocked him over. He was big. His face was on a level with mine and I stand six foot

MIKE DRURY — last night's picture

...ed him over. He was big. His face was on a level with mine and I stand six-foot five"

Mike Drury, Honorary Game Warden, in hospital after an affair with a leopard. Given that officers of the Department killed around 2,000 dangerous game animals annually, such accidents were surprisingly rare.

Yet after only going one hundred yards or so, inexplicably, I thought, "No! It may be in there dead." I was thinking of the small patch of dense bush out of which the gully emerged. Armed with the .375, I turned back to have another look. Musembi with the shotgun stood where he was with a 'what-the-hell-is-he-doing-now' look on his face. One other Scout, panga in hand, preceded me. Standing astride the gully and using the muzzle of the rifle to move the very thick undergrowth, I peered in and saw a patch of white about three to four inches in diameter and a couple of spots. I hesitated: what was I looking at?

In that split second there was a loud, harsh cough from the leopard, I pulled the trigger, the rifle went flying out of my hands over my head as the leopard made contact with the muzzle, and I was standing with my right arm across my face with the leopard firmly attached with his incisors through my right triceps.

Throwing him off, he was back in a second, front claws ripping at me, I hit him with my right fist knocking him off again, again he was back in an instant, this time I remember saying to myself you'd better hit this thing harder than you have ever hit anything in your life or you are in serious trouble. I chopped him with my left under the chin and saw him going over backwards into the gully as I went down; I was up immediately only to go down again in agony, my ankle was dislocated, I fell onto my side with a thump and a pain shot through my body and out the top of my head as the ankle went back into place; the leopard fortunately did not return.

In the short seconds all this took place, I was shouting to Musembi "Piga! Piga!" (Shoot! Shoot!). Fortunately he did not as at that range he would have shot me as well. The Game Scout with the panga was long gone and waiting for us at the Land Rover, firmly convinced I am sure, that I was dead. After a painful journey home, by nightfall I was in Nairobi Hospital with thirty-six stitches in my face and all other wounds cleaned and dressed. In the following days many friends visited me, but I particularly remember my friend George Barrington smuggling a glass of good Scotch whisky into the ward every time he visited.

As far as injuries go, the two brothers and I were very lucky; those to the upper body were quite severe but to the lower body there were none. As the leopard never used his hind quarters in the ripping motion for which the species is renowned, I can only assume that the creature had an old arrow wound that had inhibited the full use of his rear legs. My bullet had hit him somewhere in the abdomen as he sprang at me and the blood spoor suggested a fatal liver or kidney shot, but due to hard ground making tracking impossible, my Scouts never found him. There were, however, no further attacks on sheep or humans.

A Hunting Aero Survey team were surveying roads required for the Seven Forks Hydro Electric Scheme and on one occasion, I arrived at their camp to be greeted by the Chief Surveyor "Hi Mike, you're just the guy I want to see: there is an elephant giving me a lot of problems and holding up my survey work which is now well behind schedule. This dammed animal is pulling out the centre line pegs on a road I am surveying to Seven Forks and you must go out there and shoot the bloody thing."

Apparently the survey team went out daily and surveyed so many miles of road, cut a trace line and pegged the centre with special square pegs each of which had a number stamped on its top. Straight stretches were not too much of a problem as there was only one peg at each end of the straight, but corners were a different matter as the pegs were much closer together and the calculations required for positioning each one were complicated.

In the company of the Surveyor and a Game Scout, I witnessed the elephant's routine. Work had finished and every one had returned to camp with the exception of the three of us who waited to see what would happen. When all was quiet, a lone bull elephant came out of the bush and turned to follow the trace line, with the three of us behind him. Feeling the ground with his trunk as he went, when he found a peg he pulled it out of the ground held it up as if to inspect it and then tossed it into the bush. This went on for a couple of miles, when Jumbo had had enough and wandered off into the bush leaving one Chief Surveyor spitting mad. A couple of days being thunder-flashed stopped him and the Surveyor and I were friends once more.

In anti-poaching work I secured convictions against an Italian for shooting from a vehicle and against some Indians for the same offence and also for shooting after dark. In both cases the culprits were fined heavily and, in addition, had their firearms confiscated. Their vehicles could have been taken too, as was catered for in the laws, but the magistrate declined to order this confiscation.

The nephew of a very well-to-do Indian businessman was picked with several dead animals in the back of his vehicle up at a roadblock manned by my Game Scouts. He had no game licence, so he was arrested and brought to the Police who, having taken a statement and confiscated his weapons and the carcasses, bonded him and let him go. That night at about 0200 hrs a vehicle arrived at my house. It was the man caught earlier and an uncle who had come to ask that I should drop all charges and return the confiscated weapons. In return I was offered any of the firearms that they possessed including a double-barrelled Westley Richards .577. They only departed when I threatened to call the Police. Upon conviction, the Magistrate ruled that all weapons be forfeited to the State.

Naturally my family was influenced by my responsibilities and the contacts with wild animals. Typical was an involvement with a young waterbuck, which my three children – Gus, Norman and Jeanette – rescued from the Yatta furrow. Its confidence captivated them and they were broken-hearted when, despite all their ministrations it died. Nothing could have saved it because, as we found later, it had a poisoned arrowhead in one hindquarter.

My nine years as an Honorary Game Warden were overwhelmingly rewarding, encompassed many fields and in their small way, hopefully, helped conserve Kenya's wildlife for the future.

CHAPTER 21: THE DARTING TRIP

Ian Parker

Carter the Darter was the most prominent of our mob to experiment with and use darting to anaesthetise game. His speciality was, of course, capturing and translocating rhino and, as I recall, he used crossbows to deliver his projectiles. In 1964 I worked with him and Alan Root in the West Nile District of Uganda, where he caught several white rhino that were successfully translocated to the Murchison Falls National Park. In the following decade they did well and established an expanding population. It would have been a much greater success had Idi Amin not come to power. By the time he went, there were no white rhinos left and, as with so many of his legacies, much of Uganda was also bereft of evidence that white people had been there, let alone white rhinos.

I recall that, early in his experiments, Nick tried using his crossbow from inside the cab of his Land Rover, aiming out of the passenger side window. When the powerful bow was released, one arm knocked out the windscreen and Nick learned that the uncocked bow took up more space than when cocked. Jack Barrah recalled Nick's fiery temper matched his red hair and beard, and an incident when he came across Carter's Land Rover on the side of the road with a flat tyre. He then saw the Darter cursing and blinding halfway up a nearby hill. Apparently, when applied to a wheel nut, the wheel brace had slipped and hurt his finger, whereon it was hurled as far as he could throw it, and he was looking for it when Jack came upon him. It was never found.

Another early experimenter was 'Red' Palmer whose Palmer Chemical & Equipment Company Inc. of Atlanta in the USA produced much early darting equipment. His principal contact in Kenya was Billy Woodley and it was through Bill that Red came to us on the Galana. Our principal 'guru', however, was Tony Harthoorn who had had a modicum of success darting elephants in Uganda, which we wished to repeat on Galana.

With an annual quota of 200 elephants (which we never attained), selling elephant meat was not particularly profitable. While never enthusiastic about sending an elephant into a life of captivity, the zoo demand for young elephants was lucrative and there was no material reason why we should not take at least part of the quota as live elephant calves. With the dense *Commiphora* that covered much of Galana, the normal 'Carr-Hartley/Randall' technique of vehicle chase and noosing was not widely practicable. Although Nevil Steyn from Arusha had had some success with it, darting sounded more appropriate.

At the same time that we wanted to catch some elephant calves, there was also intense interest in elephant movement within the Tsavo/Galana ecosystem. Elephant destruction of woodland in Tsavo was becoming a progressively greater concern to both the National Park Authorities and the Game Department. Both wanted to know to what degree the animals moved in and out of Tsavo. To get this knowledge we needed to mark and render elephants recognisable.

It was before radio telemetry had developed and David Sheldrick's first attempt had not been a great success. At the break-pressure tank on the Mzima Pipeline (Mombasa's water supply) behind the Park Headquarters, elephants would drink within a few feet of where one sat on top of the tank. David had coupled a paint spray gun to a compressor and a startled, bright yellow bull elephant had disappeared into the night. When seen several days later from a Royal Navy helicopter, the yellow was only just discernible beneath a coating of red Tsavo dust and mud. Clearly more durable marking was called for and we thought that if we sawed off the anterior third of one tusk, the squared end would be recognisable for a long time afterwards. We were wrong of course. Tusk breaks are honed back to a point very quickly, but we weren't to know this until several years later. To cut a bit off an elephant's tusk, the animal would have to be tranquillised. And so, for both this purpose and to obtain young ones for sale we, on Galana, became darters.

* * * *

It was, of course, before the days of wonder drugs like M99 and its allied synthetic morphines and we used a 'Harthoorn cocktail'. This was a mix of four drugs. The base was 'Phenicyclidine', originally developed for human anaesthesia, but abandoned because it had such spectacular hallucinatory after-effects and became much sought by addicts. It had no antagonist so its effects could not be reversed. Animals tended to be 'out' for hours at a time; consequently, even in veterinary medicine it was soon abandoned. To the Phenicyclidine we added 'Themelon' an early synthetic morphine whose effect could be reversed by another drug – 'Lethidrone'. Its value in the cocktail derived from its reversibility. We were frightened to increase the dosage of Phenicyclidine because of the problems arising from immobilising an elephant for hours. Themelon boosted the cocktail's knockdown capacity, but because it could be neutralised, we were not so afraid of over-dosing with it. To the first two drugs these we added Largactyl, which was widely used with cattle as a tranquilliser. To control unwanted side effects like excessive salivation, we added small amounts of scopolamine and used hyalase to accelerate the effect of the other drugs. The foregoing may not be the way that Harthoorn himself would have described his cocktail, or its rationale. It is, however, what we understood.

Tony laid down no rigid ratio of drug proportions, one to another in the cocktail, or how much should be injected. He made some suggestions to start with and thereafter we proceeded very much on a suck it (metaphorically of course) and see basis. The volume of cocktail required for an adult male elephant amounted to around 20 ml which by any standards, is a large injection calling for a correspondingly large delivery dart.

Initially injections were achieved through gas pressure driving a plunger piston forward. On the reverse side of the plunger was a recess into which a 'Cap-Chur' tablet was placed and held in position by a heavy brass plug. The dart body behind the plunger was then filled with a weak acid, which in turn was retained by the dart's tailpiece. The principle was simple: on striking the victim, the brass plug fell out of the plunger recess. The tablet came into contact with the acid, effervesced, and the CO_2 gas thus generated drove the plunger forward and the injectant down the dart's hypodermic fore-end needle into the victim.

We tried several weapons to launch darts. Initially the Game Department provided a crossbow. It had two disadvantages. The first was keeping the dart on the bow while on foot, ducking and weaving through bush in pursuit of elephant. It was not a problem encountered by Carter the Darter seated in a helicopter or on a Land Rover's front seat. Moving fast through thick bush, balancing the dart on the crossbow was reminiscent of an egg and spoon race. When pursued by elephants (they disliked being darted) equipment had to be abandoned.

The crossbow's second drawback was the dart's parabolic trajectory. Its apogee in a flight of eighty metres was three metres above a straight line between point of launch and point of aim. This posed no problem in open country, but was a severe disadvantage in thick bush. Though quarry might be visible with no obstructions directly between it and hunter, twigs and branches that overhung that line of sight would deflect the dart.

Our second and very brief trial was with the Palmer CO_2 'Cap-Chur' pistol. It was too small to take darts carrying 20ml of injectant and a further 5ml of acid. More seriously, it had a rather limited range that, amongst elephants, dense Sanseviera and wait-a-bit thorn made it a kamikaze tool.

Then we tried the 'Palmer 32 gauge'. This was a lovely little weapon by Beretta, rifled and of a calibre that took normal sized 5ml darts and fired them with a wonderfully flat trajectory over distances of up to one hundred metres. The drawback was that darts capable of carrying the loads we needed and slender enough for the 32-gauge barrel resembled flying walking sticks. After two had curled up like pigs' tails on impact, the curvature blocking the plunger's forward movement, and the strikes producing two anything-but-anaesthetised elephants, we moved on to Red's next offering. This was his Palmer Five Eighths Gauge: a rifled 20-bore gun that took a correspondingly large dart.

In truth, this tool would not have been out of place in Saddam Hussein's armoury. One had to judge distance carefully, and then select an appropriate propellant cartridge. These were standard 20 bore cartridges, emptied of shot and powder, then reloaded with one of three charges: close range, medium range and long distance. The latter was sufficient to throw the massive dart on a flat trajectory for over one hundred metres. The kick was impressive, the strike would dent a Centurion tank, and if the long distance charge was mistakenly used at short range, it was virtually the equivalent of a standard .470.

With the high dart velocities and weights, we had endless problems with needles snapping, needle bores becoming plugged with cores of elephant skin and dart casings failing, all closely linked to extreme excitement in the field. Tony Harthoorn came and went and other visitors wished to watch the research. One, the son of an eminent professor, insisted on wearing a straw hat the size of a cartwheel. We left him well back as we made our final approach to a herd. The Palmer 20 bore barked, and an old lady elephant lurched forward as the missile struck her left haunch. She wheeled and, with head high, stared back in that very unfriendly down-the-nose look elephants have. We kept still and she never saw us. Yet the great yellow cartwheel of a hat, standing out like a sunflower in a coalscuttle, caught her eye and when it moved, ever so slightly, she went by us like a galleon under full sail, followed by her herd. The last we saw of the professor's son for a long time was the hat rising and falling as he jinked around and vaulted over bushes and obstacles until out of sight. Eventually the hat came off and he went on while the elephants redesigned his headgear.

It took us a while and several more failed dartings to work out why the old elephant had pursued the hat and not gone to sleep. The Cap-Chur pellet and acid were not producing enough pressure to inject all of the 20 ml cocktail. A striker and percussion cap to generate a greater force on the dart's plunger replaced them. Even this didn't work and the first clue as to why came when I happened to launch the dart dead into wind and feel a fine mist blow back over my face. Seemingly the dart had discharged its load as it was leaving the gun barrel. We proved this was indeed happening by firing a dart through a sheet of paper a metre or so from the muzzle. A wide, wet circle around the hole where the dart had passed through confirmed our suspicion. The cap was moving back and impaling itself on the striker and detonating during the initial acceleration instead of, vice versa, the striker moving forward onto the cap with deceleration at impact. The problem was rectified, but still results were unsatisfactory. Yet more pressure was needed to achieve injection. I solved this by putting some black powder in the dart's rear chamber, along with the cap.

David Sheldrick had given us permission to dart an elephant in Tsavo National Park, with the admonition "do not kill it!" The elephant was stalked to within sixty paces. The missile left the Palmer 20 gauge with a bang and took the young bull behind the left shoulder, vanishing with an even louder bang as the black powder blew the dart to smithereens. The elephant made one hundred yards at a run before staggering and falling on its side. We turned and shook one another's hands: at last – success. Soon we were swarming about the victim performing allotted duties. One poured water to keep the patient cool. I sawed a tusk in half so that the elephant would be recognisable. Having stuffed a thermometer up its bum to monitor temperature, an ever more silent Harthoorn clambered about the prostrate animal with his stethoscope, trying to pick up its heartbeat. As this had stopped he never did. In the nanoseconds before the dart disintegrated, the violent explosion had blasted 20 ml of liquid the diameter of the dart needle's bore into the victim with such force that it drilled a hole right through its heart. A .600 bullet would not have been more devastating. David's gloom was immeasurably increased when handed two tusks, one in two pieces.

If we had used a heavy rifle, we could not have done more damage than we did with Palmer's rifled 28 gauge: Harthoorn and Parker survey the result (photo Alan Root).

After that incident someone suggested that better use of the Palmer rifled 20 bore would be to take a dart, fill it with water, remove the needle, and just fire it at the side of an elephant's head. The blow alone would knock it out. The last recollection I have of Red Palmer was on a sweltering afternoon on the Tiva looking for dartable elephants. I cannot recall whether we found them, but I do remember Red's lurid reminiscences about a cute, lubricious, red-headed waitress and how she helped him while away humid afternoons back in Atlanta. Funny how the mind works: why remember that? Perhaps it was familiarity?

Elephants I could take or leave, they were everywhere in those days. Compliant, lubricious, red-headed waitresses were not, which may be why the memory sticks.

* * * *

The weapon we finally used for darting was known as the Harthoorn powder gun. It was an old single barrelled twelve-bore shotgun fitted with a .410 sleeve. Like the 20 bore, one stuffed the dart into a cartridge case loaded with a charges to suit range. It was the most effective of our many weapons.

From my records I see that thirty elephants were hit by darts. Of them only eight were immobilised, of which three were youngsters for zoos. Two more immatures never regained the use of their forelimbs and though they recovered from the drugs in all other aspects, eventually had to be put down. Two large male elephants were darted and died. One large animal was darted but escaped.

The escapee was darted at dusk and went down quickly close to a road. A truck was on site within minutes and a large hole dug next to the comatose elephant. Into this the truck was reversed so that the floor of its body was on a level with the ground. The elephant regained its feet earlier than expected, but while still groggy, we 'walked' it into the truck. This walking consisted of attaching a rope to each 'ankle', then pulling on them sequentially so that the animal moved in the desired direction. When in the truck body, the ropes were tied so that left fore leg was tethered to the forward left corner of the truck bed, the left rear leg to the rear left corner and so on, restricting the elephant's ability to move. Another rope was placed round its neck and tied to the truck body to further limit its movement. With the elephant thus secured the truck was driven out of the hole.

It was only then that all present acknowledged what had been apparent all along: the elephant was larger than any zoo would take. What on earth were we doing with an animal this size? Just how big it was really came home when the elephant, towering above us in the back of the truck, flapped its ears. Their span exceeded the width of the vehicle's body. As it stood eight feet at the shoulder, we should have reversed the truck back into the hole, dropped the tailgate, 'walked' the elephant back out, and let it go its way. Yet we didn't. With the Wata (Waliangulu) clinging to the bodywork around the elephant's hindquarters and others perched on the bonnet and wings (none would sit on the cab within reach of the elephant's nose), we headed for the pens at Dakadima.

We had not gone far when the truck blew an inner right hand rear tyre. This called for removing both rear wheels on that side. Until the truck was balanced on the jack and without its rear wheels, the elephant had been remarkably well mannered. At that point, however, it commenced to throw itself about. All hands were required to hold the vehicle steady while the wheels were replaced. It was extraordinary that we actually managed to achieve the change over without it falling off the jack. By the time we were ready to proceed, the animal was coming to and lashing out with its trunk. With no little difficulty I gave it a top-up of Themelon. At one o'clock in the morning we arrived at the Dakadima holding pens. Reversing into a hole in the ground, the elephant was walked off the truck and into a pen. As a safety measure the heavy rope round its neck was also secured to one of the pen's massive uprights.

Several young elephants were successfully darted and quickly adapted to captivity (photo Parker).

In the dawn everyone stood and stared. What would we do with our prisoner? The elephant was amazingly quiet and self-confident. All through the day it ate the food brought to it and drank from the water barrel. At five in the evening it departed: just like that. Quite gently, it destroyed the pen. Then snapping its securing neck rope as though it was no more than a cotton thread and wearing what was left of it like a tie, it ambled away, offering no threat to the people who perched in trees all around, watching in amazement. Was I not a sane and sensible person, I would have said that the elephant had tolerated the whole exercise just for the experience.

We all occasionally did crazy things. Indeed a short while before we darted and caught the big elephant, Tony Seth-Smith, his factotum Kipruto, Tony Archer and his friend Abakuna, came across a lone, young female elephant at Jara waterhole. They persuaded themselves that they could catch it, arguing that, as it was alone, it might not be well and therefore weaker than normal. Even so, it stood nearly seven feet (two metres) at the shoulder, had tusks a foot long and weighed more than a Charolais bull.

Charging out, each to an appointed limb, before the elephant was aware of what was happening, they had it trussed, hobbled and cast. By working in unison, they had it down and on its side and it was then that the single casualty occurred. Tony Seth-Smith was at the sharp end sitting on the elephant's head, when it grabbed his arm with its trunk and in a seemingly aimless move stuffed the arm into its mouth. Not appreciating the design, Tony did not resist strongly and before he realised what was afoot, the elephant had his upper left arm between its jaws and was biting down hard. He bears the scars to this day.

It was the first of a number of cases I have recorded of elephants biting. They do it routinely. Young elephants, when caught and constrained, will grab at arms and hands, pulling them towards their mouths. It looks as though they are seeking comfort and the move is almost a gesture of friendship. Let the move be carried through and its purpose will be readily apparent. In later years when catching young elephants in Uganda, several men were bitten. The most amazing case of biting happened in the precincts of Paraa Lodge in Murchison Falls National Park. It was dark and a lodge employee did not see the elephant hidden behind a hedge. A trunk shot out, grabbed the man around the upper body, hoisted him into the air then stuffed him into the owner's mouth. Fortunately it bit down on the man's jacket out of which the wildly wriggling wearer dropped, to scurry away like a crazy rodent, leaving his garment behind. Later he claimed to have saved himself by deliberately stuffing his jacket between its jaws. Such cool-headedness is unlikely in circumstances where the victim probably did not know what in fact was happening. Some guys are lucky and he was one.

Yet, returning to the start of this tale, Tony's captive was allowed to depart. If there is any lesson from his story, it may reflect on human abilities back when, as Stone Age hunters and gatherers, they preyed on big mammals. Acting in unison as a team in which everyone knew his role, a dozen men without weapons were still formidable predators.

* * * *

Quite a tale was also attached to one young elephant taken for zoo sale. We had followed tracks all day and came up with its herd far too late to dart. Yet I had done so and the young elephant had gone down quickly and easily. While I had stayed to tend the immobilised animal, the rest of the team set off through the dusk to find and bring in the truck. We knew it would be a long night.

I cut grass and fixed bundles of it in the highest nearby tree. These I would light as beacons as soon as the vehicle was within hearing. The hours passed and thirst set in. I had had no water since morning. Then I remembered the small bottle of distilled water I carried in my darting satchel. Having loaded drugs into a dart, I would top it up with water from this bottle so that all darts were full and all of equal weight. This bottle's contents would wet my lips and possibly provide a single gulp. No sooner thought than done. And no sooner done than I knew it had been a mistake.

To get water out of the small bottle I invariably used the same syringe I used to place drugs in the darts. Countless times over previous months the syringe had been dipped into the distilled water, releasing minute amounts of what it had contained into the bottle. How much of any of the drugs used were in the bottle I could not say, but one thing was certain: I had not swallowed distilled water, but a very dilute Harthoorn cocktail.

Thus started a strange, schizophrenic experience. On the one hand I was aware of where I was and what I was supposed to be doing. On the other, it was as though I looked from an immense height down on myself with the prostrate elephant in the dark. I was in the scene, yet at the same time I was outside it, far up in the sky. Periodically I tried to see the time on my watch. The match would flare, and I could see well enough. Yet when I looked at the watch face, it fizzled and flared and was impossible to read. I tried, cunningly, to look out of the corner of my eye, to catch it out. It didn't work. No matter what I did, it and only it among all that I could see fizzled and flared and refused to tell me the time. I was never so incapacitated that, when I eventually heard the truck, I could not light the grass beacons. However, we did not get out of the bush until dawn and it was weeks before I recovered from what had turned out to be a trip in more than one sense of the word. Now, decades later, mention of darting still recalls that strange experience and Harthoorn's cocktail.

Today, watching elephants and rhinos being darted on television (it is always on television these days), all seems so easy. The darters know exactly what to do. The animals go down for the prescribed period and get up on the appointed minute. Today I bet few of the practitioners know what a Harthoorn cocktail is, let alone know what it tastes like. Things used to be rough at the sharp end.

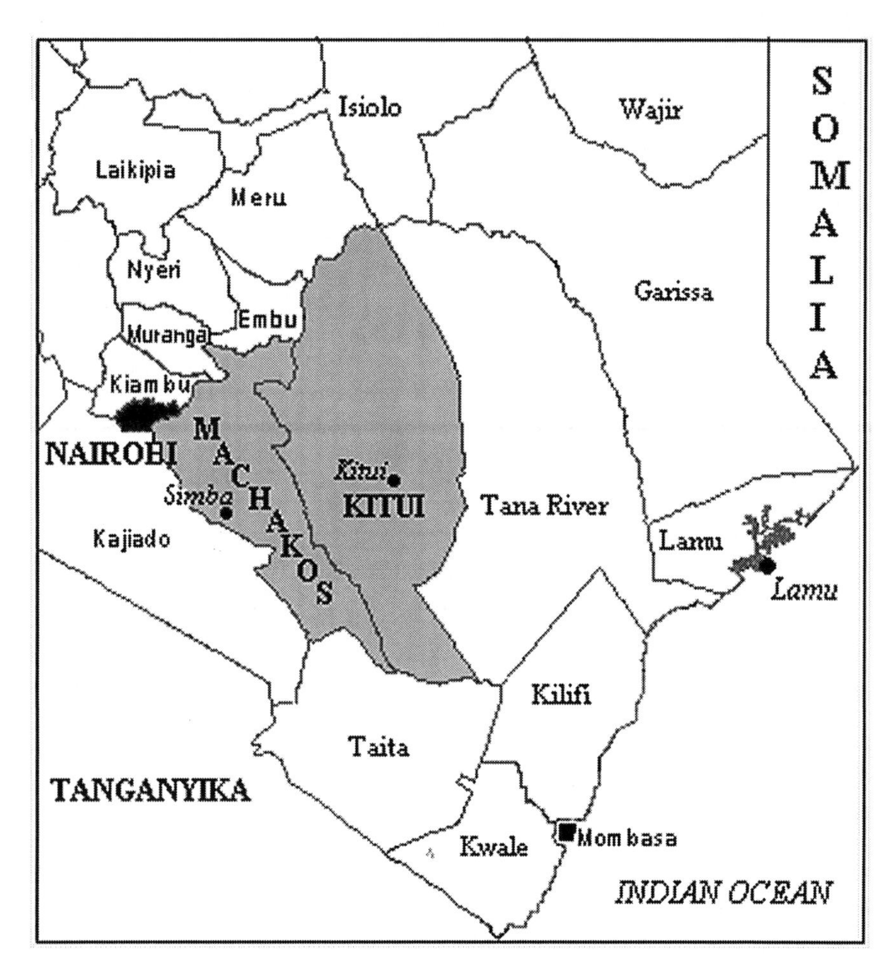

The Simba Range, being all of Ukambani

CHAPTER 22: UKAMBANI

Dave McCabe

Based at Simba my new bailiwick consisted of Ukambani, that is both Kitui and Machakos Districts. Much of this range was more or less heavily settled, devoid of game and therefore of no interest to the Game Department. Of the remainder some was coming under pressure from human settlement with consequent little long-term big game conservation potential. There remained some areas, for example, along the northern edge of the old Southern Game Reserve (and also tsetse country) where game still remained in some quantity and was worth conserving, and parts of Kitui District. The Simba station on Nguu Hill was named after the railway station of that name on the Nairobi - Mombasa line which lay a few miles to the south of our quarters. Overlooking the countryside we had a magnificent view of Mount Kilimanjaro in Tanganyika. On clear days one felt that one could reach out and touch the mountain.

Poaching appeared to be on the increase, the main target being rhino. There were plenty of them in the immediate locality, it not being unusual to encounter several in the few miles along the short cut from our house to Kiboko on the main Mombasa - Nairobi road. Kiboko was the site of the Tsetse Research Station and also, across the road, of JA's Hunter's Lodge. It was along this short cut that I once had a rhino poached right under my nose. Coming along the track that I had traversed earlier in the day we found its carcass lying almost across the track, so fresh that blood was still seeping from around where the horns had been removed. We never found either the poacher or the horns.

While rhino were still common enough to be shot on licence in many places, by 1960, the Game Department was becoming progressively more reluctant to shoot them on control. The preferred policy was to catch nuisance animals and transfer them somewhere else. Initially the Department used the country's licensed game trappers, who sold animals to zoos around the world, to undertake the capture on a share basis. That is, they could keep one of every two animals caught. They caught rhino by chasing with a vehicle and roping it. It was rather primitive with a proportion of all caught dying from the stress and after-effects.

The system was occasionally abused with deaths being concealed so that another animal could be caught on the same licence. During my time at Simba policy was changed. No further rhino would be allowed for export, and instead all those captured where they were a problem would be translocated to areas within Kenya where they could be conserved. The method of chasing to exhaustion would not only be discontinued in favour of darting, but the Game Department would handle the entire business. To this end Bryan Carter, but always called Nick, was recruited and put in charge of the project. He turned up at Simba and introduced himself.

Caught in net at Rumuruti in 1935 by Hugh Stanton, this was the first full grown black rhino caught in Kenya. Prior to World war II, motor vehicles were too costly and not robust enough to chase and lasso animals as big as a full grown rhino (photo courtesy Peter Jenkins).

I had been directed to give Nick 'every possible assistance'. A camp for his subordinates was erected at Kiboko and pens were built. Apart from his own jeep (a rather inadequate DKW), Nick had a 4 x 4 three-ton truck, rhino crates, and roller conveyor, hand winches etc. Nick had no dart-gun but a crossbow made from the tapered leaf of a car spring. Similarly, the 'dart' was a rather large metal syringe, clumsy in comparison with the modern equivalent. In retrospect, the entire set-up was primitive; no helicopters, no walkie-talkies, crude weapons, no vets, not much of anything that one expects to see nowadays. The crossbow was so powerful that it was quite impossible to cock by hand and a detachable lever was supplied for this purpose. The weapon, very well finished and assembled, was the work of a friendly Nairobi toxophilite – Chris Archer.

The drug itself was a succinylcholine based compound, which acted as a cholinesterase inhibitor that was sometimes used by anaesthetists (it was eventually abandoned because although it produced paralysis, it did not eliminate consciousness or reactions such as fear and consequently produced huge stress in the victim). After ironing out one or two teething troubles, a rhino was eventually darted. It was followed on foot and after some distance became ataxic, swaying slightly and staggering at intervals as it walked. This must have gone on for about twenty to thirty minutes after which the symptoms slowly disappeared until it was obvious we were following an unimpaired animal.

Similar failure occurred several times, the obvious deduction being that, by underestimating the weight of the rhino, the dosage was too low.

Another inexplicable occurrence on a couple of occasions at very close range, the dart bounced off the rhino instead of sticking into it. This was eventually solved when we were able to approach two rhino at very close range in a gully below us. On this occasion, instead of standing next to Nick Carter, I was some yards to one side from which angle I saw quite distinctly that on leaving the crossbow the dart tumbled end over end before bouncing off the rhino. We never discovered why, but found that after a certain distance the dart straightened out in flight and flew true.

As a result of the drug's failure to function, the dosage was increased. This was successful and a rhino collapsed unconscious and was successfully transported to a holding pen. I forget how long it lay there before showing signs of recovery. These consisted of spasms in which the rhino, lying on its side, banged its head on the ground with great force. Some straw was quickly put beneath the head as a pillow, but didn't help much. After what seemed a long time, the rhino became weaker and died.

Note the special head guard to stop the rhino from damaging its head. Severe head-banging during recovery was characteristic of the first drugs we used (photo D.McCabe).

We kept trying; reduce the dose and the rhino, after staggering about a bit, recovered and escaped. Increase the dose and many rhino still died, but a few survived. Upon veterinary advice we administered oxygen and various tranquillisers to the recovering animal and the survival rate improved. However, the horrifying head bashing that always occurred with the succinylcholine-based drug nonplused everyone, the vets included.

Those rhino which survived were translocated to various National Parks. Two – a male named JA and female called Brunie (after my wife) – were sent to South Africa's Addo Park in the Eastern Cape. They obviously did well as nearly forty years later several of their progeny were sent back to East Africa to repopulate Tanzania's Mkomazi Game Reserve and Ngorongoro Crater.

As the effects of the drug could not be reversed, and matching dose to the victim's weight was critical, our greatest difficulty in these early darting experiments was accurately guessing the victim's weight. In fairness to the animal trappers, our initial mortality was certainly higher than theirs through roping. With the arrival of the drug M99, however, results so dramatically improved that losses became rare.

* * * *

Once Nick Carter was set up (which was before M99 appeared) my presence was no longer required and, leaving him a couple of reliable Game Scouts, I returned to mundane work. Part of this was, of course, shooting on control in which I experienced incidents and excitements that all Wardens must have had.

Once, having shot one of three bull elephants, one of the survivors returned to the scene. The Game Scout and I retired a short distance and watched. We had no intention of shooting this bull that approached quite slowly until it was standing over its dead companion. It then reached out with its trunk and very gently touched the carcase. This continued for some minutes, the elephant shuffling back and forth repeatedly touching its dead companion with its trunk mainly about its head, Wondering whether it was ignorant of our presence, we shouted and threw a stone toward it, but this produced no reaction at all. Eventually the elephant slowly wandered off and disappeared. It was very touching and made me feel guilty. I described what had happened to JA who produced a clear photo of an almost identical incident he had taken years earlier, adding that he could have sworn that the elephant was weeping[63].

Perhaps my closest call was not far from the Kiangine River between Simba and Makueni. A four or five acre thicket amid cultivation was surrounded by a large and noisy crowd of Wakamba, who assured me that it contained a single angry elephant. This seemed a bit far-fetched but a tribal policeman who was present assured me it was true. To have an extra pair of eyes I bade the policeman accompany me into the thicket for a look. All went well enough until

[63] Editor's note: So many wardens had similar experiences that had they been pooled in 1960, the frequency of such behaviour would have called for explanation.

I became hooked up by the collar to a thorny creeper. It was while I was trying to unhook myself that I realised that I was more or less face to face with the elephant, of which about all I could see was its trunk. It was so close that I particularly remember noticing the hairs on it. What followed took place so quickly that I never knew what happened. I must have fired without aiming and probably without raising the rifle as the bullet struck fairly high on the trunk as we discovered later. The elephant then disappeared although I did not see it go. It may have tried to clear out of the patch of bush and been turned back by the crowd. Whatever, it next crossed my front at a run some thirty or so yards away, much of its head showing above the scrub. My second barrel, perhaps rather a lucky shot, dropped it dead. Although he was with me at the start, I had never noticed the tribal policeman's departure. I never saw him again.

Roan Antelope (photo Peter Davey)

CHAPTER 23: ROAN

Miles Coverdale

My family was always interested in wildlife, including birds, and I was brought up to take interest and to observe. Hunting animals and bird shooting was of course very common in those days (I was born in 1936), and though we now look at it with a certain amount of regret, it was part of the incentive to take an interest in wildlife. Catapults, air guns, .22s, and egg collecting, none of which are encouraged now, and are against the law, were part of one's wildlife education.

It was therefore a great honour to be asked to be an honorary Warden in the mid-sixties, in the Yatta and Thika areas. Farming at Thika left little spare time for more than dealing with problem animals, and unfortunately time was not available to take poachers to court, especially to Machakos, the administrative headquarters for the Yatta, so my anti-poaching work was minimal.

The most significant project that I was involved with as an honorary Warden was translocating roan antelope from Tana Ranch, situated between the Ithanga Hills and the Tana River down to its junction with the Thika. Tana Ranch belonged to a farming company, and had been sold to a co-operative, which would eventually split the land up into small units. One of the very few populations of roan in Kenya [since the white man arrived in Kenya, there had never been more than small pockets – see Appendix I], it was decided that they should be moved to a safer location. It was a controversial decision, with those against it arguing that roan were not rare in other countries, and that the expense was, therefore, not justified. Poaching was rife, as I had discovered while visiting the ranch. At that time little was known about roan and it was thought it would be well worth the cost to gain experience with translocation, and the East African Wildlife Society provided the finance, and the Game Department acquiesced.

The trappers John Seago, Tony Parkinson and their Grade A trapper Mwaneki Kaundu were selected, and the project was underway by September 1969. In order to keep stress minimal they decided to drive the roan between long funnel-shaped wings into a two and a half acre boma with very high walls. The wings were about a mile long, and encompassed a small hill to help deceive the roan as to what was happening. These were constructed of bush at the near end and the outer part was only a strip of polythene draped over the bushes to deflect the roan in the right direction. Tony Parkinson and his team spent weeks doing the groundwork to accustom the roan to people, while Game Scouts were seconded to deter, and if possible arrest the poachers, who had set fire to the ranch.

Because chasing animals across country could result in serious damage to vehicles, the trappers used an assortment of old models for herding the roan. This was a constant source of wry remark, and recalls a morning when Tony was driving a suitably old Land Rover and John was passenger.

John said, "the front wheel is singing." There was no reply.

"Tony, the front wheel is singing." Again, there was no reply.

"Tony, why is the front wheel singing?"

"Because it is happy."

There was no further conversation for some time!

The first drive was done on horseback. Among the steeds used, Tony was mounted on a beautifully trained American quarter horse, imported for the film *Cowboy in Africa*, and which he had subsequently acquired. The horsemen brought the roan successfully into the wings, where several vehicles, mine included, were hidden in readiness for the final push up the funnel. Once in the funnel something scared them, and they broke back and got away. Reflecting on this, it was decided to use a helicopter for greater control next time.

The helicopter was not available until Friday 13th March when pilot Andy Neale managed two successful drives that had first seven, then five roan safely in the boma. They had settled down well by the evening, and we went back to camp for a late meal and bed, both much needed. Back early next morning we were horrified to find the boma empty. The roan had escaped through a small gap in the wall, where the poles had been moved inwards. It would not have been possible for the roan themselves to move these bars inwards. The reason was not discovered, and the watchmen were doubtless having a snooze. Poachers were not beyond suspicion, but it was impossible to make anything of the tracks, as our own tracks were everywhere. Friday the thirteenth had the last say after all!

The helicopter was not available for another two months. In the meantime the rains broke, and normally dry riverbeds were flooded and the ranch was completely cut off. With the flush of green vegetation tsetse flies became a problem, and the quarter horse died as a result.

In late May the helicopter arrived and action was resumed. Dr. Don Stewart, the Game Department biologist, manned the radios to pass on instructions from the helicopter to the ground crews. The first drive was going well when Tony in the chopper saw that a herd of zebra had joined the roan, and reported this over the radio. "Take the bloody lot," replied John Seago, but the zebra were breaking up the roan group, so Tony let them all go free. On the second drive the roan were driven to within one hundred yards of the boma gate when they broke back, and a big male collided with Alexander Aaron's horse. Neither was marked, but both had broken necks, showing what heavy animals roan are. Alexander was thrown clear, luckily unhurt. It was a successful day with a total of twenty-one animals caught, though one female broke a horn off in a fight, infection set in and it died later. The boma had been lined on the outer side with strong wire mesh, and it was patrolled all night to stop further escape.

It was then known that between fifty and seventy roan remained on the ranch, and it was decided to go ahead and capture more, despite opposition on the grounds of expense. Apart from the cost of the helicopter, everything else was in place and required little extra outlay. The Wildlife Society agreed to fund one more drive when the helicopter was next available.

During the next few weeks the captured animals were divided into smaller groups and penned separately. These pens had the open transport crates forming one wall. Feeding was done near them and finally in them so that the roan became used to them and it would be no problem to get them inside when the time came to move them. They had lost weight due to the stress of capture, and had to regain condition before they could be moved. It was decided to break the journey at the Seago property in Nairobi, as the ranch road was very rough. But when the time came, the lorry failed to turn up, so the first few animals were loaded onto small vehicles, including my own. Contrary to the expected behaviour during transport, the roan lay down the whole way, which caused some abrasions on the skin, so the rest in Nairobi allowed time for these to heal for the final long trip to the Shimba Hills at the coast. This also allowed time for crates to be redesigned, and for two pregnant females to give birth, which we did not want to happen on the road. The roan were moved to the Shimba Hills in October, where they were first held in a small boma and then released into a 30 acre paddock to acclimatize and to form a territory. They were released completely the following April.

At about this time the final capture financed by the Wildlife Society took place at Tana Ranch, and twenty-four roan were caught. These settled quickly, but a week later fighting started between the two groups, and as a result twelve animals rushed into the wall of the boma in a mass, breaking it down and they escaped. Quick thinking and action by Alexander prevented the rest from escaping through the gap. The remaining twelve settled quickly and were moved to Solio Ranch at Naro Moru soon afterwards.

Yet another capture was arranged in September 1971, and this time it was to be filmed by the American Broadcasting Corporation (ABC) that partly financed the operation. Joe Kennedy (Robert F. Kennedy's son) was ABC's guest star on the show, and the final drive was to be with horses only and no vehicles. Three horses were kindly lent by Jeremy and Barbie Allen, who looked after them at Tana. Joe rode one of the horses, flanked by Tony and Alexander. A total of twenty-four roan were caught in three successful drives, but three were later killed in fighting. One big female was horned in the chest and died instantly. Another old female refused to eat and soon died.

These were moved down to the Shimba Hills and released in due course. At this point the roan operation was deemed a success. With hindsight the judgement was premature. The twelve roan that went to Solio Ranch soon died, and though those in the Shimba Hills survived and bred, they too had all died in about fifteen years. Perhaps the sceptics were right!

* * * *

Editors' Postscript :–

Following Chief Game Warden David Brown's departure in 1968, Stan Bleazard was an unwilling Acting Deputy Chief Game Warden who, for the next year, observed the development of bedlam and anarchism, which he was powerless to prevent. During this time he became aware by hearsay, of the East Africa Wild Life Society's interest in removing the remnants of a roan antelope population from Tana Ranch. It was a project that, regardless of how desirable it might be, he viewed with no great enthusiasm as the changed circumstances would make it difficult if not impossible for the Department to contribute meaningfully. Because there had been no replacement of Dr John King, the very successful Capture Unit had been disbanded and there was nobody in the Department capable of running such an exercise successfully.

The uncommon status of roan in Kenya, with a limited and diminishing distribution on the Ithanga hills, the Siria escarpment and the Lambwe valley, was the major reason that the EAWLS initiated the rescue. At the time, the Acting Chief Game Warden was an administrative Under Secretary brought in temporarily from the Ministry of Tourism and Wildlife, who had no knowledge of wildlife management whatsoever. The Wildlife Society's proposals never crossed my (S.B.) desk and I was never asked for a professional opinion on it. Possibly the final decision never involved the Acting Chief Game Warden and was made over his head at a higher political level and believing that Dr Don Stewart, Head of the Fauna Research Unit, and a member of the Wildlife Society's Scientific & Technical Committee, must have ensured the project's scientific probity.

In 1969 Ian Parker, too, was a member of EAWLS Scientific & Technical Committee that was supposed to vet all applications for funding and judge their conservation value. Absent while the roan project was conceived and adopted, he opposed the operation as soon as he returned to Kenya and learned of it. His grounds were several.

First, the Society was raising funds for the programme because 'roan were an endangered species', when they had never been more than marginally present in Kenya and were in no danger in either Uganda or Tanzania. More were shot by sportsmen in those two countries annually than were thought to exist in Kenya. Second, by implying that roan were endangered everywhere, the Society would be 'conning' donors unaware of the truth. Third, the Ithanga roan were believed endangered only because the Tana Ranch on which they occurred was changing hands from white to black owners. While it was unlikely that the new owners would be able to conserve them, he felt the Society was both morally and practically bound to find out whether the new owners might wish to retain them. Having groups of viewable roan so close to Nairobi could have been a profitable tourist draw. Fourth, the new home proposed for the roan was to be the Shimba hills on the slim basis that the related sable antelope existed there[64]. Fifth, no plans for post translocation care had been made. Sixth, if roan were really needed in the Shimba hills, Carr Hartley & Sons had offered to provide the same number from Tanzania at half the initial estimated cost of the rescue operation. When the Society went ahead with the operation despite these objections, Ian Parker felt obliged to resign from it as a matter of principle.

The roan capture operation was, in itself, a technical success. Seago, Parkinson, their staff and others like Miles Coverdale conducted a first class exercise. For the first time in Kenya, they applied 'wing-traps' with a driving helicopter, and captured numbers of a strong and intractable animal.

Unfortunately, as a conservation exercise it was a failure. All the roan died. The East African Wildlife Society did not establish why. It was as if the act of moving the animals was all the 'conservation' needed. The Society's real interest seemed to have been publicity to which the fate of the animals was incidental.

However, the principal criticism of this episode is that the Game Department took no part in it and failed to investigate and find a satisfactory solution for a resource that had been successfully conserved over many decades by the previous owners of Tana ranch.

Miles Coverdale

[64] Editor's note: At the time neither the Society nor Parker was aware that a few roan antelope had existed in the hinterland of Vanga, just south of the Shimba Hills in the late 1800s. This was mentioned by Jackson *op cit.*

Stan Bleazard with a typical box trap used the length and breadth of Kenya to catch lions and leopards (photo Stan Bleazard)

CHAPTER 24: LIONS IN SUBURBIA

Ron Jolley

The prolonged drought early in 1961 seriously affected Segenge and his pride. Nairobi National Park was barred to him by the Spivs (the lions of another pride), there was no game in the Ngong Reserve so, not for the first time, he and his pride entered Nairobi's Langata and Karen suburbs.

Reports began to come in of lions in residential gardens and of dogs being chased. Some people complained of bicycle and cars tyres being chewed, even ordinary garden hoses came in for the lion's attention. For two months commencing 6th April 1961, I spent many a sleepless night around the residential area looking for members of Segenge's pride.

Most people who telephoned in reports were prepared to put up with lions as long as they did no damage. In fact some Karen and Langata residents were inviting Nairobi City friends for sundowners, hoping to be able to show them the lions. Most reports came from properties on the Mbagathi River, whose south bank was thickly wooded and made a natural hideout for the pride.

The first casualties occurred when lions broke into chicken houses and killed chickens. Next a lion made towards a Mrs Wells and her small daughter, but was deflected by their dog, which was gashed in the process.

Next day with Dave McCabe of the Game Department, we found the pug marks of a lion and followed them to the Karen Country Club Golf Course and lost them on the third tee. Returning in the evening with rifles, we astonished many golfers, who must have thought there was an escaped convict in the area. We were particularly worried about children on ponies who often rode in the vicinity most evenings, and warned the Club Secretary of our fears. Sure enough, next day one of two girls on ponies, riding on the course was thrown when her horse reared suddenly. Both horses bolted followed by the unseated rider. Presumably the horses had scented lions.

Next lions had mauled a horse belonging to a Mr Fielding, who lived close to the Golf Course. Dave McCabe and I arrived with three rangers and a veterinary officer to stitch up the wounded horse. The ground was iron hard and we could not follow their trail. At dusk I returned to the Fieldings'. I stopped on a small rise and swept the beam of a spotlight in a circle around the property. Several pairs of eyes were reflected and three lions moved out of scrub behind the stables. They crouched on our approach and I had my first look at them.

They seemed in good condition and were not really afraid of my vehicle. Certain that if I could get them moving in the direction of the Ngong Reserve they would leave the suburbs, I put my vehicle between them and the bushes, and I slung a couple of thunder flashes at them. As these went off the lions ran round the Land Rover back into the bushes and my plan had failed. Within half an hour the lions moved out and again approached the stables. That was when I decided that one would have to be shot.

Within an hour Dave McCabe, Harry Williams and young Richard Leakey were conferring in my Land Rover while the lions, quite conscious of our presence, lolled, cleaned themselves, played around and paid us no attention.

We moved the Land Rover away from the stables to make the lions come further into the open, which they did. We shot one and he dropped immediately. We went closer and Dave put another shot into him to make sure. The two others disappeared into the bushes for a while, but when they reappeared I decided to trap them. Dave McCabe was formally responsible as the lions were in his area, and disagreed. He wanted them shot to minimise further risk and cost. However, as one against several, he agreed to one attempt at trapping.

Two box traps, one of wood and the other of metal, were put in place and a bait dragged to leave a scent trail the lions would have cross if they approached the Fieldings' horses.

Instead of the normal triggers, the two drop doors were held open by iron bars to which I attached wires that a watcher in a nearby vehicle could pull at the right moment. My watch commenced at midnight to learn that the lions had shown up after ten o'clock. They had eaten some meat scraps along the drag, then wandered near the traps, but had shown no interest in them, eventually lying down nearby just at the edge of the bush. Some time later a couple of hyaena appeared, had entered the traps and started chewing at the bait. Len Bonnett, an honorary Warden, fearing they would remove all bait, moved up in his Land Rover. The traps obstructed his view of the lions. He did not realise they, too, had noticed the hyaenas and were moving over to the traps themselves. Len and the lions reached the traps at same time, followed by the hasty departure of both lions and hyaena. Thus I took over with nothing near the traps.

It was a wonderful night with the moon making everything as clear as daylight. There was not a breath of air, and we could hear a train chugging up the gradient to Kibera. Over at the Fieldings' house all was quiet. The Press and photographers, who had been there earlier in the evening, had tired of waiting and gone home. About half an hour after we came on duty, a jackal was sniffing around. Another soon joined the first and it was not long before they smelt the bait and were eating the scraps outside the traps. We could hear them chewing the meat, and the lions did too, because they re-appeared on the scene.

The jackal moved off and the larger lion entered the metal trap making the door rattle slightly: he shot out in double quick time. He lay down and looked up at the door silhouetted against the night sky, but was soon up again, entering the wooden trap. This was too much for his companion who also came along. The first lion came out of the trap and the other went in. For a while they took it in turns to enter the wooden trap and feed, ignoring the metal trap. With time they became more confident. Once one knocked against the metal trap, which rattled, and both shot away a few feet, but were soon back feeding. The bigger lion had been in the trap for some time when the smaller one decided it was his turn to have a bite. We almost had them together in the same trap but at the last moment the bigger one reversed out and lay down outside and washed himself.

Finishing his ablutions, he rolled over on to his back and his attention was caught by the trip wires running from the traps to the Land Rover. Curious, he tried to reach them. Standing against the wooden trap he then took the iron bar holding the door up in his mouth and pulled. The door closed with a bang. There was a terrific clamour from the lion inside the trap, whilst the other beat a hasty retreat. The captive was in a frenzy and for a while we doubted if the trap would hold together, but eventually he quietened down.

An hour later the second lion came back out of the bushes and lay down in view of the traps while his companion alternately filled the night with angry roars or attacked the bait. After ten minutes the free lion rose and walked straight into the second trap. Pip Fielding pulled the trip wire and we had him.

At daybreak the Press was contacted and a message was put over the radio informing the public. Transport was laid on and just after nine o'clock we had both traps on the back of a lorry and driven to the Mokoyeti Gorge in the Nairobi Park. Both lions made headline news that morning and there was quite an audience to see their release.

All being ready I heaved on the rope, but the trap doors jammed. I was unaware that one had in fact opened about three inches. I did not know that the inmate had inserted a paw under the slightly raised door and was progressively levering the door up until he was able to emerge completely and drop to the ground. The onlookers could see this and were shouting and blowing their hooters. Why, I did not know, but it stopped me in my tracks. The lion, now free, turned my direction, but the poor animal was so frightened it just flashed past me, its only aim being to gain the safety of the scrub as quickly as possible. The other trap door was still stuck fast so I fixed it and the second lion wasted no time in joining his companion.

The eventual cost of lion activities in Karen and Langata was three hundred head of poultry killed, one horse and two dogs mauled, several people including a lady and her small child badly scared, three lions shot, four trapped, four lionesses and two cubs returned to the park or Ngong Reserve. The last in this series of incidents when lions entered suburbia is described in the *East African Standard* of Monday 22nd May 1961: -

> *"Undeterred by the sight of the Game Department officers rigging a lion trap on the edge of the fairway near the 17th hole, four semi-finalists determinedly pursued the Men's Golf Championship around the Karen Country Golf Club course at the weekend. A notice outside the Club House warned members to be on their guard near the 15th, 16th and 17th holes, and they were told that on the Friday night, a zebra meat bait hung from a tree had been*

taken. When two finalists, Mr L Griffith and Mr S A Keane, reached the course yesterday to continue the contest, they learned that a young lion had been trapped after a night long vigil by 16 year old Richard Leakey, son of Dr L S B Leakey, curator of the Coryndon Museum. But as Richard also reported seeing a young lioness in the area the warning notice stayed up outside the Club House. The Club Secretary, Mr G A Wood, said that the first he knew of the presence of lions on the Course was a Game Department warning on Friday."

Bryan (Nick) Carter: 'Carter-the-Darter'

CHAPTER 25: THE GAME CAPTURE UNIT

John King

It was October 1964 and Nick Carter's swansong. The 8th Independent Reconnaissance Squadron of the British Army Air Corps was providing an Alouette helicopter for the rhino darting. I loaded the dart for Nick, with our experimental mixture of etorphine (M99, Reckitt & Sons Ltd.) and phenicyclidine (Sernylan, Parke, Davis & Co.) and watched him fly eastwards towards the Athi River from Kiboko. He returned sometime later and informed me "it's down" and that the helicopter would take me to the rhino and then guide the vehicles in. I was whirled over the *Commiphora* woodland and deposited in a clearing near the rhino. The helicopter then departed.

The bush seemed very quiet, not even a rhino breathing. Damn it's dead, what an embarrassment! I injected an antidote into the ear vein. Whereupon the rhino stood up and stumbled off into a thicket. My next thought was: now I am going to lose it. I had no ropes with me, but managed to put a figure of eight hobble round the back legs, using the belt on my safari jacket. I then climbed a tree and waited. Fortunately the rhino was still partially drugged and remained standing in a bush which obstructed its progress. After what seemed an age, the Game Department Land Rover arrived, and Corporal Ekusi and Game Scouts from the Capture Unit quickly roped and cast it. While we waited for the lorry, Paulo the driver asked me if I was going to take over the Unit. "No," I said, "I am going back to finish my PhD at Cambridge and expect to work on breeding in race horses". Fifteen months later I was back in Kenya heading the Game Capture Unit (GCU), following the tragic death of Nick's successor, Barry Chapell[65].

Game capture was already well established when I joined the Game Department in February 1966, as Tom Carr Hartley, a professional trapper, was moved to point out in a 'welcoming' letter to a Nairobi newspaper. He was right of course. There were many professional trappers, who supplied the zoos and new safari parks of the world with practically any African animal or bird. Their expertise was frequently called upon to help in conservation efforts. There were also wildlife rescue teams in Kenya, funded by the Elsa Wild Animal Appeal, the East African Wildlife Society, and of course the GCU, headed until 1964 by Nick Carter, ex-Army Officer and Ranch Manager. Nick described his exploits, including the capture of white rhino in Uganda, in his book *'The Arm'd Rhinoceros'*, which was published in 1965.

---

[65] Editor's note: Barry Chappell and his passenger Joanna Seex died when the Piper Super Cub he was flying stalled, crashed and caught fire. Between 1900 and 1964, Barry seems to have been the only Warden of the Department to die in the course of duty.

The unconscious rhino was strapped to a sledge, then winched into a truck (courtesy John King).

The drug he used for rhinos was phenicyclidine (Sernylan, Parke, Davis & Co.). The amount required to stop a galloping adult was little short of the lethal dose, especially for pregnant cows. It caused considerable narcotic excitement. When the animal fell, it struggled violently and repeatedly thumped its head on the ground. Following these exertions, the body temperature rose to up to 40ºC (104ºF), there was profuse sweating, rapid breathing, muscle tremors and bruising of the head. During the second and third hours of recumbency the animal was quieter, becoming restless again as consciousness returned when frequent attempts to rise were thwarted by lack of equilibrium and knuckling over of the forelimbs. It was usually up within four hours but remained ataxic for a further four hours. Whether phenicyclidine was better or worse for an adult rhino than conventional roping, was irrelevant as far as I was concerned, because

I had the new experimental drug, M99, which was to revolutionise big game immobilisation once we had overcome the initial teething problems.

Back at base, rolling a now conscious rhino off the sledge (courtesy John King).

My search for an intramuscular tranquilliser had started in 1963, as a result of trying to sedate, cast and castrate one of Raymond Hook's zebroids at Nanyuki. The animal demolished Raymond's flimsy crush, and reinforced the wisdom of the time, that tranquillisers made quiet horses quieter and nervous horses more excited. I returned a year later with M99, which I had been testing at Cambridge with my supervisor, Roger Short. I had a gram of crystals in a little plastic vial. The drug looked harmless enough and in solution it was colourless and odourless. However, it adhered to glassware, was about ten thousand times as potent as morphine and reputedly was absorbed through the skin. The research chemists who synthesised it had been looking for a mild, non-addictive, morphine-like drug, and were dismayed by what they had produced, particularly as it emerged on the heels of the Thalidomide horror. I am told that M99 owed its survival to the lateral thinking of a Cambridge professor of pharmacology, who declared that the drug would be ideal for the immobilisation of big game. So conservationists owe him and the firm of Reckitts a debt of gratitude. I also like to think that my efforts to produce a coloured solution, which did not stick on glassware and had better sedative action, by adding Acepromazine (acetylpromazine, Boots Pure Drug Company Limited), contributed to the product that was finally marketed as Immobilon (Reckitt & Colman Limited). Acepromazine was yellow, which allowed me to keep tabs on the lethal cocktail as I made up my darts by the light of a pressure lamp in my tent.

Fortunately, the depressant effects of M99 could be partially reversed by morphine antagonists, but this has not prevented the occasional fatal accident amongst veterinarians. It was this potency of the drug that made it superior to the morphine-like drug cocktails developed by Tony Harthoorn and Ian Player for use on white rhino in Natal. The attention of wildlife veterinarians, notably Dr. Harthoorn at Nairobi University and Dr. Pienaar in Kruger National Park now turned to M99. I used the new mixture successfully on zebra in Ngorongoro Crater with Hans Klingel in 1964 and that same year started to use it in combination with Sernylan for Nick Carter's black rhino capture.

Kenya was well endowed with national parks and game reserves but still had large populations of game animals outside them. Some of this land destined for settlement held the country's only populations of a particular species or race (e.g. Thomas' (Uganda) kob, Rothschild's giraffe, roan, Hunter's antelope (hirola), and sitatunga) and it was Game Department policy to transfer them to safer places. The need for such action was illustrated by the fate of the kob at Lugari some thirty miles west of Eldoret. In August 1961, they numbered more than six hundred animals; by 1966 there were none left.

Translocation generated a certain amount of criticism, particularly from visiting ecologists, but the debate was largely academic, because the majority of translocations failed. For example, by the mid 60s, there was no trace of the thirteen kob released in Meru Game Reserve in 1960, or of the thirty four released in the Masai Mara Reserve in 1961. In this volume Miles Coverdale has reported the complete failure to translocate roan.

It was apparent that more thought and effort was needed to overcome the problems of translocation, for example, by catching adult females and their followers, which might stay together when let out, and holding them at the release site until they had settled in. I tried to apply these principles to the translocation of Rothschild's giraffe at the end of 1967. Mine was the seventh attempt in ten years. The first three attempts had been to drive giraffe from the Endebess plain down the rocky escarpment to the Riwa Location of West Suk, and involved two hundred Suk (today called Pokot) tribesman, forty mounted volunteers as well as Game Department staff. Dart immobilisation of animals in the Kitale area in 1959 and 1962 was not very successful, but seven out of nine giraffe roped by the Elsa Wildlife Capture Unit in 1964 made the trip to Menengai Crater (after an initial attempt to take them to Maralal proved too arduous for them). Four of these giraffe survived and one had calved by 1968. To that date there had been twenty three giraffe mortalities, to which I added a further four during crating, holding and the long arduous trip from Soy to Maralal, despite an overnight stop.

Guiding a hooded and drugged giraffe into a capture crate (photo John King).

The operation at Soy involved the capture, by darting and roping, of about fifteen giraffe, mainly from the same group, and holding them there for at least four weeks. Most of them were then transported to Maralal, because it was at a similar altitude with adequate woody vegetation, but apparently no resident giraffe. The distance from Soy to Maralal was one hundred and seventy five miles and there were about two hundred overhead obstructions to the progress of a Bedford 4 x 4 lorry carrying an adult female giraffe standing in a crate on the back. The obstructions included power lines, one of which was touched in Nakuru. The driver informed me that there was a loud report, a flash, and a panic evacuation of the lorry by the Game Scouts. The metal runner, designed to lift lines over the crate, melted but the giraffe standing in the crate escaped with singed eyelashes. A herd of eleven animals was kept in the release pen just south of Maralal adjacent to *Acacia gerrardii* woodland; the first giraffe to arrive was kept there for six weeks and the last for one week. They were released together under the watchful eye of Libby Nesbit-Evans, and immediately split into two groups, with an adult cow in one group and her calf in the other! Nevertheless the main group of eight stayed together in the area for another fourteen weeks, before extending its range and vanishing. If ever an unusually marked individual is seen amongst the reticulated giraffe on the ranches south of Maralal, it may be from an infusion of Rothschild's genes and a legacy of our fiasco!

Some of the eleven Rothschild's giraffe that were released among the reticulated giraffe at Maralal in Samburu District (photo John King)

* * * *

Fortunately, there was one success story to emerge from this period, and that was the rescue of the black rhinoceros. There were three phases to each operation: capture, translocation and release. My initial preoccupation was to catch a rhino, and I spent some months failing to do so, and in fact running away from animals presented to me by Park Warden Ted Goss and Game Warden Ken Smith, or using too heavy a charge so that the dart broke on impact or bounced out. We did not make the job any easier for ourselves, by choosing problem animals that had to be removed from where they were a danger to people. When I considered them too difficult to catch, I offered them to professional hunters for their clients, but they never took up the offers as the vegetation was too thick and despite these being the only rhinos by then available to sportsmen.

Our ultimate challenge was to remove a marooned population of about a dozen rhinos from Nyeri Forest, where their interaction with agricultural settlements demanded action from the Game Department. The animals were elusive and the bulls aggressive. They were on the alert and, head on, presented a frontal target of horns, skull and sloping shoulders which deflected the dart. The chest, although suitable, was usually hidden in foliage, but one cow was successfully immobilised when the dart stuck in her lip. We therefore called on the buffalo control packs of Bill Winter, Game Department, Nanyuki, and Ken Clark, Forestry Department, Nyeri to see if they would bay up a rhino and give me a lateral shot. I think these were the first and only attempts to capture rhinos with the use of dogs.

My field notes record that on our first sortie, Ken's dogs:–

> *...put up a large cow at 10:35 am and we caught up with her about an hour later standing in a thicket in the forest with her head held high to avoid the attentions of a 'Tumutumu' terrier. Ken persuaded me to crawl on my stomach into the thicket with Sergeant Kanampio as support gun and dart the rhino behind the shoulder.*

Following that success we spent a few fruitless and frustrating days with hunting dogs on the loose, chasing buffalo, and eventually decided to try and control the situation by taking only a few from the pack and keeping them on leads until we contacted a rhino. The first time we tried this new approach was with Jack Barrah, Game Warden Nyeri and his Sergeant Kanampio. Here is what I wrote at the time.

> *This morning we took out four of Ken Clark's buffalo dogs, with Jack Barrah and Kanampio as guns. We picked up fresh tracks, across a forest road, of two adult rhino. We turned off into the forest, Kanamapio first, with a dog and handler next, then Jack, myself, Ekusi and two other dog handlers. All the dogs were kept on leads. The cover consisted of low shrubs, reducing visibility to about 15 yards, interspersed with trees. I was just beginning to sharpen my senses for the morning's work, when there was a noise of leaves being brushed aside. For a split second I was delighted; it must be a rhino and it did not sound aggressive. Almost at once it emerged dead ahead and coming at speed. We were moving right, towards a tree but the rhino, head down, was swinging with us. Jack was just ahead and to my right; he fired; but the charge was not checked and the rhino was turning sharply towards its target. That long, hard, curved, black horn was going to hit me in the guts, and I flattened my stomach for the impact. It was surprising that I could not turn faster than the rhino; I seemed*

Perhaps the most exciting rhino darting of all: trying to bay them up in thick forest with Ken Clark's buffalo dogs (photo Peter Beard).

Ken Clark (later killed by shifta on Galana) and John King after rhino in the Nyeri forest, the tension showing (photo Peter Beard).

Rarely, in the forest, did one get a reasonable broadside shot (photo Peter Beard).

Almost more difficult than the hunt, was getting a truck to the unconscious rhino (photo Peter Beard).

leaden-footed, as in a dream. There was a second shot and the beast slipped on to its left shoulder, almost as if it was cornering too fast – but it did not get up.

So there it was; a vivid sequence, all over in the time it takes for a rhino to charge forty yards. Kanampio had seen the rhino standing watching him at thirty yards, and as he ran back to us it had charged. There had been none of the 'normal' rhino histrionics of snorts and puffs, just immediate, silent, lethal intent. Jack's first shot under the eye failed to deflect the charge, but as the animal passed he fired the second barrel. The rhino fell three to four feet in front of me. Moral: when on fresh tracks, release two dogs to prevent a surprise attack, because you hear very little when surrounded by panting dogs straining at their leashes.

Five days later we let fourteen dogs loose after the noise of departing rhinos, which turned out to be a cow and calf. The pack engulfed the calf, leaving the cow charging around the periphery, making the approach very difficult in the thick undergrowth. I climbed a tree and managed to lodge a dart in her withers and as she collapsed I shouted to photographer Peter Beard, "never mind the photos, save the calf", whereupon he hurled his camera into a bush and dived into the pack. Despite his best efforts the calf was so lacerated and sore she was rejected by her mother and died thirty hours later. After this setback, we took stock of the situation. We had darted three cows and one bull successfully at ranges of five to twenty metres after about twenty hunting hours per animal and shot two bulls in self-defence at ranges of four metres or less; we had savaged a calf and left another in the forest. It was time to abandon darting on foot.

Prior to the footwork, we had used the Wilkenair Hughes 300 helicopter, flown by Dave Woodhead, to catch rhino at Kiboko, and now decided to try it in the forest. At the altitude of Nyeri (more than 2,100 m), the helicopter performed like an autogyro, and Dave had to risk stalling (which he did once, recovering with his skids clipping the top of a tree) as he slowed for me to get a shot at a stationary rhino in the glade below. The animals came into the glades after 17:00 hours and once darted disappeared into the forest. The trick was to throw a lavatory roll down as a streamer to locate the point at which to pick up the tracks as dusk descended, because the nearest landing clearing was up to a kilometre away. The first attempt was successful, and we had a cow back in the pens at Park HQ, Mweiga, within two hours of darting.

The second occasion was more involved, because I had failed to mark the spot with a choo-roll (choo-roll a roll of toilet paper) and the ground was dry. I thought I saw the dart strike home in the rhino's neck just before he reached the trees and disappeared. Half an hour later, at 17:30 hours we picked up tracks of a rhino moving at speed deep into the forest. At 18:10 we were confronted with two sets of tracks and chose the left hand one, because the bias towards a circle was the only hint that the rhino might be slightly drugged. By 18:25 we had more or less lost the tracks and it was almost dark when we observed signs that a rhino had crashed downhill across our path. We then heard a regular noise which was either a rhino breathing or chewing.

We moved gingerly down the slope to a stream whose far bank rose vertically twenty to thirty feet. There in the stream was the rhino still standing, but wedged between steep banks with its face in the mud. It took ten minutes to get ropes on it, two hours to carry a block and tackle in and haul it out of the stream, three hours to carry the heavy sledge (160 kg) in and roll the animal onto the sledge. Meanwhile a twenty five strong labour gang was progressing through the forest armed with axes, pangas and shovels, led by Charles Moore brandishing a power saw to great effect in the dark. At midnight, seven hours after darting, the Bedford 4 x 4 lorry arrived. It took a further one and a half hours for the lorry with its load to cross the stream and clear the forest, by which time there were fears that radial paralysis might have set in because the rhino had spent too long on his side. However at 01:30 hours he was unloaded at the pens, stood up without assistance, and by 04:00 hours was eating *Euphorbia*, pushing at the walls and sniffing the cow in the next-door pen. He was a magnificent bull weighing 1150 kg and with a front horn over two feet (63 cm) long.

He was moved to Nairobi Park ten days later and released eleven days after that. As a publicity stunt, the exercise was a great success. Named the Brigadier, after Pat Hughes (Deputy Director of National Parks), the rhino even got his picture in the Brazilian press as "*questo rinoceronte, uno dei piu grandi del mondo ...verrà poi posto in libertà nel Parco nazionale.*" However, catching rhinos in the forest in the dark could hardly be recommended as a routine!

* * * *

Thereafter the strategy was changed in favour of stocking National Parks from areas due for settlement where rhinos could be darted from the Land Rover or helicopter. The latter, flown by Dave Woodhead or Stuart Whitehead, proved the most effective, but required financial support from the revolving rhino rescue fund of the East African Wildlife Society. At the height of operations, twenty eight rhinoceroses were caught during eleven hunting days in twenty five helicopter hours. The logistics of the exercise required assistance from professional trappers, notably Willie Kilian who had joined the GCU, Tony Parkinson and Barry White from the John Seago unit, and also Ken Stewart. The trappers were paid in kind with rhino calves which they often roped themselves and which we felt were best separated from their mothers anyway.

Freshly caught rhinos were put in smooth walled pens, to reduce self-inflicted injury during the first day or two. Thereafter, most animals settled down and could be fed into travelling crates and be ready to travel in about four days. On the day of departure the crate door was dropped, and the rhino loaded and transported without delay. Vehicle motion distracted the animal from smashing the crate and it travelled quietly, standing or lying down, and feeding at halts.

John King, alias 'King John'.

Rhino reception pens were built in Tsavo East and West, the Aberdares and Nairobi National Parks. They were luxurious with shade and wallows in the low country and wooden benches covered with dry grass in Nairobi. The floor required a solid base of hard core, topped with murram. The idea was to be able to keep the animals in as long as necessary (one to three weeks) after arrival. Then one evening the pen door would be opened when the staff went home. Next morning when they returned, they would sometimes find the rhino asleep in the doorway, or wandering around the outside of the pens. Usually, the new release had explored a bit further, but was very cautious about intruding on a resident rhino's home range. One bull in prime condition was found dead some weeks after release into Nairobi Park with abscesses deep in the neck muscles, presumably caused from fights. Another old bull was so marginalized that he took up residence along the Magadi Road fence line, and got his photograph into *The Daily Nation* standing amongst the chickens behind a Park Ranger's hut.

Rhino 51, named Gentian Violet, transferred to Nairobi, worked away at her pen in the middle of the night and, after breaking three six inch diameter cross poles without waking the watchman, escaped. Instead of going into the Park she made for the Warden's house, a quarter of a mile away, and crossed the game grid, skinning her legs in the process. The Park Warden, Denis Kearney, heard a noise and shone his torch through the glass sliding door, and was confronted by a rhino. Fortunately, she turned and made her way through the vegetable garden and broke through the nine-inch square barbed wire mesh into the army barracks. Next morning, army routine was somewhat disrupted until the rhino retired to some long grass and scrub by the fence. I was in Nairobi, but my dart immobilisation equipment was at Darajani. Fortunately I managed to get a radio message through to have it sent up to reach me by that afternoon. Here is what I wrote at the time:–

> *"4 p.m. We drove through the barrack gates and the sentry said something about – 'at last you've come', which seemed rather melodramatic until we followed his arm pointing across the parade grounds where a wide awake rhino had the nearest huts in a state of siege. When we were about 30 yards from her she focussed her attention on our Land Rover. Her head was very high and her ears pointing forwards. She took a few investigatory steps forward and as Paulo dithered with a three-point turn, she came in earnest. We had no choice but to trundle down the track towards the married quarters the rhino firmly latched onto the transom. After about 200 yards she veered off to the right and we tried to shape up for a shot. While Paulo tried to decipher Tony's and my conflicting instructions and extricate us from a cul-de-sac, the rhino charged again and we took flight right into the midst of the barracks, emerging on a grass pitch. The pitch had barbed wire on one side, and a monsoon drain on another – and as we burst into this enclosure we only just avoided the ditch. So this was going to be the scene of battle – I felt we were gladiators in a Roman amphitheatre – hundreds of spectators emerged from the long barrack huts on all sides. We twisted and turned trying to wrest the initiative from this aggressive animal. After each chase the rhino would veer off and stand trying to focus on the wall of noise which surrounded us and then out of the corner of its eye it would note our approach for a close shot at the rump or the neck. Spinning round furiously it would send the Land Rover scrambling out of the way with Tony complaining that we were turning on too tight a lock and could easily be rolled if that angry, armoured head and massive neck and shoulders hit the wing and not the tail board. It seemed a long time before I was presented with a shot (which would not risk a ricochet into the crowd) and planted a dart in the right buttock. We stood back and the rhino trotted through the*

crowd which melted away at its approach only to reform at once, as if expecting the animal to collapse immediately. Collapse it did, 15 minutes later in a marshy stream – no doubt crawling with bilharzia. The Capture Unit worked as best it could, hemmed in by hundreds of noisy, discourteous soldiers. When ordered off my Land Rover I noted one even picked up a rock. They were a curious mixture of naïve wonder at the rhino – feeling the skin, poking at the face – and brusque soldierlyness, which nevertheless did not hide an unpleasant discourtesy and lack of discipline.

This same rhino when returned to its pen, climbed the water trough and scraped its chin and forelegs on the top of the pen – which had to be heightened. It was now covered with scrapes and required treatment with chloromycetin, and gentian violet. The last two solutions were sprayed on to the rhino with a stirrup pump, which is how she acquired her name.

Gentian Violet was released in good order on the night of 31 March and moved about a mile into the triangle of scrub between the Warden's track and the main exit road. She frequently returned to the pens to eat browse cut for the rhinos still being held. She was often observed from cars and Land Rovers at ranges of as little as ten yards, and sometimes appeared in the headlights blocking the exit road in the evenings. There were no incidents however. On the evening of 25 April she was seen browsing the bushes in the watercourse below the main dam, and on the following days was missing from her home range below the pens. During the last week in April and the beginning of May it rained very heavily. Heavy rain often induces a change in the movements of rhino and Gentian Violet must have moved gradually eastwards out on to the plains. Because many of the roads were impassable during that week, there was little traffic in the Park and consequently little disturbance to the rhino's tentative explorations on to the open plains. On Saturday 4th May the sun shone brightly and after 24 hours without rain the cars came pouring into the Park. 'Gentian Violet' probably slept unnoticed in the long grass East of Lone Tree and at about 1700 hrs woke and started to browse the whistling thorn. She was spotted, and so harassed and hounded by cars that she decided to make a dash for the security of her old range on the edge of the forest.

I too was in the Park that afternoon with my wife and baby son, *incognito* in my Peugeot saloon, so I can give the account from my notes: -

"A sunny Saturday afternoon in Nairobi Park, not much to see as the grass is so tall. Stop and watch the baboons playing round a car, the youngsters tumbling and pulling each other's tails. Drive across the Mokoyeti river at Lone Tree drift, past microbuses stuck in their futile efforts to reach the lions. Reduced to photographing the red-feathered heads of the seeding grasses.

17.20 hrs, looking left across the valley – there is a black shape moving westwards on the far slope. I turn back the way we have come and shadow the shape. A cow rhino moving at a fast trot with her head carried high, and obviously in a very agitated state. Horn profile, sex and ears suggest that it is Gentian Violet - No.51. Parallel to her on the road is a white Mercedes hire car kicking up dust in his efforts to keep with her. At No.5 the rhino crosses the south side of the main road and disappears over the brow. The Mercedes jams on the brakes, does a three-point turn, and drives back towards us. I stop the driver who is bubbling over with enthusiasm and he tells me all about the rhino. "Why was she so upset?" I ask. He looks at me as if I am a spoilsport and drives off. We continue westwards towards No.4 the rhino has swung back on to the road. Beyond her, round the sweep of the bend I can see three cars facing in our direction, stationary amongst the baboons. The die is cast. The rhino swings round the bend head up, ears forward. Will she trot past the cars or...? Quick as a flash she lowers her head and breaks into a gallop, snorting like a locomotive. She crashes into the radiator grill in blind fury and her momentum somersaults her back legs high into the air and her body is thrown across the front of the windscreen front feet on the bonnet and she slithers down backwards off the passenger's side of the car. The thought flashes through my mind that she may be severely injured. But the moment her feet touch the ground she is skidding round the back of the car after a Citroen that is making good its escape. Then the rhino resumes her way, trotting westwards down the road. We drive up to the stricken car, a Holden Premier with a green body and white roof, registration No.KKH187. The driver winds down his window to greet us: 'there goes my no claim bonus' - the under statement of the year - and continues his drive round the Park. We do not wish to lose sight of the rhino in case she is confronted with any more obstacles in her homeward path. We take the service road via hyaena dam and find her way ahead trotting over its hard murram, tail down and wet with sweat. She joins the tarmac road by the main dam, and turns up towards the Warden's house and the triangle of tall grass and scrub below the release pens. She is home, and only then does she slow down to a walk and slip contentedly in amongst the bushes to stand quietly about 10 yards off the track. The time is 17.50 hrs and she has covered 4 miles and sorted out a car in passing all in 30 minutes. The degree of her anxiety can be judged from the ferocity of her charge at the car that blocked her escape: usually a rhino starts braking at the moment of impact and delivers powerful hooks with its horns. The momentum of this charge carried the whole rhino up and over the bonnet like a pole-vaulter.

That same evening a rhino (thought to be a bull and with a green ear tag in the right ear and identified as No.38, which had been released in April 1967) was confronted by a Ford Zephyr, KHK 613, driving down as he walked up from Mokoyeti Gorge towards the Leopard Cliffs turnoff. The driver stopped and switched the engine off. The bull continued to advance at a leisurely pace and, as he passed the car, hammered the radiator grill three times, perforating the radiator, lifting the bonnet, and smashing the near headlight.

* * * *

During my term in charge of the GCU, we successfully translocated sixty rhinos from areas where they were not wanted, to others where they were. The translocation operation to Nairobi NP was the most successful. Rhino had vanished from what became Nairobi Park before 1920. Nick Carter had made the first reintroductions since they disappeared so that there were possibly half a dozen there when I took over the GCU. To those residents we then added a further twenty two rhinos between November 66 and March 68 to bring the total population to about thirty at the end of that year (according to Patrick Hamilton). He studied the release phase and identified eighteen of the translocated animals three to thirty three months after their release. Two died, one from fighting and one from a jaw infection, leaving only two translocated animals unaccounted for.

The fate of rhinos released in Tsavo East, West and the Aberdares NP is unknown. All three parks had large rhino populations at that time, and so it was probably a case of 'coals to Newcastle', although David Sheldrick chose the location for the Tsavo East pens below the new lodge at Voi, where there seemed to be space. Then the rhino population in Tsavo and much of the low country was decimated by drought, starvation and poaching, suffering a worse fate than the British coal industry, and the perception of rhino translocation changed.

Fortunately, the story does not end there. According to figures published by Rob Brett, one-time Rhino Programme Coordinator for Kenya Wildlife Service (KWS) in the 90s, Nairobi National Park received a further half dozen rhinos in the 1970s, when the emphasis changed to stocking Solio Ranch, which received twenty two rhinos during that decade. By 1995, Nairobi National Park and Court Parfet's Solio Ranch had produced eighty seven black rhinos to stock other places. The park had sent out twenty six and retained a population of sixty four. Solio had sent sixty one rhinos to other parks and reserves, and retained fifty.

Since then other areas are producing new stock and the list of introductions (Lewa Downs twenty five, Lake Nakuru National Park twenty one, Tsavo West

National Park twenty two, Meru National Park two, Ol Pejeta Ranch twenty, Ol Jogi Ranch four, and Tsavo East National Park twenty) now tops 114.

It was in connection with the last restocking of Tsavo from Nairobi, that I found myself in correspondence with Dr Brett about the sources of the original rhinos brought to Nairobi and the risk of their succumbing to trypanosomaiasis (the disease transmitted by tsetse flies), which we discounted. He ended one letter by stating, "The success of the rhino programme here owes a lot to the continuing high breeding rates and surplus of animals available from Nairobi National Park, in turn very many thanks to your foresight and the original translocation of rhinos to Nairobi all that time ago." I have to admit that we were not that clairvoyant. Nevertheless, it is a nice thank you, and I would like to extend it to my colleagues, predecessors and successors. This story reveals an unbroken thread of determined conservation through thirty turbulent years, which Martin Mulama, the current Head of the Rhino Programme at KWS, is continuing.

Ian Grimwood

CHAPTER 26: NIGHT BLINDNESS & SHIFTA

Stan Bleazard

At the end of January 1961 I met Chief Game Warden Ian Grimwood late one afternoon in the South Horr valley, where we camped under a full moon. It was my first time on safari with my chief, and a good time for us to become acquainted. The valley was a veritable woodland of acacia trees with well-grazed grass beneath, making it ideal for camping almost anywhere. Beside us a spring fed stream ran for a few hundred yards before disappearing into the sand river and it was indeed a beautiful place. I remember it for the large numbers of galagos I saw moving in the moonlight along the treetops. During the night a leopard called, its rasping ripsaw sounds a delight to hear. As we broke camp in the morning, a large solitary bull elephant with short thick tusks, maybe a sixty-pounder, came marching down the sand river. Everyone kept dead still as he approached and passed by at fifty yards on his way to the dry country.

At Balessa Kulal we met professional hunter Andrew Holmberg and his clients who had been shooting sand grouse and had stayed on at the wells to watch falcons and lammergeyers and other activity. We motored on, up the approach track to South Kulal. Ian being a keen naturalist and ornithologist, we stopped frequently to observe all that caught his eye. We found signs of rhino on the slopes and higher up we met a small herd of greater kudu. Entering the tree zone we were dismayed to find large numbers of Samburu cattle, which were being taken to water deep inside the forest. Higher still, where there were no further signs of them, we made camp late in the afternoon.

With barely four hours of daylight remaining, we set out for a brisk walk to the summit and beyond, to view the knife-edge which joins the northern and southern halves of the mountain. The track was indistinct most of the way, as it meandered on top and along each side of a sharp ridge crest for most of the distance and we were going to be pushed to get there and back before dark. The two Scouts guiding us, Lenjetin and Lenduroni knew the way however, and we made good progress. At one place we came upon a deep hole in the path where a tree had been blown over, its roots having lifted out a great volume of earth as it fell. We had to make a careful detour of both tree roots and hole on the steep upslope, and with fortunate prescience, I asked the Scouts to remember the spot on our return.

Stepping out of forest we were favoured with clear air and a magnificent view of the setting sun across Lake Rudolf 6000 feet below. South Island and Nabuyatom (Von Höhnel's Crater), normally starkly visible from the moment the lake is in view, were from here almost indiscernible. In the distance to the southwest we could see the Cherengani Hills and possibly Mount Elgon beyond. To the south, Mount Nyiru looked impressive while to the east, Marsabit appeared insignificant. So taken were we with the panorama that we almost overlooked a greater kudu bull watching us from beyond the knife-edge, on the north side of the mountain.

A kudu bull was watching us from beyond the knife-edge (photo Peter Davey).

We did not linger. We were soon back in the forest and for a time we made a rapid descent. It was not long before decreasing visibility slowed us and while we were still stepping lively I noticed my chief was having difficulty keeping up, which had not been the case coming up. When it got completely dark, Ian kept losing his footing and stumbling and we had to proceed dead slow. Even this did not stop him falling. Finally the realization hit me that he was totally night blind. This was probably as a result of his long incarceration as a Japanese prisoner of war, in abominable conditions of forced labour on the Burma Railway. I got the lead Scout Lenduroni to remove his khaki jersey to expose the almost white merduff shirt beneath, which I could see quite clearly from behind Ian, but even this did not help much. It became obvious he would have to be physically led. Guided by holding the Scout's rifle by the muzzle, Ian could follow a step at a time and we moved along at snail's pace.

Lenduroni stopped when we arrived at the hole left by the blown-down tree, and I proposed tying Ian's trouser belt with two rifle slings to aid him across but he would have none of it. He felt confident he said, that he could safely follow if we continued the way we had been doing. In daylight there would have been no problem at all, just as we had done earlier. Now I had my doubts but not wanting to argue, I let his wish prevail. Lenjetin and I got across, then found a sapling and bent it back for Lenduroni, a short fellow, to take hold and he came over. Lenduroni and I held the sapling that Ian caught with one hand, and leaning over the hole, Lenjetin gave him the rifle muzzle to hold in the other. With two hands firmly attached I felt sure Ian would get across and I told him to step forward when he was ready.

I suppose it is always a matter of faith for a blind man to step where he cannot see and while Ian's first was firm his second, from which he would have been able to step to safety, gave way. Not being able to see, I was aware only that Ian released both hands and slid quickly into the hole, arriving at the bottom with a sickening thump. I called out to him and not immediately getting a response I feared the worst. Perhaps he was only concussed, I hoped. Climbing down to help would probably end with me falling on top of him and I hesitated. Just when I was wondering what else I could do, we heard sounds of movement in the hole. Eventually Ian muttered that he thought he was all right, but that his leg was injured. What joy, what relief to hear his voice. He was alive and I had been spared reporting to the world how I had disposed of my Chief.

I asked him if he could stand up. He said nothing for a long time, then I heard movement and he told us he was standing. We tried bending the sapling further down until it finally snapped. We broke it off, removed foliage and made a ten-foot pole of it. Lenjetin and I climbed into the hole, each of us in turn losing hold and landing on our butts. I persuaded Ian to get up and stand on Lenjetin's shoulders, from which position Lenduroni was able to heave him out with the pole. I followed but we had some difficulty getting Lenjetin out. Ian said he would be able to walk and we prepared to leave, only to find Lenjetin's rifle missing. It had not gone down the hole, we felt certain, yet search as we might we could not find it. A chill wind had started and we left the rifle until daylight. Reaching camp near midnight, a lamp showed a four-inch gash on Ian's shin, which must have been painful. He never complained and we continued our safari for another six days. Only when he returned to Nairobi did he get medical help. Though several stitches were applied, the wound took weeks to heal.

* * * *

At the beginning of my time in Kenya's Northern Frontier, the term shifta still meant equestrian brigands who came down from the Borana Ethiopian highlands to kill big game, take ivory and rhino horn and, if the opportunity arose, to attack nomadic Rendille or Samburu manyattas to secure human scrota, and livestock. Armed with rifles and lances, they came only late in a good rainy season when there was abundant forage for their mounts. At such times, big game could be caught in the open, many miles from their usual habitats. Less numerous than formerly, travelling in as few as a couple, these shifta could cover seventy miles or more overnight, alternately riding or trotting beside their stout, wooden-saddled, ponies. At dawn they would stand watch for chance opportunities; during the day they rested in shade while their ponies grazed, confident that Government vehicles never moved in the wet conditions. For sheer elusiveness and endurance, these stalwart adventurers had their secret admirers, even if their presence was abhorred. We found evidence of them every year, usually in the form of slaughtered giraffe or occasionally a rhino. Twice over the years Game Scouts on patrol had engaged them in shoot outs to good effect and without casualty to themselves, saving stolen cattle and restoring herds to their owners.

In bright sunshine on the morning of Sunday 8th December 1963, I set out from Marsabit by Land Rover with one Game Scout, planning to meet Chief Game Warden Ian Grimwood at Loyengalani on Wednesday 11th. My Bedford 4 x 4 lorry would follow with ten men. I was allowing three days for contingencies, which was just as well as it soon became clear there had been heavy unseasonable rain in the low country. There was plenty of mud and running water, even before reaching Segel, making for slow progress. On reaching the Helu luggah however, we found it flowing so I decided to wait for the truck. It was now about three o'clock and I expected my party to catch up soon.

On the far side a Rendille elder appeared and after signalling to us, he waded across using his spear to steady himself against the strong flow to report surprising news. He had seen shifta that morning and had walked to the trading post at Kargi to warn other people. Finding the place deserted, he had waited until he saw my Land Rover descending from the mountain and come out to meet us. There being no time to lose, we crossed the luggah immediately and proceeded on the short distance to Kargi, during which period Samburu Game Scout Lenduron began questioning the elder for details. Despite some similarities of language, it became necessary to stop for discussion and to draw sketches in the sand, to try and establish the location of the shifta, how far away they were, and plan an approach to their position by vehicle before trying to make contact with them on foot. With no sign of my men on the lorry, but now short of time, we set off under the direction of the Rendille to find the shifta.

Following a cattle trail, we came to a deep and impassable erosion gully and it became clear that the old man had little idea of where a vehicle could or could not travel. To detour the obstacle we had to backtrack a couple of miles. We then came onto a thick outgrowth of low acacia bush. With no way round it, we had to slowly force a passage before finally emerging into open country at the edges of the Chalbi depression, where our man announced we should dismount.

Almost at sunset we set off on foot, our guide marching at a cracking pace. We had walked for barely ten minutes when Lenduron spotted two men on horseback in full flight heading north across the Chalbi flats, their white turbans and garments streaming behind them. Without a second thought I sent a bullet past them that caused their mounts to veer into shallow water into which a rider was pitched. Thinking that I had shot him, the Rendille shouted gleefully and commenced running to the spot about half a mile away. The other rider managed to catch his partner's pony, return to collect him and make off again, with a few more mis-directed shots to hasten them on their way. We followed to where the rider fell. The shifta had lost a sandal and a cloth bag, which contained 8mm cartridges. There was no sign of blood.

Retracing their mounts' spoor, we found where they had spent the day in a shady gully, undoubtedly the same one that had caused us to detour. Like most hastily arranged plans, ours had failed, and my only encounter with these brigands remains a disappointing memory. Had we arrived earlier, we might have had some success approaching on foot down the gully.

We returned to Kargi by nightfall expecting to find the lorry. Finding no trace, we went back to the luggah, which we found in spate. By the following morning, the flow had eased considerably and we were able to cross over and eventually locate the lorry bogged in a huge mud hole. Eventually, after further nights spent with similar difficulties on the road, we met up with our Chief.

* * * *

When Kenya achieved independence, the term shifta changed to include those disenchanted Kenya Somalis who wanted their home and neighbouring lands to be ceded to Somalia. Armed with modern rifles, itinerant gangs of them took to the bush on foot, which they knew well, pursuing their political and religious objectives by challenging Government authority and terrorizing people generally.

Easter Monday 30th March 1964 passed quietly enough. In the evening, muted sounds of human activity came from the shops and village situated a half-mile from the Game Department outpost. When I went to sleep that night there were no sounds out of the ordinary.

Awaking with a start I stared through the open window into bright moonlight outside, I was unsure whether I had dreamt or actually heard the distinctive crack and thump of a bullet. The luminous hands of the clock on my bedside table were almost together at two. In the next few seconds another shot passed just above my cottage. I scrambled from my bed and in the darkness found my service rifle, loaded ten rounds in the magazine, then sat within shadow on the veranda watching the approaches. More shots, (fortunately not towards me) and distant shouting from the village, made me realise this must be the shifta attack promised by rumour since January.

Sporadic firing continued though it seemed uncoordinated and after some minutes I proceeded to the Scouts' lines and got all four available men to form a standing patrol where the forest boundary firebreak met the road, instructing them to shoot on sight. Lengthening shadows as the moon sank behind the forest gradually cast our compound into darkness, while the sounds of shooting and disturbance continued at intervals from various directions until almost dawn.

Daybreak brought typical Marsabit mist and silence, out of which Corporal Jirima, the national park Ranger emerged with his rifle slung. He lived at home on his maize plot beyond the village and he brought bad news. Like most of the the town's residents, he had taken to the bush when the disturbance started. Having only a few cartridges, he decided to use his rifle to defend himself and those gathered with him only as a last resort. They had watched the shifta moving up the ridge of settlements towards the Police lines and administrative offices, shooting as they went, assaulting anyone they found and burning many of the their empty huts. He confirmed they had come from the east and had probably returned that way.

Through a light drizzle, which further dampened our spirits, we heard a vehicle approaching. It was District Commissioner David Dale whose usual jovial demeanour was lost in the gravity of the situation. He told us all the shops had been thoroughly looted, an Indian shopkeeper killed and for the time being all Police were confined to barracks. With him were four armed Dubas (Tribal Policemen) with whom he requested I make a reconnaissance of the settled area.

Ten of us set out on foot with Jirima leading. Once in the open and away from the forest, the mist began to lift. There were no people moving and we crossed in open extended line onto the Jaldessa road where we came upon the raiders' tracks heading against us. Backtracking them, we picked up many expended .303 cartridges and one live round. All the cases bore the mark K58 that suggested to me they were of recent Kenya Government origin, though I could not recall hearing of any ammunition thefts. We moved onto the cultivated squatters' plots and there, as expected, found many burned out huts, alongside which their owners were resting in shock. Many, particularly the elderly, had been beaten during the night's onslaught.

Reaching the end of the cultivated area we crossed a thickly vegetated gully to the next ridge, intending to return around the circumference of habitation and came upon three badly shot up corpses, each instantly recognised by Jirima as a leader in the local Boran and Burji communities. They had apparently been dragged from their homes then tortured and shot.

Coming onto the ridge we followed the shiftas' departing tracks for a mile or so to where they entered thick cover. Having reconnoitred the settled area, we reported to the DC and the patrol disbanded.

After mid-morning I called my men together to review matters. What was worrying was whether our two Somali Game Scouts and two others who sympathised with the Somali cause, had been involved. All four were out on patrol separately at considerable distance from Marsabit and could not have participated. Nevertheless discussion revealed nothing except a deepening distrust of them and a fear that they might abscond with their weapons.

DC Dale made a second visit in the middle of the afternoon, wanting me to lead a fighting patrol of twenty Policemen, including a bren-gunner, to follow the shifta tracks from where we had left off in the morning. John Crossley, the senior expatriate Police officer being too busy arranging the defence and security of the station to do so. Though it was probably too late for effective action, I agreed and our patrol set off in extended file, with myself and two Scouts leading. When we reached thick cover where we had earlier left off, I split the patrol in a typical infantry flanking movement, which took some organizing, as the men had not much idea of such basic tactics. Sure enough, where they had emerged from the thicket, the shifta had ambushed their tracks, but had gone by the time we arrived. The tracks then led onto the Sagante road where the group seemed to have wandered along at a leisurely pace and we estimated their number at fourteen individuals. Further on they formed a column and moved along at a faster pace. This was to bring us along quicker and to make us less careful.

The gang left the road and followed the forest firebreak south. Approaching expansive rolling grasslands in which the route was constantly overlooked by higher ground, I split our column in two, one part moving forward, while the other remained stationary ready to give covering fire. This tactic spread us widely and made us a more difficult target at the same time as having half our force observing while the other half moved. It took time to arrange. Once the men got the hang of it, we moved along this way in dwindling daylight, alternately moving ahead then crouching until overtaken, all the time approaching a hillock which, despite its benign appearance, overlooked the firebreak.

Instinctively the men realised the threat it posed and proceeded cautiously until we were near enough for a flanking movement. The more we ascended the grassy slopes the more certain we were that there was no danger and finally reaching the top, we found a flattened area where the shifta had again lain in ambush, though this time they left us a sheet of notepaper on a stake on which was written a message. Translated, it audaciously said they had got tired of waiting all day for us and gone home!

The shifta had probably departed mid-afternoon three or four hours ahead of us and, leaving the firebreak had fanned out and split into pairs and individuals to make tracking them difficult. We selected a pair at the extreme right of the group and followed them until darkness forced a halt.

Returning to Marsabit we found defensive arrangements for the town were in place, and I made my own for the Game Department station, although it seemed a second attack was rather unlikely. Sentries were doubled and arranged in three watches, and I chose the 0300 hrs till dawn stint. To my chagrin, shots started around 2200hrs from the Police lines. This time there were intense fusillades periodically through the night that included automatic weapons. It sounded as though the shifta were trying to overrun the Police. Quite a few bullets passed us closely and peace only returned in the last hour before daylight.

As soon as it was light enough, we went into Marsabit expecting to find that the shifta had taken a fearful hiding. Disappointingly, the edgy Police had been shooting at shadows, with stray bullets damaging government buildings and the local church, wherein the Catholic priest, Father Topolini had taken refuge and recorded the night's barrage.[66] I felt compelled to have the Police exercise some arms discipline and met with ASP John Crossley, entreating him to arrange firing lanes from every sentry post, with an NCO responsible for each. A relatively quiet night followed.

The President wanted guinea fowl (photo Peter Davey).

[66] Editor's note: I have a copy. S. B.

CHAPTER 27: PRESIDENTIAL SERVICE

Stan Bleazard, David Brown & Tony Marsh

These recollections by three different authors have so much in common that, combined, they obviously make a chapter. In the three sections that follow this editorial note: the first is by Stan Bleazard, the second by David Brown and the third by Tony Marsh.

* * * *

Bleazard wrote:– In September 1964 I took leave and learned to fly. Joy Adamson's Elsa Foundation met two thirds of the costs, which for me was a great boon. Some months earlier, with encouragement from John Sutton the well known professional hunter, 'Nonnie" (Fernanda) Kellogg the American millionairess had donated a Piper Supercub aircraft to the Game Department for Wardens to use in their work.

At the end of the month, having just converted to flying the Cub, I called into headquarters for mail, where I found Ian Grimwood in somewhat of a predicament. I seem to recall that State House had just telephoned him with the request he produce a dozen guinea fowls for a banquet which His Excellency the President was giving that night, for Archbishop Makarios. Would I fly him down to Selengai, he asked?

In some haste we departed and were soon at our destination in Kajiado district searching for *kanga* (guinea fowl). We found a flock and devised a plan for me to get around the birds and drive them onto Ian. This I did successfully and Ian shot two in the air with a right and left. With his first shot however, three lionesses rocketed out of the bush behind which he had taken cover, and came bounding straight at me. I stood stock still the instant I saw the first one then, realizing in the nick of time they had not seen me, I dashed behind a substantial Acacia tortilis. Seeing me when I moved, the leader growled and changed direction, and the others followed. Ian saw them as they crossed his front and was naturally amused (perhaps thinking he had got one back on me for having dumped him in a hole on Mount Kulal). Try as we might, we succeeded in getting only another three kanga before it was time to return. Back at the office, in some desperation Ian called John Seago, who was able to supply the remainder.

Two days later I visited the office and was surprised to see a dozen dead kanga in a heap on the veranda. They had been returned by State House and apparently the Chief Game Warden was in deep disfavour. It turned out the guinea fowl had not been wanted as a gourmet dish, but to present live as a gift. Ian was absent, visiting known fowl breeders looking for a re-supply.

* * * *

Brown wrote:– Shortly after I had been appointed Head of the Kenya Game Department I received a telephone call from Assistant Commissioner of Police Ian Henderson. Henderson pioneered the use of pseudo gangs during the Emergency. He and others used to blacken their bodies and venture with their African colleagues deep into the forests of Mount Kenya and the Aberdares to locate and capture or destroy groups of terrorists. Ian's book *The Hunt for Kimathi* became a best seller.

On this occasion he was trying to help a Kikuyu fellow Police Officer called Bernard Hinga. Hinga was being groomed to command the Police Force and at that time was Head of the paramilitary General Service Unit (GSU) the armed wing of the Kenya Police. Henderson explained that President Jomo Kenyatta had contacted Hinga directly and ordered him to produce one dozen guinea fowl by Saturday morning. It was then a Monday. I asked Ian if His Excellency wanted the birds dead or alive and he was buggered if he knew. "All right," I said "Leave it with me. I'll give Bernard a call and find out. In any event I'm sure we can help you out". I called Hinga but he knew not whether quick or dead so it was arranged that I would have a dozen shot and endeavour to round up a dozen live ones to cater for both contingencies. I had in mind scrounging the live ones from my friend John Seago who trapped animals for zoos and had a menagerie at Kabete just along the road.

Alas, John had none. John Williams, the ornithologist at the Coryndon Museum, was the next hope. The museum was alongside my Headquarters and I walked across passing a very fine collection of vulturine guinea fowl in an adjacent aviary. John was busy preparing yet more bird exhibits. I explained Hinga's predicament and undertook to replace his birds if he would kindly hand over his if required. Being the generous man that he was he readily agreed but then added: – "I say. Our Chairman of Trustees, Cavendish-Bentinck, is having lunch with the old man on Wednesday. I'll ask him to have a quiet word and find out exactly what is needed." Since those close to the President were clearly absolutely terrified of him and simply did as he bade them without question, it seemed a good idea.

John said he would let me know the score first thing Thursday morning. As it happened news reached me late on the Wednesday afternoon. I forget if it was Henderson or Hinga who broke it but the message was loud and clear. Apparently His Excellency had responded to C-B's enquiry with a curt "Alive, of course" and left the table shortly afterwards. The unfortunate Hinga was then summoned to the presence. "A fine Head of the GSU you are. I ask you privately to carry out the simple task of rounding up a few kanga and two days later all of Nairobi knows about it. You are not even fit to command a night soil cart". Poor Bernard really believed he would shortly revert to constable rather than advance to Commissioner. In the event His Excellency was so impressed with the splendid Williams' birds that he almost forgave Hinga who did become Head of the Force not long afterwards.

The guinea fowl saga continued however. The very next week the Department was asked to provide another one dozen birds, on this occasion through the proper channels so to speak, in that the Minister for Wildlife & Tourism, Sam Ayodo, conveyed the directive. By great good fortune the Warden from nearby Makindu in Kamba country was in my office at the time. Barry Chappell was an adventurous do anything go anywhere tireless worker who unhappily and tragically was killed a year later when the aircraft he was piloting to spot rhinoceros for the capture team crashed and caught fire.

After the situation was explained and I said ideally we should capture, confine and care for a ready supply, Barry mentioned he had heard that if rigorously pursued, guinea fowl only flew twice and then crouched upon the ground. When you think about it, it is entirely logical. The guinea fowl is about the same size and weight as a domestic fowl with quite a small wingspan. They have to run really hard to achieve a take off and most become exhausted. The enthusiastic Chappell took off to test the theory with a couple of young fleet of foot rangers and was back within a day or two with the Presidential *kanga* in the back of his vehicle. "Worked like magic. A piece of cake," he said.

I was still a bit concerned about tying up valuable departmental resources on such trivial exercises and asked Chappell if he could leave a Kikuyu speaking Ranger with the birds, to chat up the staff and discover the purpose behind the deliveries. The word was that the Old Man wanted to stock his Githunguri property with the birds and was anxious to do so before entertaining His Highness Emperor Haile Selassie, who had been promising to pay a visit ever since the President had announced his intention to construct a highway from Nairobi to Addis Ababa. The restocking programme was not working as His Excellency had intended largely because his method was to have the birds kept on the verandah of his house until he arrived in the evening from State House in the Capital. He would then have a cup of tea or a beer, open the cage door and invite the birds to enjoy Githunguri. They immediately took wing and, with the advantage of a strong tail wind, probably first landed half way back to Makindu.

I went to see my friend and Minister. "Sam: is it possible for someone to tell the President that whereas we are honoured and delighted to provide as many guinea fowl as he likes whenever he wants them, if it is his intention to have some permanently at Githunguri they ought to be penned, fed and protected from predators otherwise they will likely try to return from whence they came."

We had no further requests for guinea fowl although that was probably because the Emperor of Ethiopia cancelled his proposed visit due to grave internal strife. But I did have one further dealing at high level so to speak. It concerned a Presidential cow.

Barry Chappell with a drugged elephant near Kiboko (photo Tony Marsh).

* * * *

Brown wrote:– Following Christmas in 1965 I arrived at my Nairobi Office to find that the Game Warden Ngong had beaten me to it. Tony Marsh was one of those happy-go-lucky types that manage to see the funny side of everything. I forget his exact words but they were along the lines of "Ha. Ha. Would you believe it? One of my Scouts has potted one of the Old Man's cows. Ha. Ha."

I confess I felt a bit like Queen Victoria. I knew that hippopotami were sometimes referred to as river cows, but a trained Game Scout should have discerned the differences between them and the domestic kind even at night. Hippo had been eating the Presidential lucerne (alfalfa). The Scout had sat up for them at night, seen the eyes of a marauding beast, and shot it stone cold dead in the lucerne. Alas, it was an imported Presidential cow that died. I told Tony that the President was presently at the coast and I would do my best to pour oil upon any troubled waters upon his return.

He departed somewhat taken aback by my serious view of the situation and muttering something about early retirement. After having telephoned the

Minister's Secretary and made an early appointment, I wondered what Archie Ritchie would have done.

"Minimise the damage. Deflect it if you can," was the imagined reply. When I met Minister Sam Ayodo I pointed out that if His Excellency's cows could get into his lucerne at night when their herder had been warned to keep them locked up lest they might be shot, it was possible that they had been causing as much damage to the Presidential lucerne as the hippo. It was difficult for Sam to go entirely ashen but he made a good attempt. I cheered him by suggesting that it was possible that the President would have such a jolly time at the coast that he would content himself with a monumental blast at the unfortunate cattle-herd. Such was probably the case because I heard no more about it.

* * * *

Marsh wrote:– It was Christmas morning, 1965, when I halted my Land Rover outside the President of Kenya's estate near Ruiru. My two Game Scouts gave unusually smart salutes, but senior Scout Digilesi Lekukuton looked terrible and thinking that he had either malaria or a monumental hangover, I asked him what was wrong... "Effendi, I have shot the President's cow."

Contemplating massive repercussions culminating in forty eight hours notice before being escorted onto an aeroplane and deported as *persona non grata* I asked Digilesi to explain.

"Bwana, we did as we were told: I walked along one bank of the river and Mbaroko the other. We had our torches on our .404s (I had managed to get clamps made which would fit a three-cell torch to the barrel of a Westley Richards .404) ready to shoot any hippo grazing on the President's lucerne." Digilesi continued, "I saw an eye in the reed bed just at the edge of the lucerne and fired."

"When did you realize that you had shot a cow and not a kiboko?" I asked.

"Effendi, it went "moo" as it went down."

I exchanged Digilesi and Mbaroko for two other Game Scouts with the object of splitting their duties over the Christmas period, and returned to my headquarters at Ngong just outside Nairobi.

As soon as the Christmas holidays were over I went to Head Office to tell Chief Warden, David Brown, what had happened. Explaining that I had received complaints from the manager of the President's estate that hippo were grazing the lucerne. I had instructed that all the cattle be put into a boma at night, as the Scouts would be patrolling during the hours of darkness. They had been told only to shoot hippo that were actually in the lucerne or in the immediate vicinity.

The Chief Game Warden retorted, "You don't seem to be treating this very seriously – I have no need to tell you what a Kikuyu thinks of his cattle, but leave the matter with me, as the President is at the coast."

Tony Marsh, who was in danger of Presidential wrath when one of his Scouts shot one of the President's cows (photo Tony Marsh).

My reply was somewhat acid: "Dave, if any disciplinary action is taken against Game Scout Digilesi Lekukuton who was on duty on Christmas Day at two o'clock in the morning, when every other Government Servant was asleep in bed – you and I included – I shall opt for early retirement and take off."

A few weeks later I was instructed by the Office of the President to kill all the hippo in the Ruiru River and that the President, who had never seen a hippopotamus close up, wanted one brought to his house on the estate. The Ruiru River is not very big and the hippo that were doing the damage lived a few miles down stream from the President's estate.

I planned to shoot the hippo on land, at night, using a .404 Westley Richards, and to use my 8x60S Brno to shoot them in the water during the day. The Brno had a set trigger and a four power scope with a post reticule, a combination I found very effective for brain shots when hippo come up for air – all that was required was patience. The hippo could not go very far without exposing their bodies as their pool was bounded by shallows for some distance both up and down stream. Shooting hippo in the water is a miserable business at the best of times but an order is an order, especially from the President.

The first hippo to float was a large male and I asked one of my Scouts to jump in the river and tie a rope round its lower jaw so that I could tow it to the bank with my lorry. No luck. All the Scouts gave varying excuses why they were unable to jump in and do the job. To show what a fearless type I was, I stripped and swam to the floating hippo, climbed aboard and paddling with my hands, got it to the bank. Then by dint of much heaving, straining and cursing we finally managed to get the dead bull onto the lorry. Taking a driver and orderly I went to the President's house where a Prison Service Corporal and the batch of convicts he was guarding provided the man-power to unload the hippo.

On returning to the hippo pool I realised why none of my Scouts had wanted to jump in to attach a rope to the dead hippo. The pool was a mass of crocodiles! Until then I had thought that crocs did not venture into comparatively small bodies of water, especially when the water was cold. You live and learn – it transpires that crocs will travel quite a way both overland and by water when a feast is in the offing. After this incident I did not hear a word about the Ruiru River hippos from either the Chief Game Warden or the Office of the President.

Eric Rundgren – 'Mchangi' – with two admirers. Ladies' man, a great hunter, Game Warden and Professional Hunter, Eric's boorishness was legendary and very funny to those who were not taken in by it (photo John Fletcher).

CHAPTER 28: KAVUMA

Ian Parker

Kavuma hill is a pimple a couple of hundred feet tall on the Kenya Tanganyika border, only slightly under halfway between Lake Jipe in the west and Vanga on the coast. Between the lake and the hill, the Kenya side was technically Tsavo West National Park. Most of the Tanganyika side, right to where the Umba River crosses the border was Mkomazi Game Reserve. Until 1957 no border was demarcated and in the flat 'nyika' plain it had been difficult to tell just which country one was in. That was why Eric Rundgren, one time member of the Game Department, took a chance.

Eric had licences to shoot four elephants in Tanganyika, but was very aware how many big elephants had been shot just over the border on Girigan, Grogan's southernmost Lake Jipe Estate that ran along the eastern edge of the lake and the Tsavo West Park. Year in and year out the Polish aristocrat, Baron Gostowski, who managed the estate took tusks that made many a hunter's eyes bulge. Rundgren, good hunter that he was, figured that the elephants were unlikely to appreciate the unmarked border any more accurately than he did, and possibly less. He was of course right and he shot four elephants. The average weight of their eight tusks was 130 lbs.

Eric's pleasure in four pairs of such large tusks was short-lived. Peter Jenkins knew the story because as a young Park Warden he was sent to investigate and with a surveyor, John Alexander (who later became a national Park Warden, then a professional hunter and guide and later still was murdered in Langata by an unknown assailant), prove that Eric had actually shot three elephants in the Tsavo Park and one right on the border. He was taken to court and fined five hundred pounds and disbarred from holding another licence for a year. It might not have been thus had he been contrite, but he was brash and challenging and by just being Rundgren, brought the temple down on his own head.

In 1957 when David Sheldrick still commanded anti-poaching, he had camped on the border below Jipe, which is where I joined up with him. After a day or so together looking around he pushed off and I patrolled on down the border to the coast. A survey team was present cutting a border trace for the first time. Among its members was Peter Day, who had been in the Kenya Regiment with me. It was the last time I saw him, there on the border and I have wondered occasionally since what became of him in the diaspora as the Empire crumbled over the next decade. With the vividness of youthful memory, I remember Peter, slight and blue-eyed, going about his survey work still wearing his Regiment slouch hat.

Recalling a Regimental slouch hat brings back other disconnected memories of days then only recently past. One is of General Kago's bugle. I had been playing variations on *Take Five* with considerable virtuosity through the keyhole of the Kangema Police Officers' mess door (good music has no fixed abode). The door had flown open and someone, probably a two-year wonder with no taste for mainstream jazz, smote the flared end of the bugle with an empty Pale Ale bottle. I remember it well.

Harking back to Kangema awakened an early recollection of Willie Hale. I had been the D.O.K.G. (District Officer – Kikuyu Guard) for Location 9 in Fort Hall and did not have to be assigned as his escort when he came trout fishing on the South Mathioya: it was a service willingly offered. Willie lost his automatic pistol and caused no end of a problem. George Grimmett the Divisional District Officer and a keen diver, had donned goggles and a snorkel tube and, with the aid of a staff had walked about bent double with his head under water. As Willie didn't know when or where the pistol had dropped out of its holster, we were pessimistic about chances of finding it, and as I had dropped a shotgun into the Tana River a week or so earlier, I was interested to see how so magisterial a person as Kenya's Chief Game Warden answered to the loss of a firearm. Fortunately for Willie, George Grimmett found the pistol and we went on fishing.

Kavuma Hill: a pimple on the Tanganyika border.

I left Peter Day's Survey Party near Lake Jipe, which then was open water and not the reed mace-choked swamp it has become, and motored away down the border. It was a slow process, weaving between newly cut stumps in relatively thick *Commiphora* woodland that extended almost as far as Kavuma. There, however, it gave way to open grass and we camped at the base of the hill. Close by were two more equally insignificant hills whose names have long escaped me. The point that lingered in my mind then was that other than for the Survey Party, I must have been among very few white men to climb Kavuma. Originally I had this number down to less than half a dozen: just Peter Jenkins (who as an Assistant Park Warden had covered this ground from all directions and to a degree achieved by no one else), the surveyors and myself and had experienced the euphoria of exploration.

The cave on the southern side of Kavuma.

Later, when I had read a little history and knew something about the First World War, I was not so sure. The Germans had established a raiding base and observation post on Kasigau Mountain and communicated with heliograph between it and the Usambara and Pare Mountains away to the south. They would never have travelled to and from Kasigau in danger of ambush by British forces all the way, without using Kavuma Hill as a lookout. By the 1950s we had forgotten how intensively both the British and Germans patrolled this uninhabited land in 1914 and 1915. Perhaps David Anstey, the Tanganyika Game Ranger (they retained the romantic label) who created Mkomazi had been there too. The possibilities grew disappointingly longer.

A little more thinking and it is obvious that exploration can only be a very personal experience. Wherever explorers went (other than Antarctica), natives had clearly preceded them. Yet if I hadn't been the first to climb Kavuma, I swear I am the first white man to explore Kavuma cave. Halfway up the southern slope, a trifle towards the west was a low rock with an opening beneath. A man could crawl into it, but not comfortably. Once through the entrance one could barely stand. Indeed it was so small a cave that few would have bothered to enter. At the time I was going through a bat-collecting phase for John Williams at the Coryndon Museum. Having just had a new subspecies of bat that I had collected on the Prince of Wales Hill at Lualeni, named after me (*Platymops barbatogularis parkeri*) by no less an authority than Harrison, I was keen. David Sheldrick had had a tiny red louse named after him and I felt that a bat, even if only a sub-species, was definitely an improvement. That my bat's anus had been described as rugose was no disadvantage, though David said otherwise. Nevertheless I was hoping to move up the scale and perhaps discover a new species. In those days we thought a species was something tangible and not merely a taxonomist's whim.

There were bats in Kavuma cave: all the grey phase of the little leaf-nosed bat *Hipposiderus caffer*. A porcupine had rested there too, and left a few quills. I suppose a leopard might have used the cave for her cubs, though it wasn't a prime site. Yet I cannot believe that any other white man has ever been into the cave, unless he, too, was collecting bats. The claim is surely not too presumptuous? The sons of herders grazing their cattle about the base of Kavuma will have poked about in the cave, generation following generation. Little over a century previously the Masai had grazed the area and before them will have been others – right back to the first Cushitic pastoralists who introduced cattle into eastern Africa. Before them in man's distant past, there will have been hunters and hunters' sons and, not impossibly, hunters' daughters. I was merely the first white to enter Kavuma cave. That no other white people wanted to is their loss.

Down near the base of Kavuma, we had come across a rhino cow and yearling calf. Climbing into the low branches of a *Commiphora* we squealed and snorted and called her. It was magic for she came like a train and stopped with her head in the branches and so close that with my ancient Box-Brownie camera, I got only the side of her head criss-crossed with branches in the view finder and a lousy photograph. More important was dropping my handkerchief on her head – which I did. Woodley introduced me to calling rhinos. They either came or they didn't. Those that did were obviously keen to see off the source of the noise. I never worked out which came and which ran, as there were males and females on both sides. Perhaps it was something to do with local dominance. Whatever the reason it was always good for a laugh and a good bush party trick.

Years earlier and beyond Kibwezi, Billy Woodley had been travelling merrily with Cogs Pearson in a wooden-bodied three-ton truck. They had called a rhino and it had come and delivered a mighty punch to the truck's rear end with its horn. Bill had stopped and from the way the truck was being bounced up and down and shoved about, it was clear that the rhino was stuck. He and Cogs went aft to see. There is not very much one can do with a stuck rhino so they decided to give it a beer. Opening one of those wonderfully large old bottles of Tusker, Bill shoved the long neck into the furious rhino's mouth. The rhino snorted and blew, frothing and blowing prodigiously while Cogs and Bill laughed and clapped their hands with the humour of it all like two brats at a party. Until the rhino broke loose that was.

Soon after Kavuma the countryside changed, betokening a higher rainfall. It had recently been burned. The grass was short and green and it was easy driving between the widely spaced trees – many of which were large specimens of *Terminalia spinosa* and another yet larger species of the same genus. Camping there for two days we wandered widely on foot. Even then, seemingly so far from centres of population, there had been a surprising abundance of bush fences with wire snares. Closer to the coast, we entered much wetter country and shortly before reaching the Umba River we were among big *Diospyros* trees in a truly coastal environment. Soon thereafter we broke out into familiar territory with forest clumps and tall grasses interspersed with thousands of doum palms. We drove through Lunga Lunga on the border, to where Vanga's main street met the seashore, just to claim to have truly traversed the whole distance from Lake Jipe to the Indian Ocean.

Vanga in those days still gave the impression of being cut off from the rest of the coast. Yet the Germans and British had fought other crazy World War I battles close by. Perhaps the strangeness of that distant war was pressed on Game Wardens more strongly than others for, by virtue of our inclinations, we spent more time in far parts where trenches and old machine gun nests were most completely out of place.

I only traversed the border between Jipe and Vanga once again with Game Warden Kilifi and that was in the following year. I got to know it better in parts when working in the Mkomazi Game Reserve, but that was years later. I went to Vanga and Lunga Lunga when the elephants came after the ripe doum palm nuts and took out crops as well. Shooting them there was like shooting them elsewhere and a purely political exercise. Two incidents pop out of the memory's trays. One was when Arabs from Vanga collected meat from a hippo shot in the rice. They said that as it was 'of the water' it didn't need its throat cut and felt my observation that hippo might be genetically linked to pigs was malicious.

The other involved space travel. One of my Turkana Game Scouts nearly pre-empted Yuri Gagarin as the first man in space. Fed up with shooting elephants I had tried to get the locals to make palisades out of doum palm logs to keep the animals from their shambas. The venture was ill-fated because I underestimated the work involved in cutting, transporting and erecting the logs – each over fourteen feet long. To unload one from a truck, its weight was taken on the shoulders of my not-so-willing bearers. As more and more of the log emerged, so it was shouldered by a succession of bearers until, without having to pick it up, the log was marched off by ten men to where it was to stand. On this occasion there was a hitch. Four bearers were in place, but as the log emerged from the truck others failed to take their allotted places. Suddenly too great a weight rested on the four and they dropped the log to pivot about its mid-point with the edge of the truck body as a fulcrum.

The Turkana had been standing astride the far end of the log deep inside the truck. As the opposite end was dropped, that between his ankles rose abruptly between his legs and he was hurled skyward with great force. At least a year before Gagarin, I saw a body tumbling slowly through space. Like a boulder from a Roman ballista the Turkana arced across the sky, to land far away on his head. This did not discomfit him unduly. It was the log's propulsive arm between his legs that had made his eyes water.

Alistair Graham, who was never meant to be a Game Warden.

CHAPTER 29: I WAS NEVER MEANT TO BE A GAME WARDEN

Alistair Graham

I was never actually meant to be a Game Warden. I had just finished university and had been recruited by the Department as a biologist. Nobody knew what they wanted a biologist for, least of all me, but the idea of engaging in biological studies had crept from somewhere into the departmental psyche, and it had been decided in some cryptic meeting or other that the Department should not allow itself to fall behind the times, whatever the times were. Several senior officers had heard of sister organisations that employed biologists, which gave good grounds for doing likewise. But after I signed my contract I was told that in fact the post had not quite been established after all and pending next year's estimates I would in the meantime have to be a Warden. I was to go to Kilgoris where the main duty would be elephant control. After a year, I was assured, I would be reassigned as a biologist. I was issued with a worn-out Bedford 3-tonner, a tent, a .470, a .404, a shotgun and enough monthly return forms to choke a hippo. I was told I would have to buy my own Land Rover. I persuaded my father to lend me fifty quid and went down to Grogan Road where I relieved some scruffy, shirt-tailed villain of a clapped out Series I Land Rover. In a twinkling I had been transformed from a common or garden Kenya hick into a Game Warden – though most latter-day Wardens were in fact only Kenya hicks with titles.

Although Ken Smith had once spent a few weeks there, Kilgoris had never been a Game Department station before I arrived and probably didn't last long after I left. It came into being because in the preceding few years the expanding population of Kisii to the north had begun to spill down onto the Lolgorien plateau in search of new land. They were confronted with large numbers of elephant, leopard, lion and assorted antelope, monkeys and pigs that naturally tucked into everything the newcomers grew or herded. The DC Narok had complained strenuously to the Game Department that it was up to them to do something about the game getting totally out of hand in the Kilgoris-Lolgorien area. So the country west of the Mara was split off from the Narok District range and made into a separate range centred on Kilgoris.

The area held a certain romance for me because Lolgorien had in the twenties been the centre of a small gold rush. My father had been one of the hopefuls who pitched up there to make his fortune and had in fact entered the local folklore - but not because of anything to do with gold. He happened to be exceptionally hairy-chested and it seems that one night while drinking in a Lolgorien bar he struck a match on the bar top to light his pipe and accidentally set fire to his chest. The flame started low down and flared up splendidly to his chin, and was considered a very fine stunt by those present. I was pleased to visit the actual scene of this legend and imagine how it must have all looked back then. In my time the place was simply a lot of holes in the ground and piles of rubble, with no clue at all as to where the bar had been.

Kilgoris wasn't really a town. It had three and a half government houses, one for the District Officer, one for the policeman and a third for the Livestock Officer. There was a Police station, a caboose and a court. One or two *dukas* and a couple of God-bothering outfits completed the place. Government had started building a fourth house for the Agricultural Officer. But he, sensible fellow, never turned up and the house was abandoned half completed. That of course was where I was quartered, it not being considered necessary for a Game Warden to be issued with a complete house.

The Livestock Officer was *Nyani* Bond (the naked hunter), a Kenya hick like me and we naturally fell into each other's company. The policeman was a swarthy, thirsty Scot, bit of a prick really, but one couldn't be too choosy and the three of us would from time to time pile into Tony's car and head off to Kisii to spend the weekend drinking the same beer we could just as easily have drunk at Kilgoris, but in greater quantities because it was a weekend in Kisii. Curious behaviour when you think about it but it seemed OK to us at the time and in any case it wasn't as if there was a lot of choice. Patel, who had the contract to run the Police canteen, was an excellent host and we passed many good evenings with him drinking whisky and eating chicken curry. But that was it for nightlife.

The fourth government officer, the District Officer (DO), was a Pongo. He was a perfectly nice, pink, well brought up fellow but not adapted to life in a waiting room for Hell like Kilgoris with only a couple of Kenya hicks for company after work. Shortly after I arrived he started behaving very strangely, spending long periods shut alone in his house. Tony and I tried hard to entice him to come and drink beer and eat curried chicken with Patel in the Police canteen but he locked himself in and refused to come out and play. We of course didn't think that possibly we were part of the problem. Anyway, we soon got really worried and composed a Police signal to the DC Narok informing him that his DO was a couple of bananas short of a complete bunch and deteriorating. The DC fortunately took us at our word and rescued him before he fell out of his tree altogether. No one came to replace him.

I was lucky that Tony was there because he'd done a fair bit of hunting in his time and managed to talk me out of some of my more foolish enterprises. He agreed to accompany me sometimes as extra firepower but always insisted on carrying his own gun. This was a .450, a relic of an earlier age with hammers. The gun was ancient enough but the ammo was something else. Cardboard cases blotchy with beer stains and chewed by silverfish, full of extremely well seasoned black powder. The bullets wiggled in the ends of the cases like hawk moth pupae. But Tony swore it was a *lekker* rifle: it never let him down.

One day we were called out to deal with an elephant that had just speared a cow to death for some incomprehensible reason. We picked out the animal with blood on its tusks and Tony said he'd like to give his musket a bit of a run, get the spiders out of the barrels. So he let rip with the old contraption, which went off like a whole box of thunder flashes and spread-eagled him on the ground in a huge cloud of dense smoke. Tony got to his feet and recovered the gun, muttering that maybe the ammo was, after all, getting a bit old. But what had happened was that he'd cocked both hammers, and when the first barrel went off it had shaken loose the hammer on the second to give him the extra thump backwards. "Think I better just cock them one at a time", said Tony.

The instrument with which I was to bring the larrikin elephants of Kilgoris to heel was a brand new Westley Richards .470. I had never been confronted with a machine as mean as this before. My father had taught me to handle firearms and shoot, and I had actually seen an elephant being shot, down on the Galana where my friend Ian Parker was working. But I'd never had to wield something like a .470, or indeed fire any sort of gun at anything more menacing than a mousebird. Neil Sandeman back in Nairobi had asked me how much experience I had had of hunting big game when he issued the .470 to me. No way was I going to admit the facts and so I drew upon my years of experience at the concentration camps I'd gone to school in, and dissembled shamelessly. Of course it didn't fool Neil Sandeman any more than it had ever fooled the masters at the Hill School or Duko (Duke of York), but I'd learnt that it often suits both parties to act as if they do believe the mendacious twaddle being dispensed. So he scowled and told me to account for every round of the measly two or three boxes he issued. I remember thinking, bloody hell, they certainly expect you to shoot straight.

Shooting straight was of course something that was preying on my mind. The mingy ration of cartridges ruled out any serious target practice but in any case, as I well knew, I'd find a lot of excuses not to fire this particular rifle cold that often. What little I did know about shooting included the realisation that a rifle like this would undoubtedly kick like a zebra. As I had a strong aversion to physical pain I managed easily to talk myself out of extended target practice. But I did manage to fire both barrels, once, and it was as well I did. Because I didn't yet know that the Game Department only bought Westley Richards Grade 3 rifles, which are not machined to anything like the same standards as Grades 1 and 2. Cold, the rifle's action was smooth enough. But after firing both barrels the action locked almost solid and the only way you could break the gun to reload was to smack it really hard across your knee. I was very glad to have discovered that little fact before getting up the nose of some large, grumpy animal in the forest somewhere. In due course I learnt that when all you see at the end of the barrel is a lion's face coming rapidly closer with an expression that tells you no prisoners will be taken, a .470's kick is no more than a Daisy airgun's and it is in fact an enormously comforting thing to have about you.

Not long after arriving in Kilgoris I was summoned to meet the Senior Game Warden, Narok, who still retained a supervisory responsibility for the Lolgorien-Kilgoris area and, of course, over me. The Warden in question was the famous TB, Major Lyn Temple-Boreham M.C., about whom I'd already heard a good deal. I'd been warned not to play the goat around TB but rather to treat him with deference and make sure to touch my forelock regularly. Part of TB's style was always to meet somewhere out in the bundu rather than in his office, as he preferred to be thought of as always out on safari somewhere. In fact it was not all an act – he really did spend a great deal of his time galloping about the Keekorok plains doing whatever it was keen Wardens did in those days. And he was super-keen, the sort of Warden that Chief Game Wardens wished all the other drones would try to be. Of course his steed was only a Land Rover, which was a shame, as he would have looked even more impressive on a horse.

Many are the would-be Allan Quatermains who have stood before their mirrors and earnestly practised the elusive pose of nonchalant bushmanship that they hoped would mark them out as masters of the bundu. But they were wasting their time as long as TB was around. For sheer style TB had no equal. If Hollywood had known of him Stewart Grainger wouldn't even have had an audition. He was a big man, tall and handsome, always dressed to perfection in a smart, not too new, not too scruffy, safari suit, the cartridge loops gorged with .470 rounds. He sported almost a caricature of a major's moustache and had an altogether very compelling presence. He always made sure he was noticed. For all that he came over to me as a bit of a dude I liked him and I've no doubt he really was on first name terms with every lion in Narok.

Actually I liked him from the start because he very tactfully avoided embarrassing both himself and me when I arrived at our first meeting place. He must have wondered what the hell Messrs Grimwood and Sandeman were up to, sending him this unprepossessing hick to bring the Kilgoris elephants to heel. A long, skinny bloke with gogs whom he must have known perfectly well had not the first clue what he was about. It was very gentlemanly of him not to ask any questions at all about my knowledge of shooting elephants and lions, arresting poachers, or whatever. He merely gave me a little pep talk about the depth of roguery professional hunters would all descend to if I so much as turned my back on them for a moment (especially such knaves as Dave Allen, Theo Potgieter, Glen Cottar, Anton Allen, Don Bousfield – the list went on and on), and reminded me that the DC Narok didn't want to hear any more complaints of crop damage in Kilgoris and invited me to send him a Police signal if I needed any help. Lastly, he said,

"I take it you remembered to take out a game licence while you were in Nairobi? We chaps have to be licensed like everybody else, you know."

I wasn't expecting this and started to mumble something evasive as of course I had remembered no such thing. But, as I came to know, TB didn't want hear what anyone else had to say, and as he no doubt figured I probably didn't have a licence he didn't wait for any damn fool answer. With that he leapt astride his mount and took off in a plume of dust across the plains to attend to some urgent, mysterious crisis in the blue beyond. I drove the long journey (all journeys are long in Series I Landys) back to Kilgoris wondering what the hell I'd been summoned for, and making a mental note to acquire a game licence quickly.

Evelyn Temple-Boreham: the legendary TB (photo Peter Davey).

Not long after, TB summoned me to another meeting at a certain spot on the Keekorok plains where he was camped. As I neared the place I saw a small group of people staring at a vehicle, evidently bogged down. It was TB and his men. His new Land Rover (Series II, very flash) was in the middle of a deep pool, listing strongly to port with the tops of the wheels just showing. The plains in these parts had many such pools that are like craters with steep sides and the middle deeper than the edges. Nasty things to drive into. Returning his earlier compliment when he refrained from asking embarrassing questions about my fitness for the job, I avoided any reference as to what lapse of nonchalant bushmanship resulted in him parking his car in this unseemly swamp. He likewise offered no answer to the intriguing question. As I had brought a couple of Game Scouts with me he reckoned he now had the manpower to push his car to dry land. He issued commands that included an order to me to get in his new car and do the driving. That made me very nervous. Why the devil me, I wondered. I could see that there was a good chance the vehicle would topple over – something that would obviously not score me any brownie points with the boss. However, I could see no way out of it and so I waded out and started the engine.

With TB bellowing orders, the men pushed and we got the vehicle moving. It heeled to the very point of toppling but I just kept hoping and going and we barged our way out. TB was very chuffed and invited me to breakfast back at his camp. Best breakfast I'd had in ages and he even allowed me to speak once or twice. I thought about it afterwards, why he got me to drive his car. I suppose he wasn't about to embarrass himself further by turning his car over with someone like me watching. If it was going to happen, better some twit to carry the can. No flies on TB, as everyone said.

TB was different to most of the younger Wardens of my generation in that he wasn't at all the Kenya hick. I suppose he represented more the type of the Department's earlier days when many Wardens were flotsam from the old *Raj*, very much the *pukka sahib* with smooth manners and a military bearing. Of course at the time I didn't see myself as a hick but looking back on it those of my generation were indeed Kenya hicks, a type with a number of distinguishing characteristics. A typical Kenya hick dressed in a shirt and shorts (but no underpants) and his language had a distinctly South African accent acquired from the *kaburus* (Boers) he'd been to school with. As they grew older and noticed that other people wore shoes they did the same, at least in polite company. But they didn't go so far as to wear real shoes. Oh no, the only acceptable footwear were *chaplis*, and not just any old *chaplis* but true *punjabis* made as far back as records were kept by Pitamber Khoda on Government Road.

A pair of vintage Pitamber Khoda chaplis (Model 7B.ii/z^{5ps}).

I don't know when the appellation Kenya hick established itself but legend has it that it was Eric Rundgren, the famous *Mchangi*, who made it really stick, albeit inadvertently. Eric had grown up barefoot and out of control, a real hick if ever there was one. Experiencing the minimum of school at which he put in the absolute minimum of effort to learn anything, the only social skill he'd acquired was how to undo a boob-strap. He did a stint as a Game Warden but drifted inevitably into safari hunting, which he always affected to despise, and acquired his nickname from his constant urge to be moving and finding new places.

I remember once sitting in Rundgren's tent on the Tana where he, To Archer and Reggie Destro were conducting a museum collecting safari for a leading American museum. It was big operation and Eric was the Ker & Downey hunter in charge. He had invited me to come over in the evening whenever I felt like it to have a few drinks and yak for a while. I felt like it most evenings as the chance to freeload the lush hospitality of a rich Yank's safari camp was something few Game Wardens could resist. As darkness fell Eric ordered one of the staff to bring him a couple of buffalo steaks. I thought it a bit odd as he'd just said we'd wander over to the mess tent soon for dinner. Anyway, two massive slabs of fresh buffalo were quickly served, which Eric got stuck into. Now, most people wouldn't have had the strength to cut meat like that, far less chew it. I was fascinated as I watched him put it away, his jaws working through the task much as I imagined Nutcracker Man's would have a million years ago or so. He saw my curiosity and simply said there was never enough stinking food at the dinner table and he had to have something to prime his guts before he got on to dinner itself. He was shaped like a gorilla and evidently had the fuel consumption of a Dodge Power Wagon to go with it.

We were soon summoned to dinner and Eric sat down and started eating as if he hadn't touched anything since lunch. Then began a scene that was a mixture of the awful and the droll. Eric didn't like the bossy Yank in charge of the safari who for his part considered Eric a gross and vulgar lout whose presence was a blunder on Ker & Downey's part. It probably was. A big bag of duck had been shot that day and these were the main course. Wild duck being fairly small after shrivelling up in the oven, large numbers had been cooked and served on big plates placed along the mess table. The staff had naturally put one serving plate in front of *Mchangi*. He sat there, elbows on the table, grasping a duck at each end. He bit the accessible flesh off, dropped the carcass and picked up another one. The head honcho of the Museum couldn't stand it. "For Christ's sake Rundgren," he shouted; "eat like a civilised human being, can't you. You are goddamn disgusting, man."

"I'll eat as I damn well please," said Eric, "and if you don't like it you can get stuffed. I'm in charge of this stinking safari, and you better remember it. I decide what goes on round here."

Of course, the Yank, whose safari it unquestionably was, leapt to his feet in a real bait and bellowed at Rundgren that he, the expedition leader was in charge of the goddamn safari and Rundgren better start understanding it. Eric just carried on ripping into the ducks like a ratel, pausing occasionally to growl out more insults and wind everyone up. The Yank was an educated, cultured man and he and his entourage were genuinely and deeply upset by the way Rundgren behaved. One cringed on their behalf. But behind the sympathetic face I couldn't deny a private grin. To a degree of course Eric was putting it on, but for the most part he was simply being himself. You had to hand it to him – nobody could act the brute as well as he could, and to hell with what anyone else thought about it.

Eric had refined a bullying and contemptuous manner to a high degree and was quick to give anyone a hard time if he felt like it. But he was one of those people who actually *was* as nasty and tough as he made out he was and very few people ever had the nerve to call his bluff, because by and large he wasn't bluffing. I saw him as a romantic figure, a swashbuckling ruffian who got away with things most of us would never have the bottle to even contemplate, and the hell with the stinking rabble around him, to use one of his trademark phrases.

Despite his manner, certain clients enjoyed *Mchangi's* company and one, a lady, invited him to join her in Europe, which he did. On his return, in his eyes at least, he was a changed man having acquired a modicum of culture and refinement. It was when this archetypical hick, himself the crudest, rudest, roughest specimen of Kenya hickdom anyone had ever come across told a gathering in the New Stanley Hotel's Long Bar that he'd moved to a higher level of awareness as a result of his trip to Europe and stated, "You stinking rabble, you know *nothing*. You don't know the first thing about stinking manners – you're nothing but a bunch of stinking Kenya hicks." Thus the term Kenya hick became fixed in the local lexicon. Yet I run ahead of my story.

It happened that *Mchangi* arrived in Kilgoris about the time I did, together with his son Donald, Jack Carlyon and John Fletcher. Carlyon it was who one day stopped for a break at the Namanga Hotel on his way somewhere or other. Jack ordered a drink at the bar and then asked the barman for a hundred shilling coins in exchange for a hundred bob note. He wanted the coins to play the fruit machine, a massive, cast-iron contraption bolted to the wall. Well, he fed the machine and pulled the handle, and fed and pulled, and in due course stuck his last coin in and pulled again. Nothing. He had won bugger all for his hundred bob. He had been quiet up till then but when the machine gulped his last offering like a hammerkop putting another plottie[67] away he swore loudly at it and stormed out of the hotel.

A couple of people at the bar heard him curse but thought nothing of it. The fruit machine had provoked a great deal of bad language in its time. But Jack soon came back in carrying a .577 he'd gone to fetch from his car. He strode up to the fruit machine and at close range gave it both barrels. The din inside the confined space was tremendous and the cast iron shattered into a thousand

---

[67] Ed's note: Plottie = clawed toad (*Xenopus*)

shards that clattered to the floor along with a cascade of coins in a fitting finale to the detonation of the gun. The drinkers at the bar were transfixed, gaping in dead silence, watching to see what would come next. Jack stood his rifle against the wall, got down on his hands and knees and carefully picked one hundred shilling coins out of the debris. Without another word he pocketed his money, shouldered his gun and drove away.

Eric had been sent to impress the Administration that the Game Department took its complaints seriously (my role was to hold the line thereafter). *Mchangi* was acknowledged by most to be by a long chalk the Mighty Hunter of his day and he and his gang soon blew away a sizeable bunch of elephants (cows and calves that rarely if ever raid crops) and decamped. But in this brief spell I got to know him and subsequently spent many enjoyable evenings in his camp in various places here and there, drinking whisky and listening to him talk in his odd, flat, drawling monologue about all sorts of bizarre people and adventures.

As soon as I arrived in Kilgoris I was besieged by angry people demanding retribution for the maize that had been ravaged by elephants. The conventional Game Department view was the notion that the elephants were misbehaving when they raided crops. The assumption seemed that basically they knew their place in the scheme of things, but like all subordinates, elephants tended to get out of hand if discipline was relaxed. Discipline would be restored by going after elephants somewhere in the general vicinity and shooting one or two. This is what Eric and his crew had done.

There was method in this madness. After all, elephants only raided crops at dead of night, in the cold and dark, when any sensible Warden or game controller was either snug in bed or pissing it up at some bar. To confront the actual culprits whilst engaged in crop raiding simply seemed a quite unnecessary and tiresome enterprise. This sort of indirect way of getting the message across to the elephants by shooting some innocent party miles from the scene of the crime seemed to me far-fetched to say the least. In addition, I had learned from Ian Parker[68] that crop raiding wasn't usually done by any old elephant. Generally, only males were involved – it was unusual for cows to try their trunks at it. So I was determined to concentrate on the actual raiders. And what I'd been told turned out to be, in the main, true. Mostly it was males that raided crops, and almost always young males. So I spent many a long cold night in fields round Kilgoris trying to intercept some sneaky elephant tip-toeing out of the forest into the maize. I got through jerry cans of adrenaline and learnt a great deal about animals and hunting in a very short time. Doing things this way rapidly reduced

[68] Editor's note: Actually the primary source of this information was the Tanganyika Game Ranger, Brian Nicholson. In the course of very extensive control work in southern Tanganyika, he had observed that young males acted as satellites to their maternal family units. If one shot one, it didn't move other elephants far. However, if one shot up a family unit, it usually did move and took all the satellites with it. Since the mid-1950s when Nicholson wrote this up as a paper, behaviourists have confirmed much of Brian's hypothesis (though they never acknowledge it).

the incidence of crop raiding but of course it was all pointless really as the elephants were doomed anyway and disappeared altogether not long after.

* * * *

I'd started with the Department in April 1961 and I stayed at Kilgoris until December the following year, when I was told to hand over to The Vulture, also known as Alec Forbes-Watson, and proceed to Garissa where at last I was to begin the much-vaunted biologist's job studying Hunter's antelope. I pitched up in Garissa late one evening in January 1963 and was directed to the Curling Club where I was told I would find Dave McCabe, the Game Warden with whom I was to work. *Kebi* and his wife Brunie were indeed there making sure the beer didn't go stale. I was obliged to pitch in and help, which I did by flattening a couple of bottles as fast as I could, thinking that was *de rigueur* in the Curling Club. Suddenly my knees caved in and I went down backwards like a brain-shot elephant, out to the world. *Kebi* was convinced, and I suspect remains so to this day, that I had some undisclosed brain disorder that left me prone to unpredictable fits of this sort, and that sooner or later I would die on him. He couldn't believe that Grimwood had lumbered him with such a gratuitous responsibility. Why else would I have done what I did? There was nothing wrong with the beer. In his time he'd seen a lot of people become legless at bars but never so fast and unexpectedly. After he'd propped me up at the bar again like a doll, and I'd recovered my senses, I swore it had never happened before. But I can still see the utter scepticism on his face that evening. He was sure I was going to die on him.

Luckily I quickly became good friends with *Kebi* and Brunie because whereas at Kilgoris I had rated a half-finished house at Garissa I rated nothing at all, it being vaguely assumed that Kebi would take care of that little detail. So they put me up and in my time with them we had a thousand good laughs and great times. The day I arrived hadn't been a good one for *Kebi*, quite apart from my unnerving (for him) stunt at the Club. That morning he had decided to type a long-overdue letter to headquarters. He had a government-issue typewriter and was an accomplished touch-typist. That is, he could type with two fingers provided he focussed hard on the keyboard to make sure he touched the right keys. Touch-typing takes concentration and Dave was at the yours faithfully stage when relief begins to unknot the brow, retract the tongue and loosen the shoulder muscles. At last, cc to and the job was done. Dave sat back and yelled for coffee. He then reached forward to drag the letter out. But something was wrong, something was very wrong. There where the keys hit the paper was a big huddle of keys, frozen in the act of all trying to get at the paper simultaneously. The letter consisted of 'Dear Sir' and a smudgy black hole in the paper, carbon and copy, and probably the roller too. I'd heard how *Kebi* was prone to respond when fate behaved in this cavalier way and true to form he had let out a dreadful roar that made the children cry and woke up a lion three miles away, and hurled the typewriter through the office window. It hit the ground at an angle that caused it to unravel the bunched keys really nicely, but also the rest of the machine as well. It took many patient hours to get it working again.

My task was to study Hunter's antelope and determine whether or not the habitat of Tsavo East National Park was suitable for the creature. This was because their future in their natural habitat in northeast Kenya was thought to be uncertain and so the idea was to transfer some to the park to ensure their survival. After poking about for a while I pronounced the Tsavo habitat quite fine and *Kebi* and I were then instructed to catch and move enough Hunter's to start the species off in the park. *Kebi* observed from the outset that if God had intended Hunter's antelope to live in Tsavo East he'd have given them water wings to cross the Tana with. All the same he organised the operation and we set to and caught more than seventy.

Although I'd recently been on an exercise in Uganda to dart elephants with Red Palmer's new-fangled Cap-Chur Gun, and found it quite straightforward and effective, elephants were of course very easy to creep up close to, and the biggest targets in the business. Darting something as skitsy as a Hunter's antelope was altogether another matter and we didn't even contemplate it. Instead we simply applied the good old tally-ho method perfected by the likes of Ken Randall, tearing about in a car lassoing young adults. When you're young and stupid this sort of rodeo is great sport and we had a fine time racing about catching antelope until, as described later in this book, we had pens full. Those that didn't die of the after-effects of stress we drove or flew down to Tsavo East where David Sheldrick pampered them in a boma for a while before turning them loose. As no one saw much of them after their release, it was assumed that the local lions had taken care of them. Many years later, however, it transpired that these hirola must have holed up somewhere and bred, for they started to be seen regularly not far from their original release site.

It was now March 1964 and my contract was up for renewal. Time to figure out where I was going. Sitting around playing the goat with the likes of Dave and Brunie was as good as it gets from the point of view of plain enjoyment but was it a proper job with a haircut? Ian Parker and I had long talked about bailing out and starting a private consulting business. We would show everyone that game could be put on an economically sound basis through private enterprise. This would save wild animals from what would otherwise be inevitable obliteration and ensure their permanent future in the jolly old scheme of things. Everything would come good and at the same time maybe we could continue to enjoy the drone's life from a different vantage point, though of course we didn't mention that. Maybe this was the moment to set to and put things straight.

And so I sat and thought about it all for a long time. It was certainly very tempting to continue in the Department as a paid drone, farting about here and there filling in monthly returns and cultivating that desirable but elusive image of nonchalant bushmanship that seemed to preoccupy so many of us. True, there were some who'd made a fine art of it, and why not, what was life to get so serious about? TB, George Adamson, *Mchangi* – each in his way – were Old Masters of an enviable art form. But few are destined to become great artists and I was certain that I was among the many. And all sorts of other thoughts (about girls, for example) intervened to spoil the sylvan fantasy of a Mowgli prince in the Peaceable Kingdom, forever Land Rovering into the sunset on some pointless but romantic mission. A recurring, chilling thought was that some of the oldest virgins in the Colony were Game Wardens. This looked suspiciously like a warning signal to be taken very seriously indeed: long-term game keeping evidently had its occupational hazards.

If I was ever going to jack up the nerve to walk into Nairobi's posh hairdressers, *Salon Laura,* with all the swish bints sitting watching from under their space helmets, and ask the beautiful, aloof Laura herself to go to the flicks, I'd sure as hell better bail out of places like Garissa and take a crash chat-up course. Maybe even try on a pair of underpants when I'd built up a bit of confidence. And so I stopped being a Game Warden.

CHAPTER 30: THE KAPITI LION

Ken Levett

I joined the Game Department just before Chief Game Warden Ian Grimwood left, after Peter McLinton, John Mutinda and Perez Olindo. I was on a two and a half year contract and posted to Thomson's Falls to establish a game control station. From this base I undertook game control between Maralal in the north, Nanyuki in the east, Naivasha in the south across the Rift to Kabarnet in the west. Control work was increasing in this period because the new African settlers were cultivating previously uninhabited forest areas, and their crops were too much of a temptation for buffalo and elephant.

Most junior staff had to live under canvas as hardly any money was provided for the new station. Indeed it was only sufficient for temporary living quarters for some Game Scouts and some dog pens for my hunting pack. My dogs came from sources ranging from gifts from farmers leaving the country, to others confiscated from poachers or to just strays that came to join the fray. Most adapted to life in the pack and their main work was baying up buffalo: the only method of obtaining much success with these animals in forest and in thick bush.

In Laikipia lions were a problem. Their control was usually undertaken by sitting up over a kill with a spotlight. Normally this was successful unless other hunters or farmers had already tried shooting or poisoning and made a bosh of it, teaching the lions not to return to kills. In such cases other tactics had to be employed. Other than tracking them up and hoping to find them in the open, which happened rarely, I used dogs to bay them up and hold their attention long enough for me to get in a telling shot. Yet dogs are not usually keen on chasing lions. Our first attempt to bay up a lion was a complete failure, with some dogs taking off never to be seen again.

Gilbert Colville, a well-known Laikipia cattle rancher, kept a lion in a cage just to train dogs to hunt them. The dogs were brought into proximity of the lion's cage when it was being fed, so they became familiar with his majesty. All hell was usually let loose with the lion snarling and growling and the dogs barking in frantic excitement. After a couple of introductions, most but not all dogs lost their fear of lions and were ready to hunt them. I subjected some of my dogs to the Colville schooling.

As luck would have it, it was not long before Gerry Edwards, whose place was nearby, had a bull killed by a lion. The dogs turned up trumps and, within an hour of picking up the tracks, bayed up and held the culprit long enough for us to arrive and dispatch him. After this first success the pack was used on a number of occasions. From then on, new dogs received their training from experienced pack members. Some turned out better than the originals: those too foolhardy were short-lived.

Ken Clark's buffalo pack. It was a mob such as this that Ken Levett also trained for lion. The motley packs were known generically as 'Tumu-Tumu terriers'. Tumu Tumu being a Kikuyu village beset with pariahs and mongrels of all sorts (photo Peter Beard).

My experiences of two years shooting buffalo and other troublesome big game will have been similar to those of many other Wardens down the years. It was a physical life, there were occasional close calls, and like most hunters, I had my favourite weapon (mine was my personal .375 rifle). My contract passed quickly and it was soon time to hand over to an African successor.

The man detailed to take over from me was an ex-army Major who, because he was a Somali, had been forced to retire early. In the mid-1960's the Somali 'shifta' war was in full swing, Kenya's relations with Somalia were very bad, and the powers that be felt it too great a security risk to have Somalis with divided loyalties in the military. Having handed over to Major Mohamed I thought I would have an easy time showing him over the area before leaving for good, but the Chief Game Warden had other ideas for me that led to perhaps the most interesting of all my control work hunts. My quarry was the Kapiti lion.

The Kapiti lion was killing cattle down on the Ulu Kapiti plains area southeast of Nairobi. A number of hunters, including other Game Wardens, had tried unsuccessfully over several months to dispose of this rustler and their many failed attempts had made him so wary and crafty that his disposal called for something more than a normal spot of control work. The area, with which I was unfamiliar, comprised several hundred square kilometres of plains and rolling hills bisected by the Nairobi-Mombasa railway. To its south were nomadic Masai pastoralists; to its north were European owned ranches. The lion did not kill frequently and roamed widely across this big territory.

I was given a Land Rover, six dogs and two Game Scouts, Labuny and Legeria, one of whom was from Thomson's Falls and the other from Nairobi headquarters. Les Mousley's guesthouse was put at my disposal. First we visited all the farmers in the area who had been troubled by the lion, gathered any information we could from locals and livestock herders, informed them that I was in the area and could be contacted at Les Mousley's place who would then pass on information to myself or to my wife, Heather. Three or four days passed with no reports of a kill, or sightings, but we spent the time checking all known watering holes and cattle troughs in the area for fresh signs or tracks. As the lion also affected the Masai, we visited them as well, but they were on the whole uncooperative. They said that nobody, even themselves, was capable of killing this lion because they had often tried and knew the creature well. We did pick up some tracks in the Masai area, but they led us to a pride of thirteen, all spread out lazily sunning themselves in a glade. As our quarry was reputedly a loner, we made a quiet retreat without disturbing them.

On the fifth day, Les Mousley lost a steer. Half of a hind leg was eaten, unquestionably by a lion. We followed the tracks to the edge of a gully that looked a likely lie-up site. Collecting the dogs, we descended into the gully with them leashed and took up the tracks. When the dogs' agitation suggested we were close, we let them go. From the barking and growling the lion was certainly in the gully, but would not bay up and took off with the small pack in hot pursuit. We followed as fast as we could but to no avail. The lion gave the dogs the slip and they eventually returned to us after about half an hour, very tired and thirsty. The next day we picked up the tracks again but when we lost them after several hours, we did at least know he was heading towards a set of hills drained by the Il Mulungush watercourse.

A few days later a kill was reported on Ulu Estate ten miles away. We followed the same procedure, followed tracks, eventually losing them, but again they had been heading towards the same set of hills as when we had previously trailed the lion. On both occasions it had not revisited its kills. In the following days there were no kills, but we found lion tracks at a cattle trough on the Sands' property, nearly ten miles northwest of our last clues. We followed them into a likely gully where we put the dogs in. Lots of barking ensued and we were sure it must be the lion. This time the dogs had tried to bay up a bull giraffe that was most indignant, coming for me with front legs stamping and in the process struck one dog stone dead.

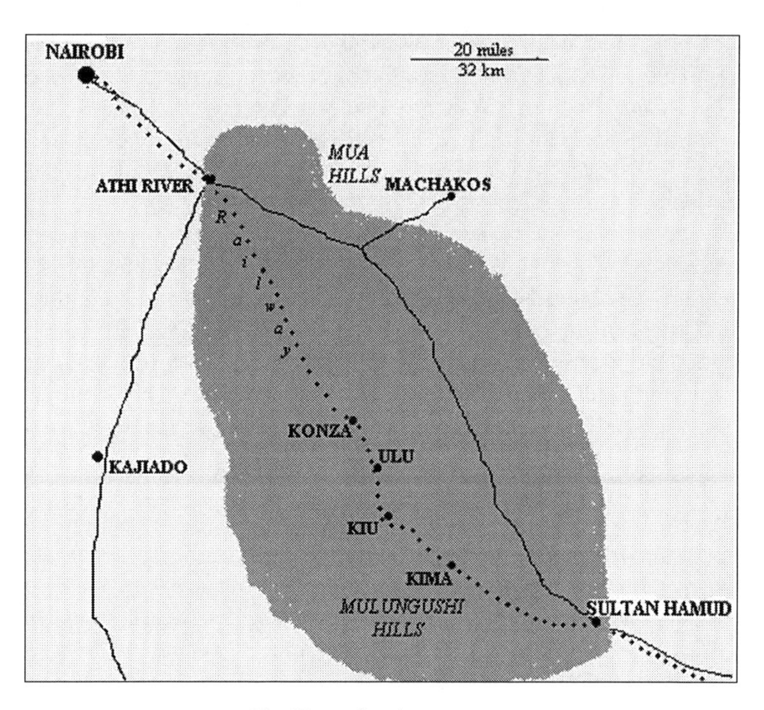

The Kapiti lion's territory.

We detached ourselves from this encounter and continued on the lion's tracks to where he had lain up, but had obviously been disturbed by the commotion and taken off. Once more we lost him, but noted that the general line of retreat was the same as in the previous two pursuits. Over the next few days we visited all the known waterholes in the area but the lion had not used any of them. We then placed baits widely, hoping that he would be tempted to one of them. To stop vultures consuming them, we covered the kills with brush early in the mornings and opened them up every evening, but no luck. He was not tempted. After a few days we replaced the baits and changed their positions but still no luck.

We had covered the ground so extensively that soon after the giraffe incident all the dogs became lame. A combination of very hot soil and stony ground had left them with no soles to their feet, so Heather went to the local boot maker, obtained some soft pliable leather and fitted all the dogs with little bootees. Training the dogs to wear them was a problem but they eventually learnt and their soles soon recovered.

Lions like to drink frequently and when, day after day, our routine patrols to all known water points in the Kapiti lion's range failed to yield tracks, I became certain that he must have a secret waterhole. In view of the times that its tracks had headed towards the hills drained by the seasonal Il Mulungush watercourse, I guessed they were where this water source would be. After days of patrol and investigation we found what we suspected must exist, a very small spring under a rock, which filled a small depression about a yard wide that spilled over before disappearing again underground. There were lion tracks everywhere about it, and we hoped we had at last found our quarry's hidden water supply. We scouted around without disturbing the place too much and noted the hills had a series of wooded gullies separated by open ridges, which gradually descended towards the Il Mulungush watercourse. All these gullies could have hidden the lion.

The following morning we took the dogs and visited the spring with high expectations, but found no fresh tracks. With hopes dashed yet again, we returned to base to be greeted with the news that at Sultan Hamud Estate owned by a Mr Sergeant, a cow had been lost to a lion overnight. Despite the lateness in the day, we went there, easily found the tracks in very dry and dusty black cotton soil and followed them. Despite being about six miles as the crow flies the from spring, we were sure from the preference for prime rump steak and an early exit to distance himself from the scene while it was still dark, that this was our lion. Sure enough, the tracks crossed the main road and railway and headed for the hills above the Il Mulungush watercourse, where we lost them on the stony ground just before dark. As the lion had drunk at a cattle trough on the way it was unlikely to need any more water that day, so we decided a visit to the spring next morning would not be worthwhile.

Instead, on the following day, we placed new fresh baits in the area of the spring, having dragged them in and around the gullies and hidden them from the vultures. The following morning we found the lion had at last been tempted and had eaten a good portion of rump steak. The net was closing in on this illusive animal and we felt certain we had the right one. We made no attempt to track that morning, leaving the area undisturbed and planning to return the next morning early. If he had fed we would then have some fresh tracks to follow.

This was the right tactic. Returning early the following morning we found he had taken a drink at the spring, leaving fresh tracks. With the dogs on leashes we quietly followed them to the first wooded gully, where the pack showed excitement and apprehension. Releasing the dogs as usual all hell was soon let loose in a cacophony of barks growls and snarls. Unfortunately, the lion broke away before we saw him, crossing over an open ridge and down into the next gully where the dogs again tried to bay him up. Again he escaped back up the gully and over the next ridge top, across open ground and into a third gully. The dogs were now very thirsty and tired. One by one they returned to us.

Feeling sure that the lion would stay in the third gully and that it was pointless to try to bay him up again so soon, we returned to the spring to quench our thirst, cool off and rest until nearly three p.m. before resuming. With the rest of the afternoon ahead of us we would take our time, because we did not want to lose the lion again for weeks.

Returning to the third gully, I sent Legeria to the top end, left Labuny at the lower end, where I entered the thicket with the dogs on leashes, intending to work along its whole length at the bottom of the gully. I had not gone far when the pack became excited. Less than a minute after unleashing the dogs there was a rumpus ahead and I glimpsed the lion racing up the gully with the dogs in hot pursuit. I shouted a warning to Legeria, who took a shot as it emerged towards him. The bullet clipped its shoulder and turned the lion back towards me. The pack held him in view for a few seconds during which I was unable to shoot at a vital area without risking a dog, so fired at a back leg, breaking it at the hip. The lion now took off again, considerably slowed down, heading straight to Labuny, who killed him as he broke cover, still fighting off the dogs.

He had been in the prime of life, in beautiful condition but with only a poor scraggy mane. After skinning him and leaving his carcass for the vultures, we set off back to the car, carrying a dog that was suffering badly from being cuffed by the lion. The dog was stiff next morning but recovered completely during the following days. But for the giraffe casualty, the pack was still intact.

While at breakfast with Les and Maria Mousley the following morning one of Les's herders came in to say that a lion had killed a steer near the cattle yards. I couldn't believe it. Indeed a large calf had been killed but not by a lion. Following tracks of a leopard, we unleashed the dogs and within five minutes had the spotted villain in the back of the Land Rover. Maria was presented with the skin in some recompense for the lost steer and all the bait meat they had provided for the Kapiti lion exercise.

The Kapiti lion was unusual in that booking it had taken almost six weeks. We did not often have to deal with individual animals that were so difficult to account for and time involved was measured more usually in days than weeks.

* * * *

I returned to my private trout farm and had already put some ponds in action when I got a frantic message from Divisional Warden Jack Barrah, asking me go to Thomson's Falls and find out what was happening there. Nothing had been heard from Major Mohamed since I handed over to him two months previously. Nobody was sure where all the rifles and ammunition, together with the keys of the armoury and other vital Government property were.

Mohamed had absconded to Somalia, leaving everything with the Sergeant Game Scout, all in order and nothing missing. The reason why no office work had been done before he left was because Mohamed was illiterate and only able to sign his name, which of course was all that had been necessary on the hand over documents. His single achievement as Warden was, sadly, to arrange for all the Thomson's Falls hippo to be shot.

For the next six weeks until a replacement became available, I again ran the station. As I was no longer on the pay roll, I could not be paid any salary for this service. In lieu, I was given two free elephant licences. Thus ended my service with the Game Department. Remuneration had been pathetic, but I had enjoyed it and when I left, it was not without regrets.

The graves and the haunted house at Kipini
(photo of house Tony Carn, graves Monty Brown).

CHAPTER 31: KIPINI'S GHOSTS

Tony Carn

On August Bank Holiday 1960 we went to Kipini. It had rained heavily and getting the old Austin lorry through a twenty-two mile stretch of black cotton soil had given us much trouble. Eventually, in the late evening, we reached Kipini, exhausted and covered in black mud.

A small port town near the mouth of the Tana River, Kipini was very much off the beaten track, even though it had once been the District headquarters. It is littered with Arab ruins, and has an all-pervasive atmosphere of having been greater long ago. Even when it was District headquarters, Kipini was a back water: the sort of place that Administrators on their first tours or who would rise no further were posted to, to serve out their final tours of duty.

As the Tana River was the single artery around which the District's life revolved and little ever went on in the arid wastes away from it, the District Commissioner had a boat (the 'Barge' – a shallow draft vessel encased in mosquito netting to control these pests which whined both day and night in Tana River District) as his main means of transport. His safaris were mainly up and down the hundred-mile length of the river within his district. This, alone, imparted a 'Sanders of the River' ambience to the position of DC, Tana River. To my eyes, the place was attractive: sandy beaches, good fishing, bird shooting and a chance to learn Kiswahili and Arabic. This was obviously not perceived by a certain Mr Pitt, who was posted there as an Assistant District Commissioner in 1915. He wrote a poem, one of twelve verses reading:–

I'm sick of spicy breezes,
I loathe your coral strand
And the surf that roars
On the reef girt shores
Of this God-forsaken land

It betrays a somewhat different vision of Kipini to mine.

The final blow to Kipini came in 1958 when it lost its status as district headquarters. Things had changed almost overnight because of the 'Hola incident'. As implied by the name itself, Hola is truly a hole: the type of hole to which one can attach many adjectives. It is hot, dusty, mosquito-ridden and remote: all good reasons why it was made a detention centre for the very hardest of the hard core who evaded the hangman's noose in Kenya's Mau Mau Emergency. And it was here that in 1958, some of these detainees died of mistreatment at the hands of prisons warders.

The overseas press got hold of the news and such was the outcry that the Commissioner of Prisons had to resign and, *inter alia*, the district headquarters were moved there, the better to control events. It was a strange decision, almost as strange as changing the name of the place to Galole, as though this would expiate the inhumanity with which Hola had become associated. Losing headquarter status pushed Kipini yet further of the beaten track, and though the little hospital still functioned and the postal agency sold stamps, the airstrip was overgrown and the petrol pump no longer worked. It was all a bit sad.

Normally I and my Scouts camped when on safari, but on that August Bank Holiday evening in 1960, we were so weary and mud-spattered that I decided to bed down in the abandoned DC's house, while the Scouts made themselves comfortable in the surrounding out-houses. It saved us the chore of pitching tents. On the morrow I would attend to the hippo that was giving trouble and then, perhaps, stay on for a day or so wandering about this historic outpost.

The DC's house was unusual and had been built by Germans in the German colonial style at the end of the 1890's. Double-storied, thick-walled, with a corrugated iron roof and netted-in upstairs and downstairs verandahs, it had been altogether more substantial than was normal in British district headquarters. There were at least four bedrooms upstairs and at least as many rooms downstairs, all with wooden shutters and lofty ceilings that kept temperatures cool even in the hottest seasons. Although it was only two years since the last DC had resided in it, dereliction was already well advanced. Yet, on that evening in 1960, this mattered little. I had a roof over my head, even if the whole house did smell strongly of bats.

My gear was brought into one of the lower rooms and my servant, who had been with me since Forest Department days, rapidly erected my camp bed, produced a bottle of beer, a hot meal and hot water for a shower: no slumming for me! Well set for the night, I personally went round the entire house, fastening all the wooden shutters so that if the wind rose in the night, they would not rattle and bang. As dark fell I lit my Tilley pressure lamp. This produced excellent white light, but it was temperamental and needed careful handling. Its vaporiser needed thorough pre-heating with a little methylated spirit pad to ensure that the kerosene was vaporised fully before opening the cock that allowed it to ignite. Any attempt to hasten the process, to short circuit the full and careful routine, produced a swirling, smoking orange flame that, in an instant, coated the lamp glass with soot. If this happened there was no recourse but to let it all cool down, remove the glass, clean it and start again from the beginning. Lighting the Tilley called for strict routine and a large measure of patience. Its other disadvantage was that it got very hot and, in an enclosed room, smelt of kerosene.

Sometime after seven thirty the wind rose a little and the old house creaked and groaned to itself making a variety of companionable noises. I was tired, so turned off the light and was soon asleep. It must have been around midnight that I awoke to footsteps on the wooden upstairs verandah. Though my first reaction had been without question that they were footsteps, I quickly reasoned that the sounds must come from the old planks expanding and contracting. Then, just as distinctly, I heard footsteps on the stairs. Again, I reasoned, old stairs are always noisy. Then a shattering thought hit me: the stairs were cold, silent concrete and not creaking, warping wood. Then there was a scream; a woman's scream from somewhere upstairs and I was upright in bed sweating and thoroughly frightened. I needed light: quickly. One part of my mind refused to accept the prospect of ghosts, I was in no doubt whatsoever about the screams I had heard.

Fumbling in the dark I located the Tilley, matches and methylated spirits and, willing myself to follow the routine procedure, set about lighting it. I was in the midst of the process when the woman upstairs screamed again, jangling my now over-stretched nerves and in haste I twiddled the little black knob that regulated the vaporiser. There was a sheet of swirling yellow and orange flame, and I turned the knob to the off position, but the damage had been done and I had burned a finger badly. The lamp glass was coated in black soot and would have to be stripped out and cleaned. Yet there was no time for this and as I struggled to restart the lighting process, there were several loud knocks on the door from my room onto the outside verandah. Forcing myself to go through the lighting regime slowly, I managed to get the Tilley working, but the light was dim for the glass was well and truly blackened.

By now I was angry and I had an impression that someone was trying to evict me from the bedroom. At this time of night I was going nowhere. There was a crash from upstairs followed by a noise like a cannon ball being rolled over the wooden floor. This was ridiculous: I didn't believe in ghosts. Indeed my old Forest Department house on Mount Kenya was supposed to have been haunted, but it had never worried me. I was used to being alone. Yet reaching for my Winchester rifle, loading it and pointing it at the double doors made me feel better. So there I sat on the edge of my bed, prepared to blast anything that came through the doors, though nothing on earth would have induced me to open them, let alone go upstairs where most of the action was taking place. I prayed that the Tilley had enough fuel to last until dawn, which miraculously it did.

Things quietened down after two o'clock. The crashings and bangings gradually subsided though the old house still moaned to itself in the wind and the smell of bats became more pronounced. With my rifle to hand I dozed on and off, but never went back to sleep properly. At dawn I was weary and out of sorts, but there was still that hippo to deal with. Going down to the little jetty alongside the slipway where the DC's boat was still careened every six months, I met with the two Pokomo who were to show me the troublesome hippo. Getting in to their leaky canoe, I half hoped that the hippo would not appear and I could leave in peace to mull over the night's events. I had no such luck. We had barely reached deep water when several canoe lengths away, up shot a large hippo head with jaws agape. Yelling at the two paddlers to hold still and give me a steady platform for a shot, I had my rifle up. It was to no avail as they panicked, the canoe rocked wildly on its outrigger and my snap shot hit the hippo, but was not lethal and the hippo submerged. Now we were for it. The two Pokomo were desperate to get ashore despite my bad language. In the midst of this very unsettled state there was a whoosh and there was the hippo so close that water splashed into the canoe. I got off another snap shot at almost point blank range. Again it was not lethal and the hippo disappeared under water. By now we had a crowd of observers on the shore. The hippo came after us again, noticeably more slowly, and again the heavy rifle crashed out. Eventually it surfaced dead, the many bullets having taken effect and Kipini's hippo problem was resolved. Yet it had not been a good performance on my part and I was glad no one in authority had witnessed this unedifying exercise in game control.

A tetchy hippo is among the most dangerous of animals (photo Peter Davey).

Back on shore my Scouts divined my bad mood and were silent. We packed up the old lorry and I shelved any plans to stay on and go over Kipini's ruins, though not before I noted three graves in front of the District Commissioner's house that I had missed the previous evening. The black-cotton soil that had given us such problems the day before had dried out a little and we were back at my house at Hindi on the Lamu mainland by late morning. I write house: in fact I lived in a converted chicken run in the Agriculture Department compound. It had a hard floor, mud walls and a leaky grass roof, but it was my home in those bachelor years. It contrasted badly with my previous Forest Department station with its double storey house and ample space. That night I was not disturbed by thumps and bangs, but my burned finger gave me considerable pain.

Next morning I took the boat over to Lamu Island to get it treated and went to see District Commissioner John Simpson. John was a bachelor and of the old school who, for all that he was most hospitable, demanded due deference to his rank and was a bit of a stickler for proper procedure. Once, when staying with him, he gave me a rocket for appearing in his court without a tie. He had been in Lamu for a long time, resisting transfers elsewhere, and regarded the District as his personal kingdom. His pride and joy was his official boat – the *Rasini*. Indeed, I had an impression that if any part of Lamu District could not be reached by *Rasini*, in his eyes it was not worth reaching.

I recounted my experiences of a night in Kipini and waved my bandaged finger to make the points. John had been amused. "Which room did you make your bed in?" he had asked. When I told him he had replied, "that was a mistake. Officers over-nighting in Kipini are always advised to sleep upstairs or they will be disturbed. I have slept there several times and just ignored the noises you hear. There is no need for alarm and getting burned fingers! But, you really should avoid wandering at night near the old Sultan's Fort here in Lamu, for *there* you really can get chased by spirits." He had been grinning to himself at the time, but then we had gone on to discuss elephant damage in cotton fields at Witu.

Returning to my little house on the mainland I called for my Game Scout Corporal, who had lived at the coast all his life, and told him about my experiences in the DC's house at Kipini. Just as had John Simpson, he had replied, "Oh Bwana, everyone knows about Kipini and the mzuka (ghost) and no one enters the old house at night. The out-houses, are quite all right however."

As was often the case, I was the last to find out about local lore and history. No one had ever mentioned the DC's house in Kipini, though in truth, neither had I ever asked. What I learned that morning in August 1960 set me on my own line of enquiry. In the Agricultural Office at Lamu there was a confidential file compiled by one of the last DCs to live at Kipini before the district headquarters moved to Galole. It was a contentious document that had never been either sanctioned or accepted by the DC's superiors. The elements of contention suggested that Somali claims to some areas on the Tana River had substance. At the time the Government in Mogadishu was agitating for large sections of northern Kenya to be ceded to Somalia and any official British document giving even remote credence to such claims was political dynamite. Yet the file read well and may have, in parts, been written slightly with tongue in cheek.

My interest was Appendix 14 on page 145 headed 'Ghosts of Kipini'. The historical facts surrounding the building of the Kipini DC's house were not entirely accurate, but I was intrigued by reference to the Mr Pitt whose verse I have already mentioned and from which it is clear that he loathed Kipini. In 1915 he had set off on safari up the Tana in his official barge, but only went a short way before collapsing in a malarial coma. The boat returned to Kipini, but Pitt died and was buried in front of the house.

Next I read of one of Pitt's successors, a Mr Duff. He, too, was stricken with melancholia and so distressed by his circumstances that he committed suicide. How, the report did not say, but local legend has it that he hanged himself somewhere inside the house. He occupied the second grave in front of the house.

Whether Duff knew that his mother was coming to visit him when he departed this world, we will never now know. Yet this was so, and when the poor lady arrived from overseas to stay with her son, it was to learn that he was no more. She nonetheless did reach Kipini where, for reasons unknown, she, too, died and was buried next to her son.

Those then, are the bones of the Kipini ghost legends. As with all such tales, they acquire additions and embellishments. One of them was that the DC Kipini of the time was a certain Mr Luckman, a harsh man who drove his assistants Pitt and Duff to their deaths and no doubt contributed to Mrs Duff's too. The story was well known to the residents of Kipini and many visitors to the DC's house, even before it was vacated, had heard tappings and voices at night. In 1955 a Mr Rawl saw the wraith of a white woman, and several of the local caretakers say they have seen figures in the house. My own experience was thus one among many, none of which I had heard before Bank Holiday, August 1960.

CHAPTER 32: FROM NGONG TO GARISSA

Dave McCabe

Towards the end of 1960, I was transferred to open a new station at Ngong, a few miles west of Nairobi. The need for this post had arisen from a rising tide of complaints about game depredations around the fringe of Nairobi's expanding suburbia and the nearby ranches east to Sultan Hamud as well as those in the Rift Valley as far west as Mau Narok and as far north as the Kinangop Plateau. In recent months matters had been made worse due to the serious 1960 - 61 drought which had left much of the countryside, especially in Masailand, denuded of grazing. Very many Masai cattle had died and much game had moved into settled areas, concentrating on the better managed grazing. Predators of all kinds had, of course, followed and had had a field day among the debilitated herds and domestic livestock. Hitherto the staff of Nairobi National Park had dealt with these peri-urban problems, but it had all become too much for them to handle.

My main occupation initially was shooting and trapping lions. Those trapped were translocated to a national park. On one or two occasions a trapped lion was 'claimed' by the Nairobi Park people as being one of theirs and they insisted that it be sent back there. I was not happy with this. Nairobi Park was too close to the place of capture. One such lion, a rather fine male, again left the park soon after being returned and was once again causing trouble in the Ngong area. It now avoided traps and I shot it, which was not popular.

Zebra, literally in their thousands, had moved into the ranching areas from Athi River to the Ulu hills. The ranchers were not only losing what little grazing they had left, but their fences were continually broken and their water troughs emptied as fast as they could be filled. Given the scale of the drought, I could provide them with very limited assistance. The only answer was to shoot the zebra. In an effort to recover some of the costs of this work, we erected a small shed adjacent to the Scouts' quarters at the end of the Ngong Hills to accommodate the zebra hides, which were salted and sold 'green' to the public (Shs 10/= for a 'run of the mill' hide and Shs 15/= for the better-marked skins).

Some days were spent dealing with a hyaena problem at the back of the extinct volcano Mount Suswa in the Masai Reserve. In daylight, many holed up in hollows along the slopes of the lava flows. Shooting with a very accurate telescopic sighted .22 Hornet as they emerged in late evening worked for some days, after which we resorted to poisoning with strychnine baits. At first light I recovered all uneaten baits. On one morning I had just crossed a lava flow when, slightly below me, a hyaena shambled across my front. Hotfoot some sixty to seventy yards behind came a Masai Moran with a spear. This may not sound very spectacular, but in fact he was a wonderful sight, travelling at a tremendous pace, leaping and bounding over the most broken ground imaginable, in many places real ankle-twisting terrain, his red 'shuka'(toga) trailing but otherwise stark naked. The entire scene was lit up by the rising sun. Foolishly I brought it to an end by shooting the hyaena. The Masai, previously unaware of my presence, stopped abruptly, stared at me for a second or two, and stalked off. That he could attain such a speed over that awful surface was incredible: an unforgettable sight!

* * * *

Towards the end of 1961, I was moved yet again, this time to Garissa which has already been described by Ken Smith so I will forego the details and refer to an unusual operation, which took place during my tenure as Warden there. For sometime there had been rumours of a project to dam the Tana with a huge barrage some distance downstream from Garissa to facilitate large-scale settlement and irrigation. If this was to go ahead, much of the surrounding countryside would, due to the topography, become flooded. Suffice it that the chances of this project going ahead seemed strong[69]. Somebody thought the inundation would affect the Hunter's antelope habitat[70]. Another somebody, or perhaps the same somebody, must have decided that the possibility existed, and that the feasibility of relocating as many of the species as possible to a safe haven should be examined.

Hunter's antelope has a limited distribution in Garissa District north of the Tana and into a small part of contiguous Somalia. The species seems to have first been described by Sir R. G. Harvey in a letter to Sir J. V. C. Willoughby. This letter is appended to a book written by Willoughby published in 1889. Hunter had been Harvey's companion on a shooting trip and it was he who shot the first specimen known to western science.

The feasibility study was handed to Alistair Graham, a qualified zoologist at that time employed by the Game Department. An alternative home for the Hunter's had been suggested as the Dika plains, a tract of rather open country within the Tsavo East National Park between the Voi River and the Mombasa/Nairobi Railway.

Alistair was initially based with us, but later set up camp at Bura on the north bank of the Tana downstream from Garissa. This turned out to be inconvenient so camp was moved eastwards to Madahaduni some few miles from Ijara and adjacent to the Lamu road. Madahaduni was an artificially deepened natural water hole that contained semi-permanent water. Together with my family I joined Alistair at Madahaduni.

Once Alistair could see no reason why their intended new home would not be suitable for the Hunter's, the next step was planning the movement of animals

---

[69] Editor's note: it did.

[70] Editor's note: it didn't.

captured to Tsavo. Chief of the problems was distance. From the point of capture to Tsavo via the Tana River bridge many miles upstream at Garissa was considered altogether too great. However, this was solved by an arrangement made in Nairobi whereby the British Army's Royal Electrical & Mechanical Engineers (REME) undertook to install a ferry across the Tana if we indicated a suitable site. Alistair chose Wadesa on the south bank not far from Bura. By chance this was where the South African forces had installed a ferry during the Second World War during their advance to Somalia. Nearby was the old SA Airforce airfield which required little work to renovate. The presence of the ferry shortened the distance to Tsavo very considerably.

To reduce the distance even more, an old Shell oil-prospecting track heading roughly southwest from a point on the Garsen-Garissa road into the Galana Game Management Scheme was renovated and connected to the Blixen/Finch-Hatton road at Dakadima. The route would then be down this road to the Sabaki and thence to the Dika plains where the antelope were to be released.

Once the route was organised we all moved to Wadesa to establish a base for the actual capture operation. The World Wildlife Fund provided funding for the project. While we were busy building holding pens for the Hunter's antelope, the REME contingent turned up with their prefabricated ferry. This may be worth describing. Forty-gallon drums contained in a massive timber case provided flotation. The entire upper frame was decked with substantial planking. In both length and width it exceeded any vehicle we were likely to load on it. The upstream side of the wooden cage was fully covered to act with the current as a paraplane. Both fore and aft were three sheave pulley blocks, which were attached to similar blocks on an overhead cable that had been stretched tightly across the river secured at each end to a large tree (scars of the S African cable still showed on the same tree on the north bank). Tightening the ropes at one end of the ferry platform while slackening them at the other, angled the ferry so that the current against the upstream boarded-up side produced a paraplaning effect and drove it one way. Reversing the process drove it in the opposite direction.

The antelope holding pens were constructed of bush pole uprights laced laterally at intervals with purlins and the sides were thatched with palm leaves to restrict the inmates' visibility beyond the pens entirely. They had no roofs. Being hartebeests we though it unlikely that Hunter's were jumpers of note, but to be safe, walls were made 12 feet tall. Each pen enclosed an area of 8 x 8 metres and we made twelve of them. In addition we made timber transport crates in which to confine the animals when they were transported to Voi. When all was ready, the capture team arrived.

In charge was Tony Macguire who had had previous experience with a private game capture company. Anaesthetising techniques had not yet been developed for antelope and Tony was going to use the old-fashioned chase and noose system. The catching car, originally a Ford V8 pick-up, had been modified so

Hunter's Antelope:(a) The chase, (b) captured and (c) unloaded (photos Dave McCabe).

Hunter's Antelope: (a) Penned, (b) crated and (c) flown to Tsavo (photos Dave McCabe).

that it was completely open with a wide timber flat bed at the rear. The noose man stood behind the driver and wielded a long pole with a lasso attached to the business end, and clung on to the roll bar over the driver's position. Tony, as driver, would cut an animal out of a herd and give chase until in a position from which the catcher could drop the lasso over the animal's head. The vehicle then came to a halt, helpers leapt off the back and overpowered the animal. Once restrained, the victim was blindfolded, which stopped it struggling.

Tony usually returned to camp after catching two or three antelope each day. These were released into the pens before removal of the blindfold. Several antelope were held in each, although never more than one adult male to a pen. Feed consisted of lucerne and hay. I cannot remember whether the Hunter's drank at all; certainly they lived in a seasonally waterless area in their wild state. While the males were aggressive, we were pleasantly surprised at how quickly the rest of the penned animals became docile. A few days after delivering the first ten or so antelope to their holding pens in the Tsavo Park, David Sheldrick radio-ed that some had died and others were not looking too good. We put this down to stress from the thirteen hour drive from the Tana to Tsavo Park. While chewing this over, David Sheldrick radio-ed again to say that the Royal Air Force was prepared to help. As a trial run, four Hunter's were flown from our airstrip to Tsavo in a Twin Pioneer. All survived. Hopes of this being the solution to our problems were dashed when the RAF said that there would be no further flights.

None of the animals moved to Voi had been held long at our Tana camp. Perhaps the casualties could be avoided by holding them for a longer period to permit recovery from the capture trauma and improveme their stamina before the move. So new captures were temporarily stopped.

During the enforced delay we amused ourselves in various ways. A pilot friend wished to shoot a crocodile and I accompanied him some miles upstream where he achieved his wish. It was while waiting for him to walk back to camp and fetch our boat (a large dug-out with an outrigger and driven by a small outboard), that I had to perform an imperative natural function. Having no paper of any description I resorted to a handful of leaves from a nearby shrub. Within a few minutes I had strange feelings from my fundament which seemed to be shrinking and soon felt as though it ceased to exist. Extremely worried with visions of surgery and replacement parts, I asked George Adamson, who was with us, if he had ever heard of this phenomenon. George was amused, but although having no similar experience himself, knew of the plant and that Somalis used it as a treatment for piles. Happily the constriction cleared up after a few days and all returned to normal.

At almost the last minute before recommencing road trips, David Sheldrick radio-ed to say that the Royal Navy thought they might be able to help with helicopters of *HMS Ark Royal* currently anchored at Mombasa for a few weeks. An RN Officer would be arriving shortly in our camp to see what was required.

Welcome news indeed. The Royal Navy ground contingent arrived and impressed us all with their efficiency and enthusiasm. While flight crew used our camp, a second camp was established for the ground crew. The men were interested in all around them: from the lavatory, a long drop type whose seat was a large elephant's inverted lower jawbone (large backside, sit further back, and vice versa), to the kitchen with its open fire and oven consisting of an old steel ammunition box in which the cook turned out loaf after loaf of excellent bread daily, to the messing arrangements and 'bar'. To this day it is a wonder to me how my wife managed to run this huge domestic operation with such success[71].

At the time the Fleet Air Arm Squadrons on *HMS Ark Royal* were flying Westland Wessex helicopters. A daily shuttle of five or six crated antelope at a time was started. At one point, with two helicopters in use, we nearly ran out of crates, and Tony Macguire was kept busy catching fresh antelope to replace those being flown out. Thoughts of acclimatising the animals before relocation had to be abandoned in order to avoid delaying the helicopters.

The operation ran remarkably smoothly. Word of it soon reached the media and a stream of journalists began to turn up from Nairobi. Invariably they came by air, buzzing the camp so that someone had to collect them from the airfield. We were soon fed up with these very demanding visitors. There was little unobtrusive about them and simple ground rules such as not making holes in the holding pen walls or taking flashlight pictures of the antelope were continually breached. One wretch even had the gall to tell us that his aircraft would be collecting him the following day as he wished to stay overnight. Except for a toothbrush and pyjamas he had brought nothing. From then on any buzzing aircraft without prior approval via the radio were ignored. A great exception was Des and Jen Bartlett, professional wildlife photographers, who arrived completely self-contained even bringing us the odd luxuries.

Capture slowed down. Tony Macguire was finding the herds becoming wilder as time passed. Chases prior to roping were taking longer and may have caused a number of deaths in the holding pens. Post mortems indicated a high incidence of the muscular dystrophy associated with excessive exertion. Consequently actual chase time was limited to a maximum of three minutes. Whether this had the desired effect I cannot remember, but it reduced the inflow of captured animals to a trickle. As the *Ark Royal*'s departure date was approaching, catching ceased and, after the last antelope had been crated and flown out, we all packed up and went our different ways. In all, over seventy Hunter's antelope were delivered to Voi, a substantially greater catch than I had initially hoped for.

David Sheldrick held as many animals as possible and then released them *en masse*, hoping that they would make off in groups rather than individually. I

---

[71] Editor's note: Wardens' wives (and sometimes girl friends) were the Department's unsung heroines. Without any pay they actually managed a great deal of the Department's behind-the-scenes administration.

gather that this never happened since each animal headed for the horizon individually as it emerged from the pen. For some years it was thought that the operation had failed. Yet, in recent times (the 1990s) it was confirmed that a small population of Hunter's antelope was established on the Dika plains and the project had indeed been successful. There was a second operation in the 1990s to augment them with fresh blood from north of the Tana.

Our success was due to the Royal Navy and the *Ark Royal*'s helicopters. Had all relocation been done by road, I have little doubt that deaths would have been far higher. The Royal Navy's involvement with conservation on the Kenya coast had started earlier in 1962 when squadrons from the carriers *HMS Albion* and *HMS Bulwark* flew in both Tsavo East and the Galana Scheme, helping with elephant counts. It had developed into something of a tradition that when a Royal Navy helicopter-equipped ship called at Mombasa, the helicopters' services were offered to either Game Department or National Park projects at Her Majesty's expense. A highlight I will long remember was while flying low over Malindi one day, the pilot pulled the helicopter up short to hover over a block of flats. Lying sunbathing on the roof below us, flat on her back and perfectly naked was an attractive young lady. Most generously she never batted an eyelid or moved, allowing those above to inspect her very considerable charms in detail. Presumably she assumed that the helicopter crew would never make her acquaintance. Had she known I was in the helicopter she might not have been so revealing, as I knew her well.

* * * *

Towards the end of my tenure in Garissa, the Somali rebellion to make the NFD part of Somalia was developing apace and making work north of the Tana all but impossible. I was transferred to take over the Galana Game Management Scheme whose origins and purpose are described elsewhere in this volume. I had to take over Galana before handing over Garissa to my successor (in fact I never did hand over the Garissa station, and to all intents and purposes, it was abandoned by the Game Department for several years) and for several months was responsible, not only for running both stations, but also for settling my family in Malindi. Consequently I had to travel frequently between my two responsibilities. One such trip stands out in my memory.

I left Malindi with a bad hangover and a Garissa Game Scout for company. Fifty miles beyond Galole (a.k.a. Hola) there had been a freak wash-away. After waiting several hours for the water to subside, damage to the road was so severe that it was no longer negotiable except on foot. Being Easter, the likelihood of another vehicle along the road was slight. I have never understood quite why we did not simply drive back the fifty miles to Hola and radio via the Police there for Garissa to send a vehicle to meet us at the wash-away. Perhaps the hangover was worse than I realised, but I elected to walk the sixty or so miles to Garissa.

The Game Scout and I walked most of that night, sleeping in the sand for an hour or two before setting off again as it got light. It was soon very hot. We had only one water bottle between us, which didn't last long. In view of this we agreed that the Scout should make for Garissa via the parallel Tana River and therefore have water, while I continued to follow the road. Whoever reached Garissa first would send a vehicle to collect the other.

The road was practically dead straight; coming over one of the slight rises more miles of straight road stretching into the distance met the eye. A very late night celebrating Easter with strong drink, and then having had no food since the previous morning had a cumulative effect as the day wore on. I felt awful and very thirsty. Then, way in the distance, I saw a road grader heading my way. Relief flooded through me. Then, two hundred yards short of me, it swung into the bush, reversed out again and set off back the way it had come. Absolutely incensed with rage, it took me some time to work out a probable cause for the grader driver's strange behaviour.

It was logical for him to assume that a gun-toting figure on the road was likely to be a Somali shifta. The prospect of a lone white Government official walking down the Garissa road was so unlikely that his reaction was understandable. I must be rid of the rifle lest the next potential saviour also make the same mistake. Selecting two small adjoining anthills as recognisable marks some fifty yards off the road, I hid the rifle in the grass behind them.

Having done this I returned to the road, hoping that the grader driver would report seeing a shifta, which would result in an armed patrol being sent out. This never happened. It must have been at about this time that I could no longer stand the heat and knew that I should find shade and lie up until evening. There was no foliage left on any of the local thorn trees and the remaining thin sticks provided no shade. I really cannot remember much that occurred after this except that I kept walking. I do recollect finding myself imitating the call of nearby turtledoves at one stage. I also remember a compulsion to remove my clothing but managed to resist it, as I knew it to be a bad thing to do. I must have been seriously dehydrated and hyperthermic. When within sight of the T-junction at the Garissa-Nairobi road a lorry passed across my front but failed to see me. However, I only covered a short distance of the remaining five miles to Garissa before being picked up by a rescue party sent out by Brunie. The Game Scout had beaten me by a short head but was so exhausted that he had had difficulty in explaining the situation.

Once revived two days later, I went to recover the hidden rifle. The number of similar small adjoining anthills in a hundred mile stretch of dry, 'nyika' bush is unbelievable. I thought I recognised my landmarks, but we couldn't find a rifle near them and as there were no signs of any humans having been there since I had left the gun, I had presumably selected the wrong pair. Suffice it that after driving back and forth for miles in either direction searching all likely ant heaps, we returned to the original spot as I was still convinced that this was the right place. Again we searched and searched futilely in widening circles until a Scout returning to the road about two hundred yards away stumbled on the rifle in the grass a couple of feet from the road edge where I must have dropped it two days earlier.

Yet to this day I still have a clear image in my mind not only of the twin anthills, but also of carefully placing the rifle directly behind them in the grass. The incident was salutary in more ways than one!

Netty McCabe and two stock killers on the banks of the Tana. Wardens' children were the greatest beneficiaries of the life style (photo Dave McCabe).

CHAPTER 33: THE CLOSING PHASE

Dave McCabe

At Galana, my 'house' was a rather primitive affair of 3 rooms under a thatched roof[72]. There were no doors or windows as such; merely gaps in the walls, the bedroom windows I think had wire netting screens. Sometime during the night I was awakened by a presence in the bedroom. The smell was unmistakably that of a lion, which presently began pushing itself against the mosquito net. 'Petrified' aptly describes an extreme state of fear. This was alleviated to a certain extent by the recollection that a previous Warden, Gilfrid Powys, had reared a lion cub which had become semi-tame and that this might be it. The beast made off into the living room from where came strange sounds followed by tearing noises outside. Torchlight through the 'window' revealed the lion tearing a sofa to pieces, which it had dragged out from the living room. The previous evening I had removed this sofa from the rafters, unable to understand why anyone would want to hoist it up there.

On the lighter side: 'Tiva', the lion, and I soon became great friends. At the time he must have been some three quarters grown and weighed perhaps 250 lbs. After spending his day lying up in the riverine saltbush, he would visit the house immediately after dark but would only come close after satisfying himself that I was alone. Once in the living room he became quite affectionate, mewing with pleasure and rubbing himself against my legs. He would become playful but he did not realise his own strength (which was phenomenal) and which, at times, needed to be controlled. A really hard blow on the nose, which he never seemed to resent, prevented too much roughness.

Tiva could not abide Africans and had no hesitation in demonstrating his hostility. Once, when Brunie and the children had arrived from Malindi accompanied by our house servant, I had forgotten to warn him and to keep out of sight. The wretched man, ignorant of the existence of Tiva, entered from the kitchen at the rear of the house to lay the dinner table. Tiva was lying about twenty paces away at the edge of the pool of light cast from the house. Although I immediately realised the danger, I was a fraction too late. Tiva, who must have got his legs under him on first sighting the man, was already coming in fast and obviously meant business. I was just in time to tackle him as he came through the front and hold him round the neck. By this time the servant had wheel spin on the polished floor with Tiva's wheels also slipping about trying to get after him. Still clasping Tiva I managed to calm him. At no time during our acquaintance had he ever extended claws in my presence, but I suspect that they would have come into use had he caught up with the servant. Tiva eventually ended up in the

[72] Editor's note: built in April 1960, it was temporary and planned to last eighteen months. It in fact stood for morc than twenty years.

Animal Orphanage at the Nairobi Park. I had had to trap him after he chased our two children. Shortly after sending him to Nairobi, the Kenya Govt presented Tiva to Emperor Haile Selassie of Ethiopia but he escaped from his cage en route to Nairobi airport and broke a leg. This was repaired but the lion of Galana never was sent to the Lion of Judah, (perhaps this was just as well in view of Tiva's racist attitudes) seeing out his days at the orphanage.

Things were not going well at Galana. Recurrent expenditure was exceeding income. Few of the original ex-poachers recruited by Ian Parker at the inception of the scheme remained and its role, where the Wata were concerned, was not being met. As foreseen in Ian's final report on the Scheme, Government could (or would) not provide any development capital. As had been the case from the very outset in 1960, the annual elephant quotas were still not being secured. Shortfalls in revenue were attributed to an apparent scarcity of elephant within the scheme boundaries[73]; elephant and the proceeds of their cropping - the sale of ivory, meat, feet, ears and various portions of skin – being the primary sources of income. Those few elephant that were located proved unusually nervous and wild, frequently clearing right out of the vicinity for miles at the slightest whiff of humans[74]. Government still accepted Ian's recommendation that Galana should be handed over to private enterprise, which is what happened in 1967. Until the hand over, however, the project was kept going very much as a hand-to-mouth holding operation, responsibility of which I was soon relieved to concentrate on other duties based at Malindi.

Through the mid-1960s, the security situation across northern and northeastern Kenya deteriorated in the face of Somali revolt. Normal Game Wardening north of the Tana River became impossible. My Game Department truck was burnt by Shifta in 1968 at Mbalambala, south of the Tana. A few Scouts were left based in Garissa itself and the rest I withdrew to Malindi. From there we attempted to manage game affairs over the three hundred mile stretch between Garissa and Malindi south of the Tana, as well as along the coast south of Malindi. As if this wasn't enough, Peter Saw, Game Warden Lamu, resigned at about this time, and I was instructed to keep an eye on the Lamu/Tana River range (also severely influenced by the Somali guerrillas) pending the return of normality.

In these early years after Kenya's independence from Britain, there was a powerful trend to centralise all administration and for the centre to control all government activity in the field. Whereas, under British rule, field officers were given as much freedom as possible to carry out their duties (and nowhere was this

---

[73] Editor's note: Aerial counting from 1968 through to the mid-1970s proved the scarcity more apparent than real and the Galana area consistently held >5,000 elephants.

[74] Editor's note: The intensity of hunting during the seven years that the Galana Scheme ran was far less than in the decades preceding its inception. If there was a local reaction to human presence, it will have been the cumulative result of hunting over a very long period.

more the case than in the Game Department), under African rule the reverse was true. Everything had to be sanctioned from the top. And by the top, I do not mean by the Chief Game Warden, but the Ministry under which the Department came. I have never really analysed why this happened, but observe that it wasn't peculiar to Kenya, but to all African states on their receipt of political freedom. By gathering all power unto themselves, by demanding that they make all decisions, the men at the top were soon overcome by the sheer volume of decisions that had to be made, and the whole machinery of governance wound down. As an aside, this centralisation also greatly facilitated the spread of corruption.

What we experienced was an ever increasing flow of paper, a large proportion of it bureaucratic rubbish, emanating from our ministry. Handling it progressively eroded the time we could spend in the field and became a real curse. Some field Wardens had no typewriter. Handwritten correspondence, formerly quite acceptable, was now "non-U" and was largely unread by Ministry petty bureaucrats whose sole interest in life was drawing their monthly salary. After official efforts to acquire a typewriter failed, I removed a brand new model from an empty office in the Ministry's chief storekeeper's building (I believe Rodney Elliott acquired one by the same method but was later called to account). I never heard another word - I wonder how the storekeeper sorted it out, perhaps he never missed it, it was that kind of set up. Suffice it that we rapidly developed a clerical wing to handle paper that had never existed before.

There were also more ominous signs appearing from the field. Sometime in 1969, I think, one of my foot-patrols encountered a Land Rover near the Ukambani border west of Hola in which there were several tusks. The driver was a Kikuyu woman who apparently showed the Scouts a letter authorising her to collect 'found' ivory. This document was purportedly signed, or had some connection with, President Kenyatta's wife. The Land Rover was without number plates and the two Wakamba accompanying her were strangers to the Scouts[75]. Issues such as these came to dominate my final years as Game Warden Malindi.

* * * *

I received an urgent call from Robin Pereira, Warden i/c the Ivory Room Mombasa. As the Senior Game Warden, Mombasa, was away; Robin requested my presence in Mombasa as soon as possible. Much of the ivory on the auction floor had been shoved to one side to accommodate a huge number of rhino

---

[75] Editor's note: The occupant of the Land Rover had produced a "collector's permit", the first of which were awarded by Presidential directive to ex-Mau Mau Freedom Fighters, ostensibly so that they could benefit from the trophies they collected and hid while in the forests seven years earlier. This was the foot in the door that developed into a spate of such collector's permits which undermined the already ineffectual State monopoly over all ivory other than tusks taken on licence.

horns, each pair of which had been removed from the parent carcase as a single unit. I am not certain how many there were[76] but recall Robin saying that there were seven hundred horns: that is three hundred and fifty pairs. Without exception, they were white rhino horns and therefore not Kenyan in origin. They had arrived in Kenya from Uganda, and while that country may have still had a few white rhino, they had fallen below a hundred early in the 1960s[77]. Most of the horns are thus likely to have originated in the Southern Sudan.

Robin Pereira who ran the Ivory Room for many years.

It transpired that Robin had received information of the shipment and, in conjunction with Customs, had just been in time to recover the whole lot at the dockside, arrest the Asian smuggler responsible and have him remanded in custody. The Asian was released the following morning, his case having been heard, not in open court, but by a Magistrate in chambers at 8a.m., that is an hour before courts normally opened. The accused pleaded guilty and was fined an insignificant amount. No witnesses had been called. I gather the Magistrate concerned subsequently had his hand smacked as a disciplinary measure. The smuggler quickly disappeared. Sadly it was not the last of our failures to secure convictions despite blatantly obvious guilt.

Mohamed, a Baluchi Assistant Game Warden sent to help me in Malindi, was immensely keen and had an uncanny nose for all forms of malfeasance. He also

---

[76] Editor's note: To have needed the floor of the Ivory Room cleared; there must have been at least one hundred and possibly several hundred pairs.

[77] Editor's note: Nick Carter darted some of the few survivors, which were transferred to Murchison Falls National Park in 1964.

had an incredible and detailed knowledge of Mombasa, its seamier characters and less salubrious neighbourhoods. Mohamed was sent to investigate the very recent killing of three elephant in the Mackinnon Road area. He returned with a number of spent cartridge cases collected at the scene. He also said he had a pretty good idea of which three men had shot the elephant. They all held current elephant licences, seemingly issued before the elephant were shot and that therefore all was in order. However, a physical check of licence counterfoils revealed that in fact all three had been issued after the elephants had been shot and that a collaborator in the Department's Licensing Section had backdated the licences.

The Central Firearms Bureau called in the three suspects' rifles and submitted them to ballistics tests against the cartridge cases collected. Every single case was matched. A clerk in the Licensing Section then vanished. Obviously he was the party who had back-dated the three elephant licences, but with the counterfoils in the prosecutor's hands, there could be no doubting that the three hunters had shot three elephants before they had licences to do so.

Once it was clear that prosecutions were inevitable, one of the three accused visited me by arrangement late one evening. He offered to compromise his two co-poachers in exchange for dropping the charges against himself, unaware that our conversation was being taped. As he was not prepared to provide a written statement, I declined the offer.

Among those outside the Mombasa Courts on the day of the hearing, were some members of the Nairobi Press. The Chief Game Warden was also present which was understandable. Less so, was the fact that he had brought his own private lawyer. Read into that what you will. Very shortly after the court hearing started, and while I was giving evidence, the magistrate stopped the proceedings. Two men entered the court and conferred with him after which he announced, to the amazement of all present including the prosecutors, that the State had entered a *nolle prosequi*. One of the men who entered the court and conferred with the magistrate was Kenya's Attorney General.

So that was almost that. Almost because we still held the three accuseds' rifles and their ivory which Mohamed had confiscated and was holding at the Ivory Room. The three poachers arrived at the Ivory Room several days later and demanded their ivory be given to them. Robin Pereira phoned me about this and I told him to hold onto the ivory as, so far as the Game Department was concerned, the tusks had not been legally acquired. The three stormed off saying that they were going straight to State House Mombasa and also that they would kill McCabe. To forestall any further nonsense with the ivory, Robin immediately took the tusks to the Collector of Customs, an old school friend of mine. I think this was the end of the matter so far as the ivory was concerned. Not so with the rifles as the Officer i/c the Central Firearms Bureau phoned to say that he had had instructions from "very high up" to return the weapons to their owners. He declined to go along with my suggestion that very slight bending of the barrels would finalise things once and for all.

Abdulla Sood Al-Busaidi (grandson of Sir Ali bin Salim, the highly respected Chief Liwali of Mombasa in colonial times), another very effective Arab Game Warden, suddenly disappeared. At home one day in Lamu and on the following morning he was nowhere to be found. His Land Rover was parked at the Scouts' quarters on the mainland. A thin air job: nobody knew anything about Abdulla's disappearance over which the Police were very cagey and positively obstructive. Finding no leads anywhere on the Coast, I mentioned Abdulla's disappearance to a close friend, an ex-Police Special Branch (SB) man. He in turn passed the mystery onto another ex-SB man now working in a similar capacity with the British Govt in Nairobi.

Abdulla was located under house arrest in Nairobi. However, once enquiries into his disappearance had gathered a certain momentum, he was released and returned to Lamu. The reasons for this detention without charge – a virtual official kidnapping - were never established. Abdulla himself said he never knew why, although he had been rapped over the knuckles just previously for some alleged remark denigrating the Govt. This incident occurred when a number of enquiries were in hand regarding the movement of illicit trophies along the coast, and Abdulla may have been suspected as having initiated one or more of them and his removal was merely to have him temporarily out of the way.

A gentleman I knew as Hatim had a large curio shop in Malindi and traded in game skins etc. Most curio dealers were suspect and Hatim was no exception, but his books were always in order. Years earlier he had had a run-in over illicit gold transactions with a Senior Superintendent of Nairobi Criminal Investigation Department who happened to be my brother. Perhaps this connection is what led him to paying me a visit.

Hatim was almost incoherent with rage and had to be calmed down before I could make sense of what he had to say. Apparently he was out for revenge as someone in Game Department headquarters had compromised some of his personal interests. The long and the short of it was that Hatim poured out a torrent of accusations and information concerning the skulduggery taking place with game trophies, naming senior members of the Game Department and other top civil servants. He had referred to ivory being flown out of the country from Nairobi International Airport. The scale of it was countrywide with ramifications as far afield as Uganda and clearly beyond my position as Game Warden Malindi to investigate. I told Hatim that Nairobi CID would have to be brought into it. He didn't like this but agreed to it if I was present when he was interviewed. Having got his agreement, I made the necessary contacts with the Police in Nairobi.

I had made Hatim's condition very clear to Nairobi, but for some reason Supt. Bell of Nairobi CID, who came to Malindi, left me out of it, and went straight to Hatim. What I do know is that Bell hot-footed it back to Nairobi and was killed a day or two later in a motor accident near the Uganda border. There were rumours that the accident had been contrived. I think Hatim believed this as he refused any further contact and clammed up about what he had already told me. Perhaps he feared being the victim of a similar 'accident'. A few weeks later Hatim died after leaving the road between Kilifi and Malindi and colliding with a tree. There may have been nothing more sinister than coincidence in this as he habitually drove like a maniac, but …?

I kept a private file with numerous items of information. Among them, for example, were copies of counterfoils removed from the Nairobi Licensing section by CID (and shown to me by a CID friend off the record) revealing how licences and permits were irregularly but routinely issued to certain people including officials. Also how CID attempts to generate prosecutions were all blocked from higher up in the Police or from the Attorney General's office. We were always looking over our shoulders and, sadly, in a fit of paranoia I destroyed my file.

My growing awareness of events on a scale never previously known in Kenya led to Assistant Game Warden Mohamed and I being invited to the house of Dr Mohamed Hyder, an Mswahili and a member of Kenya's National Park Board of Trustees. I believed him a man of integrity and thought the private meeting might be a move in the right direction. I was wrong as the Minister for Wildlife & Tourism under whom the Game Department fell was also present and, by then we Wardens were so suspicious of Government's higher echelons, that neither of us were happy to discuss anything but generalities in his presence. The foregoing gives some idea of the state of mind into which we fell after the upper ranks of the Game Department had been Africanised.

Ironically, I started my time in the Game Department on anti-poaching and ended it in the same way. The only difference being that in the beginning we succeeded. In the end there seemed no hope.

Inevitably, as part of the Africanization process, my own enforced retirement took place. When this time came, I was not sorry to leave, as matters seemed to be spiralling irretrievably out of control. Yet I still look back with nostalgia on the rather wonderful life we all led in the 'happy years'. When we started we really thought we were doing great things and yet were always pulling one another's legs. Therein lies a tale.

I admit to a slightly volatile temper: more accurately, perhaps, I am given to explosive outbursts that greatly relieve frustrations of the moment. They are cathartic – which is sometimes not understood. The idiosyncrasy had not gone unremarked by my colleagues. That is the background to an occasion when my truck became stuck for nearly two days when crossing the dry Tiva River. With only an elderly driver and 'kitchen toto', this involved not just digging the lorry out of the sand and cutting sticks to make a corduroy to drive on over the sand, but unloading and reloading several drums of water. It was both arduous and frustrating and at some point I had fetched the back of the truck some bad-tempered whacks with a stick.

In no time the incident reached Voi. Thereafter Sheldrick and Co gleefully embroidered the facts to suit the circumstances and their mood. A story, whose veracity would be sworn to on books that were holy, by a host of improbable eye-witnesses, then went to the far corners of Kenya and beyond. McCabe had ordered his men to cut sticks and thrash the truck until, like a recalcitrant mule it heaved itself clear of the sand. The legend survives to this day and anything I say simply affixes it more firmly. They were good times when that story took root.

CHAPTER 34: CALL ME AL

Stan Bleazard

With great regret, I learned of my transfer to Coast Province to take over from Perez Olindo, who had been selected as Director (Supernumerary) of Kenya National Parks. I had always viewed Mombasa as an iniquitous place, so it was with many misgivings I left the Northern Frontier.

On Tuesday 23rd March 1965 I arrived in Mombasa. Next morning Perez still being absent on safari, I set about examining records and soon discovered all was not well. Accounts were not up to date by many weeks and there was a nine-month backlog of papers unanswered and unfiled.

Mid Friday morning a hefty woman dressed in hunting garb marched into the office. Dr Sylvia Sykes, accompanied by her partner introduced herself with a letter from headquarters authorizing her to shoot a hippo for research purposes under the direction of a Game Warden wherever it was found necessary to remove such animal. When I told her I could not immediately help her, having just arrived, she complained that Perez was out hunting elephant with an American named Sparks. She wasn't complaining mark you: just intimating that she would be happy to receive similar attention, but at least I now knew where Perez was.

On the fourth morning after my arrival, Perez breezed into the office briefly, greeting me with the news that a rifle was missing. Pointed words were exchanged about his unpreparedness for handover, after which he became a little contrite, explaining he had not had sufficient time to arrange things in good order. At the time I did not believe him. I soon discovered, however, there was always so much happening at Mombasa that routine administration could indeed quickly get out of kilter, but I long ago forgave him for another reason.

On Monday 29th March, most Game Department staff felt obliged to attend a political rally for Tom Mboya[78], so that it was not until the next day 30th March that Perez could start the handover. Expecting to meet the District Commissioner at Kwale later in the day, Perez arrived at the office dressed in his best grey pinstripe suit, with dapper black sharply pointed shoes to match. We set out in my Land Rover and went first to Gazi to pick up a couple of Scouts he had left there to shoot a buffalo, then to Lukore and the Shimba Hills Settlement Scheme where elephants were damaging the new plot holders' crops.

---

[78] Editor's note: It was a sign of how quickly times were changing. Prior to Independence civil servants were not allowed to indulge in political activity, let alone take time off to attend rallies. Now, fifteen months after Independence, though still nominally apolitical, civil servants were expected to attend them.

Perez Olindo went on from the Game Department to be the first Kenyan Director of Kenya's National Parks.

Proceeding slowly along a firebreak next to the forest checking for elephant signs, we saw a pack of dogs emerge followed by a big man carrying a sack on his shoulder. Such circumstance could mean only one thing: poaching! By good luck the man never glanced in our direction but continued walking away from us. We got very close before he realized a vehicle was approaching whereupon he dropped his partly filled sack and ran. I wanted to chase him until he tired, but Perez demanded I stop for him and the Scouts to dismount.

Perez was first away and I raced after him, hardly believing what I next witnessed. Notwithstanding his fancy attire, Perez made a flying tackle in the best rugby tradition and brought the big man heavily to ground. They commenced wrestling and in the nick of time I arrived to seize the man's outstretched arm in which he had a panga intended to slash Perez's head. The man was so powerful that even the two of us could not hold him and although I had managed to remove the panga from him, he was about to escape our hold when the Scouts began to drub him with their rifle butts. There were many hard and telling blows which I could feel shaking his massive frame, every one weakening him more. Finally he realized the futility of fighting, submitted and was handcuffed. His dogs had fled at the first signs of trouble.

Perez stood up unharmed and happy, his crinkly hair stuck with grass and his best suit stained and possibly ruined, but with that broadest of grins only Africans can display. I had expected no less an effort from the Scouts, but I greatly admired the way Perez entered the fray so unexpectedly, yet wholeheartedly. The contents of the sack were, as expected, pieces of smoked meat attached to broken bones. For a long time none of us could identify the source of the meat until I found part of an upper jaw with large incisors intact. It could not be other than a cane rat which was an animal not covered by the game laws.

Nevertheless, our prisoner was charged with illegally hunting with dogs, for resisting arrest and for assaulting Government Officers and, convicted on all counts, sentenced to two years jail[79]. But, getting back to the point of this tale: I could forgive anyone for inefficiency behind a desk if he performed in the field as Perez had done.

Sable antelope: their presence was the primary reason why the Shimba Hills became a sanctuary (photo Peter Davey).

---

[79] Editor's note: Little wonder that Africans at large hated the Game Department! Catching cane rats was no crime. Using dogs to catch cane rats was no crime. And a lawyer would have argued that finding himself pursued without prior challenge, the man only acted in terrified self-defence. He went to jail, not because he had committed a crime, but because he was ignorant. Such is the wisdom of hindsight!

* * * *

Among Mombasa residents there were numerous sport hunters a few of whom were rumoured to overshoot their licence or hunt areas without a permit. So it was only natural whenever a free weekend approached I took the opportunity to patrol some of the areas they frequented, if only to show the flag as it were, and keep matters under reasonable control. Bill Wilkinson, the Fisheries Officer accompanied me on an overnight trip to Msimizi via Kilibasi 21st January 1966, having collected a Game Scout at Mackinnon Road on the way.

Late in the afternoon we were quietly motoring towards the Tanzania border following a well used meandering track in extensive mature *Commiphora* woodland. We had seen very little game and it was unusually dry and hot. We stopped for some time examining elephant spoor which was recent but not fresh. We drove on, up a slight incline where we met a native walking towards us, who fled immediately he saw us. His unnatural behaviour caused us to follow and catch up with him, even though he zigzagged through the woodland. Just when I began to wonder how long he could keep running, I saw that he was desperately trying to reach a rifle he had left hanging by its sling from a tree branch. Accelerating the Land Rover to within a few feet of him just as he managed to grab the rifle, I hooted the instant he tried to load the weapon. Realizing I intended to run him over before he could close the bolt, he threw the rifle to one side where I stopped the vehicle on top of it. Within seconds the Scout was on top of the man and had him handcuffed.

As the East African Game Departments, but few others, used Westley Richards .404 rifles, we suspected that the prisoner's rifle was a Government firearm. We interrogated him beside the racks of giraffe meat gently sizzling above an almost smokeless fire. He was a Jaluo from Tanga, across the border in Tanzania, and had hired the rifle from a policeman in that country.

A week later Peter Odipo Opade was convicted of various offences and sentenced to two years jail[80] and the rifle be surrendered to the Chief Game Warden. However, the matter did not end there as, for once, the Police continued investigating the matter. On 27th October I attended a Tanzanian court in Tanga with the .404 rifle as a witness against the owner of the firearm, Tanzania Police Sergeant Masudi Kazipombe who pleaded guilty as charged. Claiming overnight expenses next morning at the courthouse, I almost missed my return flight because the clerk took almost two hours to prepare a refund voucher for one hundred and thirty three shillings, then insisted paying me in shilling coins!

* * * *

[80] Editor's note: The same sentence given to a man who had only hunted cane rats quite legitimately.

The Ivory Room was always something of an attraction to Wardens and hunters visiting Mombasa. As its fate will interest my contemporaries I present this historical note by Judy Aldrick, an historian who lives in Mombasa:–

> *It is sad news that the old Ivory Room in Mombasa was pulled down in August 1999. The present owners, the Kenya Wildlife Services, who though concerned in the preservation of wildlife, unfortunately seem less interested in other fields of conservation, did this.*
>
> *This old government warehouse was used for the storage and grading of ivory before it became a banned commodity. At one time auctions were held here and the ivory tusks and animal skins would be laid out for general viewing. When the warehouse was built in the early years of the century a railway siding passed alongside, so it was very convenient for offloading the ivory brought from the interior. The main Mombasa station was located nearby at Treasury Square until 1933, when it was moved to its present site.*
>
> *Originally a private godown used as an ammunition store by a German businessman it was taken over by the government during the First World War. At that time it was the Customs Department that dealt with ivory and organised the ivory auctions. In 1956 the Game Department took over the collection, grading and sale of ivory, in 1976 it was taken over by the Game Department's successor – the Wildlife Conservation and Management Department (WCMD), then in turn in 1989 by the Kenya Wildlife Service which has either burned or stored ivory and officially sold none.*
>
> *The building was put on a list for gazettement as a historic building not only because it was a good example of early warehouse architecture but also situated just off Treasury Square, in the old centre of Mombasa, it could have made an excellent museum showing the history of the ivory trade and hunting in Kenya. It is disappointing that the KWS did not consider this proposal a worthwhile project.*
>
> *Judy Aldrick*

The Ivory Room in Mombasa (photo Tony Marsh).

* * * *

The Permanent Secretary to the Ministry for Tourism and Wildlife, Alois Achieng, made many visits to Mombasa during my wardenship there. If I received advance warning of a visit I would be on safari when he turned up. Alois had taken his degree in America and some of his professors and lecturers were huntin', fishin' and shootin' men who had no shame in taking advantage of their pupil's position in charge of Kenya's conservation, to experience some big game hunting. Thus, when Alois visited field stations, he was often accompanied by one of this group or their acquaintances. On their behalf, Alois would 'lean' on Wardens to take his friends when they were doing control work and they, unwilling to offend their Chief, would agree and provide the free hunting. This is why I ran away if I knew Achieng was coming.

Perhaps the most persistent of Alois's friends was an American whose habit at each meeting was to step forward aggressively, clasp my hand and greet me with the words: – "Call me Al." I never took to him and liked him even less when he began phoning me to enquire the chance of accompanying me hunting. I usually gave him the slip, but was annoyed at having to do so.

On Friday 11th June 1965 I was on safari, but conditions were extremely wet making travel on foot or vehicle difficult and I had stopped off in the deserted White Horse Inn at Mackinnon Road. Heavy rain fell for some hours while I slept. I awoke to the sound of a vehicle arriving. It was past midnight, rain had ceased and I could think of no one moving at this hour except Police. It was Perez Olindo and I was displeased to learn he had been suckered to take Al hunting, and wanted to know if there was any possibility of elephant control nearby. Making it plain I did not relish the intrusion, I directed them (with a tinge of malice I must admit) to Selaloni from whence I had come the day before. I learned later they spent most of the weekend bogged in deep black-cotton soil.

A year later Al was again on the scene, this time at headquarters where I was now stationed. On the authority of Alois Achieng, he was pestering David Brown – now Chief Game Warden – with futile enquiries and suggesting inimical schemes for wildlife use. DB also saw avoidance and non-engagement as the only means of handling the fellow, who he had nicknamed 'Call Me Al'. On several occasions the American arrived hoping to see DB and not finding him present never deigned to speak with me or even leave a message, for which I was grateful. The weekend at Selaloni was paying dividends.

DB was nearly caught on one occasion, but by chance he espied Al parking his car. Being a relative newcomer to headquarters, I had often wondered why an up-ended forty-four gallon drum was directly below the Chief Game Warden's office window. Hearing the drum fall over at the same moment as Al appeared on the veranda, I realized immediately what had happened and wondered how many times the escape route had been used previously (until preparing this book, I did not realise that DB had learned the trick from Willie Hale). Call Me Al checked DB's empty office and departed. A few moments later DB mysteriously reappeared from the clerk's office. This was clever because if Alois later checked to find out where the Chief Game Warden had been at the time and day that Call Me Al had reported him absent, the clerical staff (who were Alois' spies) would aver that he had been in their office.

Several months later Al somehow became privy to information that allowed him to profit at Game Department expense. In the headquarters armoury were several classic firearms of considerable value, and which the Department never used because it could not get ammunition for them. How Al learned they existed was never discovered, but out of the blue a letter arrived from our Permanent Secretary Alois Achieng requesting the Chief Game Warden to let Al inspect them with a view to purchasing three.

As the officer responsible for firearms, I had the unenviable task of showing Call Me Al into the armoury. He immediately seized upon a ten bore Paradox gun in mint condition made by Hollands, which was a prize worth possessing at any cost. Looking over other rifles we could no longer use, he asked my advice. I had no hesitation in recommending a .600 double in poor condition, saying it was the ultimate elephant gun, but knowing no one would use it as the stock was not only too light but also much too short, even for a short person. Of several others, I recommended a well used .577 by Gibbs but he selected a .500 in slightly better condition. I then had to take these three guns to be valued by Shaw and Hunter, local gun dealers who were not best qualified to give a market appraisal. Thus, without going through normal Government processes of disposal by public tender, Al acquired the firearms at valuation with approval from his mate Alois and exported them, realizing an immediate increase in value that I believe was at least five hundred per cent. Among other things, this showed abuse of position was not monopolised by Africans in newly independent Kenya.

In early 1984 I made a final visit to Kora to see George Adamson. Since his retirement in 1961 I had seen him infrequently but always enjoyed his company. Although I had by this time also retired in the interests of Africanization, he enquired in passing if I knew what became of the Holland & Holland Paradox ten bore gun[81] which his father had used in India. It had been in mint condition and was engraved "Specially Made for Sir H. G. C. Swayne, Governor of Somaliland." George had given the gun to David McCabe who had left it in the Game Department armoury for safe keeping when he was briefly out of the country. Angry about the crime to which I had unwittingly been a party, I had not the heart to tell him what had happened to it.

George Adamson: the Department's great romantic (courtesy Jack Barrah).

---

[81] I have since learned that Holland & Holland made a number of these guns for use in India and that today they are worth tens of thousands of pounds if in good condition. S.B.

CHAPTER 35: POLICY IN 1967

David Brown

On March 15th, 16th and 17th 1967, the Animal Husbandry Division of Kenya's Ministry of Agriculture held a conference on livestock development. Specifically, it revolved about the East African Livestock Development Survey and Kenya's prevailing Development Plan. Item VI on the conference agenda was 'The Utilization of Wildlife in relation to the Livestock Development Survey'. The principal speaker for this section of the agenda was Kenya's Chief Game Warden – David Brown. Because so little archival material remains on official conservation policy, the editors feel the points DB made are worth recording here. What follows in this chapter is his speech, edited heavily and abbreviated (while on the ball, DB nevertheless waffled somewhat!).

* * * *

I am grateful for this opportunity to address you on a subject which is dear to my heart as Chief Game Warden: the question of wildlife in our country today. I will confine my remarks in the short time available, to a resumé of the conclusions in Chapter 8 *The Utilization of Wildlife*, of the East African Livestock Development Survey Report.

I make the point that tourism in Kenya today depends almost entirely upon the variety of wild animals to be seen in our parks and reserves[82]. You all know that the gross income from it is somewhere in the region of ten to fifteen million pounds sterling annually, when the total recurrent estimates for the whole of the Government of Kenya, are a little in excess of fifty million, and the total development estimates something in excess of twenty million.

The hunting industry generates foreign exchange, and of course, through taxation, contributes quite heavily to the Government coffers, in addition to the direct annual returns of some seventy thousand pounds sterling from licenses, permits and fees. In addition, local authorities receive a further nearly thirty thousand pounds sterling from controlled area fees. So the direct return to government both central and local is around a hundred thousand pounds yearly. On top of this are the benefits accruing indirectly from sport hunting tourism.

Three years ago one hundred and fifty people were prepared to pay about £2,000 for a month's hunting; now it is well in excess of three hundred parties every year. So they have had to turn more and more to private land. On private land no controlled area charge is raised, the landowner is permitted to levy his

[82] Editor's note: At the time (1967) this was true, but by a decade later, beach tourism based on the four S's (sea, sun, sex and sand) was accounting for over 70% of tourist arrivals in Kenya.

own fees, and these are probably sometimes in excess of what we would charge for a controlled area. Some landowners, particularly in the Rumuruti area where wildlife is varied and plentiful, are making quite good returns from this source. I am hopeful that these will go up. Of course, in certain cases, culling is necessary and we listen sympathetically to any rancher who feels that his land is carrying too many wild animals. Our policy is for the local Warden to discuss the problem with the landowner concerned and decide on the numbers, by species, which could be carried on his land. If agreement is reached, we then permit him to cull the natural increase and in some cases to cull down to the agreed figure. Then, of course, he will either invite hunters to shoot these animals for a fee or he can cull them himself. If he does this, we allow him to sell the hide. We do not allow the sale of meat as yet, but this is often used to feed the labour in these areas.

Game cropping for meat and hides was an obvious prospect on many Kenya ranches (photo Parker).

Having covered game viewing and sport hunting very rapidly I would like to turn to the major findings of the members of the Survey Team. They are quite right, when they suggest that the renewable resource of wild animals outside the national parks and game reserves is, at the moment, largely untapped. It is suggested that this is an obvious source of meat and protein for under-nourished peoples and every attempt should be made to tap this resource. I have no quarrel with the argument, but it is a new field. With the limited resources available we have developed healthy tourist and sport hunting industries, but have no experience in other commercial usage of wildlife. Government wishes, as soon as it is possible, to turn our attention towards the possibility of using wild animals economically for meat and other products.

I agree also that such utilization or exploitation comes broadly under three headings. First, culling as a management technique to maintain equilibrium between wild animals and their habitats within parks and reserves. Second, ranching free ranging wild animals either on their own or possibly in association with domestic stock and third, the possibility of domesticating some species.

The Government considers that the immediate priority of the Game Department now lies in perfecting cropping techniques, and using the meat and other by-products of animals which are routinely destroyed in defence of human life and property. At this present time my own Department kills well in excess of two thousand head of wild animals every year. Some 1,300 are buffalo and 600 are elephants. These are killed defending human life or agriculture. Presently, little use is made of the products, even though they are often shot in accessible places. The tragedy is that we have not used or processed them economically.

Government is also keen to develop cropping for sustained yields in, or on the peripheries of game reserves and national parks for two reasons. Firstly to take off maximum natural increases for sale, secondly to regulate populations. If ecologists were to prove to us that one species was increasing to the detriment of the other species, or to the habitat, then we could use our utilization teams to reduce that particular species. The reasons why we have found it difficult to branch out into this field until now are several.

We have the problem of disease. Endemic rinderpest, for example, is one of the most serious making it dangerous to move carcasses of freshly killed wild animals over any distance because of the risk of spreading disease. Therefore, one would have to be very careful, and we would want a qualified veterinary officer in any pilot project of this nature. There are, of course, and wisely so, public health restrictions to be taken into consideration, but we can overcome these I am sure with trained manpower. Do we try and sell fresh meat locally or frozen fresh meat overseas? Do we process meat into fertilizers, meat extract, and bone meal? What is the most economic form of processing? These tasks lie largely outside the Game Department's experience. We will have to broaden our department if we are to tackle this type of work or we must employ qualified manpower from international organisations.

It is argued quite strongly in Chapter 8 [of the Livestock Development Survey Report], that use of game meat would help, or even overcome in time, the general protein deficiency of the African continent. I suggest here today, that this would only be possible if the commodity was cheap or subsidised in price. It is possible in Kenya today, to buy cuts of beef for as little as a shilling or shs 1/50 per pound (shs 2.20 or shs 3.31 per kg), and I think that with the added difficulties of killing and marketing game meat it would be impossible to market game meat profitably at these prices. If a man cannot afford to pay one shilling for beef, he is not going to pay one shilling or 1/50, for impala, or any other game meat.

If there were a desperate shortage of beef by 1970, as some people suggest, then game meat would be invaluable. But from the point of view of wise management and making game pay, it has profitable. If the sale of game meat could be put on a proper footing, there would be that much more encouragement for a man to keep wild animals[83].

DB with the farewell gift from his colleagues in the Department (photo DB)

[83] Editor's note: David Brown's policy statement in 1967 is still broadly the official attitude in 2001. The legal marketing of game meat commenced privately in 1971 and was augmented by a massive FAO aid programme 1972-1976. This collapsed with the hunting ban imposed through Legal Notice 120 of 1977. In the 1980s the Hopcraft ranch at Athi River was allowed to recommence selling game meat commercially, and in the 1990s quotas to produce game meat were given to a number of other ranches. However, the sale of trophies was restricted. Overall, and while paying lip-service to the 1967 policy, Kenya's conservation authorities have been obstructive and philosophically against wildlife use on private land, other than through game viewing tourism. I.P.

CHAPTER 36: A TRIBUTE TO SHELDRICK

David Brown

It was on a hot, sunny day early in February 1957, that I found myself cruising along the old dirt road from Nairobi towards Mombasa in my recently acquired Short Wheel-base Land Rover KFL 930. As I neared my destination at Voi my apprehension rose on two counts. Firstly, I was concerned about the Land Rover. In those days the Game Department had no light vehicles of its own. Recruits were expected to purchase their own with loans from the Government to be repaid by deductions from one's salary. In order to meet those payments a certain number of cents per mile had to be earned by the use of the vehicle on official business. During my three months at Nanyuki I had scarcely used the vehicle at all and it seemed certain there would be no use for it at Voi. I concluded that little would be achieved by threatening Willie with a False Pretences claim and, since the mileage claim from Nanyuki to Voi would nearly cover that month's deduction, a "wait and see" attitude was indicated.

The second concern was the sort of reception I would receive from those assembled at Voi. David Sheldrick already enjoyed a considerable reputation as a former Company Commander in the King's African Rifles and hunter of note as well as a passionate, competent, completely dedicated Warden. His two Assistant Wardens were also proven men of enormous ability.

It was therefore a very diffident twenty two year old who proceeded with caution along the old coast road with all his worldly goods in the rear. They did not amount to much; one medium sized cardboard suitcase stuffed with clothes, one camp bed and mosquito net, one tin box with kettle, teapot, frying pan and sundry utensils, and a wooden box which housed a double barrelled single trigger Westley Richards .470 elephant gun with ammunition therefor, and an ex-army .303. The Westley Richards was nicely balanced and looked good but it had a nasty habit of discharging both barrels at once. Not only did this give the right shoulder the father and mother of a jolt; it left one somewhat embarrassed if the first discharge did not down the target. With either Fred Bartlett or Jack Barrah in the vicinity the consequence was mere embarrassment but I would have to get the trigger seen to before setting out on my own. I reminded myself that I would be chasing poachers at Voi and not nasty tempered *Loxodonta africana*.

I arrived at Voi in the late afternoon and halted at the Tsavo East National Park gate on the left hand side of the road. A smartly turned out park Ranger emerged from the gatehouse and politely told me the entry fee. Having explained my presence I was asked to sign a book instead of parting with money and advised to take the first left hand turn to reach the head quarter office up a slight rise. Also travelling up the road were two young elephant calves followed closely by an African minder. They went ahead of me towards a dwelling further up the hill and I stopped outside the office block. I went through the open doorway and there was the man himself.

David Sheldrick (courtesy Jack Barrah).

He was tallish at six foot or thereabout, swarthy, clean shaven with slightly receding brown hair and comfortably dressed in tailored, pressed khaki shorts under a loose fitting piped khaki bush jacket and feet ensconced in light leather chapli style sandals. Somewhat to my surprise he knew who I was. He came quickly across, grasped my hand firmly in his, and said "David. I can't tell you how pleased I am to see you. Welcome to Tsavo. I very much hope your stay here will be a happy one." His welcome was expressed in such a way that I immediately felt reassured and some of my diffidence began to ease there and then. He left whatever he was doing and took me to his house where the young elephant played in the pond in the front garden, ushered me into a bedroom, explained the layout of the house, supervised the stowage of my few goods and left me to wash and brush up before he and some others would join me for a drink before dinner. I was quite simply overwhelmed by his hospitality. Afterwards I concluded that this spontaneous generosity of spirit was the key to his undoubted charisma.

Billy Woodley at the dawn of his service with the Royal National Parks of Kenya in 1948 (photo courtesy A. Dyer).

This was in sharp contrast to that of Billy Woodley which sprang from sparkling eyes, a wide smile and an endless stream of beguiling patter; David was somewhat taciturn and generally of a serious nature. It was not that he lacked a sense of humour, for he had one and it was acute; but he concealed it by an almost sombre countenance, so it was perhaps all the more delightful when revealed. The generosity of which I speak expressed itself not only in his praise and absolutely unqualified support for those under his command but also in the manner in which he entertained a continuous stream of visitors both official and otherwise to Tsavo.

At the time I knew him he was living a bachelor's life away from his wife and children. To him, therefore, fell the chore of accommodating and feeding this variety of human life. At any one time there might be six guests living in his house and others in tents in and about the garden. The provisioning logistics were considerable. Remember, this was a bush station with only sparsely stocked Indian shops in Voi township. Nevertheless, Sheldrick did not just manage, but ran like clockwork a busy wireless network, an equally busy office, an armed Ranger Force, a national park and attended to the thousand and one problems that continually arose but still managed to organise his bachelor household like a first class hotel. Cooked breakfasts, luncheon and dinner of seemingly endless variety appeared as if by magic.

All of this might appear mundane but I firmly believe that the continual pressure of that particular year of intense activity heaped more stress upon David than is or was generally appreciated. The Africans called him "Saa Nane" literally "the eighth hour" (the eighth hour after dawn = two in the afternoon in western time) because he started work at six o'clock in the morning and ended at two in the afternoon. He felt, that given the hot environment of Voi, men would work better starting in the cool hours of dawn and having the hot afternoon off.

After the anti-poaching campaign had been brilliantly concluded there followed a few years of stress free progress. These were Tsavo's best years when elephant numbers increased and the black rhinoceros, today near extinction, was so well represented that those relocated from threatened areas to the north had difficulty finding territory in which to resettle. Unfortunately there soon followed the enormous dilemma of how to tackle an obvious over-population of elephants with a consequential and inevitable destruction of the *Commiphora* bush. Regrettably, no radical management programme was instituted and the eventual drought and mass starvation of wild life must have been heart breaking.

Returning to the anti-poaching campaign, an early undertaking was to reconnoitre the northern boundary and the country bordering it as far as the Tana River. This was very hot, desert scrub, dry save for a few water holes kept accessible by elephant and containing small quantities of murky liquid. The two objectives were, to locate and renovate an air-strip at Ndiandaza made by von Blixen twenty years earlier, and to search for elephant remains, particularly ivory, of those killed by Waliangulu poisoned arrows or from natural mortality.

Billy and I undertook this long foot safari. It was very hard going indeed and only made tolerable by our long evening chat sessions. One remarkable feature that springs to mind is the recollection of our brief halts to avoid the worst of the midday sun. Apart from cigarettes, freshly cooked wild animal parts and beer, Billy was very partial to ice cream. When we eventually arrived at Ndiandaza and restored the air-strip, our first visitor was David Sheldrick, a passenger in a Kenya Police Tri Pacer piloted by Roy Drummond, clutching between his legs an enormous vacuum jug filled with ice-cream. Morale was all-important in those days. Operating as we did in very primitive conditions and in some danger, David was an exemplary Commanding Officer.

Another example of his spontaneous generosity was to be found at the Voi Hotel. Occasionally, all three teams would conclude operations at the same time and the personnel would gather in the Hotel bar. David would always put in an appearance and, if the party was going well at closing time, would buy a bottle of whisky and a crate of beer or two to keep it going. Since the hotelier charged it out at the bar price per tot the expense was not inconsiderable. If the whisky and beer lasted, as it sometimes did, until opening time the next day, the party would continue for another twelve hours at least.

Just one more illustration of Sheldrick's kindness: I went down with a particularly vicious attack of malaria. After a week at death's door at Malindi I was given a week's convalescent leave and put on the night train at Mombasa to travel to Nairobi. The train always stopped at Voi in the middle of the night. When it did there was a smiling David brandishing grapes. Goodness knows where he got them or how he learned I would be on the train. I was immensely cheered by his appearance and still recall his parting words. "Don't worry about a thing. Stay in Nairobi until you are absolutely fit" - an 'order' well received and duly acted upon.

I left Kenya in 1969 and when I returned for a brief visit some ten years later David had died. I was especially saddened to learn that he had shortly before been moved from his beloved Tsavo. A question often asked is "So what did he achieve?" The Tsavo we all knew in the 50s and 60s had all but disappeared. An enormous human population increase, a corrupt and inefficient Government and its agencies aided and abetted by foreign speculators and manipulators, a breakdown in law and order threatening the tourist trade and an ever increasing demand for illicit wild animal products such as ivory and rhinoceros horn has exacted a huge toll of Kenya's wildlife. It was a wasted life the critics said.

My answer is to remind them that the prospect of an early independence from Britain was never seriously contemplated until Harold MacMillan's icy wind of change blew through the African continent with all the force and destruction of a cyclone. By then, of course, David had already committed some twenty years to the conservation of Tsavo. At least the Park has survived and future generations of Africans may achieve its restoration to mirror its former grandeur. At the end of the day I am sure that Sheldrick would have chosen the same path that he did. Under the pre-Independence regime he would certainly have become at least the Director of Kenya National Parks. More important, if today I were to find an elderly native leaning upon his stick gazing from Voi hill across the scrub towards the Sabaki River and enquire if he recalled "Saa Nane" he would likely smile and say, "Ah Yes. He was a Man among Men". There can be no higher accolade than that.[84]

---

[84] Editor's note: Although in attitude and outlook Shedrick epitomised much of the Colonial ethos that newly Independent Africa so disliked, his contribution to Kenya National Parks and his genuineness had so impressed Kenya's leaders that when he died they made a unique gesture to his widow, Daphne, by granting her fifteen years free accommodation in Nairobi National Park.

Jack Barrah

CHAPTER 37: PERSONALITIES

Jack Barrah

My maternal grandfather started his career as a forester in the Forest of Dean in Wales. He was a keen athlete and was representing the United Kingdom in South Africa when the Boer War broke out. Presented with a uniform and told to fall in by the authorities, he then served with the British forces for the duration. During that war he learned something about oxen and ox wagons. In 1903 he disembarked at Mombasa with his wife, my mother aged six months and an ox wagon complete with trained team of oxen. He trekked four hundred miles from the coast to the northwestern slopes of Mount Kenya and there he built a forest station at Gathiuru which stands to this day. He never left Kenya. Coincidentally, Gathiuru is where Fred Bartlett and his wife Jock built the first Game Department station in Nanyuki District. My father was Australian, arrived in Kenya after the First World War and farmed at Solai.

I was schooled at Pembroke House at Gilgil, then at Michaelhouse in South Africa. On leaving school, my ambition was to become a Vet. However, with the flood of wartime servicemen leaving the forces after the Second World War, I could not get a place in any U.K. university, so abandoned the idea and became a Livestock Officer in the Kenya Veterinary Department. With the declaration of the Mau Mau State of Emergency, I joined the Kenya Regiment and was commissioned before being seconded to the Administration as a D. O. K. G. My ambition then was to convert from this position, which was a temporary Mau Mau Emergency post, into the permanent Colonial Administrative Service.

As a D.O.K.G. I was posted to Narok and was privileged to work with that District's Game Warden – Lyn Temple-Boreham. Major Temple-Boreham, M.C., better known as TB, ran his Game Scouts as a quasi-military unit during the Mau Mau years, as did many other Wardens in areas affected by the rebellion. We worked together, he with his Scouts and I with my tribal policemen, and we jointly liaised with the local Masai moran (warrior age set). I was much impressed by the morans' discipline and order. Every evening they held an "O" group to decide on tactics, the next day's events and where they would all meet up the following evening after the day's activities, to join elders who had arrived in advance and slaughtered sheep, goats or cattle for the moran to eat that night.

What really got the Masai excited was when one of the few Mau Mau gangs occasionally rustled Masai stock. Expert at tracking, they usually recovered most of the stolen stock, but seldom caught any Mau Mau. The rustlers invariably rested up on high ground overlooking the plains they had just crossed, so that they could see anyone following them. When they saw moran approaching on their tracks, the Mau Mau would abandon the stolen stock and split up, each man going his own way to a predetermined rendezvous, but leaving single sets of tracks that are hard to follow.

Through this work in the Emergency I came to know TB well. A gentle giant of a man, formidable when aroused, he was the scourge of hunters who did not follow the game laws meticulously. He knew his district backwards and frequently travelled around it, cross-country and off the roads. He went to great lengths to cover his tracks, hide his favourite campsites, and establish hidden fuel depots. Consequently he was apt to appear suddenly from 'out of the blue' and from unexpected directions. Bill Woodley recalled the first time that he met TB. He had just left school in 1946 and was hunting with a friend near Longonot and had shot a tommy in the evening. On the next morning TB drove into their camp and having established that they were properly licensed, recounted their hunt, move by move, having watched them through binoculars from a nearby hilltop.

TB, who had started life as a Livestock Officer in Narok, was well acquainted with Masai stock problems, and developed a particularly close relationship with these people. Liking and respecting him, he may have been a Government official, but the Masai would consult him on many issues far removed from game affairs. Given this great rapport, they provided him with a vast intelligence gathering system and few things that visitors to the district did, failed to be reported to him in due course.

Certain issues were anathema to TB. One was hunting for biltong. He had nothing against making game meat into biltong as such: but when farmers took out game licences, not only in their own names, but in the names of their parents, grand-parents and wives so that they could legitimately shoot many animals in order to feed their farm labour on biltong, he took exception. Such hunting parties had such large legitimate bags that they acted as cover for even bigger illicit bags. Once made into biltong, it was impossible to separate the legal from the illegal. It was not unknown for such hunters to evade his roadblocks in Narok, but find him waiting for them at their own farm gates on returning home.

Wounding a dangerous animal, failing to follow it up, and not reporting the fact was another particularly heinous crime in his book. The offence carried a mandatory jail sentence. Leaving a dirty campsite was a third issue that raised TB's ire. On one occasion, when garbage had not been effectively buried and the latrines not correctly filled in, he collected the offending matter, packed it in a parcel and sent it to the professional hunter concerned c.o.d. and care of the well known safari firm for whom he worked.

While he was a stickler for licensed hunters abiding by the game laws and hunting in a manner he deemed ethical, he took a very different line with the natives who were hunters and gatherers by tradition. As reported by several other authors in this volume, his Nelsonian blind eye towards traditional hunting has already been described.

It was TB who induced the Masai to create the Masai-Mara National Reserve. His powers of persuasion were equally effective in convincing philanthropists, to donate to both local Masai and game conservation causes. Victims, who included Kenya's colonial Governors, were given a polished performance, and invited to his special camp on the Mara River. This came to be called 'Governors Camp' and, in due course, its cachet was usurped by an eighty-bed tourist lodge. In fact the lodge does not stand on TB's original site.

Like David Sheldrick, TB died prematurely from a heart attack aged 58. This happened in 1969, and today he exists in my mind as not only a great character, but one of the colonial era's great Game Wardens. More than once in his career, he had been offered the Chief Game Warden's post but turned it down, preferring to stay in the field. It was in those Mau Mau Emergency days that I became very envious of TB's whole life style. I, too, wanted to become a Game Warden. With some trepidation I approached him towards the end of 1955 and enquired whether I should even consider applying for one of two posts advertised. In those days the Department was regarded very much as an old boys club, membership of which was reserved for senior ex-Army Officers and other illustrious characters. The two new posts would bring the establishment up to twelve Wardens and some two hundred or so Game Scouts.

I was particularly apprehensive about applying for a Game Warden's post because if I failed, it would blot my copy-book with the Administration, which was also an elite body that didn't take kindly to being ranked second to other organisations, least of all by one yet to be formally accepted.

"Not a problem," said TB, "I'll fix that."

And fix it he did. Despite having to appear before a board of peppery old civil servants who wanted to know why I had wasted their time by applying to join the Colonial Administrative Service (I had replied:- "because I now realise that I would prefer to deal with animals rather than people," which raised a smile or two), I received one of the posts and my good friend, Ken Smith the other.

* * * *

Thanks to TB putting in a good word for me, I commenced thirty-six years in conservation. The first nine of which were as a field Warden in Kenya's Colonial Game Department; these were followed by seven years after Independence working my way up the new field Warden ranks to Divisional Warden (higher than which was closed to expatriates like me); followed by twenty years seconded to the Kenya Game Department (which became the Wildlife Conservation & Management Department when Game Department merged with National Parks, and later still the Kenya Wildlife Service) under the auspices of British Overseas Development Administration titled a 'Wildlife Advisor'.

Looking back, the most striking aspect of my thirty-six year service must be the immense changes that took place across this relatively brief span. In the mid 1950s we field Wardens had almost complete autonomy for conservation in the huge areas for which we were responsible. We dealt with many tribes, all of them interesting and all very different. All of us were amateurs as, in those days, there were no schools or training courses for Wardens. We tried to uphold the game laws and outside of that applied common sense. We 'controlled' (the word is probably a misnomer) dangerous, marauding animals, undertook anti-poaching law-enforcement, flew light aircraft, tried to create and develop game reserves and permanent sanctuaries for wildlife; tried to keep sport hunters 'in line'; tried to persuade farmers and ranchers to tolerate as much game as possible on their land; safaried to many out of the way places that others had small chance of seeing and, naturally, were continually meeting interesting personalities.

How effective we were in conserving Kenya's wildlife is not so obvious now as it seemed to be then. If one takes Ian Parker's long historical perspective, for example, I think we must admit that we were spread too wide, too thinly, to have ever achieved a great deal. None of us really comprehended population increase. We read the statistics, but at the time they meant nothing much. I suppose if we had sat down and tried to work these figures out and what they meant, it might have changed what we did a little. Yet I am not sure: population increase only means something to me when I compare what were wildernesses then with the wall-to-wall cultivation they are now. I don't think that I could ever have imagined what things would become.

There are certain aspects of our work that, looking back now, make me cringe. Shooting rhinos, for example. They were common animals in many parts of Kenya and one thought no more about shooting one for damaging crops or property, than one did shooting a buffalo for example. Had anyone said that they would virtually disappear from Kenya within thirty years, we would have laughed at him. Yet while it is important we acknowledge that we may not have conserved very effectively, I think that at the time it seemed that we were doing the right things and it is that which matters, for one cannot do more. Being a Warden in those far off days certainly was a wonderful life.

Others, either independently or in this volume, have written autobiographies or recounted what we used to do, so I do not wish to cover the same ground. Instead, I shall dwell more on the characters of some of those who were my colleagues in distant times.

My first posting was to Maralal under the eagle eye of 'The Major':– Major Rodney Elliott, whose range covered Samburu District and the ranch lands of western Laikipia around Rumuruti. Where the professional hunting fraternity were concerned, Rodney had a reputation of being something of a martinet and a stickler for the rules. He was one of the very few colleagues that TB would allow to stand in for him in Narok when he went on leave and his Game Wardening was done rather in the TB mould. He shared TB's outlook towards natives hunting and ignored the traditional taking of animals for meat. Like TB, he drew the line at the valuable commercial species – elephant, rhino and leopard – and jumped on any hunting that was 'commercial'. Rodney encouraged local Samburu moran to deal with troublesome animals themselves, and welcomed their help *provided* that it was reported back to him without delay and the trophies handed in. His local intelligence system matched TB's and it was wiser for all licensed hunters to his area to assume that he had an informer in their retinues, than believe otherwise.

A case that was typical of the Elliott informers' style, though in this case it involved 'Coley' Coles, another Warden, and an unlettered Njemps fisherman on Lake Baringo who was Coley's man. A white man had been shooting hippos at night which – unless it was in defence of crops or property – was unlawful, as was shooting without a licence as this case was. Getting himself employed as a 'boat boy', the Njemps soon reported back that the suspect had indeed shot a hippo in the lake after dark. In fact he was very specific: the hippo had been shot at 0230 hours. In court the accused's defence was to deny the charge and that it had been cooked up by the Njemps.

"How did the witness know it was 0230 hrs when he alleges that I shot a hippo when, by his own admission, he doesn't own a watch? And even if he did have access to a watch, how would he have known it was 0230 when, by his own admission, he does not know how to tell the time?"

The Njemps's replied, "It was the Bwana who said that the time was 0230. You see, I asked him the time immediately after he had shot the hippo. He looked at his watch and told me 0230: it was he who had the watch and he who told me what the time was."

The accused was convicted; but the informer had been well prepared to collect evidence that would stand in court before he ever went out on the hippo hunt. Where most Wardens may have occasionally had a 'coup' of this nature, it was routine in the Elliott range in which licensed hunting was perhaps better managed than in any other save, perhaps, TB's.

When posted to gain experience under Rodney, I arrived in some trepidation. Years earlier in my youth and during Rodney's first spell as relief Warden of Narok while TB was on leave, I had wounded a lion with a .275 rifle. The Department insisted on hunters using much heavier calibres on the big six classified as dangerous game. Not only was I using too light a calibre (under-clubbing it was called), but also I had done so across the bonnet of my Land Rover – an offence because I was shooting less than 200 yards from a motor vehicle. Early next morning I tried to follow up the wounded animal with a scratch pack of untrained dogs owned by the local 'duka wallah', who had been sworn to secrecy because it was an offence to hunt with dogs. The dogs were useless and I failed to find the lion. In apprehension I set off to report the wounding, because failure to do so with a dangerous animal carried a mandatory jail sentence.

I found Rodney on the road and told him about the wounding, but not the calibre rifle I had used nor that I had shot across the bonnet of a vehicle. Little did I realise that, at the time, he already knew these details and was on his way to find me when we bumped into one another. Had I not reported the wounding to him, I would have been in deep trouble. That I had done so ameliorated the situation somewhat. Rodney followed up the wounded lion and killed it, but I was not allowed to have the skin which was a particularly fine trophy and from then on I was on the Elliott list of characters to be watched closely.

That was the background to my arrival at Maralal to learn from Elliott how to be a Game Warden. Among the first things he did was to go to his safe, extract an envelope and hand it to me. On it was my name, time, date and place where I wounded the lion years earlier, and in it was my .275 bullet that he had extracted from the lion. "Now you can tell me the full story," he had said with a grin. Needless to say, I learned a great deal from the Major.

* * * *

While learning and working under Rodney Elliott, I enjoyed visiting George and Joy Adamson in Isiolo. George was based there and ran the next-door range that took in the rest of northern Kenya east of Lake Turkana (Rudolf as it then was). George has written two books about himself[85] and Adrian House wrote his biography[86]. There is little point in repeating what was written in them here, so I shall confine comment to my own personal impressions. George was a great raconteur: he loved yarning about his experiences and particularly his long foot treks into virgin terrain with Joy, a few Scouts and his pack donkeys. Even in his vehicles he preferred driving for miles across country to following tracks. Consequently he knew more of remote northern Kenya than any one else I knew.

While George was easy-going, his wife Joy was the opposite – opinionated, with strong views on most matters and saw the world in black and white. Hardly surprising, their marriage was tempestuous. Joy had an obsession to stop George drinking whisky and became so strident on the subject that George arranged to have his purchases put on Jerry Dalton's account at the local duka (shop), settling up with him at the end of each month (Jerry was the National Park Warden in charge of the Marsabit National Reserve and also based at Isiolo).

As his trainee, George would inform Joy that he was taking me to sit up for a stock-killing lion every evening. There was of course no lion, but we would drive into the bush and have a sun-downer or two, before driving back to the Adamsons' house for dinner with Joy. Somehow or other the Asian duka owner let the cat out of the bag about the whisky purchases and the sitting up for lions. Joy was so infuriated by the deceptions that she lay in ambush for George one evening. When he returned she went for him wielding a dining room chair and cracked several of his ribs.

---

[85] Adamson G. 1968. *Bwana Game*. Collins & Harvill Press. London and Adamson G. 1986. *My Pride and Joy*. Collins Harvill. London

[86] House A. 1993. *The Great Safari*. ISBN 0 00 272082 5. Harper Collins. London

Fearsome and eccentric though Joy was, she was a talented artist, a botanist and musician who, for the most part directed her volatile temper at George. He seemed to take it all in his stride, puffing at his pipe, only removing it from his mouth from time to time to say "Oh shut up Joy," before her next tirade. I got to know the couple at the dawn of the "Elsa" era when their involvement with this soon-to-be world famous lioness was to so radically change their lives. What was not clearly told in the Adamsons' books about her was Elsa's infuriating habit of knocking visitors down. With a full-grown lioness upon them, the victims often ended up scratched and bleeding and very much the worse for wear. Well do I remember an afternoon when professional hunter Reggie Destro dropped in for tea while Elsa was sprawled on the floor. Joy left the room and Reggie disappeared for a wee. Elsa came to life and set an ambush, when Reggie returned she fell on him from behind, flattening him on the floor, then sprawled out again as though nothing had happened. Reggie was not amused and when Joy left the room again, he leapt out of his chair, and delivered a mighty boot to the recumbent lioness, who jumped to her feet and departed grunting. Joy soon reappeared wondering what was wrong with Elsa. Reggie innocently suggested "may be she has a guts ache."

Elsa was to become a major source of wealth for Joy, most of which she committed to conservation through her 'Elsa Fund'. Among the many benefits provided by the fund was the cost of teaching Wardens to fly; I being one of them. Though integral to the whole Elsa phenomenon, George did not benefit quite as handsomely as Joy. Consequently he made the wry claim that he had all the fame, but none of the fortune. It was inevitable that George and Joy would part once she was financially independent. They lived separately pursuing their obsessions with big cats, but still retained strong proprietory interests in one another. The ultimate irony was of course that both should be murdered: George by Somali shifta and Joy by a Turkana teenager with whom she had fallen out. These were sad endings to two colourful characters, both becoming legends in their own lifetimes through their involvements with wildlife in Kenya.

* * * *

After training with Rodney and George, I was posted to take over the Nanyuki range from Fred Bartlett. This was above all, *the* buffalo range, as the species was both abundant and given to constantly grazing and raiding the farms. Yet elephants were also a perennial problem along the forest edges and lion and leopard constant fixtures on the ranches – with an occasional aggressive rhino thrown in for good measure. This constant control work was exhilarating which, as a young man, I enjoyed. The buffalo hunting kept me very fit as it entailed running after a pack of dogs. As this was often in thick bush, dense forest or bamboo, it was dangerous as one had to get very close to the baying dogs before one could see the animal to shoot. This often resulted in buffalo (and sometimes lion) charging over the dogs at close range.

Overall, I held the buffalo in highest regard because it has all senses equally well developed – sight, hearing and scent – and it had unlimited courage. My personal choice of rifle was heavy bore and double-barrelled, and a quick shot with the second barrel of my .470 that would not have been possible with a magazine rifle, got me out of trouble time and again.

Fred Bartlett gave me valuable experience before I was left on my own. Among the Wardens who knew him, Fred was considered the most experienced and competent hunter of us all. He probably shot more buffalo than anyone before or since his time. Modest and unassuming, he thought like a wild animal, anticipating their moves time and again. He was the quickest shot that I have ever seen, superbly accurate who seldom wasted a second barrel, confident that the first had found its mark. He was also the best white tracker that I ever met. Fred believed in using solid bullets on all big game, as they were less likely than soft-nose bullets to be deflected by twigs and branches or break up on impact with bone. It was sound advice that I have adhered to ever since. What Fred taught me about game control is probably the reason that I am still around to tell the story.

My next posting after Nanyuki was to take over the Makindu range from another legend: the venerable JA Hunter. Speaking with a soft Scottish burr, and with an almost dreamy manner, the appearance belied the man within. Like George Adamson, he was a raconteur and wrote books[87] about his hunting life that I have no need to repeat here. Taking over from JA was a trip back into the Game Department's distant past when Game Rangers were so expected to shun paper work that no one took it amiss. By the time that I was ordered to take over JA's establishment, the civil service bureaucracy was still lax where we were concerned, but had moved ahead (perhaps backward would be more appropriate) from JA's day. When I asked him for the files he would hand over to me and what records he kept, he pointed to his "too difficult file": a large tin box crammed with many years' instructions and requests from Headquarters. When I asked him to give me a list of his Game Scouts and their dispositions about the range, he had little idea of where they were – other than those whom he had under his thumb at Hunter's Lodge – his retirement project at Kiboko – where he had them welcoming the guests and carrying their suitcases etc. as supernumerary porters and waiters etc. It took me a while to track down the rest who were wandering around Ukambani doing control work, with rifles slung over their shoulders and wearing no uniforms[88]. They claimed that uniforms had

---

[87] Hunter JA 1952. *Hunter*. Hamish Hamilton. London
Hunter JA 1957 *Hunter's Tracks*. Hamish Hamilton. London

[88] Editor's note: Before the Second World War, Game Scouts were never issued uniforms, and JA obviously still clung to old ways.

not been issued to them for many years. When Don Bousfield was a Game Warden and doing control with JA, he told me that he saw JA knock down fifteen elephants with sixteen shots, all brain shots from a wide variety of angles and on the run, and then complain of failing eyesight because he had had to fire twice at one of them. David Sheldrick related how he saw JA shoot a wounded leopard off the back of a Masai who was running for dear life when it sprang on him. The man was untouched by JA's shot.

When I took over from JA he was advanced into his twilight years and the once legendary shot and ladies' man was past it. Nevertheless, his reputation from the pre-war years was still alive and 'Hunter' was a name that 'sold'. Thus Vernon-Smith, the feared Kenya Police Firearms Bureau Chief Licensing Officer, capitalising on the name, persuaded JA to take two German clients on a hunting safari (I never established how he became involved in setting up this safari while still a serving Policeman). I visited his camp and taking the clients out was so far beyond JA that the poor old man broke down and asked me to help him out. For a few days I broke the rules and performed as a professional hunter in his stead. It seemed the least I could do to save a venerable reputation from a situation in which he should never have been placed.

Later as a field Warden based at Nyeri, I worked closely with Bill Woodley. Again, he was one of those larger than life characters about whom others have already written a great deal that I would not wish to repeat. Yet there are memories which surface whenever I think of Bill. He loved the ladies, and when we were both invited to the opening of 'The Ark' on the Aberdares, he went in high anticipation. Among the guests was a group of Travel Agents that included a party of American girls. One of them had written to Bill in advance of the visit and wished to meet him. He was crowing because I had not had similar luck.

We sat at the bar watching them file in, with Bill picking out the best lookers in the hopes that one of them was her. Among them all, one stood out: she looked like a parody of a dumpy St Trinian's girl, with plaited hair and thick glasses. With a look in our direction she walked over and said, "either of you guys Bill Woodley?" Try as he would, and to my great amusement, he could not shake her off and for the entire visit she clung to him like glue. He was philosophical about the incident saying, "You cannot win them all Jack!"

On another occasion, having received the all clear of cancer after the mandatory five years since having part of his stomach removed, Bill and I went on a major pub-crawl in Liverpool. We ended up on the banks of the Mersey to find a pretty girl closing the bar shutters.

"Don't do that," said Bill with his usual charm, "we have come all the way from Africa to have a drink with you."

"O.K.," she said reopening the bar, "now I suppose that you will tell me that you are Game Wardens or white hunters!" I am certain she felt we were just pulling her leg, but took it in very good heart.

Bill Woodley was a natural leader who displayed great courage, be it hunting, flying, suffering from illness, or in the Kenya Regiment where he earned the Military Cross. We shared many experiences and were the closest of friends.

The list of personalities and incidents from the old days is endless. David Brown or DB learning to fly under the tuition of a peppery ex-R.A.F. instructor Les Bolton reacted to Bolton's "Fire in the engine. Action?" with "Panic!" It did not amuse Les, but he got his own back. They flew down to Meru in a Super Cub, which, as with most American light aircraft, has a cabin heating system designed for sub-zero northern winters. Unbeknown to DB, Les surreptiously switched on the heat to maximum. In no time DB was sweating copiously. "Hell," he said turning to Les, "I knew it was hot here, but don't recollect it being *this* bad!"

Then there was Kenneth Archibald Smith, who joined the Department at the same time that I did. He was a quiet spoken Scot who served mainly in Isiolo, Garissa and Lamu and was also a great friend. Like all of us who spent time with George in Isiolo, Ken was extremely wary of Joy and her tantrums. Eventually, after George had to duck a kitchen knife Joy had thrown at him from close range, Ken's nerve broke and he went to stay with other friends.

For quite a while Ken distrusted my advice. I had heard from George Adamson I think, that an effective antidote to a scorpion sting was to plunge the injured part into petrol. As stings were usually on a hand or foot, this was easy. On safari in Garissa Ken climbed into bed and had the misfortune to be stung on a buttock. It was a bad sting and sufficient to make him roar with pain. Desperate to ease the agony, he recalled my advice, and yelled for help. However, there was no receptacle large enough to encompass one of Ken's buttocks, so laying himself naked across the bonnet of his Land Rover, he ordered a very astonished Game Department driver to pour a jerry can of petrol over his bottom. The man did as he was bidden and, as was only to be expected, the fluid penetrated hidden crevices and other nearby parts where the skin is very thin and sensitive, burning Ken as effectively as if someone had put a match to it. He blamed me for this and gave me hell when next we met. A man who appreciated a joke or the funny side of things, this was one incident that he never found amusing.

* * * *

In my later role as wildlife advisor I no longer held executive powers, but was prevailed upon to escort some of Kenya's V.I.P. guests when they wished to see wildlife – or hunt it. Thus when President Tito of Yugoslavia and his wife Madame Broz wished to shoot a buffalo, a lion and a rhino in three days, I was detailed to act as his professional hunter. It was a tall order which I would never have fulfilled without adequate advance notice to deploy Game Scouts to locate the quarry and keep it under surveillance.

President Tito, an impressive man by any standard, his wife Madame Broz and in the background, John Mutinda, Chief Game Warden

I based the operation in Keekorok Lodge to accommodate his retinue of some twenty people. This meant rising in the early hours of the morning to get out of the Masai Mara National Reserve and be in the hunting grounds as dawn broke. I asked Tito whether he preferred tea or coffee upon being woken, to which he grunted "whisky soda". That is how it went all day and a cool box of whisky and soda was readily to hand in the Land Rover.

Our first target was a lone bull buffalo and the hunt went badly wrong. To my horror, Tito insisted upon using a 9mm calibre with soft-nosed bullets. When I tentatively offered him my double-barrelled .470, he declined it snapping, "Everything I kill, one shot."

Thinking, so be it, I let him proceed. He put a well-placed shot in the buffalo's shoulder that, had calibre and bullet been adequate, would have been lethal. However, the buffalo took off and disappeared into a dense thicket nearby. When I raised my rifle to put in a back-up shot, an irate Tito pushed the barrels aside reiterating "I told you, everything I kill one shot, come, we go and find it."

There was no way that I would allow him to follow it up, which nearly caused a Cabinet crisis, with his attendant entourage siding with me, and Tito going off in a huff to sit in his vehicle while I found the so-called dead buffalo. Very soon after entering the thicket with my tracker Game Scout, it exploded upon us in full charge. We could not see it until it was almost on us and I was lucky to kill it with a single shot through its boss.

Upon reporting back to Tito, he accused me of firing a shot into the air to conceal having found the buffalo dead. That was easy to disprove when I returned to the thicket and pointed out the blood trail, a pool of blood where the buff had lain down, and then the tracks and blood from where it charged to where it was shot. Again, Tito stormed off back to his Land Rover in another huff. That evening at dinner I was summoned over to his table, wondering in some trepidation, what now? Fishing in his pocket he presented me with a valuable gold wrist watch with his signature engraved on the back saying, "good show for the buffalo," and not another word. That watch is a treasured souvenir.

His next victim was a rhino. We stalked up to it with Tito still carrying his 9mm loaded with soft-nosed bullets. I never said a word, nor did he, until we got within range when he turned to me with a big smile and whispered, "Now I take your rifle!" With it he knocked over the rhino with a single shot and we were two down and one to go. On the third morning he despatched his lion. When hunting he was calm and indisputably, a good shot.

While with me, a Masai reported an elephant had just killed a woman, so I asked Tito if he would like to accompany me to shoot it. To my surprise he replied with disdain, "I do not shoot elephants," quickly closing the subject.

As happens with hunting, one quickly gets to know a character, and in spite of his tantrums I admired Tito enormously. His rages may have come about through finding that, for once, he was out of his depth – as was so obviously the case with the buffalo. That and being told what to do, which was obviously something few in his retinue ever dared.

During his safari the Russians had marched into Afghanistan, which prompted me to ask whether he was concerned for Yugoslavia. "No," he replied emphatically. "They may capture our cities like the Nazis did, but they will never drive us out of the caves in the hills." It brought to mind how this man of truly Churchillian stature had unified Yugoslavia and with his guerrilla partisans had kept the Nazis on the run. His personality was awesome: the sort of character for whom everyone would stand up. His penchant for whisky and cigars merely added to his unique aura. Perhaps the only person not intimidated by him was Madame Broz, his wife. Charming and very feminine, she, too, had inner steel for during the Second World War she had commanded her own guerrilla partisans in the caves to which Tito referred. She was on my side in 'handling' her husband.

Another very down-to-earth character I took on safari as a V.I.P. three times was H. R. H. Prince Bernhard of the Netherlands. On all three he was wearing his hat of President of the World Wildlife Fund (WWF) of which he was one of the founder members. As a hunter his ambition was to shoot a fifty-inch buffalo (one whose horns spanned fifty inches), but we never found one.

PB as he was known, hated pomp and ceremony or being made a fuss of. On his visits he requested the Kenya Government to keep official reception committees away, which it was always very good about and complied with. The overall relaxed atmosphere and laughter dominate my recollections of PB's presence. Once, when camped at Garissa with him and Ken Smith, we were to fly to Lamu in a Cessna 206. The last to clamber aboard was Ken who was, shall we say, a trifle overweight. Getting into the rearmost seat he so changed the aircraft's centre of gravity that the nose wheel came off the ground – to Ken's embarrassment and our laughter. We tried to persuade him to move further forward, exchanging places with someone lighter, but he refused and opted to drive to Lamu instead.

PB was an excellent pilot who flew his own jet on international visits and thoroughly enjoyed taking the controls of my Government Cessna 180 or 182. On one occasion after take-off he pointed out to me that I had forgotten to remove the pitot head cover and hence had no reading of airspeed. He was not in the least fazed by this oversight and just to accentuate my embarrassment put his hat over the rest of my instruments as I prepared to land and rectify my mistake.

I asked him which Heads of State he held in high regard, he had replied Haile Selassie, Tito and Kenyatta were in a class of their own. One was never in any doubt as to who was the boss when in their presence.

PB – His Royal Highness Prince Bernhard of the Netherlands (courtesy Jack Barrah).

* * * *

'Daddy' Probyn was a famous Kenya character whom I had known since my days as a field Warden in Nyeri. His exploits with home built aircraft had intrigued generations of those who knew him. At one point when over ninety years old, he had been the oldest licensed pilot still flying, having started with the Royal Flying Corps in the First World War in the very earliest days of aviation. To honour his ninetieth birthday there was a fly-past of all models and makes of civilian light aircraft, followed by a flight of Kenya Air Force Lockheed F 105 fighters. What those of us in Kenya were apt to forget was that Daddy Probyn was more than just a local character. In the annals of the Royal Air Force he had very high standing as the commander of Biggin Hill air base during the Battle of Britain. Not only was he a first class leader, but also highly innovative. The essence of pragmatism and economy and something that probably saved many pilots' lives, were his training exercises. Flying formations were mounted on bicycles at each end of the station rugby pitch and followed Daddy's instructions to intercept one another in simulated combat. Thus when his name was mentioned while I was taking H. R. H. Prince Charles on safari and we were camping with Bill and Ruth Woodley in the Aberdare National Park, the Prince, who like PB had asked for privacy, exclaimed that Daddy was one person he really would like to meet.

Daddy Probyn: aviator extraordinary.

So Daddy was invited to lunch wearing his Royal Flying Corps scarf, and hatband, with his RFC tie round his waist holding up his trousers. When Daddy entered the Royal presence, Prince Charles in a gesture of respect, rose to his feet and taking Daddy by the hand said, "What a privilege to meet you Sir."

Daddy in turn had replied, "Nice to meet you young man. I knew both your grandfather and father." He had, of course, been decorated by both monarchs, but this meeting between him and the United Kingdom's next King in such informal circumstances was so natural and unaffected and reflected such mutually impeccable manners, that it was a privilege to have witnessed. Introductions over, there had then followed a lively and fascinating conversation about the old RFC days, with Daddy relating his memories of evading and avoiding the Red Baron and German 'Archie' (anti-aircraft fire) over the trenches and, last but not least, his disgust at being shot down because his gunner was off the mark with his shotgun: – "Never should have happened!"

One of the problems when we were with Prince Charles was keeping the British Press at bay. On the ground this was relatively easy by posting armed rangers on all access routes, but we could not stop them prying from light aircraft flying over our camp, forever snooping for scoops through their long lenses. Consequently a report did go out that the Prince had a blonde bird in his party, which was quite true. It was Pat, my wife.

Lord Carrington, at the time the British Foreign Secretary, camped with us in the Mara. The excitement on that trip was that a Tanzania Airways aircraft had been hi-jacked and that the hi-jackers were demanding to speak with him, unaware that he was camped within spitting distance of the Tanzanian border. He was rather disinterested in their request and confident that Willy Whitelaw (the British Deputy Prime Minister at the time), would persuade them to land at Stansted Airport which as it was well known to the SAS was, in his words, entering the jaws of death, which is exactly what happened.

As a joke on me, and knowing that I am not a birdman, the Deputy British High Commissioner to Kenya – John Edwards – led me to believe that Lord Carrington was a keen ornithologist. At the same time, he had asked his Lordship to go along with the pretence. It led to a stream of embarrassing enquiries about birds that I was unable to identify. Eventually one appeared that I did know and when Lord Carrington asked, "What is that" I had replied "a purple grenadier." He had burst out laughing, saying, "This joke has gone too far." He thought it was a leg-pull on my part because during the war he had served with the Grenadier Guards (he commanded the first tank over the Nimegen Bridge spanning the Rhine, for which he received the Military Cross).

* * * *

What did I achieve during these memorable years? As a Warden I influenced channelling controlled areas fees towards local landholders. I look back with satisfaction at having persuaded local communities to establish Lake Bogoria and Shaba National Reserves. As wildlife advisor to the Kenya Government I was able to assist some young Wardens in the field, but more impressive, negotiated the $35 million Wildlife & Tourism loan to Kenya by the World Bank to finance a variety of projects throughout the country. Sadly much of it was later misused.

Come what may, I shall always feel privileged to have been an officer of the Department, experienced a unique era and seen things that are gone forever in the face of the ever mounting encroachment and displacement of wild Africa.

CHAPTER 38: REQUIEM FOR A WHITE ELEPHANT

Ian Parker

As the 1960s progressed, the Game Department acquired civil service characteristics previously lacking. There was a rapid expansion of clerks and secretaries. Who they were related to rather than ability, determined who was employed. Inability to write or read back shorthand, coupled to no knowledge of wildlife produced some odd results. I have read Departmental minutes referring to lanner kaleous, perequin kaleous, white-bellied Germany birds and red-naped shydabis[89]. Such strange species put focus on clerical competence, which has always been the Game Department's Achille's heel.

Ivory had been an important source of income throughout the colonial era. Until 1910 at least, it, together with income from sport hunters provided more than fifty per cent of the British East Africa Protectorate's income. That proportion fell progressively, yet it was still important at independence. In 1967, as indicated by DB in his policy chapter, tourism and game revenues were still 21% of the country's recurrent and development budget of £70 million. As ivory was revenue, its handling was not originally seen as a Game Department responsibility. Rather, the bulk of tusks that came into Government hands – even those from Game Department control work – went to District Revenue Officers who periodically passed them on to the Customs & Excise Department's Ivory Room in Mombasa. There, it was graded, placed in lots and auctioned twice a year. The auctions were co-ordinated with the Tanganyika Ivory Room in Dar-es-Salaam so that there was an East African ivory auction in each quarter of the year. The Ivory Room in Mombasa handled all Uganda's ivory. Some tusks did move along Game Department channels from field stations to headquarters and thence to the Ivory Room, but never very many.

The system changed in 1956 as the anti-poaching campaign got under way. Suddenly it was decided that as ivory came from elephants, and elephant conservation was a Game Department responsibility, the disposal of ivory and the Ivory Rooms in both Mombasa and Dar-es-Salaam should become respective Game Department responsibilities too. This was a non sequitur and the thinking was flawed. Ivory was revenue, with all the valuing, grading, accounting and accountability that the management of revenue calls for, and should have been left in Customs hands. After all, handling and collecting revenue is what Customs are about. Game Departments were probably the least numerate of all Government's arms, and least competent to keep tabs on a revenue collecting exercise. If, as alleged, the Customs men were not picking up illicit ivory dealers, the reason did not stem from ignorance about elephants. The Customs & Excise investigation

[89] Minutes of the Game Department's Advisory Committee for the Capture and Export of Wild Animals for the 9th July and the 6th of October 1970.

branches were larger than both Game Departments combined and professionally trained to detect fraud and theft. Their deficiencies where illicit ivory was concerned should have been analysed and corrected. Instead, Nixon's Law[90] was applied and the illicit trade continued to flourish.

The degree of the Department's administrative incompetence eventually floated into public view when DB followed a hunch over revenue from trophy sales, which led to an investigation, which in turn led to the two clerical officers in headquarters being prosecuted. The magistrate who convicted them in 1960 recorded in his judgement that the state of the Game Department was 'Gilbertian', and because of this he imposed a three year suspended sentence on the senior of the two men because, even if only through negligence, more senior members of the Department were culpable. Rather unfairly, I thought, the junior of the two who had stolen less, got nine months in the 'slammer'. The value of the ivory the senior man had got away with was said to be £30,000 (worth more than ten times that in today's terms). Interestingly, when the two officers were formally charged, their counterpart in the Fisheries Section fled the country. Quite what his role had been in the long-running scam remains a secret to this day, though his flight suggests complicity.

Receipt.

ORIGINAL

COLONY AND PROTECTORATE OF KENYA

ISSUE NOTE No. 6635

GAME DEPARTMENT

The following stores ~~issued to~~ ~~returned by~~ from Mr. R. T. Elliott Game Ranger have been received in good order viz:—

Description of Article	Quantity	Amount Paid		Remarks
Rhino horn	One			Rotten
Ivory	five			
Lion skins	three			

Please acknowledge receipt on this form and return it at once to Game Warden, Nairobi.

Date of receipt 5. 8. 55

Signature of recipient

When Wardens accepted receipts for ivory and rhino horn on which the weights were not recorded, it was inviting corruption.

[90] Nixon's Law = "If two wrongs don't make a right: try three."

When Wardens accepted receipts for ivory and rhino they handed in without the weights being recorded, it was an open invitation for small tusks to be substituted for the far bigger ones handed in. Ivory, rhino horn and other trophies coming into headquarters had been accounted for in so slack a manner for so long that the two clerical officers simply couldn't resist the opportunity to better themselves financially. After the court case, the Department should have issued new, stringent trophy accounting procedures. This was not done and when, after independence, locals took over, they inherited a slack system.

The issuing of permits for game trophies illustrated how 'unclerical' the Game Department was. Under Section 34(2) & (3) of the Wild Animals Protection Ordinance #18 of 1951, the seller of a legal game trophy had to ensure that the person to whom the sale was made received a sale permit covering the item concerned. The growth of the tourist trade and the sale of game trophies through the 1950s made this legal requirement a progressively greater burden to the Department. Technically each zebra skin watchstrap needed a permit and a single zebra skin that had started off covered by a single sale permit, could spawn a hundred watchstraps that required a hundred separate permits. By the late 1950s the number of such permits being issued annually was of the order of 60,000 – 70,000 and overwhelming the Department's clerical capacity. The solution was novel, if nothing else. Sale permit books were issued to the trophy dealers and the burden of issuing the permits was passed to them. As these dealers had always been weak links in the law enforcement chain, handing them responsibility for issuing sale permits was tacit acceptance that the legal requirement was unrealistic. The Department should have reviewed the law rather than perpetuate something so clearly pointless.

A third illustration of Departmental weakness concerns what were known from their inception as 'forest elephant licences'. The rationale for such licences was straightforward enough. The Department wished to spread the hunting 'load' on elephants to include those in the highland forests. In parallel, it was hoped that such hunting as might happen would lighten the control load on the Department. However, as many people were not as enthusiastic about hunting elephants in dense forest as they were in savannah, an incentive for them to do so was needed. That incentive was a lower price: instead of £75, only £25 was charged for a 'forest elephant licence'.

Correctly, the creation of such a new licence should have been properly gazetted and added to one of the Wild Animals Protection Ordinance licence schedules. This meant going through the bureaucratic minuet such promulgations called for: the sort of work officers in the Department hated. Someone (whose name went up in the smoke of burned files when the Department's records were destroyed) had a bright idea. "We don't need to gazette new licences if we use Chief Game Warden's Permits instead." If one ignores the philosophical base for this class of permit, this was technically true.

Section 14 of the Ordinance (and all subsequent revisions thereof) is worth quoting at length: -

> *"1. Notwithstanding anything to the contrary in this Ordinance, the Chief Game Warden, with the approval of the Minister, may in his discretion grant to any person, or may refuse without assigning any reason for his refusal, a permit (in this Ordinance called a Chief Game Warden's permit) which shall entitle such person, subject to the provisions of Sections 18, 19 and 20 of this Ordinance* [18 = areas where entry required a DC's permit; 19 = private land; 20 = National Parks], *to hunt and kill any animal in any place, at any time and by any means.*
>
> *"2. A Chief Game Warden's permit shall be subject to whatever conditions the Chief Game Warden may impose in his absolute discretion.*
>
> *"3. There shall be paid for a Chief Game Warden's permit such fee, if any, as the Chief Game Warden may, at the time of the grant of such permit, fix."*

The power Section 14 gave the Chief Game Warden was immense. Yet the purpose of Chief Game Warden's permits was to cater for one-off situations that were otherwise not covered by the Ordinance. Most commonly they were used to legalise museum and scientific collecting. They were never intended to cover any form of regular sport hunting. Yet this is what the Department did when it started issuing Chief Game Warden's permits as Forest Elephant Licences. The strategy may have been innocent, but it was rooted in bureaucratic indolence.

The Game Department was never seriously hauled over the coals for its deficiencies. When a young Government Auditor tried to analyse my Kilifi station books in 1958, he was dumbfounded to find my filing system was a triplicate book, that there was no station type-writer, that the station vehicle was my personal Land Rover and that, because there was no clerical staff, the station effectively closed down while I was on safari. He had recoiled in horror when on lifting a jar from my safe he found it contained potassium cyanide and that another held strychnine. Asked how I accounted for both, I had told him quite simply that I didn't (both were inherited from predecessors and, eventually, disappeared down a long-drop). And when he asked to see the stores vouchers for the silver Game Scout badges I got Walimohamed to make for the Kilifi and Kajiado Ranges, and learned that Zaphiro and Parker had paid for them from their own pockets, he gave up. Perhaps he was right: the Game Department was beyond or outside normal Government auditing.

Here it is worth reiterating a point made in the Introduction. Among the strongest reasons for Departmental accounting laxity was rooted in western cultural perceptions of conservation's practitioners. The cause is held to be inherently good, not through reasoning or assessing evidence, but as part of one's upbringing. Being kind to animals and treating them humanely is more an issue of faith than reason. Following on from this, those who devote their careers to conserving animals are also seen as good. Wardens and rangers are thought to have vocations and missions in life, much in the same way as priests and religious ministers. Such people do not fiddle the books – or are not supposed to! In parallel, and because they are driven by vocation, they do not demand high salaries. Like parsons, their pay is meagre and always has been. Consequently, no one saw it incongruous that Game Wardens were among the most lowly on government pay scales, yet charged with looking after elephants and rhinos whose trophies were easily taken and worth huge sums of money, but which appeared on no auditable inventory. Of course there were always exceptions but, looking back over the record, by and large colonial Wardens and rangers did not abuse this public trust. It was this cultural link to a high sense of probity that underlay the latitude encoded in Section 14 of the Ordinance.

The issuance of forest elephant licences did not even follow the loose demands of Section 14 that the Chief Game Warden's permits only be issued with the Minister's approval. This approval may have been given in principle at the outset, but it was not sought thereafter for the issuance of each permit granted – as it should have been.

The Kenyans who replaced us pale-face Game Wardens inherited a lax bureaucracy, no hard and fast rules on how Wardens should dispose of trophies, and trophy permits that – at least in part – were being issued by the very dealers that they were supposed to control. They found themselves in charge of huge mobile, uncounted and unauditable treasuries. It was a situation inviting pillage. More important though, their cultures did not give Game Wardens special status or associate them with any sense of vocation. They were simply civil servants in whom probity was obviously desirable, but Wardens were not expected to exhibit it to a greater or lesser degree than, say, Public Works Department officials.

'Forest elephant licences' were quickly appreciated. Over 15 months in 1970/71, 31 members of the Department took out Chief Game Warden's permits for 82 forest elephants. Though these were supposed to be for elephants in highland forests, some were certainly used for elephants elsewhere. Some who bought forest elephant licences were clerical officers with no hunting knowledge. The Asian hunter they hired to shoot the elephants for them was caught doing so in the Coast Province by Dave McCabe. This abuse of 'forest elephant licences' was among the earliest to become general among members of the Department and drew attention to the much greater possibilities offered by Section 14.

In 1973 the number of elephants being shot on licences was so high that public outcry temporarily stopped elephant hunting. The ban was lifted briefly in 1974 then reintroduced permanently. An ignorant public was unaware that the ban related to normal licences only. Hunting on Chief Game Warden's permits continued and the number issued jumped from under 200 a year to over 2,000[91], many as cheap forest elephant licences and many more for tens of elephants at a time. Even after a ban on hunting was introduced in 1977[92], and the Game Department had merged with the National Parks into the Wildlife Conservation & Management Department (WCMD), Special Director's permits which replaced Chief Game Warden's permits continued to be issued for hunting. The general perception that there was a complete hunting ban was a fiction.

The new men in the Department combed the laws for further opportunities. Section 15 gave the Chief Game Warden the same virtually absolute power to issue capture permits whose conditions and costs were left to his discretion. Section 39(3) gave the Chief Game Warden power to waive Government's ownership of any game animal, trophy or meat, which included ivory. Section 54 allowed the Chief Game Warden to appoint anyone to be an Honorary Game Warden. Section 55 allowed him to delegate any of his powers and responsibilities including all those listed above to any officer in the Department, *including* Honorary Game Wardens.

In a nutshell, the law allowed the Chief Game Warden or any person to whom he might delegate all or any of his powers, to set aside the law. And that, quite literally, is what happened. When Police did investigate the Game Department, they concluded that most of what had been happening was technically legal, for all that it was at odds with the Game Department's publicly perceived role, and that there were technically no grounds for prosecuting the large number of Wardens and Scouts who appeared to have been breaking the rules.

What happened with ivory encapsulated the general trends. In 1964, immediately after Independence and by Presidential edict, certain allegedly ex-Mau Mau figures were to be allowed to bring in and sell ivory that they had cached during their years in the forests. Ian Grimwood foresaw this order, to be effected through Chief Game Warden's permits, would be a catastrophe. However, at best he could only fight a rearguard action and he tried to prevent these ivory collectors selling their ivory freely. Initially he was successful and their tusks had to be sold to the Game Department at a fixed price. The Department then sold them through the regular Ivory Room auctions.

It was not long before the 'collectors' were disputing the prices paid by the Game Department and pressing for freedom to sell to buyers of their choice.

[91] Casebeer Robert L. 1975. *Summaries of Statistics & Regulations Pertaining to Wildlife, Parks & Reserves in Kenya.* UNDP/FAO Project KEN:71/526 Project Working Document 8. FAO Rome.
[92] Legal Notice 120 of 1977.

These pressures played a substantial role in bringing about Grimwood's resignation. In due course the collectors had their way. Little of the ivory they brought in came from the Aberdare and Mount Kenya forests – the only areas in which Mau Mau could have cached tusks. Instead it came through a network of collectors' employees cast across the whole country, drawing ivory from the furthest reaches of the NFD and the far interior of Tsavo. While they could not openly operate within the Parks, they stood on the borders where they 'legally' relieved those bold enough to get tusks to them from inside.

Government officials bought ivory directly from both the Ivory Room and from headquarters in Nairobi, not through auctions, but by private treaty and at preferential prices. Among those who took tusks from headquarters were a Foreign Minister and an Assistant Minister in the Ministry of Tourism & Wildlife. Ivory registers documented this erosion of the established system. In 1974 85% of tusks (50.8% by weight) arriving in Nairobi headquarters were still forwarded to the Ivory Room. The missing balance had been sold by private treaty. In 1975 this dropped to 18% of tusks (14% of weight) and in 1976 when National Parks came under the merged WCMD, it dropped to nothing. In 1976 the last Mombasa Ivory Room auction took place[93]. While no ivory from the Ivory Room arrived in Nairobi in either 1974 or 1975, from 1976 onwards most Mombasa tusks went to Nairobi, which had become the country's ivory marketing centre. The majority of registered buyers from WCMD headquarters were Asian Curio dealers. However, among the biggest purchasers were several of the people originally given permission to bring in ex-Mau Mau caches. With Asian backing, they became major buyers of the Government's own ivory.

Also listed among the buyers of ivory for their own rather than commercial ends were judges, court prosecutors, senior policemen and other officials across the higher echelons of the hierarchy. Both the Game Department/WCMD headquarters and the Ivory Room should have had registers in which trophies coming in were recorded in sequential order as they arrived. Both stations did have such registers: not one in each, but at least two each operated in parallel at any one time. Some ivory was registered in one and some in the other of these parallel registers. Every tusk was supposed to have its own unique identity number. Yet, not only did the same number appear twice in the same register, but sometimes in both registers. In all cases tusks with the same numbers had different weights. Clearly they were not the same tusks being erroneously entered more than once, but different tusks being given the same number.

The registers showed large gaps in numerical sequences, had instances in which while numbers appeared, they were not in sequential order and even the dates were out of sequence. The trophy registers, with their thousands of entries,

---

[93] Editor's note: A set of auction catalogues was printed in 1978, but it was circulated to eight buyers secretly and was just a front so that the officials selling the ivory could say that they had held an auction.

were an accounting nightmare. Indeed, until I entered their data on computer discs (720 man/hours), I don't think anyone had seriously checked them. Once computerised, checking became a matter of seconds and the facts obvious.

Seeing that trophies coming in at either Nairobi or Mombasa were logged in a 'proper' register, fooled most observers that they were being accounted for. The degree to which it was all a front comes both from comparing exports of ivory reported in Kenya's Customs statistics with the Game Department and/or WCMD ivory registers. The latter recorded only tens of tons where the Customs documented hundreds annually. This disparity was even greater when one compares what Kenya said it exported to Hong Kong with what Hong Kong said it imported from Kenya[94].

A great deal was said about the Kenyattas' involvement with ivory. While I am unaware of President Kenyatta acknowledging in public that he had commanded the issuance of the 'collector's permits' to a few ex-Mau Mau people, I do not doubt that he did do so. The issue was not one that his henchmen would have done in his name, as the risk of the President finding out was too high. From what I observed, I believe Jomo Kenyatta never sold ivory for personal financial gain, but used it politically. He did give the largest tusks held in the Tsavo East armoury to friends – among them Bruce Mackenzie, the Minister of Agriculture. However, that was not ivory trading.

Much was said about his wife, Mama Ngina, being deeply involved in ivory exporting, yet I never came across evidence that she was. This may reflect ignorance on my part, but I believe the charge came out of Kenya's renowned capacity for rumour. Where the President's daughter Margaret was concerned, well, that is another tale. Her United Africa Company exported ivory on a substantial scale. I saw and filmed consignments destined for mainland China, and photocopied airwaybills (mostly Pakistan International Airlines) that proved it was a regular business. On behalf of media clients I interviewed her manager (a Mr Pusey – an ex-banker who went by the nickname of Pissy) several times, on each occasion very much against his will. He was not forthcoming and iterated endlessly that the ivory the United Africa Company handled was legal, was covered by all necessary legal documentation, came mainly from government sources and was traded openly. While the last of these statements was not wholly accurate, the others were. There was nothing illegal in the United Africa Company's ivory exports.

Technically, a loophole was a slit or narrow opening in a castle wall through which one could fire at targets below. Figuratively a loophole in a law is an opening that permits actions or behaviour that the law was otherwise intended to

---

[94] See Parker I.S.C. 1979. *The Ivory Trade*. Report to the US Fish & Wildlife Service, Washington DC, USA. & Parker I. S. C. 1987. *The Ivory Trade 1978 – 1987*. Report to the CITES Secretariat, Lausanne, Switzerland.

prevent. Under our colonial game laws the Chief Game Warden's manifest powers were so great that they constituted far more than loopholes. They were gaping chasms that all but nullified the Ordinance. In pre-independence times, all that prevented their dimensions being apparent was the cultural connection between probity and Wardens. Where this cultural perspective was lacking, as was the case with the men whom replaced the expatriates, they appreciated the bonanza offered by the law and took advantage of it.

It would be very wide of the mark to say that the Game Department became as corrupt as it did (and that was very corrupt indeed) purely from the legacy of bureaucratic laxity it inherited from the colonial era. The breadth of corruption throughout government in many fields far removed from conservation is proof of a more general cause. In 2001 Kenya has the dubious distinction of being among the four most corrupt countries in the world. Yet the speed, scale and boldness of the Game Department in leading this charge was influenced by a disrespect for bureaucracy that can be traced back into the colonial Department and, even more, by the laxity of our laws.

The Africans who succeeded us did not believe that our use of Chief Game Warden's permits as forest elephant licences came about through mere laziness. Logically, they thought that we exploited the loophole (chasm) for exactly the same reasons that they did (to get elephants cheaply), only they were more thorough! Unwittingly, we did significantly influence the pace at which the wheels came off the old Game Department. Germany birds and red-naped shydabis were innocuous signs of its impending demise.

* * * *

Reading the old Game Department annual reports there is a curious mix of reality and make believe. In 1911 Woosnam set up the first water-for-wild-animals project by planting tsama melon seed from the Kalahari all over the Southern Game Reserve, to be a source of water for the animals as they were in the southern deserts. In 1926 Archie Ritchie wrote with approval of Sir John Ramsden who had brought out seventeen young red deer from his deer forest in Inverness-shire and was holding them in a paddock at Kipipiri. His approved aim was to release their progeny to go wild on the Aberdare moorlands. Ritchie himself wanted to introduce black buck from India and establish them on the Athi Plains. Clearly the Victorian wish to improve nature still flourished.

Yet perhaps the most striking false assumption of which we, as a group, were guilty, was that we were achieving more in our time than had been achieved before. When I sent first drafts of these texts to Peter Jenkins for criticism, and indicated that greater tracts were conserved in 1900 than in 2000, he was amazed. When I presented the results of MacArthur's anti-poaching he was so doubtful that I had to show him the original reports. How was it, he demanded, that none of us who joined up as callow youngsters, were told these facts as part of our basic training? There was no answer to that other, perhaps, than that we had received precious little training. Yet one cannot doubt that the conservation vision of a century and more ago, was far broader than it is today. The inescapable conclusion is that the great dream was untenable and that what has been conservable has been becoming progressively less. This is understandable in the face of human increase and 'development', but it is something that we have yet to really come to grips with. Our never-ending control work is more readily explained. We hoped we were the buffer between opposing forces whereas in fact we were the cutting edge of expanding humanity. It explains, too, why so many of us were keen to establish reserves of different sorts. It would take another book to open this one up, so suffice it that we recognise that in many respects we were riding a great white elephant.

When we look back at the enjoyable times we had and the relatively high level of probity that prevailed, it is all too easy to criticise what happened subsequently and ignore that it grew logically from the system we passed on. As an historian looking back, there were vast flaws in our conservation policies, foremost among them was making no provision for Africans to hunt. The greater of our Wardens (TB, for example), were never happy over this and, recognising its iniquity, allowed them to do so through a Nelsonian blind eye. The Galana Scheme was a far more deliberate move to redress the issue, but it was too little, too late and not fully thought out. Yet at the time, it seemed appropriate. Therein lies the rub.

Had we been aware of how closely Kenya's independence was upon us, had we had the foresight to see how inconsequential white opinions and wishes were to become, we would have had conservation policies (and much more besides) that were far more African-oriented for no other reason than logic. Yet we were denied such wisdom and it is now all in the realm of ifs and ans and pots and pans and little pigs flying. The period that is the core of this book – the 1950s and early 1960s – saw developments such as the Baring anti-poaching campaign, the Galana Scheme, the formation of the Game Policy Committee and the translocation of animals as a conservation strategy. These were novel and departures from the past, and perhaps they kept us from appreciating just how fast the wild was receding.

One cannot do more than what appears to be right at the time and that, I think, most of us did. If there is anything left for us to do that might be of use to posterity, it is to acknowledge that for all our certitude that we were right at the time, we did get some things wrong and that we were indubitably too few on the ground to have ever had any great impact on what was happening. That is not to say that the game laws were of no consequence. They were an expression of society's attitude and reflected what our imperial community believed. There were always poachers among us, but overall, it was very much part of our traditions to abide by game (and other) laws. Today one sees remnants of this adherence to a code in New Zealand's licensing for trout fishing. Having fished there over several years, I have yet to be approached by any official asking to see my licence. The populace at large does not have to be continually checked. One gets one's licence at the local post office, not for fear of prosecution for going fishing without one, but simply because it is the right thing to do. That ethic once manifest itself across the Empire and, come to think of it, was one of its most admirable features. It was that which influenced our attitudes to game and produced such successes as can be attributed to colonial conservation.

Now, we can sit around and analyse what went wrong and bemoan the passing of the good old days. Then, given our youth, it was natural that we acted rather than thought. Yet, even if we had thought things through, I don't think we would have been very good at it. We were by inclination not of the thinkers' ilk. Our Game Department days were great fun, we led lives that, with good reason, were widely envied and, for a while at least, we were indeed the Heaven-born.

APPENDIX I

The Native Question with Reference to Game by A. Blayney Percival Game Ranger

(This document was delivered to the Deputy Commissioner F. J. Jackson as evidence in his case for creating a Game Department)

So long as the natives do not hunt outside their own district, and use only their own weapons, I do not consider that they will do very much harm. In November 1901, when so many Wakamba were hunting on the Athi Plains, there was a small famine in Ukamba country, and every man who could use a bow was out. Since then much less has been seen of the Wakamba on this part of the Athi, though they still hunt at certain times of the year in the Southern Reserve.

Natives using bows and arrows are only likely to do real damage when big drives are arranged, and the only district where this goes on to any extent is in the bush country between the Tzavo [sic] River and Serengati Plains. The method employed here is to build a thorn fence for a mile or more, and drive the game along this, bowmen being hidden in the fence who fix poisoned arrows into the game as it passes.

Elephants suffer at the hands of the natives as cows and calves are as often killed by natives as bulls. If all trade in cow ivory could be stopped it might do something to prevent the killing of cows. Pitfalls and drop-spears are also used, and of course there is no chance for the cow or calf who walks into one or other of these. At the same time the condition of the herds of elephants on the Kenia and Kinangop Forests is most satisfactory, any number of cows and calves as well as plenty of young bulls. But the very few big bulls on the range, such as there are, are mostly solitary.

Owing to the huge distances ranged over by the elephant it is impossible to estimate numbers; a troop of elephants may be seen during the dry season in one district, and a month or two later, should the rains be on, they may be seen a hundred or more miles away.

During the dry season elephants may be found in the following districts: - Near Lake Victoria, Mount Elgon, Ingongo [Ngong] Hills, Mau Forest, Abadare [sic] Range, Mount Kenia, Tzavo River, Tana River, Mumoni District, Lorian Swamp, Umtondea [Mtondia near Kilifi] on the coast, and in the Northern Reserve, where they are numerous on Mount Marsabit, Rendili and Samburu country. In the Baringo District elephants come from the east every year to Soli [Solai] and afterwards pass the western side of the lake Baringo going northwards.

Rhinoceros. If any animal in British East Africa could be counted it would be the rhinoceros, but he is spread over such a huge extent of the country that it is impossible to make even a guess at their numbers. They are found over more than half of the Protectorate in fair numbers, and in smaller numbers over the rest.

They are most numerous in the following districts: - Southern Reserve (here I myself saw more than 150 while crossing to Kilimanjaro, several times having six or eight in view at once. On my return via another route 100 miles to the east I saw them in similar numbers). On Likipia, Thika and Tana Rivers, Kitui District and over the Northern Reserve. In smaller numbers they are found on Athi Plains, and in the bush country near Kiu and Machakos Road.

Hippopotamus. Very generally distributed in most of the large rivers, lakes and swamps. In Lake Victoria, on the coast, in the creeks and mouths of rivers, and in the Tana River they are numerous, and often prove a danger to canoes and small boats. Great damage is done by them to the shambas on shores of the lake, and to the rice crops in Vanga District on the coast.

Buffalo. Most numerous near the Tana River. On the Athi Plains there are three troops – one of 40-50, one of 37-40-, one of 15-20, and a few solitary bulls. A few on Kikuyu escarpment. Several small troops on the coast north of Mombasa, also on the Sabaki River, and up into Jubaland. A fair number in the Forest on Mau; as well as many solitary animals and small herds scattered over Likipia, Northern Reserve, and near Lake Rudolf.

Giraffe. One or other species is commonly found over the drier parts of the Protectorate, viz., The Tana River, Voi, Seringati Plains, and from there up the Rift valley from Kilimanjaro to Sosian, Baringo District, Gusso [sic] Nyiro, and the Northern Reserve, Turkwell River, and Gusso Nguisho.

A few only are found on the Athi, and in the Rift valley, south of the equator, until Sosian is reached.

They breed freely in October and November, and appear to have few enemies.

At Sultan Hamud I counted 130 adult animals in about eight miles, and nearly every cow had a calf with her.

Eland. No animal has repaid protection more than the eland. Within the last five years they have on the Athi Plains increased greatly in numbers. I recently saw and counted a troop consisting of 58 eland; of these at least 20 were calves not more than a few months old.

In the following districts eland are very plentiful: - Baringo, Likipia, Tana River, and in parts of the Northern Reserve. While in Voi, Tzavo, Kitui Districts they are fairly numerous. In Rift valley a few troops only are found.

Neuman's [sic] **Hartebeest.** An extremely local animal found only in the Rift valley south of the equator to about the Gil Gil [sic] River. Total number not more than 600 or 700. Almost the whole of the country inhabited by this animal will within a very short time be settled up.

Jackson's Hartebeest. Numerous from the Lake Victoria to the Rift valley where it meets Neuman's [sic] Hartebeest. A few at Baringo and on Likipia.

Coke's Hartebeest. The chief haunt of this animal is the Athi Plains, but it is found from the coast south of Mombasa to Naivasha, north-east to Kitui District and south to Kilimanjaro into German territory. On the Athi it is a usual sight to have several thousands of these animals in view at one time, extending as far as the eye can see.

Hunter's Antelope. A very local animal found only in one small district on the Tana River. Its habitat is roughly triangular in shape extending north-west from the River for about 50 miles then east to within 30 miles of the coast, and back to the Tana along the northern bank of which it extends for about 20 miles.

Topi. Extremely common in Jubaland, on the Tana and near the Anglo-German border south of Sotik. A few only, on Mau and near Lake Victoria, in the Nyando Valley.

Wildebeeste. The habitat of this fine beast is in the Southern Reserve, where it equals even Coke's Hartebeest in numbers, but only over a comparatively small area. At certain times of the year they come north, and spread over the Athi Plains to as far as the Thika River, some few crossing. The main body of the Wildebeeste does not leave the reserve.

Bohor Reedbuck. Wherever swamps and marshes are to be found these buck exist, but mostly in small numbers. On Mau, however, they are the common buck, and go about in parties of four or five.

Chanler's Reedbuck. Commonly found on rocky hills from Simba and northward through the Rift valley. Most numerous on El Donyo Sabuk, where they are carefully preserved on private land, and on Elburru [sic] they are in considerable numbers.

Steinbuck. Numerous all over the open country with the exception of the coast and Mau.

Klipspringer. Found in fair numbers on rocky hills from Makindu to north of Kenia and Baringo, but never really numerous.

Common Waterbuck. From the coast to Taveta, and from there northward to the Kikuyu escarpment and Kenia. One of the most evenly distributed animals. Fairly plentiful on most rivers and swamps whether in the open or in forest.

Waterbuck Defassa. Takes the place of the common waterbuck on the western side of the Kikuyu escarpment, and extends along the Rift valley to Baringo, and into the Northern Reserve, Likipia, Lake Victoria.

Thomas's cob. Rare in this Protectorate, a few only, found along the shores of Lake Victoria. True habitat being on Uganda side of the lake.

Duiker. Common everywhere.

Harvey's and Isaac's duikers. These being bush antelopes they are seldom seen. Found from coast to Mau in forest.

Other species of red duiker will most likely be found as the country becomes better known.

Dik-dik. Kirk's, Hind's, Cavendish's; Gunther's. All over the dry country dik-dik are found in great numbers. More like rabbits and hares than anything else. Particularly numerous in the Taru Desert, around Kilimanjaro, Lake Baringo, and on Gusso Nyiro, Likipia.

Oribi. Haggard's Found near Lamu, in Jubaland, on the coast for about 50 miles. Very local but numerous where found.

Abyssinian. Extremely common on Mau Nandi and Nyando Valley.

Kenia. Local and in small numbers near Fort Hall.

Zanzibar Antelope[95]. Common along the coast, in thick scrub; used to be particularly so on Mombasa Island. Also found in forest on Kenia and Kikuyu Escarpment.

Impalla [sic]. One of the most numerous of the antelope, being found evenly distributed over a large part of the Protectorate. From the Taru Desert to the Rift valley and as far north as the Gusso Nyiro; around Baringo herds run large. Near Lake Victoria they are found but in smaller numbers.

Thomson's Gazelle. Over the whole of the open country from Tzavo River, throughout the Rift valley all over Athi and Likipia as far as Gusso Nyiro this delightful little gazelle is still very plentiful, but much reduced in numbers in the Rift valley between Naivasha and the equator.

Grant's Gazelle. Very much the same range as Thomson's, but in slightly smaller numbers except in the Southern Reserve. There are several types of this animal in different districts varying chiefly in the horns.

Peter's Gazelle. Found on the coast from the Sabaki to Jubaland and inland to Voi. Nowhere in large numbers.

Waller's Gazelle. Numerous in Jubaland and on the Tana River. A few found in the Serengati and in the lower part of the Rift valley from Kilimanjaro to Sosian. Also in the Gusso Nyiro, north of Kenia.

---

[95] Editor's note: Here, Blayney was referring to suni (*Neotragus moschatus*).

Sable. One of the most local antelopes in the country, and only found on and around the Shimba Hills. I should not think that there can be more than two or three hundred in all, including the few that are found north of the railway and on the Anglo-German border.

Roan. Very local, but fairly distributed over the country. Nowhere are there more than one hundred or so in one locality. But there are a number of isolated hills that hold small troops, particularly in the bush country near Sultan Hamud.

I know some four or five troops in the reserve, and outside there are two troops near Machakos Hills, one on Kiangundu Hills, one between there and El Donyo Sabuk, a few along the edge of the Kikuyu Forest. On Chania River, on hills near Thika River, north of Kenia, Nyandu Valley, about three troops on Anglo-German border and Kulungu on Lake Victoria.[96]

Oryx callotis. Headquarters of these animals appear to be around Lakes Jipi and Nyiri, near Mount Kilimanjaro, where they are in considerable numbers; from there they extend northwards to Simba, Makindu, and Voi. They also follow the Rift Valley to Lake Magadi.

Oryx beisa. In fair numbers on Likipia and Baringo, but in great numbers on Gusso Nyiro; by far the commonest animal north of Kenia and throughout the Northern Reserve.

Bushbuck. Where the bush is thick enough there will bushbuck be found, from the coast to the lake. Common on the Mau and on the Abadare Range.

Bongo. Only found, and then but rarely, in the Mau Forest.

Greater Kudu. Extremely scarce in East Africa, only found in any numbers near Baringo. A few inhabit the Ingongo Hills, Eldonyo Narok Hills, on south of Naivasha, Sultan Hamud, Makindu, Serengati, Tzavo River, and at mile 70 on the railway. Some time ago I heard that there were a few between Wasin on Coast and Taveta on the old road, but this has never been confirmed.

Lesser Kudu. Freely distributed throughout the bush country from the coast to Makindu, and following the belt of bush country north to the Tana River and Jubaland; common all through the Northern Reserve.

Zebra. In countless troops all over the plains of Athi and Rift Valley. These animals have undoubtedly increased in numbers, and are I consider becoming far too numerous, they do more damage to crops than all other game put together, and if it should be decided to give up the zebra catching as a failure I should suppose that zebra be put into the class where 10 of a sort are allowed, and into a settler's license

Grevey's [sic] **Zebra.** Commonly found over the whole of the Northern Reserve coming as far south as Gusso Mara on north of Kenia.

Wart Hog. Extremely numerous along the edge of the Kikuyu Forest. Near Nakuru and Molo, and generally distributed over the country from the coast to Lake Victoria.

Bush Pig. Numerous in thick scrub, seldom seen plentiful on coast and along Mau Forest.

Giant Pig. Apparently common in Bamboo Forest on Mau and Kenia where it feeds on bamboo shoots.

---

[96] Editor's note: Sir Frederick Jackson (*op cit*) recorded roan from the coastal hinterland of Vanga before the turn of the century, and Theodore Roosevelt hunted roan successfully in the Timboroa/Burnt Forest area: see Roosevelt T. *op cit.*

Lion. Lion appear to be as common as ever on the Athi Plains and in the Southern Reserve. As these animals are not in the schedules they are not shown in game returns as a rule, but I should say that some 50 are killed every year, about two-thirds of these on the Athi Plains between Nairobi and Machakos Road. They undoubtedly migrate at certain times of the year, for during November, December and January more are to be seen on the Athi than at any other time of year. From November, 1905, to end of January, 1906, I know of 27 bagged, but many sportsmen have been down whose bags I do not at present know.

Big manes are, however, scarce, at least eight females and young males being seen for one with a mane.

Leopard. Numerous in forest and hill country.

Cheeta [sic]. In certain parts of the country they are still fairly numerous, but very local.

Wild Dogs. These, the worst vermin in the country, are, I regret to say, numerous. They do a great deal of harm amongst the game. A large pack has lately been hunting near Athi River, and has been seen to move about from place to place, staying in one district for a week or two, and then moving on.

A. B. Percival 1906

APPENDIX II

AN INCOMPLETE RECORD OF COLONIAL ERA KENYA GAME DEPARTMENT RANGERS/WARDENS & FISHERIES OFFICERS

Head of Department

	Year <	
Crawshay R	1900	1900
Percival B. (acting)	1900	1907
Patterson J. H.	1907	1908
Percival B. (acting)	1908	1910
Woosnam R. B.	1910	1914
Percival B. (acting)	1914	1922
Caldwell K. (acting)	1923	1924
Ritchie A.	1924	1948
Hale W.	1949	1959
Sandeman N. (acting)	1959	1960
Grimwood I. R.	1960	1964
Brown D. W. J.	1964	1967

Rangers/Wardens

Percival B.	1901	1923
Goldfinch G. H.	1907	
Ross C. J.	1907	
Woodhouse C. W.	1907	
Seth-Smith M. P.	1911	1914
Clarke F. H.	1920?	
Erskine E. N. Capt	1924	
MacArthur C. S.	1927	1945
Oulton Capt	1928	
Hilton W. R.	1929	
Dawson H. C	1931	
Adamson G.	1938	1961
Temple-Boreham L.	1939	1969
Hunter JA	1942	1957
Bonham J	1942	1952
Salmon T. R. P.	1945	1955
Rundgren E.	1944	1952
Simms J	1946	1951
Turner M.	1945	1949
Henley A. H.	1948	1950
Kirkpatrick Sir A.	1949	1950
Bartlett F.	1949	1957
Elliott R. T.	1949	1971
Hurt R. A. F.	1950	1962
Bousfield D	1950	1955
Coles W. L.	1950	1967
Teague	1950	1954
Zaphiro D.	1951	1973
Harvey G.	1953	1956
Sandeman N. 1	1954	1962
Orchardson J. A.	1955	1955
Foster R. W.	1955	1955
Smith K. A.	1955	1967
Barrah J.	1955	1976
Brown D. W. J.	1956	1968
Parker I. S. C.	1956	1964
Morris-Smith S.	1956	1961
McCabe D.H.	1956	1973
Kearney D	1956	1958
Massey H.	1956	1956
McKeand J.	1957	1959
Harvard R.	1957	1958
Grey M.	1957	1958
Allen D.	1958	1960
Pereira R.	1958	1976
Bleazard S.	1959	1968
Forbes-Watson A.	1959	1963
Saw P.	1959	1964
Carn A.	1960	1969
Winterburn R.	1960	
Jenkins A.	1960	
Winter W.	1960	1971
Seth-Smith A.	1961	1963
Graham A. D.	1961	1964
Marsh A	1962	1967
Chappell B.	1962	1965
Powys G.	1963	1964
Allison G.	1963	1964
Olindo P.	1963	1976
Mutinda J.	1963	1979

FISHERIES SECTION

Fish Warden

	Year>	
Dent	1926	1937
Copley H.	1937	1948
Smith D. F.	1948	1960
Watson P.		

Fisheries Officers

Van Someren V. D.	1947	
Allfree T. E.	1948	1961?
Martindale N.	1949	1963?
Brown J. M.	1951	1959
Hamilton G.	1953	
Holness P.	1953	1953
Whitehead P. J. P.	1953	1963
Paul H. J. A.	1954	
Wilkinson W.	1954	
Harris C. J. R.	1959	
McConnell R.	1961	1976

INDEX

A

Aaron, A., 198
Abakuna Gumundi, 59, 109, 110, 111
ABC – American Broadcasting Corpn, 199
Abdulla (Somali clan), 68
Abdulla Sood Al-Busaidi, 288
Abdwak (Somali clan), 68
Aberdare National Park, 322
Acacia gerrardii, 211
Acacia tortilis, 233
Acepromazine, 210
acetylpromazine, 210
Achieng, A., 296, 297
Acokanthera, 107
acovenocide A, 107
Adamson, G., 2, 22, 53, 65, 68, 73, 119, 125, 145, 147, 148, 150, 151, 164, 258, 278, 298, 316, 318
Adamson, J., 119, 121, 233, 314
Administration, 2, 11, 22, 24, 31, 39, 40, 41, 47, 65, 68, 70, 93, 95, 98, 99, 100, 112, 119, 126, 157, 166, 167, 255, 309, 311
African District Council, 57, 91, 140, 167, 175
Afrikaner, 5
Agricultural Development Corpn, 173
Agriculture Department, 2, 140, 270
Ahmed, 122
Ahmed, Diwan bin, 93
Ainsworth, J., 15, 24
Aldrick, J., 295
Alexander, J., 241
Ali bin Salim, 288
Allen, Anton, 250
Allen, Bunny, 53
Allen, Dave, 250
Allen, Jeremy & Barbie., 199
Allison, brothers, 39, 40
Alouette helicopter, 207
American Museum of Natural History, 59, 62
Amhara, 47
Amin Dada, Idi (Dr, Field Marshall etc. etc.), 44, 181
Anderson, M., 173
Animal Husbandry Division, 299
Animal Orphanage, 284
Annual Reports, 2, 11, 24, 28, 52, 62, 84, 93, 94, 99
Anstey, D., 243
anti-poaching, 3, 28, 29, 35, 60, 61, 68, 86, 87, 93, 94, 96, 99, 100, 101, 102, 103, 105, 111, 112, 116, 119, 125, 141, 143, 165, 166, 176, 180, 197, 241, 289, 306, 312, 325, 334
Arabs, 10, 27, 35, 68, 74, 102, 116, 130, 134, 137, 245, 267, 288
Archbishop Makarios, 233
Archer, C., 192
Archer, Tony, 63, 130
arrows, 17, 50, 101, 105, 106, 107, 108, 109, 141, 148, 168, 174, 177, 179, 306, 337
arsenite of soda, 43, 69
Asian girls drowning, 33
askari, 49
Astles, 'Major' Bob, 44
Attorney General, 87, 287, 289
Aulihan (Somali clan), 68
Ayodo, Sam, 235, 237

B

baboons, 69, 70, 128, 139, 140, 220, 221
badges, 49, 68, 328
Bajun, 127, 130
Baluchi, 10, 16, 286
Banbury, H., 36
Baring Biscuit Factory, 120
Baring, Sir Evelyn, 33, 87, 98, 99, 166
Barrah, Jack, 65, 119, 121, 181, 213, 264, 303, 308, 309, 341
Barrington, G., 179
Bartlett, Des. & Jen., 279
Bartlett, Fred, 65, 119, 303, 309, 315, 316
Bartlett, 'Jock', 2, 309
Bateman, R., 122
Batiaan, 26
Bearcroft, P., 111
Beard, P., 216
Beer, W., 48
Bell, Karamoja, 9, 130
Bell, Superintendent, 288
Berkeley, E. J., 7
Bertie, F., 8
biltong, 5, 310
bison, 6
black buck, 333
Blanche, E., 159
Bleazard, Jim., 147
Bleazard, Stan, 1, 65, 121, 144, 145, 147, 161, 164, 200, 202, 225, 233, 291
Blixen, Baron Bror von, 59, 113, 169, 275, 306
Block, Jack, 37, 84
Board of Trustees, 89, 289
Boer, 15, 24, 309
Bolton, L., 318
bomas, 70, 135, 177, 197, 198, 199, 237, 257
Bond, Tony (Nyani), 123, 248, 249
Bonham, J., 65, 67, 126, 130, 341
Boni (Waboni, Bon), 26, 71, 93, 94, 105, 106, 112, 128, 129, 130, 133, 141
Boni, (Waboni, Bon), 17, 93
Bonnett, L., 204
boomslang, 163
Boots Pure Drug Company, 210
Borana, 7, 47, 67, 70, 73, 173, 227, 230
borassus, 127, 133
Bousfield, D., 65, 126, 130, 250, 316, 341
bovine pleuro-pneumonia, 26
bows, 17, 101, 105, 106, 108, 168, 174, 337
Bows, 106
Brett, R., 222, 223
British Army Air Corps, 207
British Museum of Natural History, 59
brown olives, 150
Brown, David (DB), 2, 3, 100, 101, 112, 113, 118, 119, 121, 168, 200, 233, 237, 297, 299, 302, 303, 318, 325, 326
Brown, Monty, 9
Browning, P., 149, 154
Broz, Madame, 318, 320
Buechner, H., 86
buffalo, 13, 19, 50, 52, 55, 56, 65, 68, 70, 101, 119, 120, 122, 128, 129, 139, 143, 145, 147, 150, 175, 176, 213, 214, 253, 259, 260, 291, 301, 312, 315, 316, 318, 319, 320, 321
bundu, 250
Burma Railway, 6, 41, 226
Burton, J., 73
Burton, Mr, 50

C

Caldwell, Capt K., 27, 341
camels, 57, 68, 70, 71, 72, 130, 147, 154, 159, 161, 164
cane rats, 293, 294
Cap-Chur, 183, 184, 257
Capture Unit, 200, 207, 220
caracal, 154
card index system, 108
Carlyon, J., 254
carmine bee-eater, 153
Carn, Tony, 2, 65, 127, 135, 137, 138, 267, 341
Carr-Hartley, T., 41, 43, 181
Carrington, Lord, 323
Carter, B. (Nick), 30, 181, 183, 191, 193, 194, 206, 207, 210, 222, 286
Cathedral, 75
Catling, Sir Richard, 87
cattle, 26, 41, 50, 56, 68, 72, 130, 131, 132, 133, 155, 156, 159, 173, 182, 225, 228, 237, 244, 259, 260, 261, 263, 264, 273, 309
Catzler, Jack, 37
Cavendish-Bentinck, Sir F., 234
Central Firearms Bureau, 287
Cessna, 321
chaplis, 252
Chapman, A, 83
Chappell, B., 207, 235, 236
cheetah, 51, 52, 153, 340
Chief Game Warden's Permits, 327
Chief Justice, 87
chloromycetin, 220
CITES, 11, 332
Clark, K., 173, 213, 214
Clarke, Dr D., 159, 341
Closed Districts Ordinance, 22
Coles, W. L. (Coley), 173, 313, 341
colobus, 120, 147
Colonial Office, 6, 25
Colville, G., 259
Combretum, 176
Commiphora, 115, 170, 181, 207, 242, 244, 294, 306
Commissioner of Prisons, 268
Conservator of Forests, 87, 159
controlled area fees, 140
controlled areas, 57, 70, 91, 172, 299, 300, 324
Convention for the Preservation of Wild Animals, Birds and Fish in Africa, 10
Convention on International Trade in Endangered Species of Fauna and Flora (CITES), 11
convictions, 28, 35, 51, 55, 117, 141, 180, 286
Cook, J. (Cookie), 51
Corbett, J., 53, 78
corporal punishment, 5
Coryndon Museum, 91, 145, 206, 234, 243
Cottar, G., 250
Cotton, P., 59, 62
County Councils, 57, 69, 73, 146, 167
Coverdale, M., 197, 201, 210
Cowie, M., 29, 30, 31, 34, 84, 87, 89, 91, 158, 159
Crauford, C., 6
Crawshay, R., 11, 341
crocodiles, 70, 278
Cromer, Lord, 98
cropping, 40, 87, 284, 300, 301
crossbow, 181, 183, 192, 193
Crossley, J., 231, 232
Croton, 150
Cullen, Tony, 84, 98
culling, 41, 139, 300, 301
Cunningham, General, 72
Customs, 16, 17, 18, 54, 55, 86, 286, 287, 295, 325, 332

D

D.O.K.G., 100, 242, 309
Dahalo, 93
Dale, D., 230, 231
Dalton, J., 47, 48, 314
Day, P., 241, 242
debe, 134
deer, red, 333
Delamere, Hugh Cholmondley 3rd Baron, 11, 25, 75
Destro, R., 155, 159, 253, 315
dhow, 127
Digilesi Lekukuton, Game Scout, 237, 238
Digiri, 93
Digo, 93
dik-dik, 106, 339
Dineh, Corporal, 127
Diospyros, 245
Dodosa, 17
dogs, 52, 77, 80, 128, 203, 205, 213, 214, 216, 259, 261, 262, 263, 264, 292, 293, 313, 315
Donohew, M., 52
Dorobo, (Wandorobo), 17, 28, 29, 55
doum palm, 107, 245
Downey, S., 37, 84, 159
Dreschfield, Uganda Attorney General, 145
Drummond, R., 306
Dubas, 230
Duff, 272
Duff, Mrs, 272
Dugmore, J., 159
duka, 40, 134, 313, 314
Duke of Windsor, 72
Duke of York School, 249
During, a missionary, 133
Duruma, 93
Dutch, 5
Dyer, T., 173, 305

E

East African Land & Development Company, 33
East African Livestock Development Survey, 299
East African Professional Hunters' Association, 166
East African Standard, 205
East African Wildlife Journal, 84
East African Wildlife Society, (EAWLS), 197, 201, 207, 217
Eastman Kodak Expedition, 147
Edwards, Gerry, 259
Edwards, John, 323
Ekusi, Coporal, 207, 213
eland, 13, 19, 50, 78, 338
elephants, 3, 6, 7, 8, 9, 10, 16, 17, 26, 29, 35, 37, 41, 44, 51, 52, 53, 55, 56, 59, 60, 61, 62, 67, 68, 70, 72, 73, 86, 87, 88, 93, 94, 95, 96, 101, 105, 107, 110, 111, 113, 115, 116, 119, 120, 121, 122, 125, 126, 127, 128, 129, 130, 133, 137, 138, 139, 141, 143, 149, 150, 152, 154, 159, 165, 170, 171, 174, 176, 177, 179, 180, 181, 182, 183, 184, 185, 186, 187, 188, 189, 194, 195, 225, 236, 241, 245, 247, 249, 250, 255, 256, 257, 259, 265, 271, 279, 280, 284, 287, 291, 292, 294, 297, 298, 301, 303, 304, 306, 312, 315, 317, 320, 325, 327, 329, 330, 333, 334, 337
Elgeyo, 8
Elgin, Earl of, 13
Elliott, Rodney, 46, 47, 73, 75, 93, 161, 164, 167, 285, 312, 313, 314, 341
Ellis, Steven, 77
Elsa, 67, 147, 151, 152, 207, 210, 233, 315
Elsa Foundation, 233
Elsa Fund, 315
Elsa Wild Animal Appeal, 207

Elsa Wildlife Capture Unit, 210
Elui, Ace Kamba hunter, 59
etorphine, 207
Euphorbia, 217
Euphorbia robecchii, 114, 115
European, 5, 13, 35, 36, 41, 121, 261

F

falcons, 225
famine, 26, 39, 337
Fatah Morgana, 131
Fauna Preservation Society, 161
Field Force, 87, 96, 100, 101, 102, 105, 108, 109, 111, 113, 120
Fielding, Pip, 203
Finch-Hatton, D., 113, 275
Fleet Air Arm, 98, 279
Fletcher, John, 240, 254
Foran, R., 9
Forbes-Watson, Alec, 256, 341
Ford Foundation, 121
Ford V8, 39, 40, 275
Foreign Office, 6
Forest Department, 137, 268, 269, 271
Forest Elephant Licences, 328
Foster, R. W., 126, 130, 341
Fox, G., 50
Francolin, 70, 83
Fraser-Darling, Dr F., 166
Fred, Wilson, 34
French Foreign Legion, 33
Fulbright Scholar, 86, 89, 90

G

Gagarin, Yuri, 245, 246
Gailey & Roberts Ltd, 96
galagos, 225
Galana Game & Ranching Ltd, 173, 174
Galana Game Management Scheme, 35, 60, 129, 141, 165, 168, 169, 170, 171, 173, 174, 275, 280, 284, 334
Galla, 47
Galogalo Kafonde, 59, 60, 63, 107, 117
Game Policy Committee, 86, 88, 146, 165, 334
game preserve, 11
game ranges, 66
Game Regulations, 7, 15, 17, 88
game reserve, 6, 8, 11, 23, 25,73, 92, 210, 300, 301, 312
Garissa Curling Club, 71
Gavaghan, T., 119
General Service Unit (GSU), 234
Gentian Violet, 218, 220, 221
gerenuk, 153
giraffes, 8, 10, 41, 50, 51, 146, 151, 152, 153, 164, 210, 211, 212, 228, 261, 262, 264, 294
Giriama, 95, 107
glycocide, 107
Gostowski, Baron, 241
Government Chemist, 148
Governor, 6, 9, 10, 13, 33, 65, 72, 87, 98, 99, 100, 117, 119, 159, 166, 167, 298
Graham, Alistair, 2, 3, 246, 247, 255, 274, 275, 282
Grainger, Stewart, 250
Grant's gazelle, 50
Grenadier Guards, 33, 323
Grevy's zebra, 51, 153, 154, 163
Grey, M., 126
Griffith, L., 206
Grimwood, Ian, 89, 121, 154, 158, 161, 168, 172, 224, 225, 228, 233, 250, 256, 259, 330, 332, 341
ground hornbills, 153
ground squirrels, 44
Guest, R., 63
Guest, W., 59, 62, 63
guinea fowl, 70, 149, 232, 233, 234, 235
gun law, 7
gunsmith, 36

H

Habash, 47
hadama, 115
Haile Selassie, Emperor of Ethiopia, 235, 284, 321
Hale, Willie, 22, 28, 48, 50, 51, 89, 119, 120, 165, 167, 242, 297, 341
Hall, F., 6
Hamilton, P., 222
Hardinge, Sir Arthur, 7, 37
hartebeest, 33, 52, 61
Harthoorn, Tony, 181, 182, 184, 185, 186, 189, 210
Hartley, Lionel, 43, 45
Harvey, Gordon, 65, 67, 116
Harvey, John, 63
Harvey, Sir R. G., 274
Harvey, William, 58, 59, 61, 62, 63
Hatim, 288
Hayashi, Tom, 159
Hayes Sadler, Sir James, 13
Henderson, Ian, 234
Henley, Tony, 126, 130, 341
Heuglin's bustard, 153
Heyer, Chas. A., 36, 37
Higginson, Henry, 39, 40
Higginson, Phil., 39
Higgs, Cecil, 37
Hill School, 249
Hillaby, John, 161, 162, 163, 164
Hilton, Jack, 86, 341
Hinga, Bernard, 234, 235
hippo, 50, 68, 72, 139, 143, 153, 236, 237, 238, 239, 245, 247, 265, 268, 269, 270, 291, 313
Hipposiderus caffer, 244
hirola, 70, 210, 256, 257, 274, 275, 278, 279, 280, 338
HMS Albion, 280
HMS Ark Royal, 278, 279
HMS Bulwark, 280
Hobson, Valerie, 72
Hoffmann, Prof. Reino, 53
Hola Force, 112
Hola Mau Mau Detention Camp, 137
Holden, Bill, 159, 221
Holmberg, Andrew, 225
Honorary Game Wardens, 1, 31, 38, 41, 52, 54, 55, 65, 126, 145, 175, 178, 180, 330
Hook, R., 209
Hopcraft, D., 302
hornbills, 44
horses, 21, 22, 57, 198, 199, 203, 204, 205, 207, 209, 250
Houghton, Mr & Mrs, 59, 131, 132
House, A., 314
Houses of Parliament, 5
Howick, Lord, 33
Hughes 299 helicopter, 216
Hughes, Brig. P., 217
Hunter & Higgs Limited, 37
Hunter, after whom the antelope was named, 274
Hunter, J. A., 36, 37, 60, 100, 113, 191, 194, 316, 317, 341
Hunter's Lodge, 37, 191,316
hunting ban, 302, 330
hunting blocks, 57, 70, 150
hunting industry, 299
Hurt, Col. Roger D. S. O., 48, 126, 127, 165, 166
Hutchings & Biemer Ltd, 37
hyaena, 41, 73, 150, 204, 221, 273
hyalase, 182
Hyder, Dr M., 159, 289
Hyparrhenia, 128

I

Immobilon, 210
impala, 55, 150, 302
Imperial British East Africa Company, 6, 7, 107

Imperial Government, 6
Independence, 1, 3, 57, 73, 74, 121, 172, 291, 307, 311, 330
Independent Reconnaissance Squadron (8th), 207
Ionides, C. J. P., 159, 163
Isiolo Bath Club, 72
ivory, 6, 7, 8, 9, 17, 22, 26, 29, 34, 39, 41, 47, 56, 59, 60, 61, 62, 70, 71, 73, 86, 93, 94, 95, 99, 102, 103, 108, 109, 111, 113, 114, 115, 116, 126, 130, 134, 141, 149, 168, 170, 171, 173, 176, 177, 227, 284, 285, 287, 288, 295, 306, 307, 325, 326, 327, 330, 332, 332, 337
ivory collector's permits, 285, 332
ivory collectors, 330
Ivory Room, 87, 170, 285, 286, 287, 295, 296, 325, 330, 332
ivory trade, 295

J

jackal, 67, 204
Jackson, Sir Frederick, 9, 12, 14, 20, 22, 25, 28, 30, 129, 131, 132, 201, 337, 338, 339
Jafferali, 40
Jaluo, 72, 294
Jenkins, Bryan, 2, 40
Jenkins, Peter, 2, 25, 33, 38, 39, 43, 63, 94, 101, 102, 105, 113, 169, 192, 241, 243, 333
Jirima, Corporal, 230
Johnson, Martin & Osa, 147
Johnson, Osa, 150
Johnston, Sir Harry, 7
Journey to the Jade Sea, 164
Jumbe Kimemeta, 59

K

Kago, General, 241
Kamba, 39, 59, 95, 102, 105, 116, 235
Kanampio, Sergeant, 213, 216
Karen Country Club, 203
Kavirondo, 17
Keane, S. A., 206
Kearney, Denis, 2, 101, 112, 113, 125, 127, 128, 141, 170, 219, 341
Keekorok, 250, 252, 319
Keith, Stuart, 159
Kellogg, Fernanda, 233
Kelly, Nora, 5, 6
Kelly, O'Brien, 117
Kennedy, Joe, 199
Kenya Bunduki Ltd, 37
Kenya Land Commission, 30, 34, 47, 157
Kenya Regiment, 96, 112, 148, 172, 241, 309, 318
Kenya Weekly News, 84, 98
Kenya Wild Life Society, 84, 86, 91, 99
Kenya Wildlife Service (KWS), 26, 222, 223, 295, 311
Kenyatta, Mama Ngina, 285
Kenyatta, Margaret, 332
Kenyatta, President Jomo, 234, 321, 332
Ker & Downey Safaris Ltd, 37, 51, 253
Ker, Donald, 37, 84
Kibwana, Sergeant, 127
Kikuyu, 6, 55, 72, 100, 234, 235, 237, 242, 285, 337, 338, 339, 340
Kilian, Willie, 217
King, Dr John, 200, 207, 218
King's African Rifles (KAR), 65
Kipsigis, 72, 73
Kirkman, Dr J., 130
Klingel, Dr Hans, 210
klipspringer, 150
kob, Uganda or Thomas', 210
Korokoro, 68
Kruger National Park, 29, 95, 210
kudu, greater, 13, 19, 51, 53, 150, 154, 156, 225, 226
kudu, lesser, 153
Kushi Mohamed, 40

L

Labuny, Game Scout, 261, 264
Laikipiak, 26
Lake Nakuru National Park, 90, 91, 223
lammergeyers, 225
Land Rover, 3, 68, 113, 134, 147, 155, 156, 161, 179, 181, 183, 197, 203, 204, 205, 207, 217, 219, 228, 237, 247, 250, 252, 261, 264, 285, 288, 291, 294, 303, 313, 318, 319, 320, 328
Largactyl, 182
Lawrence, John, 95, 166
Laws, Dr Dick, 121
Leakey, Dr Louis, 91
Leakey, Dr Richard, 204, 206
Lebesoi Lelisimon, 50
Legal Notice 120 of 1977., 302, 330
Legeria, Game Scout, 261, 264
Legislative Council, 25, 30, 34
leleshwa, 57
Lenjetin, Game Scout, 225, 227
leopard, 29, 52, 53, 54, 55, 56, 70, 73, 78, 79, 80, 102, 120, 121, 139, 141, 147, 150, 153, 154, 171, 177, 178, 179, 202, 225, 244, 247, 264, 312, 315, 317
Lepus saxatilis crawshayi, 11
Leth, Peter, 53
Lethidrone, 182
Levett, Heather, 261, 262
lion, 41, 56, 57, 66, 70, 75, 76, 77, 78, 80, 133, 134, 135, 139, 143, 147, 151, 154, 155, 159, 164, 202, 203, 204, 205, 206, 221, 247, 249, 250, 257, 259, 260, 261, 262, 263, 264, 273, 283, 284, 313, 314, 315, 318, 320
Lockheed F 105, 322
locust hoppers, 83
locusts, 43, 83
Logie, Conservator of Forests, 159
longbow, 174
lucerne (alfalfa), 72, 236, 237, 278
Luckman, Mr, 272
Lugard, Lord, 107
Lumbwa, 18

M

M99, 182, 194, 207, 209, 210
Mac's Inn, 35
MacArthur, G. C., 28, 29, 34, 35, 36, 59, 61, 62, 63, 93, 95, 169, 334, 341
Macguire, Tony, 275, 279
machine belting, 39, 40
Mackinnon Road, 44, 287, 294, 297
MacMillan, Sir Harold, 92, 307
Magdalen College, 33
maize, 68, 128, 230, 255, 256
Makau, 131, 132
Makindu Force, 112
Malakote, 68
Mandera Whaling Club, 72
Markham, Beryl, 59, 113
Marsabit National Park, 154, 158
Marsabit National Reserve, 47, 48, 146, 157, 314
Marsden, Mr, 16
Marsh, Tony, 123, 233, 236, 237, 238, 341
Martin Mulama, 223
Masai, 18, 26, 39, 40, 41, 47, 56, 57, 72, 85, 91, 131, 132, 138, 210, 244, 261, 273, 309, 310, 317, 319, 320
Masai Mara National Reserve, 72, 319
Masai-Mara National Reserve, 310

Massey, Major Hugh, 101, 112, 341
Masudi Kazipombe, 294
Mathews, Dennis, 84
Mau Mau, 92, 96, 112, 126, 173, 285, 309, 330, 332, 332
Mau Mau Emergency, 50, 65, 100, 105, 267, 309, 311
Mayers, Roy, 41
Mbaroko, 237
Mboya, Tom, 291
McCabe, Brunie, 194, 256, 257, 281, 283
McCabe, David (Kebi), 2, 65, 100, 101, 104, 105, 120, 125, 140, 141, 148, 173, 191, 203, 204, 256, 273, 282, 283, 287, 290, 298, 329, 341
McKeand, Julian, 151, 341
McLinton, Peter, 259
Merille, 152
Meru District Game Reserve, 91, 167
Meru Game Reserve, 210
Meru National Park, 223
Mijikenda, 95
Millard, John, 59
Mills, the murdered rancher, 48
Minister for Wildlife & Tourism, 235, 289
Ministry of Forest Development, Game & Fisheries, 166
Ministry of Tourism & Wildlife, 159, 332
Mkomazi Game Reserve, 194, 241, 245
Mohamed, Asst Game Warden, 286, 287, 289
Mohamed, Major, 260, 264
monkey, 120, 147, 247
Moore, Charles, 217
moran, 56, 57, 132, 309, 313
mosquitoes, 113, 135
Mount Kenya Safari Club, 173
Mousley, Les, 261
Mousley, Maria, 264
Mowat, Christine, 169
Mudir, 137
Mudirates, 137
Murchison Falls National Park, 181, 188, 286
Musembi, Sergeant, 176, 177, 179
Mutinda, John Kimanzi, 259, 341
Mwaneki Kaundu, 197
Mzima Pipeline, 182

N

Nairobi National Park, 77, 89, 96, 203, 222, 223, 273, 307
Nairobi University, 53, 210
Nandi, 18, 339
National Park Trustees, 159
National Parks Ordinance, 47, 98
National Reserves, 47
Neale, Andy, 198
Nesbit-Evans, Libby, 211
Neumann, Arthur, 8, 9
New Stanley Hotel, 167, 254
Nicholson, Brian, 255
Nihill, Sir Barclay, 85
Njemps, 313
nolle prosequi, 287
Northern Game Reserve, 9, 24, 47, 156
Nuffield Foundation, 166, 171

O

Odipo Opade, Peter, 294
Olindo, Perez, 259, 291, 292, 297
Orma, 95, 132
Oromo, 47, 95, 154, 169
Oron River, 8
oryx, 41, 50, 112, 152, 153, 155, 164
ostrich, 51, 72
ouabain, 107
Outlying Districts Ordinance, 16

P

Pakistan International Airlines, 332
Palmer Chemical & Equipment Company Inc, 181
Palmer, 'Red', 181, 183, 184, 185, 257
Paradox gun, 298
Parfet, Courtland, 222
Park Inn, 43
Parke, Davis & Co, 207, 208
Parker, Ian, 1, 2, 3, 5, 13, 59, 92, 93, 102, 112, 119, 126, 165, 167, 181, 200, 201, 241, 249, 255, 257, 284, 312, 325
Parkinson, Tony, 197, 201, 217
Partridge, David, 55
passenger pigeon, 6
Patel, Dr Fatal, 135
Patel, of Kisii, 248
Patterson, Colonel J. H., 22, 24, 341
Peace Parks, 92
Pearsall, Prof. W., 86
Pearson, Cogs, 244
penalties, 117
Pereira, Robin, 285, 286, 287, 341
Peterson, Roger Tory, 90
Petrides, Dr George, 89
Pienaar, Dr T., 210
Pitamber Khoda, 252
Pitman, Captain Charles, 33
Pitt, Mr, 267, 271
Platymops barbatogularis parkeri, 244
Player, Ian, 210
poison, 41, 48, 50, 69, 98, 105, 106, 107, 141, 148, 174
Pokomo, 269
Pokot, 210
Police, 2, 9, 11, 14, 21, 22, 31, 34, 50, 53, 54, 55, 65, 68, 73, 75, 87, 95, 98, 99, 100, 101, 102, 109, 119, 130, 159, 161, 180, 230, 231, 232, 234, 242, 248, 250, 280, 288, 289, 294, 297, 306, 317, 330
Police Air Wing, 99, 102
Police Special Branch, 54, 55, 288
Poole, Guy, 161, 162, 163
Poppleton, Frank, 145
porcupine, 244
Potgieter, Superintendent Rassie, 87, 101, 102
Potgieter, Theo, 250
Powys, Gilfrid, 173, 283, 341
Premna, 150
Prince Bernhard, H.R.H., 320, 321, 322
Prince of Wales, H.R.H., 244
Prisoners of War, 41
Probyn, Daddy, 322
professional hunters, 8, 36, 37, 41, 51, 53, 59, 107, 120, 126, 161, 172, 212, 225, 233, 241, 250, 310, 315, 317, 318
prosecutions, 28, 108, 116, 117, 148, 156, 287, 289, 335
Pusey, Pissy, 332

Q

Quatermain, Allan, 250
Queen Victoria, 6, 236

R

railway, 16, 18, 21, 61, 86, 101, 191, 261, 263, 295, 339, 340
Randall brothers, 41
Randall, Ken, 257
Rasini, 271
ratel, 254
rats, 48, 80, 293
Reckitt & Colman Ltd, 210
Reckitt & Sons Ltd., 207
Red Baron, the, 323
reed mace, 242
Reeve, F., 52
Rendille, 47, 227, 228, 229
Rennison, Sir Patrick, 159

Retherford, J. M., 52
rhino, 3, 13, 24, 26, 29, 34, 37, 40, 44, 45, 46, 50, 51, 52, 55, 56, 70, 71, 73, 96, 99, 101, 103, 105, 115, 116, 121, 123, 139, 147, 150, 151, 152, 164, 175, 176, 181, 189, 191, 192, 193, 194, 207, 208, 209, 210, 212, 213, 214, 216, 216, 217, 218, 219, 220, 221, 222, 223, 225, 227, 235, 236, 244, 285, 306, 307, 312, 315, 318, 320, 326, 327, 329, 337
rice, 68, 245, 337
Rider Haggard, 131
rifle, 18, 39, 48, 57, 68, 69, 75, 109, 123, 127, 129, 134, 147, 149, 150, 155, 156, 168, 174, 175, 176, 177, 179, 185, 195, 203, 226, 227, 229, 230, 248, 249, 255, 260, 264, 269, 281, 282, 287, 291, 292, 294, 298, 313, 316, 319, 320
rinderpest, 13, 19, 26, 131, 159, 301
Ritchie, Capt Archie, 27, 28, 30, 32, 33, 34, 35, 37, 39, 41, 86, 146, 156, 175, 237, 333, 341
Ritchie, Queenie, 34
roan antelope, 13, 197, 198, 199, 200, 201, 210, 339
Roberts, Alick & Boyce, 41
Rodwell, Edward, 61, 63
Root, Alan, 106, 181, 185
Ross, Iain, 149
Rossinger, Dr, 34
Round-Turner, David & Betty, 72
Royal Air Force, (RAF), 278, 322
Royal Electrical & Mechanical Engineers (REME), 275
Royal Flying Corps, (RFC), 322, 323
Royal National Parks of Kenya, 31, 86, 156, 159
Royal National Parks of Kenya Ordinance, 31
Royal Navy, 98, 182, 278, 280
Ruben, Eddie, 37
Rundgren, Donald, 254
Rundgren, Eric, 2, 41, 107, 126, 127, 130, 240, 241, 253, 254, 341
Ryan, R. W. (Bill), 51
Ryan, Ray, 172, 173

S

Sabie Game Reserve, 29
sable antelope, 13, 129, 201, 293
Safariland Ltd, 35, 37, 44
Safaris Africa Ltd, 44
Salisbury, Marquess of, 7, 8, 30
Salon Laura, 258
Salter, Clive QC, 85
Samburu, 47, 48, 49, 50, 51, 52, 55, 56, 73, 112, 119, 212, 225, 227, 228, 312, 337
Sandeman, Colonel Neil, 65, 73, 75, 77, 78, 120, 145, 147, 167, 249, 250, 341
sand-grouse, 70
Sanseviera, 44, 183
Sanye (Wasanye, Wasania), 1, 17, 28, 93, 95, 141
Sauvage, Gilbert, 50
Saw, Peter, 53, 135, 284
scopolamine, 182
scorpions, 169
scrub hare, 11
Seago, John, 197, 198, 199, 201, 217, 233, 234
Seex, J., 207, 236
Selous, F. C., 65, 67
Serengeti Committee of Inquiry, 84
Serengeti National Park, 85
Sergeant Mr, Machakos rancher, 263
Sernylan, 207, 208, 210
Sessional Paper No 1 of 1959/60, 88
Seth-Smith, Martin, 169
Seth-Smith, Renny, 170
Seth-Smith, Tony, 169, 170, 188
Sharpe, H. B., 149, 150, 154, 165
Shaw & Hunter Limited, 37, 298
Shaw, R., 37
Sheldrick, Daphne, 108
Sheldrick, David, 36, 45, 86, 87, 88, 93, 95, 96, 98, 99, 100, 101, 102, 105, 112, 120, 121, 125, 165, 166, 167, 168, 182, 184, 222, 241, 244, 257, 278, 279, 290, 303, 304, 306, 307, 311, 317
Shell Co. Ltd, 275
shifta, 73, 93, 110, 143, 173, 174, 214, 227, 228, 229, 230, 231, 232, 260, 281, 315
Short, Prof. R., 209
shotguns, 69, 77, 128, 177, 179, 186, 242, 247, 323
Simon, Noel, 1, 5, 82, 83, 98, 99, 164, 165, 166, 167, 168
Simpson, John, 271
sitatunga, 210
slaves, 47
Smith, Clive, 154
Smith, D.F., 3
Smith, Ken, 2, 5, 64, 65, 71, 120, 134, 169, 188, 212, 247, 274, 311, 317, 318, 321, 341, 342
Someren, V.G.L. van, 30, 342
Sorsbie, Sir M. & Lady C., 159
Southern Game Reserve, 11, 15, 18, 21, 191
Southey, Mr, 50
Sparks, Mr, 291
Spinage, Dr Clive, 5
Sporck, Mr, 16
State House, 173, 233, 235, 287
Stephens, Ron, 43, 95
Stevenson-Hamilton, Major, 15
Stewart, Dr Don, 198, 200
Stewart, Ken, 217
Stewart, Sir Donald, 17
Steyn, Nevil, 181
Stigand, Capt C. H., 130
Stonier, P., 123
succinylcholine, 192, 194
Sugota Game Reserve, 8
Suk, 16, 210
Swahili, 10, 95
Swayne, Sir H.G.C., 298
Swynnerton, Gerry, 51
Sykes, Dr Sylvia, 291

T

Tanganyika National Parks, 84
Tannerhill, Ginty, 119
Tarconanthus camphoratus, 57
taxidermist, 53
Taylor, Vivian, 34
telemetry, 182
Temple-Boreham, Lyn (TB), 2, 29, 40, 41, 55, 56, 72, 167, 250, 252, 252, 258, 309, 310, 311, 312, 313, 334, 341
Terminalia spinosa, 245
Thalidomide, 209
Tharaka, 28
The Arm'd Rhinoceros, 207
The Daily Nation, 218
The Hunt for Kimathi, 234
The Mombasa Times, 61, 63
Themelon, 182, 187
Thesiger, Wilfred, 159
Thoms, W., 52
Thomson's gazelle, 55
thunder-flashes, 68
Tito, President Josep, 318, 319, 320, 321
topi, 153, 164
Topolini, Father, 232
Touche, G. E., 50
tourism, 299, 302, 325
Trans-Mara Game Reserve, 91
triplicate book, 2, 48, 49, 328
trypanosomaiasis, 223
tsama melon, 333

Tsavo East National Park, 35, 43, 45, 60, 86, 87, 95, 96, 100, 102, 112, 116, 165, 169, 170, 218, 222, 223, 257, 274, 280, 303, 332
Tsavo National Park, 35, 43, 44, 59, 87, 95, 105, 170, 184
Tsavo West National Park, 21, 87, 95, 102, 223, 241
tusks, 9, 17, 26, 53, 58, 59, 60, 61, 62, 63, 94, 101, 103, 108, 111, 114, 115, 116, 117, 134, 138, 141, 145, 157, 171, 182, 184, 185, 225, 241, 249, 285, 287, 295, 325, 327, 330, 332, 332

U

United Africa Company, 332
United Nations, 10, 121

V

vermin, 70, 139, 340
Veterinary Department, 167, 309
Voi Hotel, 44, 306
vultures, 114, 115, 262, 263, 264

W

wabayo, 107
Wajir Yacht Club, 72
Wakefield, Mr, 132
Wakwafi (Masai), 131
Waliangulu, 61, 86, 87, 91, 93, 95, 113, 115, 120, 121, 126, 165, 166, 167, 168, 174, 186, 306
Walimohamed & Co. Ltd, 328
Waller, Sydney, 42, 43, 339
WaNyika, 27
Wata, 59, 61, 93, 95, 101, 105, 106, 107, 108, 109, 110, 112, 116, 165, 168, 171, 174, 186, 284
Waterbuck, 143,180,337
Wateridge, Larry, 167
Webster, John, 119, 167
Wells, Mrs, 203
Westland Wessex helicopters, 279
wheat, 72, 83
white rhino, 181, 286
white settlers, 11, 27, 72
White, Barry, 217
Whitehead, Major Stuart, 217
Whitelaw, Sir William, 323
Wild Animals' Protection Ordinance #18 of 1951, 22
wildebeest, 39, 40
Wildlife Conservation & Management Department (WCMD), 295, 311, 330, 331, 332
Wilkenair, 216
Wilkinson, Bill, 294
Williams, Harry, 204
Williams, John G., 91, 234, 243
Winter, Bill, 213, 260
Wissman, Major H. von, 10
Wood, G. A., 206
Woodhead, David, 216, 217
Woodley, Bill, 34, 35, 45, 62, 93, 94, 95, 96, 98, 99, 100, 101, 102, 105, 108, 109, 111, 112, 113, 116, 117, 120, 121, 141, 158, 159, 165, 181, 244, 305, 310, 317, 318
Woodley, Daphne, 108
Woodley, Ruth, 322
Woosnam, R. B., 24, 27, 333, 341
World War I, 6, 27, 33, 37, 47, 130, 243, 295, 309, 322
World War II, 1, 34, 39, 47, 71, 83, 90, 129, 156, 169, 275, 309, 316, 320
World Wildlife Fund (WWF), 275, 321
Wreford-Smith, John, 48

Y

Yardley, J., 10
Yutzy, Mr, 52

Z

Zaphiro, Dennis, 328, 341
zebra, 8, 17, 39, 40, 41, 52, 55, 67, 83, 150, 164, 198, 206, 210, 249, 273, 327, 340
zebroids, 209
Zimmermann's Ltd, 53

ABOUT THE EDITORS

Stan Bleazard, born 1930, and Ian Parker, born 1936, were brought up in Kenya and, as young men, joined the Kenya Game Department in the decade before the British Empire closed down. It was a small and exclusive organisation in those days, and, while the pay was paltry, the way of life was such that all vacancies were hotly contested. Both Stan and Ian intended making their life careers in the Department, but were overtaken by political events over which they had no control when their posts were 'Africanised'.

Stan obtained his Commercial Flying Licence and, keeping close to conservation, worked for the United Nations Food & Agricultural Organisation as pilot for a wildlife project in Zambia's Luangwa Valley. Having completed his contract there, he joined the Malawi Department of National Parks & Wildlife Conservation. After a decade away from Kenya, he returned and flew commercially for a while, before emigrating to Western Australia with his two daughters. The idea for this book was his, and he contacted old Game Department colleagues with the intention of recording some of their memories before it was too late. One of these colleagues was Ian Parker who, having some experience in writing and book production, agreed to manage the editing and production of such contributions as were produced.

Ian stayed in the wildlife field as a management and research consultant, operating widely in Africa. Still based in Kenya, with his wife and grown up family, he became progressively more involved in writing about conservation and its historical and political ramifications. At the same time, he claims that he only writes under duress and would prefer to spend all of his time in the outdoors, fishing and doing things of no concern to tax collectors.

Cover Design:	The Digital Canvas Company Forres Scotland bookcovers@digican.co.uk
Layout:	Stephen M.L. Young Elgin Scotland stephenmlyoung@aol.com
Font:	Adobe Garamond (11pt)

Copies of this book can be ordered via the Internet:

www.librario.com

or from:

Librario Publishing Ltd
Brough House
Milton Brodie
Kinloss
Moray IV36 2UA
Tel /Fax No 01343 850 617